AutoCAD® 2013 FOR DUMMIES®

by David Byrnes and Bill Fane

WILEY

John Wiley & Sons, Inc.

AutoCAD® 2013 For Dummies®

Published by
John Wiley & Sons, Inc.
111 River Street
Hoboken, NJ 07030-5774
www.wiley.com

Copyright © 2012 by John Wiley & Sons, Inc., Hoboken, New Jersey

Published by John Wiley & Sons, Inc., Hoboken, New Jersey

Published simultaneously in Canada

For general information on our other products and services, please contact our Customer Care Department within the U.S. at 877-762-2974, outside the U.S. at 317-572-3993, or fax 317-572-4002.

For technical support, please visit www.wiley.com/techsupport.

Wiley also publishes its books in a variety of electronic formats and by print-on-demand. Not all content that is available in standard print versions of this book may appear or be packaged in all book formats. If you have purchased a version of this book that did not include media that is referenced by or accompanies a standard print version, you may request this media by visiting http://booksupport.wiley.com. For more information about Wiley products, visit us at www.wiley.com.

Library of Congress Control Number: 2012936846

ISBN 978-1-118-28112-3 (pbk); ISBN 978-1-118-33352-5 (ebk); ISBN 978-1-118-33465-2 (ebk); ISBN 978-1-118-39217-1 (ebk)

Manufactured in the United States of America

10 9 8 7 6 5 4 3 2 1

WILEY

About the Authors

David Byrnes is one of those grizzled old-timers you'll find mentioned every so often in *AutoCAD 2013 For Dummies*. He began his drafting career on the boards in 1979, and first learned AutoCAD with version 1.4. Dave is based in Vancouver, British Columbia, where he works as a civil/structural drafter. He taught AutoCAD for fifteen years at Emily Carr University of Art + Design and British Columbia Institute of Technology in Vancouver. Dave has authored or co-authored over a dozen AutoCAD books and was sole author of this title from *AutoCAD 2008 For Dummies* to *AutoCAD 2012 For Dummies*.

Bill Fane is a recovering doorknob designer. He was a product engineer and then product engineering manager for Weiser Lock in Vancouver, Canada for 27 years and holds 12 U.S. patents. He has been using AutoCAD for design work since Version 2.17g (1986), and Inventor since version 1.0 beta (1996). He is a retired professional engineer and an Autodesk Authorized Training Center (ATC) certified instructor.

He began teaching mechanical design in 1996 at the British Columbia Institute of Technology (BCIT) in Vancouver, including such courses as AutoCAD, Mechanical Desktop, Inventor, SolidWorks, machine design, term projects, manufacturing processes, and design procedures. He retired from this position in 2008.

He has lectured on a wide range of AutoCAD and Inventor subjects at Autodesk University since 1995 and at Destination Desktop since 2003. He is the AUGI CAD Camp National Team instructor for the manufacturing track. He has written over 220 "The Learning Curve" columns for *CADalyst* magazine since 1986 and claims to be a close personal friend of Captain LearnCurve. He also writes software product reviews for *CADalyst, Design Product News,* and *Machine Design*. He is an active member of the Vancouver AutoCAD Users Society, "the world's oldest and most dangerous."

In his spare time he skis, water skis, windsurfs, scuba dives, sails a Hobie Cat, rides an off-road motorcycle, drives his '37 Rolls-Royce limousine, or his wife's '89 Bentley Turbo R, travels extensively with his wife, and plays with his grandchildren.

Dedication

From Dave: I left the bohemian lifestyle of the AutoCAD consultant at the beginning of 2008 and rejoined the engineering company I last worked for in 1988 (luckily they'd forgotten all about that chandelier). Working full-time (oh! the horror!) and keeping up with AutoCAD so I can revise this book has made me somewhat inaccessible for three months a year, and I'm forever grateful to Annie and Delia, still and always the two women in my life, who remind me there are other things besides keyboards and mice (and sometimes they have to try *really* hard).

From Bill: Back in the last millennium I wrote a book about AutoCAD 13, after which my wife Bev swore "Never again!" This time around she was smart enough to go on a two-week South Pacific cruise while I worked on the final author review files, and so our marriage stands a chance of surviving another 46 years.

Authors' Acknowledgments

Dave thanks former author Mark Middlebrook for bringing him into the *AutoCAD For Dummies* world by asking him first to tech edit *AutoCAD 2000 For Dummies*, then to join him as co-author of *AutoCAD 2006 For Dummies*, and finally to take over the title altogether.

Bill was both honored and flattered when Dave invited him to co-author this edition of the prestigious *AutoCAD For Dummies* title, with a view to his taking it over completely next year. Dave's support and assistance through Bill's teething period on this project know no bounds, and no matter where the book goes from here, there will always be parts of Dave's soul lurking in it somewhere.

We both thank colleagues and friends at Autodesk: above all Heidi Hewett and Bud Schroeder, who never seem to mind being asked even the dumbest questions. At Wiley, Acquisitions Editor Kyle Looper was a reliable source of calm but firm direction. It was a pleasure to work with project editor Mark Enochs, and copy editor Heidi Unger pointed out where we mixed up our Ps and our Qs. And thanks, finally, to Ralph Grabowski who did a sterling job of tech editing.

Publisher's Acknowledgments

We're proud of this book; please send us your comments at http://dummies.custhelp.com. For other comments, please contact our Customer Care Department within the U.S. at 877-762-2974, outside the U.S. at 317-572-3993, or fax 317-572-4002.

Some of the people who helped bring this book to market include the following:

Acquisitions and Editorial

Sr. Project Editor: Mark Enochs

Acquisitions Editor: Kyle Looper

Copy Editors: Heidi Unger, Teresa Artman, Amanda Graham

Technical Editor: Ralph Grabowski

Editorial Manager: Leah Michael

Editorial Assistant: Amanda Graham

Sr. Editorial Assistant: Cherie Case

Cover Photo: ©iStockphoto.com/-Vladimir-

Cartoons: Rich Tennant (www.the5thwave.com)

Composition Services

Project Coordinator: Sheree Montgomery

Layout and Graphics: Claudia Bell, Carl Byers, Joyce Haughey

Proofreader: Bonnie Mikkelson

Indexer: Infodex Indexing Services, Inc.

Publishing and Editorial for Technology Dummies

 Richard Swadley, Vice President and Executive Group Publisher

 Andy Cummings, Vice President and Publisher

 Mary Bednarek, Executive Acquisitions Director

 Mary C. Corder, Editorial Director

Publishing for Consumer Dummies

 Kathy Nebenhaus, Vice President and Executive Publisher

Composition Services

 Debbie Stailey, Director of Composition Services

Contents at a Glance

Table of Contents

Introduction

*L*et's get something straight upfront. You may have heard that AutoCAD is difficult, complex, or hard to learn and use. Well, it has been our observation that the easier any software is to learn and use, the sooner you bump up against the software's limitations. Yes, AutoCAD is complex, but that's the secret to its success. Some claim that few people use more than 10 percent of AutoCAD's capabilities. Closer analysis reveals that pretty much everyone uses the same basic 5 percent, but everyone else uses a different 5 percent after that. The trick is to find *your* 5 percent, the sweet spot that suits your particular industry.

It should also be perfectly clear that if your career path has put you in a position where you need to learn AutoCAD, then you're no dummy!

It's amazing to think that AutoCAD came into being more than a quarter of a *century* ago, back in the last millennium, at a time when most people thought that personal computers weren't capable of industrial-strength tasks like CAD. (The acronym stands for Computer-Aided Drafting, Computer-Aided Design, or both, depending on whom you talk to.) What's equally amazing is the fact that many of today's hotshot AutoCAD users weren't even born when the program first hit the street and the grizzled old-timers writing these words began using it! It's almost as amazing that, 29 years and counting after its birth in December of 1982, AutoCAD remains the king of the micro-computer CAD hill by a tall margin, making it one of the longest-lived PC programs ever, and it will probably be a year older next year. It's conceivable that the long-term future of CAD may belong to special-purpose, 3D-based software such as the Autodesk Inventor and Revit programs, or to specialized market-specific variations built on top of AutoCAD. At any rate, AutoCAD's .DWG file format is the de facto standard, and so AutoCAD will be where the CAD action is for the foreseeable future.

AutoCAD has grown more complex over the years, in part to keep up with the increasing complexity of the design and drafting processes that AutoCAD is intended to serve. It's not enough just to draw nice-looking lines anymore. If you want to play CAD with the big boys and girls, you need to carefully orga-nize the objects you draw, their properties, and the files in which they reside. You need to coordinate your CAD work with other people in your office who will be working on or making use of the same drawings. You need to be savvy about shipping drawings around via the Internet. You may even need to be a little cognizant of working with AutoCAD in three dimensions.

AutoCAD provides the tools for doing all these things, but it's not always easy to figure out which hammer to pick up or which nail to bang on first. With this book, you have an excellent chance of creating a presentable, usable, printable, and sharable drawing on your first (or at least your second) try without putting a T-square through your computer screen in frustration.

What's Not (And What Is) in This Book

This book is not *Drafting For Dummies*, or *Engineering For Dummies*, or *Crash-Testing For Dummies*, or anything similar. We cover the basic principles of how to use AutoCAD to create and edit the objects (lines, circles, arcs, and so on) that make up engineering, architectural, and similar technical drawings. We do not cover drafting standards and practices for any particular industry or profession. For example, we teach you how to create dashed lines, but don't tell you specifically how and when they should be used to indicate hidden edges in solid objects.

Unlike many other *For Dummies* books, this one often *does* tell you to consult the official software documentation. AutoCAD is just too big and complicated for a single book to attempt to describe it completely.

AutoCAD is also too big and complicated for a book like this to cover every feature. We don't address advanced topics, like database connectivity, customization, or programming, in the interest of bringing you a book of a reasonable size — one that you'll read rather than stick on your shelf with those other 1,000-page tomes! The ultimate book that covered *everything* to do with AutoCAD would need a fork truck to move it.

Autodesk likes to keep its users (and us authors!) guessing about new features in future releases of the software. AutoCAD 2009 surprised users and authors alike with a totally revamped user interface, replacing the drop-down menus and toolbars of previous versions with a Microsoft Office 2007–style Ribbon (happily, Autodesk doesn't *force* its users to adopt the new look the way Microsoft does — there's still an "AutoCAD Classic" interface available). AutoCAD's interface gets some tweaking in each succeeding release, if for no other reason than to include new functionality, so even seasoned users will always find something that's a little different. This book focuses on AutoCAD 2013 and addresses its slightlyless-capable but much-lower-priced sibling, AutoCAD LT 2013.

We do occasionally mention differences with previous releases so that everyone has some context and upgraders can more readily understand the differences, and you are bound to encounter a few of the millions and millions of drawings out there that were created with older methods. We also mention

the important differences between AutoCAD and AutoCAD LT so you'll know what you — or your LT-using colleagues — are missing so far as this book is concerned; the major difference is the almost-total absence of 3D capabilities in AutoCAD LT.

This book does *not* cover the discipline-specific features in AutoCAD-based products such as AutoCAD Architecture or AutoCAD Mechanical (except for some general discussion in Chapter 1), but most of the information in this book applies to the general-purpose AutoCAD features in the AutoCAD-based versions of those programs as well.

Mac attack!

Late in 2010, Autodesk released the first non–Microsoft Windows version of AutoCAD in 20 years. AutoCAD for Mac is out there today, but this book covers the Windows versions only. Although the two versions are file compatible, there are many differences in how they look and what they can do. If you have AutoCAD for Mac, you should be able to gain some understanding of concepts, but you might be better off with a Mac-specific book such as *Mastering AutoCAD For Mac* by George Omura and Rick Graham (Sybex Publishing).

Who Do We Think You Are?

AutoCAD has a large, loyal, dedicated group of longtime users. This book is not for the sort of people who have been using AutoCAD for a decade or more, who plan their vacation time around Autodesk University, or who consider 1,000-page-plus technical tomes about AutoCAD to be pleasure reading. This book *is* for people who want to get going quickly with AutoCAD but who also know the importance of developing proper CAD techniques from the beginning.

However, you do need to have some idea of how to use your computer system before tackling AutoCAD — and this book. You need to have a computer system with AutoCAD or AutoCAD LT (preferably the 2013 version). A printer or plotter and a connection to the Internet will be big helps, too.

You also need to know how to use your version of Windows to copy and delete files, create a folder, and find a file. You need to know how to use a mouse to select (highlight) or to choose (activate) commands, how to close a window, and how to minimize and maximize windows. Make sure that you're familiar with the basics of your operating system before you start with AutoCAD.

How This Book Is Organized

Appearances can be deceptive. For example, had you wandered into our office and seen the apparently random piles of stuff that covered our desks while we were writing this book, you might wonder how we could possibly organize a sentence, let alone an entire book. But — given a suitable degree of concerted thought — Bill knows *exactly* where to put his hands on that list of new dimension variables, and Dave can always find that bagel and cream cheese he started at coffee break yesterday. In the words of the philosopher, "A tidy desk is the sign of a sick mind." Boy, are we healthy!

We hope you find that the book also reflects some concerted thought about how to present AutoCAD in a way that's both easy-to-dip-into and smoothly-flowing-from-beginning-to-end.

The organization of this book into parts — collections of related chapters — is one of the most important, uh, *parts* of this book. You really can get to know AutoCAD one piece at a time, and each part represents a group of closely related topics. The order of parts also says something about priority; yes, you have our permission to ignore the stuff in later parts until you master most of the stuff in the early ones. This kind of building-block approach can be especially valuable in a program as complex as AutoCAD.

The following sections describe the parts that the book breaks down into.

Part I: AutoCAD 101

Need to know your way around the AutoCAD screen? Why does AutoCAD even exist, anyway? What are all the different AutoCAD-based products that Autodesk sells, and should you be using one of them — for example, AutoCAD LT — instead of AutoCAD? Is everything so slooow because it's supposed to be slow, or do you have too wimpy a machine to use this wonder of modern-day computing? And why do you have to do this stuff in the first place?

Part I answers all these questions and more. This part also includes what may seem like a great deal of excruciating detail about setting up a new drawing in AutoCAD. But what's even more excruciating is doing your setup work incorrectly and then feeling as if AutoCAD is fighting you every step of the way. With a little drawing setup work done in advance, it won't.

Part II: Let There Be Lines

In this part, you discover some essential concepts, including object properties and CAD precision techniques. We know you're rarin' to make some drawings, but if you don't get a handle on this stuff early on, you'll be terminally confused when you try to draw and edit objects. If you want to make drawings that look good, plot good, and *are* good, read this stuff!

After the concepts preamble, the bulk of this part covers the trio of activities that you'll probably spend most of your time in AutoCAD doing: drawing objects, editing them, and zooming and panning to see them better on the screen. These are the things that you do in order to create the *geometry* — that is, the CAD representations of the objects in the real world that you're designing. By the end of Part II, you should be pretty good at geometry, even if your ninth-grade math teacher told you otherwise.

Part III: If Drawings Could Talk

CAD drawings don't live on lines alone — most of them require quite a bit of text, dimensioning, and hatching in order to make the design intent clear to the poor chump who has to build your amazing creation. (Whoever said "a picture is worth a thousand words" must not have counted up the number of words on the average architectural drawing!) This part shows you how to add these essential features to your drawings.

After you've gussied up your drawing with text, dimensions, and hatching, you'll probably want to create a snapshot of it to show off to your client, contractor, or grandma. Normal people call this process *printing,* but CAD people call it *plotting.* Whatever you decide to call it, we show you how to do it.

Part IV: Advancing with AutoCAD

A good CAD user, like a good kindergartner, plays well with others. AutoCAD encourages this behavior with a host of drawing- and data-sharing features. Blocks, external reference files, and raster images encourage reuse of parts of drawings, entire drawings, and bitmap image files. You can create symbols with changeable text or appearance, and you can apply parametric "rules" to drawing objects so they help maintain design intent. This part of the book ends by explaining how to use AutoCAD's Internet features to enable sharing of drawings well beyond your hard drive and local network.

The drawing- and data-sharing features in AutoCAD take you way beyond old-style, pencil-and-paper design and drafting. After you've discovered how to apply the techniques in this part, you'll be well on your way to full CAD nerdhood. (You may want to warn your family beforehand.)

Part V: On a 3D Spree

In this part, you learn the basics of 3D modeling in AutoCAD 2013. Beginning with the 3D environment — how to change its appearance, how to move around in it, how to examine the model itself in different ways — the chapters introduce different modeling techniques, from solid models to generating 2D working drawings from your 3D models.

Part VI: The Part of Tens

This part contains a concise catalog of differences between AutoCAD and AutoCAD LT, and lists of resources and settings that can make the time you spend in AutoCADland more enjoyable. There's a lot of meat packed into these three chapters — juicy tidbits from years of drafting, experimentation, and fist-shaking at things that don't work right — not to mention years of compulsive list-making. We hope that these lists help you get on the right track quickly and stay there.

But wait . . . there's more!

AutoCAD 2013 For Dummies has a companion website. Point your browser at www.dummies.com/go/autocad2013fd to find many of the drawing files we use to demonstrate commands and procedures in this book. The drawings are posted to the website in Zip format; just download and unzip them and they're ready to open in AutoCAD. The Zip files are named for the chapters and contain one or more drawing files. For example, afd03.zip contains the versions of the drawing for the base plate exercise in Chapter 3 of the book (refer to the downloadable Read Me file for an explanation of the naming conventions used for the drawing files). Note that not all chapters have associated drawing files.

Most of the drawing files are saved in AutoCAD 2010 format and can be opened in AutoCAD 2010 or any later release.

The reverse is *not* true. AutoCAD 2013 files *cannot* be opened in earlier releases. You can SAVEAS all the way back to Release 11 (1990), but features added later won't be supported and may translate poorly.

If you don't have *any* AutoCAD release and just want to get a taste of the program before you buy, you can also download a free 30-day trial version of either AutoCAD 2013 or AutoCAD LT 2013. Just browse to

`www.autodesk.com/autocad` or `www.autodesk.com/autocadlt`

and look for the Product Trial button.

You can also find the cheat sheet that's mentioned here and there in the book at

`www.dummies.com/cheatsheet/autocad2013`

Icons Used in This Book

Throughout this book, we point out certain morsels of particularly important or useful information by placing handy little icons in the margin. Naturally, different icons indicate different types of information:

This icon tells you that herein lies a pointed insight that can save you time and trouble as you use AutoCAD. In many cases, Tips act as a funnel on AutoCAD's impressive but sometimes overwhelming flexibility: After telling you all the ways that you *can* do something, we tell you the way that you *should* do it in most cases.

The Technical Stuff icon points out places where we delve a little more deeply into AutoCAD's inner workings or point out something that most people don't need to know most of the time. These paragraphs definitely are not required reading the first time through, so if you come to one at a time when you've reached your techie-detail threshold, feel free to skip over it.

This icon points out text that tells you how to stay out of trouble when living close to the edge. Failure to heed its message may have unpleasant consequences for you or your drawing — or both.

There's a lot to remember when you're using AutoCAD, so we've remembered to remind you not to forget about some of those things that you should remember. These paragraphs usually refer to a crucial point earlier in the chapter or in a previous chapter. So if you're reading sequentially, a Remember paragraph serves as a friendly reminder. If you're not reading sequentially, this kind of paragraph may help you realize that you need to review a central concept or technique before proceeding.

This icon points to new stuff in AutoCAD 2013 (and sometimes AutoCAD LT 2013). It's mostly designed for people who are somewhat familiar with a previous version of AutoCAD and want to be alerted to what's new or different in this release. New AutoCAD users starting out their CAD working lives with AutoCAD 2013 will find this stuff interesting, too — especially when they can show off their new book-learnin' to the grizzled AutoCAD veterans in the office who don't yet know about all the cool new features.

This icon highlights text that shows the differences between AutoCAD LT and AutoCAD. If you're using AutoCAD LT, you'll find out what you're missing compared to "full" AutoCAD. If your friend is using LT, you'll know where to look to find stuff in AutoCAD to brag about.

This icon points out places where you don't have to draw stuff from scratch. Just visit the book's companion website at

```
www.dummies.com/go/autocad2013fd
```

and download the specified file or files.

A Few Conventions — Just in Case

You can probably figure out for yourself all the information in this section, but here are the details just in case.

Commanding from the keyboard

Text you type into the program at the command line, in a dialog box, in a text box, and so on appears in **boldface type**. Examples of AutoCAD prompts appear in a `special typeface`, as does any other text in the book that echoes a message, a word, or one or more lines of text that actually appear on-screen. Sequences of prompts that appear in the AutoCAD command-line area have a shaded background, like so:

```
Specify lower left corner or [ON/OFF] <0.0000,0.0000>:
```

Many of the figures — especially in Chapters 8 through 11 — also show AutoCAD command-line sequences that demonstrate AutoCAD's prompts and example responses.

Many AutoCAD commands have *aliases* — shortcut (fewer-letter) versions for the benefit of those who like to type commands at the AutoCAD command line, and in the long run, this is the way the real power users work. In this book, we show command names in uppercase letters. Chapters throughout the book include tables listing the most commonly used drawing and editing commands, and for each table we list both the full command name and its alias in parentheses; for example, LINE (L), ARRAY (AR), and so forth. If you're using the keyboard to enter commands, this means that you can type either **LINE** or simply **L**, and then press Enter to execute the command. Command input is not case-sensitive, so LINE, line, Line, liNe, LiNe, and so on will all work. You can view a list of all the command aliases in both AutoCAD and AutoCAD LT by clicking Edit Aliases on the Manage tab's Customization panel — *but just look, and be careful not to change anything!*

Tying things up with the Ribbon

As you've noticed if you've skimmed through the book and looked at a few of the figures, AutoCAD uses an Office 2007–style Application Menu and Ribbon interface. The Ribbon is organized into a series of task-based tabs, and each tab has a number of panels containing specific tool buttons. We tell you where to find each command.

Where to Go from Here

If you read this Introduction, you're like us — you like to read. (The cut-to-the-chase people tend to flip to the index right away and look up what they need to know at that instant.) If you're a total AutoCAD newbie, you can read this book in order, from front to back; it follows a straightforward route from setting up your drawing environment, to outputting your masterworks to hard copy, to sharing your work with others.

If you're an experienced user, you'll probably be one of those index-flippers looking for the missing information you need to complete a specific task. You can probably find the index on your own, but we encourage you to browse through the book anyway, with a highlighter or sticky notes in hand, so you can find those particularly important places when you need them again. If you're competent in most areas of AutoCAD and pretty familiar with the previous version, look for the New In 2013 icons in the margins to find out the latest features you never knew you couldn't live without.

Whichever route you choose, we hope you enjoy your time with *AutoCAD 2013 For Dummies*. And . . . *you're off!*

Occasionally, we have updates to our technology books. If this book does have technical updates, they will be posted at:

www.dummies.com/go/autocad2013fdupdates

Part I
AutoCAD 101

AutoCAD 2013 is more than just another drawing program; it's a complete environment for drafting and design. So if you're new to AutoCAD, you need to know several things to get off to a good start — especially how to use the command-line area and how to set up your drawing properly. These key techniques are described in this part of the book.

If you've used earlier versions of AutoCAD, you'll be most interested in the high points of the new release, including some newer interface components. The lowdown on what's new is here, too.

Introducing AutoCAD and AutoCAD LT

Maybe you're one of the few remaining holdouts who continue to practice the ancient art of manual drafting with pencil and vellum. If so, we must tell you that you belong to a dwindling breed. Or maybe you're completely new to drafting and yearn for the wealth and fame (would we lead you on?) of the drafter's life. Maybe you're an engineer or architect who needs to catch up with the young CAD hotshots in your office. Maybe you tried to use AutoCAD a long time ago, but gave up in frustration or just got rusty. Or maybe you currently use an older release, such as AutoCAD 2006 or even (if you're into antiques) AutoCAD 2000.

Whatever your current situation or motivation, we hope that you enjoy the process of becoming proficient with AutoCAD. Drawing with AutoCAD is challenging at first, but it's a challenge worth meeting. AutoCAD rewards those who think creatively about their work and look for ways to do it better. You can always find out more, discover a new trick, or improve the efficiency and quality of your drawing production.

AutoCAD first hit the bricks in the early 1980s, around the same time as the first IBM PCs. It was offered for a bewildering variety of operating systems, including CP/M (ask your granddad about that one!), various flavors of Unix,

and even the Apple II and then the Macintosh. By far the most popular of those early versions was for MS-DOS (your dad can tell you about that one). In 1997, Autodesk settled on Microsoft Windows as the sole operating system for AutoCAD, and that was the case for the next 13 years. Then in 2010, Autodesk released its first non-Windows version for many years: AutoCAD for Mac. The last version of AutoCAD to run on the Mac was Release 12, which appeared as long ago as 1992. It's taken a while, but it looks like the Mac is back!

In this book, we cover only the Windows versions of AutoCAD 2013 and AutoCAD LT 2013. AutoCAD for Mac is different enough — in both capabilities and interface — from the Windows versions that we simply can't cover it all here. If you're a Mac user with an interest in running AutoCAD, check out *Mastering AutoCAD for Mac,* by George Omura and Rick Graham (Sybex Publishing), and/or *What's Inside? AutoCAD for Macintosh,* by Ralph Grabowski, available as an e-book at www.upfrontezine.com/wiam.

AutoCAD 2013 and AutoCAD LT 2013 are supported in the following Windows flavors, including both 32- and 64-bit versions:

- ✔ Windows 7 and Windows Vista Home Premium
- ✔ Windows 7 Professional
- ✔ Windows 7 and Windows Vista Enterprise
- ✔ Windows 7 and Windows Vista Ultimate
- ✔ Windows Vista Business
- ✔ Windows XP Professional
- ✔ Windows XP Home (32-bit only)

Although not officially supported, AutoCAD 2013 (and AutoCAD LT 2013) can also run in Windows XP Tablet PC 2005 Edition, and make use of the tablet functionality included in Windows Vista and Windows 7. Trying to do production drafting on a tablet isn't a great idea because of limitations in the graphics system, but we know it works. In fact, between the two of us, we are also running it on an Acer notebook with only 1024 x 600 resolution. When AutoCAD starts, it complains that it needs a minimum 1024 x 768 resolution but starts running anyway. The secret is to set up the notebook's graphics in dual-monitor extended-desktop mode and plug it into a higher-resolution monitor or even a digital TV and then drag AutoCAD onto that screen.

Because of AutoCAD's MS-DOS heritage and its emphasis on efficiency for production drafters, it's not the easiest program to master, but it *has* gotten easier and more consistent over the past decade or so. AutoCAD is pretty well integrated into the Windows environment now, but you still bump into some vestiges of its MS-DOS legacy — especially the *command line* (that text area lurking at the bottom of the AutoCAD screen — see Chapter 2 for details). But even the command line — oops! command *window* — is kinder

and gentler in AutoCAD 2013. This book guides you around the bumps and minimizes the bruises.

Why AutoCAD?

AutoCAD has been around a long time — since 1982, which we suspect, dear readers, is longer than many of you! AutoCAD ushered in the transition from *really expensive* mainframe and minicomputer CAD systems costing tens of thousands of dollars to merely *somewhat expensive* microcomputer CAD programs costing a thousand dollars.

AutoCAD's 3D capabilities have grown by leaps and bounds over the last several releases, and 3D modeling is becoming a common way of checking designs *before* they're drafted. Nevertheless, AutoCAD is, first and foremost, a program for creating *two-dimensional technical drawings,* drawings in which measurements and precision are important because these kinds of drawings are often used to build something. The drawings that you create with AutoCAD must adhere to standards established long ago for hand-drafted drawings. The upfront investment to use AutoCAD is certainly more expensive than the investment needed to use pencil and paper, and the learning curve is much steeper, too. So why bother? The key reasons for using AutoCAD rather than pencil and paper are

- **Precision:** Creating lines, circles, and other shapes of the exact dimensions is easier with AutoCAD than with pencils.

- **Modifiability:** Drawings are much easier to modify on the computer screen than on paper. CAD modifications are a lot cleaner, too.

- **Efficiency:** Creating many kinds of drawings is faster with a CAD program — especially drawings that involve repetition, such as floor plans in a multistory building. But that efficiency takes skill and practice. If you're an accomplished pencil-and-paper drafter, don't expect CAD to be faster at first!

Figure 1-1 shows several kinds of drawings in AutoCAD 2013.

Why choose AutoCAD? AutoCAD is just the starting point of a whole industry of software products designed to work with AutoCAD. Autodesk (the software corporation that develops and sells AutoCAD along with a host of other design software) has helped this process along immensely by providing a series of programming interfaces to AutoCAD (although, alas, not to AutoCAD LT — see the "Seeing the LT" section, later in the chapter) that other companies — and Autodesk itself — have used to extend the application. Some of the add-on products became such winners that Autodesk acquired them and incorporated them into its own products. When you compare all the resources — including the add-ons, extensions, training courses, books, and so on — AutoCAD doesn't have much PC CAD competition.

Figure 1-1: Cities, houses, little toy trains — what do you want to draw today?

Here's one more reason for choosing AutoCAD: You may need to discuss and share your drawings with people who don't use AutoCAD, such as clients or vendors. Autodesk offers a free service called AutoCAD WS. You simply upload your files to an Autodesk web server and then invite people to access them. Now here's the cunning part: They don't need to have AutoCAD or any special plug-ins installed on their computer. Any standard web browser can open your files and perform basic creation, editing, markup, and printing functions. Better yet, several people can access the same file at the same time. Everyone can chat, and everyone can see everyone else's edits and markups at the same time, live, from anywhere in the world. There's even a free app for iPods and similar portable devices. See Chapter 20 for more details.

The Importance of Being DWG

To take full advantage of AutoCAD in your work environment, you need to be aware of the *DWG* file format, the format in which AutoCAD saves drawings. Here are some DWG facts to keep in mind:

- **In many cases, an older release of AutoCAD can't open a DWG file that's been saved by a newer AutoCAD release.** Table 1-1 shows the relationship between AutoCAD versions and their corresponding file formats.

- **A newer release of AutoCAD can *always* open files saved by older versions.** We have sample files going back to 1984 that open in AutoCAD 2013.

✔ *Some* **previous AutoCAD releases can open files saved by the subsequent one or two versions.** As Table 1-1 shows, the DWG file format changes every three years starting with 2000, so AutoCAD 2013 has a new format.

✔ **You can use the Save As option in newer releases to save the file to older DWG formats.** In fact, AutoCAD 2013 can save as far back as AutoCAD Release 14, which dates all the way back to 1997! In addition, you can Save As to the simple text-based DXF format back as far as Release 11.

The earlier formats don't support all the features of the later ones. AutoCAD does its best at translating, but some items may be lost or won't fully survive a round trip back into a newer release.

Table 1-1 shows which versions (described later in this chapter) use which DWG file formats.

Table 1-1	AutoCAD Versions and DWG File Formats		
AutoCAD Version	*AutoCAD LT Version*	*Release Year*	*DWG File Format*
AutoCAD 2013	AutoCAD LT 2013	2012	Acad 2013
AutoCAD 2012	AutoCAD LT 2012	2011	Acad 2010
AutoCAD 2011	AutoCAD LT 2011	2010	Acad 2010
AutoCAD 2010	AutoCAD LT 2010	2009	Acad 2010
AutoCAD 2009	AutoCAD LT 2009	2008	Acad 2007
AutoCAD 2008	AutoCAD LT 2008	2007	Acad 2007
AutoCAD 2007	AutoCAD LT 2007	2006	Acad 2007
AutoCAD 2006	AutoCAD LT 2006	2005	Acad 2004
AutoCAD 2005	AutoCAD LT 2005	2004	Acad 2004
AutoCAD 2004	AutoCAD LT 2004	2003	Acad 2004
AutoCAD 2002	AutoCAD LT 2002	2001	Acad 2000
AutoCAD 2000i	AutoCAD LT 2000i	2000	Acad 2000
AutoCAD 2000	AutoCAD LT 2000	1999	Acad 2000
AutoCAD Release 14	AutoCAD LT 98 and 97	1997	Acad R14
AutoCAD Release 13	AutoCAD LT 95	1994	Acad R13
AutoCAD Release 12	AutoCAD LT Release 2	1992	Acad R12

Working with AutoCAD is easier when your co-workers and colleagues in other companies all use the same release of AutoCAD and AutoCAD-related tools. That way, your DWG files, add-on tools, and even the details of your CAD knowledge can be mixed and matched among your workgroup and partners. In the real world, you may work with people, probably from other companies, who use AutoCAD releases as old as AutoCAD 2006 — or even older.

Many programs claim to be *DWG-compatible* — that is, capable of converting data to and from the AutoCAD DWG format. Achieving this compatibility is, however, a difficult thing to do well. Even a small error in file conversion can have results ranging in severity from annoying to appalling. Every time you open a drawing file, AutoCAD checks its parentage and warns you if a non-Autodesk program created the drawing. If you exchange DWG files with people who use other CAD programs, you may have to spend time finding and fixing translation problems.

Seeing the LT

AutoCAD LT is one of the best deals around, a shining example of the old 80/20 rule: roughly 80 percent of the capabilities of AutoCAD for roughly 20 percent of the money. (Actually, with recent price creep, it's now more like a 67/33 rule.) Like AutoCAD, AutoCAD LT runs on mainstream Windows computers and doesn't require any additional hardware devices. With AutoCAD LT, you can be a player in the world of AutoCAD, the world's leading CAD program, for a comparatively low starting cost.

AutoCAD LT is a very close cousin to AutoCAD. Autodesk creates AutoCAD LT by starting with the AutoCAD program, taking out a few features to justify charging a far lower price, and then adding a couple of features to enhance ease of use versus full AutoCAD. As a result, AutoCAD LT looks and works much like AutoCAD. The drawing areas, the Ribbon, and Application Menu of the two programs are nearly identical. (LT is missing a few Ribbon tabs, panels, and commands.)

In fact, the major difference between the programs has nothing to do with the programs themselves. The major difference is that AutoCAD LT lacks support for most customization and programming languages that are used to develop AutoCAD add-ons. That means that almost none of the add-on programs or utilities offered by Autodesk and others are available to LT users.

AutoCAD LT has limited 3D support. You can view and edit 3D objects in AutoCAD LT, so you can work with drawings created in AutoCAD that contain 3D objects. However, you can't create true 3D objects in LT.

Although you may hear claims that AutoCAD LT is easier to master and use than AutoCAD, the truth is that they're about equally difficult (or easy, depending on your *NQ* [nerd quotient]). The LT learning curve doesn't differ significantly from that of AutoCAD, which was originally designed for maximum power and then modified somewhat to improve ease of use. AutoCAD LT shares this same heritage.

Fortunately, the minimal differences between LT and AutoCAD mean that after you climb that learning curve, you have the same great view. You have almost the full range of the AutoCAD 2D drafting tools, and you can exchange DWG files with AutoCAD users without data loss.

This book covers AutoCAD 2013, but most of the information in it (except for the 3D chapters in Part V) applies to AutoCAD LT 2013 as well. The icon that you see to the left of this paragraph highlights significant differences.

Checking System Requirements

If you're upgrading from AutoCAD 2012 or another recent release and you work mostly or entirely in 2D, you're probably already current with system requirements. In fact, if your work is mostly or entirely 2D — and therefore, this applies especially for LT users — AutoCAD 2013 will run fine on pretty well any recent computer that will run Windows 7, Vista, or XP.

AutoCAD's requirements for running in Windows 7 or Vista are substantially higher than for running in XP. This section covers the details.

You should know the following before you upgrade from any older AutoCAD release:

✔ **Wash those old Windows:** AutoCAD 2013 does *not* support older versions of Windows, such as Windows 2000, NT, 98, or Me. For AutoCAD 2013, you have three choices of operating system:

 • *Windows XP* (Home or Professional, SP3 or later)

 • *Windows Vista* (Enterprise, Business, Ultimate, or Home Premium, SP2 or later)

 • *Windows 7* (Enterprise, Ultimate, Professional, or Home Premium)

There are 64-bit versions of AutoCAD 2013 and AutoCAD LT 2013 that run in the 64-bit versions of XP, Vista, and Windows 7. 64-bit versions can access much more system memory for faster operation, while 32-bit systems are limited to 2GB or 3GB of RAM.

✔ **Application compatibility:** If you use third-party applications with a previous AutoCAD release, they may not work with AutoCAD 2013. AutoCAD applications developed with the .NET or the ObjectARX (AutoCAD Runtime eXtension) interfaces may or may not need to be recompiled. Many LSP (AutoLISP) programs written for the last several versions of AutoCAD should work without change.

Built-in support for VBA (Visual Basic for Applications, a Microsoft programming language) applications isn't included in AutoCAD 2013. You can continue to run VBA applications, but you first have to download and install the VBA installer from the Autodesk website. At the time this book went to press, the URL wasn't finalized; just go to www.autodesk.com and enter **VBA installer** in the Search box. There are 32- and 64-bit versions, so make sure that you download the right one for your system.

✔ **Computer system requirements:** For AutoCAD 2013, Autodesk recommends a 1.6 GHz or better Intel or AMD processor with at least 2GB of RAM if it's running in Windows XP, and a 3.0 GHz or better chip and 2GB of RAM if it's running in Windows Vista or Windows 7. The recommended operating system is Windows 7 (64-bit). Multiple and dual-core processors are supported. You also need a 1024 x 768 or higher display resolution with True Color graphics, 1GB to 2GB of available hard drive space, an Internet connection, and Microsoft Internet Explorer 7 or later.

✔ **Additional requirements for working in 3D:** AutoCAD recommends a 3 GHz or better processor; 4GB or more of RAM; a workstation-class, Direct3D-capable graphics card with at least 128MB of memory; and an additional 2GB of hard drive space beyond the 1GB required for installation.

I find even the recommended system requirements to be on the minimal side. For example, between the two of us we run a desktop computer at screen resolutions of 1600 x 1200 and 1280 x 1024 (yes, dual monitors), a tablet computer at 1400 x 1050, a desktop at 1280 x 1024, and a laptop at 1920 x 1200. The figures in this book were shot at a resolution of 1024 x 768, and as you can see, things can get pretty crowded at that resolution. The problem is that things like icons and dialog boxes display at a fixed number of pixels, so at lower resolutions, they take up more of the screen.

When you're running AutoCAD, there is no such thing as too much RAM.

You should also note that a gaming graphics card is different from an engineering graphics card. It's well worth the few extra dollars to get an engineering card, especially when working in 3D. So how can you tell the difference? First, check the price. Engineering boards will usually be a little more expensive, but not outrageously so. Next, check the name. Engineering boards often have dull and boring names, while gaming boards have names that

hint at violence and action. For example, the NVIDIA product line contains GeForce and Quadro series. Can you tell which one is the Engineering series? Finally, check the manufacturer's specifications. They usually spell out quite clearly which is which.

Suddenly, It's 2013!

There's been a new release of AutoCAD every spring since AutoCAD 2004 was launched in 2003. That's not much time for even an army of programmers to deliver a compelling new feature set that's going to convince all users that they just have to upgrade. What seems to have been happening is a concentration on particular areas in recent releases. For example, AutoCAD 2007 was a 3D release; the 3D modeling engine was made much easier to use, but there was relatively little to please the 2D crowd. By contrast, AutoCAD 2008 was deemed to be "the drafter's release" because of the number of enhancements to 2D drawing capabilities — above all, the introduction of annotative documentation objects.

In AutoCAD 2009, the new interface got the lion's share of development (suddenly, it's Office 2007!); major new features were limited to some 3D navigation tools, the very useful Quick Properties tool, and a palettized Layer Properties Manager. AutoCAD 2010 offered significant enhancements to both 2D and 3D users, in parametric drafting tools and free-form mesh modeling, and AutoCAD 2011 introduced some workflow changes and a welcome new object property, *transparency*.

The big news in AutoCAD 2012 was associative arrays. Arrays allow you to very quickly create a repeated pattern of objects, such as building columns or bolt-hole patterns. Previously, they were just multiple copies, but with AutoCAD 2012, they became linked objects. For example, if you edit one item in the array, then all copies of it in the array also update. We cover arrays in more detail in Chapters 11 and 18.

Each new release of AutoCAD typically includes about 200 new or enhanced features. It would take a full chapter just to outline the *What's New* guide issued by Autodesk. Rather than listing everything, we just hit the high spots here.

As noted earlier, what's new in each new AutoCAD release tends to have a theme. This time, it's mainly 3D enhancements for mechanical designers, including the ability to directly open Autodesk Inventor 3D model files, and to automatically create 2D working views from them. The files remain linked so that any changes made in Inventor reflect through to the AutoCAD drawing. A

full discussion of this is beyond the scope of this book, but we do introduce 3D in Part V.

Some of the additions, changes, and improvements of interest to us include the following:

- ✔ **Command line:** Improvements to displaying and accessing the command history.

- ✔ **Visual previewing:** Many editing operations display a preview. For example, you can see what a new color will look like before actually applying the color to the object.

- ✔ **Arrays:** Enhancements to the creation and editing of arrays.

- ✔ **Crosshatching:** Improved editing of hatch patterns.

Okay, let's do it!

Le Tour de AutoCAD 2013

*A*utoCAD 2013 is a full-fledged and thoroughly up-to-date member of the Windows world, but if your last kick at the software was AutoCAD 2008, or you're using Windows XP, or you've yet to kick the tires of the Microsoft Office 2007 suite, you may not recognize much in AutoCAD's newest release. But the title bar says "AutoCAD 2013," so you must be in the right place!

Like the rest of the book, this chapter is written for someone who has used other Windows programs but has little or no experience with AutoCAD. If you *are* experienced with recent releases of AutoCAD, some of this chapter may be old hat (even if it does *look* different). Here and throughout the rest of the book, we show you how to do things by using AutoCAD's implementation of Microsoft's Fluent User Interface (or FUI for short; pronounced *fooey*). In the "Going for that classic look" sidebar later in this chapter, we show you how to make the new version look a lot like an old one.

By default, AutoCAD 2013 opens in the Drafting & Annotation workspace, and will continue to do so until you make another workspace current. (We explain workspaces in the section "And They're Off: AutoCAD's Opening Screens," later in this chapter.) If you've been away from AutoCAD for a while, right now you may be asking yourself, "Where are my toolbars? Where is my menu bar? Where is the text-only side screen menu (if you have been away for a *long* time)?" Unlike older Windows programs, AutoCAD 2013 sports just one toolbar — the Quick Access Toolbar, on the application title bar, right next to the Application button (known informally as the "Big Red A") — and doesn't show a menu bar in this environment. Instead, the Drafting & Annotation workspace displays two major interface items:

- **The Application Menu:** Clicking the Application button at the top-left corner of the AutoCAD window opens the AutoCAD 2013 Application Menu, which presents file-related commands only; here you can create new drawings, open existing drawings, save files, or print your masterpieces.

- **The Ribbon:** The Ribbon replaces the menus, toolbars, many of the palettes, and the dashboard of earlier releases. Whereas the Application Menu focuses on file management, the Ribbon is where you find commands to create and modify drawing objects. The Autodesk programmers made a best guess at a task-based approach to drafting and organized the old interface items into panels of related tools.

We discuss both of these items in more detail in the following sections. For the dyed-in-the-wool traditionalists, you can reset the AutoCAD 2013 environment so it looks pretty much like it did in AutoCAD 2008. We show you how in the "Going for that classic look" sidebar, later in this chapter.

AutoCAD Does Windows (And Office)

Whether you're a total newcomer or an experienced user from a few releases back, we can guarantee that finding your way around AutoCAD 2013 is going to be an interesting experience.

If you're already familiar with the Microsoft Office 2007 suite, you may recognize some program features, such as the Ribbon and the Application Menu, which you use for choosing commands or changing system settings. But even if AutoCAD's new look does seem a little familiar in places, many aspects of the program's appearance — and some of the ways in which you work with it — are quite different from other Windows programs. Depending on the workspace you've chosen to use, you can, in many cases, tell the program what to do in at least five ways — pick a toolbar button, pick from a pull-down menu, pick a tool button from a Ribbon panel, type at the keyboard, or choose from a right-click menu — none of which is necessarily the best method to use for every task.

Profiling your display

The illustrations and descriptions in this chapter and throughout the book show the *default* configuration of the AutoCAD 2013 Drafting & Annotation workspace — that is, the way the screen looks if you use the standard version of AutoCAD 2013 (not a flavored version, such as AutoCAD Architecture 2013 or AutoCAD Mechanical 2013) and don't change any display settings. You can change workspaces by clicking either the Workspace Switching button on the status bar or the Workspace drop-down menu on the Quick Access Toolbar, and then choosing a different workspace from the menu. You can change the appearance of the workspace itself with settings on the Display tab of the Options dialog box (click the Application button, and then click Options at the bottom of the Application Menu) and by dragging toolbars and other screen components.

The main change from AutoCAD's default settings that we make for this book is to configure the drawing area background to be white because the figures show up better that way when printed in the book. The default background color in both AutoCAD 2013 and AutoCAD LT 2013 is dark gray, but many long-time users prefer a pure black background because they believe there's less glare that way. (This is much less of an issue with LCD flat-panel displays.) You may want to set a black or a white background on your own system or stay with the default gray background — it's your choice, and there's no right or wrong way. Some AutoCAD object colors show up better on a light background, and some are better on a black one.

You can reset the default AutoCAD 2013 color scheme from the Options dialog box Display tab. Click Colors to open the Drawing Window Colors dialog box, and then click the Restore Classic Colors button. AutoCAD 2013 includes a couple of skinlike color schemes, also accessible from the Display tab of the Options dialog box. Designed to enhance the look of the Ribbon-based interface and ingeniously named Light and Dark, the differences between them are pretty subtle and apply to Windows elements (such as the title and taskbar), not to AutoCAD elements like crosshairs or background colors.

Slick as they are, navigating Ribbon panels and browsing through the Application Menu aren't always the most efficient way of doing things. When you want to get real work done, you need to combine the Ribbon panels with other methods — especially entering options at the keyboard or choosing them from the right-click menus. We show you how throughout this book.

And They're Off: AutoCAD's Opening Screens

In addition to the Drafting & Annotation workspace, a few additional pre-configured workspaces are available from the Workspace Switching button. However, for most of this book, we stick with the out-of-the-box Drafting & Annotation workspace (the exception is Part V, which deals with 3D modeling), and we recommend you do the same as you read along.

A *workspace* is a collection of menus, palettes, toolbars, and/or Ribbon panels tailored for specific tasks, such as 3D modeling or 2D drafting.

After you switch workspaces, AutoCAD remembers which one you last used and opens in that one. Four standard workspaces are created when you install AutoCAD 2013 (only two come with AutoCAD LT 2013):

- ✏ **Drafting & Annotation:** This workspace (shown in Figure 2-1) is configured for a 2D drafting environment, with Ribbon tabs and panels optimized for technical drawing in two dimensions.

- ✏ **3D Basics:** This workspace is designed to help you get your feet wet with 3D modeling in AutoCAD 2013. It leaves out the Solid, Surface, and Mesh object creation tabs, and provides simplified panels in the other tabs. We cover modeling in 3D in Part V of this book, and there we use (and recommend that you do the same) the full 3D Modeling workspace Ribbon. This workspace isn't included in AutoCAD LT because LT doesn't do 3D.

Application button

In-canvas viewport controls Title bar

Quick Access toolbar InfoCenter

Status bar Command window Navigation bar

Welcome screen

Figure 2-1: Where's my AutoCAD?: The AutoCAD 2013 Drafting & Annotation workspace.

✔ **3D Modeling:** This Ribbon-based workspace is configured for a 3D modeling environment, with navigation, visualization, and modeling tools suitable for working in 3D. This workspace isn't included in AutoCAD LT, either.

✔ **AutoCAD Classic:** This workspace is configured for a 2D drafting environment, with toolbars and tool palette arrangements similar to those in AutoCAD 2008 and earlier. In AutoCAD LT, this workspace is called AutoCAD LT Classic.

AutoCAD 2013 added the Welcome screen, as shown in Figure 2-1. It appears when you first launch AutoCAD, and contains a number of quick links to recent drawings, What's New and Getting Started tutorials, and so on. If (or more likely, *when*) you begin finding it to be irksome it can be turned off. In fact, if you're using a computer that belongs to someone else, such as a school or office, you will probably find that it has already been turned off.

Going for that classic look

Like it or not, the Ribbon-based user interface isn't going away any time soon. We didn't care for the 2D Drafting & Annotation workspace when it first showed up in AutoCAD 2008, but thanks to the Ribbon, we're now more or less sold on it. AutoCAD 2013's Drafting & Annotation workspace is where we spend most of our time, and that's what nearly all the figures in this book (including the figure here) show.

(continued)

(continued)

Unlike the Microsoft Office 2007 suite, which dragged longtime users kicking and screaming into the new Fluent User Interface (except for one of us who went back to Office 2003 with the Microsoft Compatibility Pack), AutoCAD users have the option of staying with the old interface. The easiest way to go back to the future is to switch workspaces by using (what else?) the Workspace Switching button on the status bar, or the Workspace drop-down menu on the Quick Access Toolbar. Select AutoCAD Classic, and presto! — this is (almost) your father's AutoCAD! You end up with a menu bar; some familiar-looking toolbars docked to the top, left, and right sides of the drawing area; and a floating tool palette near the middle of the display.

The Ribbon-based interface lets you add bits of the old one, too. You can display the classic drop-down menu system by clicking the down arrow at the right end of the Quick Access Toolbar and choosing Show Menu Bar. You can also stay mostly in the Ribbon but display your favorite classic toolbars at the same time. Just click Toolbars on the Windows panel of the View tab, click AutoCAD to display the entire list of toolbars, and then select the ones you want.

Running with Ribbons

Whether you're running AutoCAD 2013 in Windows 7, Vista, or XP, most of the AutoCAD default screen (refer to Figure 2-1) is pretty different from traditional Windows fare. Yes, you have title bars and a status bar, but the rest of the interface might look foreign. We cover the familiar stuff first.

A hierarchy of title bars

Like most Windows programs, AutoCAD has a *title bar* at the top of its application window, which reminds you which program you're in (not that you'd ever mistake the AutoCAD 2013 window for, say, FreeCell — or even AutoCAD 2008!). After you open a drawing or start a new one, it shows the filename.

- **On the program's title bar:** At the right side of the program title bar is the standard set of three Windows control buttons: Minimize, Maximize/Restore, and Close.

- **On the file's title bar:** Each nonmaximized drawing window within the AutoCAD program window has its own title bar, as shown in Figure 2-2. You can use the control buttons on a drawing window's title bar to minimize, maximize/restore, or close that drawing instead of the entire AutoCAD program.

As in other Windows programs, if you maximize a drawing's window, it expands to fill the entire drawing area. In the AutoCAD 2013 Drafting & Annotation workspace, a maximized drawing window's control buttons have migrated south, from the menu bar (which isn't there anymore) to the upper-right corner of the drawing area itself. To un-maximize (restore) the drawing so that you can see any other drawings that you have open, click the lower Restore button.

Drawing window title bar Drawing window control buttons

Figure 2-2: The AutoCAD screen with several windowed drawings in view.

The program title or drawing name is centered in the title bar instead of being off to the left. The AutoCAD title bar also has these couple of devices added to it:

- **InfoCenter:** Located at the right side of the program title bar, this is Information Central for AutoCAD. Type a keyword and then click the binoculars for more information, or sign in to your Autodesk account if you have one. The next two buttons both open the Autodesk Exchange for AutoCAD window. The button that looks like a half-positive, half-negative X opens the Exchange window home page with links to What's New videos and the Autodesk Subscription Center (alas, not included in the price of admission). You can download free or inexpensive add-on programs from the Apps page. Clicking the question mark button in the InfoCenter area, as you can probably figure out for yourself, opens the Exchange window Help page.

- **Quick Access Toolbar:** This permanent toolbar (the only one common to all workspaces) contains frequently used commands in an easily accessible location. You can add and remove tool buttons by clicking the down arrow at the right end of the Quick Access Toolbar and selecting or deselecting the ones you want to add or remove, respectively.

If you're floundering around looking for the commands you used to be able to find, a life preserver is hiding in the drop-down menu at the right end of the Quick Access Toolbar. Click Show Menu Bar, and the old familiar classic menu appears above the Ribbon.

Making choices from the Application Menu

The Application Menu is accessible from all workspaces. The AutoCAD 2013 Application Menu follows the Microsoft FUI guidelines in placing file management commands here, and all drawing and editing commands on the Ribbon. The Application Menu is divided into nine categories, as follows:

- **New:** Create a new drawing from a list of templates or create a new *sheet set* (a named collection of drawing layouts derived from one or more drawing files that can be printed or archived at one go). Sheet sets are included in AutoCAD 2013 and LT 2013, but we don't cover them in this book.

- **Open:** Open an existing drawing or sheet set for editing, or import data from a MicroStation DGN file into a new AutoCAD drawing.

- **Save:** Save the current drawing in the current location; if the current drawing hasn't been saved, you're prompted for a filename and a location.

- **Save As:** Save the current drawing to a new filename and/or location and make the newly named or located file the current drawing. Also save the drawing as a template (DWT) or standards (DWS) file, or export a paper space layout to a new drawing.

 Use the DWG Convert tool to save drawing files to different DWG formats as far back as AutoCAD 2000. Yes, you can already do that with the regular SAVEAS command, but DWG Convert can do batch conversions of groups of files and entire file folders.

- **Export:** Save the current drawing to a variety of Design Web Format (DWF) files, a PDF, a DGN, or several other CAD file formats. We discuss many of these formats in Chapters 18 and 20.

 AutoCAD 2013 exports to FBX format (that's one we don't discuss in this book). FBX is specifically designed to export lights and materials — even animation data (and haven't we come a long way from lines and circles?) from AutoCAD drawings to more specialized 3D programs like Autodesk Maya or Max. In short: If you need this format, you already know about it.

- **Publish:** Send a 3D model to an outside 3D printing service or create an archived sheet set. (AutoCAD LT doesn't support 3D.) Use eTransmit to create a package that includes all files referenced by the selected drawings, or e-mail the current drawing by using your configured e-mail client.

- **Print:** Print a single drawing or batch plot multiple drawings, create or modify named page setups, and manage plotters and plot styles. We cover most of these operations in Chapter 16.

- **Drawing Utilities:** Set file properties or drawing units; purge unused blocks, layers, and styles from the current drawing; and audit or recover damaged drawings.

✔ **Close:** Close the current drawing or close all drawings. If any drawings have been changed, you're prompted to save before AutoCAD closes the file.

But wait! There's more under the Big Red A

In addition to the Application Menu's actual file menu items, a few other features are worth a mention:

✔ **Recent Documents:** If you choose this option, the right pane displays a list of drawings that you recently edited but that aren't currently open. You can show them in a simple list or as thumbnail images, as shown in Figure 2-3. You can also pin them to stop them from scrolling off the list. Naturally enough, clicking one of the icons opens the drawing.

✔ **Open Documents:** Choose this option to see what's already open, and click an item to switch to it. This is equivalent to pressing Alt+Tab to switch between open documents in any Windows program and works the same basic way as the Quick View Drawings feature, described in the "Looking for Mr. Status Bar" section, later in the chapter.

✔ **Options:** Click this button to open the Options dialog box, where you can make hundreds of system settings. You can also open Options by typing **OP** (the alias for the OPTIONS command).

Figure 2-3: Find that drawing you know that you worked on yesterday.

✔ **Search:** If you're not sure of a command name or you want help on a topic, just start typing in the Application Menu's search bar. AutoCAD 2013 very quickly displays a categorized list, complete with links to start commands or to access the online help (see Figure 2-4).

Figure 2-4: If you can't find it in the Ribbon or tool buttons, just start typing!

A quick way to close AutoCAD is to double-click the big red A. AutoCAD asks if you want to save unsaved drawings, and then shuts down.

Unraveling the Ribbon

The primary interface element in the Drafting & Annotation, 3D Basics, and 3D Modeling workspaces is the *Ribbon,* an adjustable area that contains different collections of tabbed, task-oriented collections of panels. Some panels — those marked with a little black triangle on the panel label — have more tools concealed on a slideout (see Figure 2-5). Click the panel label to open the slideout. You can click the pushpin icon to pin the slideout open — otherwise, it will slide away home after you click a button.

In AutoCAD 2013, you can click and drag a Ribbon panel and pull it into the drawing area. So if, for example, you find yourself doing a whack of dimensioning, but you also want to move away from the Annotate tab to other Ribbon tabs, you can drag the Dimensions panel into the drawing, and it will stay put, even as you switch to other panels or tabs. Just be sure to put it back where it came from when you're finished with it (as your mom used to say).

Panel slideout

Figure 2-5: More tools than you can wave a Ribbon at.

Autodesk's programmers see the Ribbon as an alternative way of interacting with the program. Theoretically, the Ribbon eliminates the need for menus and separate toolbars, although the change-averse may think otherwise. The Ribbon is fully customizable, but we don't get into customizing AutoCAD in this book. If you want to find out more, click Customization Guide in the AutoCAD 2013 online help Home page.

By default, the Ribbon is docked at the top of the screen, but it can be docked against any edge, anchored to the left or right side of the AutoCAD window, or floated. To gain some screen space, you can click the little white button to the right of the last tab on the Ribbon's tab bar to reduce the amount of space the Ribbon takes, or use the drop-down menu next to the little white button to tailor the Ribbon's display to just the way you want it.

Instead of menus of grouped commands like Draw, Modify, Insert, and so forth, the tabs are organized by task as follows:

✔ **Home:** The Home tab contains Draw, Modify, Layers, Annotation, Block, Properties, Groups, Utilities, and Clipboard panels. Some panels may be displayed as collapsed, depending on your screen resolution. As an example, the five panels at the right end of the Annotate tab in Figure 2-5 are in a collapsed state. We cover most of the commands in these panels in other parts of the book.

✔ **Insert:** This tab groups Block and Reference panels, as well as Point Cloud tools, Import commands, and a series of commands for working with nongraphical information, including attributes, fields, and data links. We do cover blocks (Chapter 17) and external references (Chapter 18), but point clouds, importing, and data tools are beyond the scope of this book and aren't covered.

✔ **Annotate:** The Annotate tab expands on the minimalist Annotation panel on the Home tab, with many more options for creating text, dimensions, leaders, and tables, as well as markup functions and a few annotation scaling tools.

✔ **Layout:** This tab includes a series of panels used to create and modify paper space layouts, and to create 2D drawing views from 3D models. We cover paper space layouts in Chapters 4 and 5 and introduce 3D in Part V.

✔ **Parametric:** This tab is home for one of AutoCAD 2013's most powerful features — parametric drawing. You can apply geometric or dimensional parameters or constraints to drawing objects so that, say, two circles are always concentric or the length of a rectangle is always twice its width. (AutoCAD LT is limited in this department: You can modify or delete existing constraints, but you need the full version of AutoCAD to create them.) We introduce parametric drawing in Chapter 19.

✔ **View:** The View tab contains tools and panels for controlling drawing display, working with viewports, loading various palettes, and organizing Windows functions such as cascading open files or displaying different parts of the application window. We explain most of the features on this tab later in the book.

✔ **Manage:** This tab contains panels that access the Action Recorder, CAD Standards (neither of which is in AutoCAD LT), and a set of drawing management and customization tools. We don't cover anything on the Manage tab in this book.

✔ **Output:** Panels on this tab allow you to get those drawings off your hands by printing (also known as *plotting*), publishing, exporting to PDF or DWF files, or simply sending them electronically to others. We cover some of these functions in Chapter 16.

✔ **Plug-Ins:** This tab is present in both AutoCAD and AutoCAD LT, although in LT, there is only one panel instead of two. Both versions have a Content panel with a single Explore button that runs the new Content Explorer tool. After you let it index your file folders, Content Explorer can winnow through all your drawings looking for specific blocks, layers, layouts, and even text strings. AutoCAD itself also has an Inventor Fusion panel, from which you can edit solids and surfaces in a stripped-down version of Autodesk Inventor.

✔ **Online:** This tab is also present in both AutoCAD and AutoCAD LT, and this time, the tabs are identical. Most of the buttons fire up a login screen for the AutoCAD WS service. With an AutoCAD WS account, you can upload drawings to a secure website, and then access them on your iPad (you *do* have an iPad, right?), Android device, or on any computer with a web browser. You can also invite non-AutoCAD users to view and mark up your drawings, using a standard web browser.

No Express service?

If your Ribbon doesn't include the Express Tools tab (at the far right in Figure 2-1), you should consider installing the Express Tools from your AutoCAD DVD. (AutoCAD LT does not include or support the Express Tools.)

When you first install AutoCAD, you choose between a Typical and a Custom installation. If you choose Typical, the next screen asks whether you want to install the Express Tools. If you choose a Custom installation, in the next screen, make sure to select the Express Tools item in the list of components. If you don't install the Express Tools during initial setup, you'll have to rerun the setup routine from your AutoCAD DVD or USB stick. If you haven't installed AutoCAD yet, we strongly recommend that you choose the Typical installation option — or at least make sure that the Express Tools check box is selected checked during a Custom installation.

✓ **Express Tools:** The Express Tools are an invaluable set of custom commands that streamline your work procedures in pretty well every aspect of AutoCAD. They're officially unsupported, but they've been an install option for many releases now, and mostly, they work very well. You get this tab only if you have the full version of AutoCAD — Express Tools aren't available in AutoCAD LT.

Other Ribbon tabs may exist if you purchased AutoCAD as part of a suite. AutoCAD *suites* are series of collections of related Autodesk products sold in one package under one serial number.

Getting with the Program

In most of this book, we focus on 2D drafting, which is by far the easiest way of getting your feet wet with AutoCAD. (Just don't be dripping water on your computer.) And if you're not already in the Drafting & Annotation workspace, we suggest that you use the Workspace Switching button to return to it. After you make the switch to this workspace, AutoCAD displays the interface shown earlier in Figure 2-1.

Like all good Windows programs, AutoCAD has *tooltips,* those short descriptions that appear in little text boxes when you hover the mouse pointer over a button. In AutoCAD 2013, tooltips display two levels of information. When you hover the mouse pointer over a tool button, you first see a quick identification of the command. If you keep hovering, a longer description of the icon's function, often with a graphic image, appears in an extended tooltip. Helpful as they are when you're starting with AutoCAD, you'll probably want to remove these training wheels sooner or later. You can do so in the Options dialog box. (See the online help for more information.)

Looking for Mr. Status Bar

The *application status bar* (see Figure 2-6) appears at the bottom of the AutoCAD screen. The status bar displays and allows you to change several important drawing modes, aids, and settings that affect how you draw and edit in the current drawing. We introduce them in this section.

You can set status bar buttons to display icons or the traditional text labels that will be familiar to users of earlier releases. To switch from one style to the other, right-click any of the drawing mode buttons at the left side of the status bar and select or deselect Use Icons.

Status bar buttons showing icons

Status bar buttons showing text labels

Figure 2-6: Status (bars) check.

Some of these status bar settings won't make complete sense until you've used the AutoCAD commands that they influence, but here's a brief description, with references to detailed descriptions of how to use each setting, starting at the left end of the status bar (and note that not all buttons are displayed at all times, so Figure 2-6 doesn't show all the buttons listed):

- ✔ **Coordinates of the crosshairs:** The coordinates readout displays the current X,Y,Z location of the crosshairs in the drawing area, with respect to the origin point, whose coordinates are 0,0,0. (AutoCAD LT displays only the X,Y crosshairs location.) Chapter 7 describes AutoCAD's coordinate conventions and how to use this area of the status bar.

 If the coordinates in the lower-left corner of the screen are grayed out, coordinate tracking is turned off. Click the coordinates so that they appear in dark numbers that change when you move the crosshairs in the drawing area.

- ✔ **Infer Constraints (INFER):** Parametric constraints were new in AutoCAD 2010. (The inferred constraints feature isn't available in AutoCAD LT.) When Infer Constraints is enabled, you automatically set geometry-based constraints as you draw. We cover geometric and dimensional constraints in Chapter 19.

- ✔ **Snap Mode (SNAP):** Constrains the crosshairs to regularly spaced intervals, enabling you to draw objects a fixed distance apart more easily.

✔ **Grid Display (GRID):** Displays a series of graph paper–style lines or regularly spaced dots, which serve as a distance reference.

✔ **Ortho Mode (ORTHO):** Constrains the crosshairs to horizontal and vertical movement, which makes drawing *orthogonal* (straight horizontal and vertical) lines easy.

See Chapter 4 for instructions on how to configure these modes and Chapter 7 for information about why, when, and how to use them in actual drawing operations.

✔ **Polar Tracking (POLAR):** Polar tracking causes the crosshairs to jump to certain angles when you draw and edit objects. The default angle settings are multiples of 90 degrees, but you can specify other angle increments, such as 45 or 30 degrees. See Chapter 7 for instructions on specifying the polar tracking angles that you prefer. Clicking the Polar button toggles polar tracking on and off. Ortho and polar tracking are *mutually exclusive* — turning on one mode disables the other.

✔ **Object Snap (OSNAP):** Object snap is another AutoCAD tool for ensuring precision drawing and editing. You use object snaps to grab points on existing objects — for example, the endpoint of a line or the center of a circle. Chapter 7 contains detailed instructions on how to use this feature.

✔ **3D Object Snap (3DOSNAP):** With AutoCAD's enhanced 3D capabilities, an extension of object snaps into the third dimension was a given (not in AutoCAD LT, of course). Enabling this mode lets you snap to the precise center of a face, a vertex, the midpoint of an edge, or a number of similar 3D points you can't get to with regular object snaps.

✔ **Object Snap Tracking (OTRACK):** When you turn on *object snap tracking,* AutoCAD hunts in a more sophisticated way for points that are derived from object snap points. Chapter 7 briefly describes this advanced feature.

✔ **Allow/Disallow Dynamic UCS (DUCS):** This one's for 3D object creation (and so isn't included in AutoCAD LT). Most AutoCAD primitive objects, such as lines, arcs, and circles, are planar, and you have to set an appropriate 2D plane in three dimensions if you want to work in 3D. You can set planes with the UCS command — we explain how in Chapter 22 — but enabling Dynamic UCS automatically sets the workplane by simply hovering the mouse over the face of an object.

✔ **Dynamic Input (DYN):** *Dynamic Input* displays commands, options, prompts, and user input in a tooltip adjacent to the crosshairs and enables you to keep focused on what you're drawing. In addition, the Dynamic Input tooltip displays what you type in response to prompts. We describe Dynamic Input later in this chapter.

✔ **Show/Hide Lineweight (LWT):** One of the properties that you can assign to objects in AutoCAD is *lineweight* — the thickness that lines appear when you plot the drawing. This button controls whether you see the lineweights on the screen. (This button doesn't control whether lineweights appear on plots; that's a separate setting in the Plot dialog box.) Chapter 6 gives you the skinny (and the wide) on lineweights.

✔ **Show/Hide Transparency (TPY):** You can assign transparency to individual objects or to all objects on a given layer. Similar to the Lineweight button, this button controls whether objects assigned the transparency property appear transparent or opaque. We introduce you to object transparency in Chapter 6.

✔ **Quick Properties (QP):** When *Quick Properties* is enabled, selecting an object in the drawing displays a pop-up window that lists a selection of properties of that object. You can choose which properties you want displayed by right-clicking the QP button and choosing Settings. We fill you in on object properties in Chapter 6.

✔ **Selection Cycling (SC):** It's remarkably easy in AutoCAD to draw objects on top of other objects and not be able to tell you've done so. When Selection Cycling is enabled, an icon showing two overlapping rectangles appears beside the crosshairs if AutoCAD finds more than one object under them. If you then click to select, a Selection window pops up showing you how many objects, and of what type, are under the point that you picked (see Figure 2-7).

✔ **Annotation Monitor:** When using associative annotations, such as dimensions, it's possible for the link between the annotation and the object it's annotating to get broken. When turned on, the Annotation Monitor warns you of this and highlights the offending objects.

MODEL
PAPER

✔ **Model or Paper Space (MODEL/PAPER):** Clicking this button toggles between model space and paper space.

Figure 2-7: Overlapping objects listed in the Selection window.

As we describe in the upcoming section, "Down the main stretch: The drawing area," AutoCAD's drawing area is composed of two overlapping environments: *Model space* is where you create your model geometry, and *paper space* is where you compose your drawing sheet to document that geometry. Clicking this button when the Model *tab* is active (that is, you're in full-screen model space) switches you to a paper space layout. A completed layout includes *viewports,* which reveal the objects in model space at a particular scale. (We tell you more about viewports and layouts in Chapter 5.) After you switch to a paper space layout, clicking this button toggles between paper space and model space *within the layout.* The button label switches from MODEL to PAPER to show you which space you're in.

- **Model and <Layout>:** These two buttons disappear if Model and Layout tabs are displayed. Clicking the Model button switches you out of the layout and back to full-screen model space. (If Model and Layout tabs are displayed, you click the Model *tab* to switch to full-screen model space.) Clicking Layout switches you to whichever paper space layout was active when you switched to model space. Also note that the tooltip for the Layout button displays the name of the layout, which might be changed from the default Layout1 or Layout2.

- **Quick View Layouts:** Clicking this button displays a horizontal row of graphic images of all layouts in the current drawing. Click a layout image to make that layout current. The Quick View toolbar below the layout images contains buttons for pinning the Quick View Layouts bar so it stays open, creating a new layout, publishing the selected layout, and closing Quick View Layouts. We cover layout creation in Chapter 5 and publishing in Chapter 16.

- **Quick View Drawings:** Clicking this button displays a row of graphic images of all open drawings. Click a drawing image to make it active. Quick View Drawings includes the same Quick View toolbar as Quick View Layouts. We cover this in Chapter 5.

- **Maximize/Minimize Viewport (appears on paper space layouts only):** When you're looking at one of the Layout tabs instead of the Model tab, the status bar displays an additional Maximize Viewport button. Click this button to expand the current paper space viewport so that it fills the entire drawing area. Click the button — now called Minimize Viewport — again to restore the viewport to its normal size. (Chapter 5 describes viewports.)

The next group of buttons controls the size and appearance of AutoCAD's annotative objects — things like text, dimensions, hatching, and so forth. Annotative objects appear to be complex, so don't worry if you don't understand at this point. For now, just remember that, in this chapter, we're just showing you what the buttons do. Because *annotative objects* means text more than anything else, we explain this powerful feature that actually simplifies drawing processes in Chapter 13.

✔ **Lock/Unlock Viewport:** When you're satisfied with the display inside your viewport, and you've assigned a viewport scale, use this button to lock the viewport display so you don't accidentally pan or zoom inside it. (See Chapter 5 for more on viewports.)

✔ **Annotation Scale (appears in full-screen model space only):** Clicking Annotation Scale displays a list of preset annotation scales; if the Automatically Add Scales button is toggled on, changing a scale here causes all annotative objects to update to the new scale.

✔ **Viewport Scale:** This button appears only in a layout, when a model space viewport is activated. If the viewport is locked, this button is inactive. If the viewport is unlocked, clicking the button displays a list of scales; choose the desired scale from the list.

✔ **Annotation Scale Is Not Equal To Viewport Scale:** If the scale assigned to annotative objects within the viewport differs from the scale assigned to the viewport itself, clicking this button will synchronize the annotation scale to the viewport scale.

✔ **Annotation Visibility:** This button toggles the visibility of annotative objects. When the light bulb is off (gray), only annotative objects of the current annotative scale are visible; when the light bulb is on (yellow), all annotative objects in the drawing, regardless of scale, are visible.

✔ **Automatically Add Scales:** When this button is toggled on, additional annotative scales are automatically added to objects inside the viewport when you change the viewport scale.

✔ **Workspace Switching:** Clicking this button displays a list of saved workspaces, including the four default workspaces (two in AutoCAD LT): AutoCAD Classic, Drafting & Annotation, 3D Basics, and 3D Modeling (the latter two aren't included in AutoCAD LT), plus any user-defined and saved workspaces.

✔ **Lock/Unlock Toolbar/Window Positions:** "Now, where did we leave that Properties palette?" You'll never have to ask yourself that question again because you can click this button to lock the Ribbon, toolbars, or palettes in position, so you'll always know where they are.

✔ **Hardware Acceleration:** You can quickly toggle hardware acceleration on and off from the status bar. Prior to AutoCAD 2011, you had to run the 3DCONFIG command and proceed through a couple of dialog boxes. Visit the online help to find out more about improved graphics performance and better rendering options by using hardware acceleration; hardware acceleration is available in both AutoCAD and AutoCAD LT.

The remaining status bar icons, with the exception of Clean Screen at the very end, live in a special area of the status bar called the *tray*. The tray displays icons that represent drawing services, and most do not appear at all times. These tray icons include

 ✓ **Trusted Autodesk DWG:** A *trusted drawing* is one created by AutoCAD, AutoCAD LT, or any program developed by Autodesk. In recent years, more and more programs have been able to save in DWG format, but in Autodesk's eyes, these files are not to be trusted. If you open such a drawing file, you'll get a warning dialog box and a little yellow danger sign over the trusted DWG icon (make sure that you know where your wallet is when you work on one of these files).

 ✓ **Object Isolation:** You don't need to turn a layer — and everything on it — off if you want a clearer view of something in a crowded drawing. Now you can select an object and either hide it (so it disappears) or isolate it (so everything else disappears). If the light bulb on this button is dim, one or more objects are either hidden or isolated; click the button and choose Unisolate Objects to turn everything else — including the light bulb icon — back on.

 ✓ **Associated Standards File:** You see this button if you've enabled CAD standards-checking and configured a drawing standards (DWS) file. Clicking this button displays the Check Standards dialog box. AutoCAD's CAD Standards functions are not included in AutoCAD LT. We don't cover standards-checking in this book.

 ✓ **Manage Xrefs:** You won't see this combination button and notification symbol until you open a drawing that contains *xrefs* (external DWG files that are incorporated into the current drawing). Chapter 18 tells you how to use xrefs and what the Manage Xrefs button does.

✓ **Status Bar Menu:** When you click the easy-to-miss, downward-pointing arrow near the right end of the status bar, you open a menu with options for toggling off or on each status bar button. Now you can decorate your status bar to your taste. You can also turn on the *drawing status bar*. Doing so moves any of these tray icons and the three annotation scaling buttons described earlier to a separate drawing-specific status bar. (My personal preference is to leave it turned off.)

✓ **Clean Screen:** No, this button doesn't squeegee your monitor. Clicking this button frees up a bit more screen space by first maximizing the AutoCAD window and then turning off the title bar, toolbars, palettes, and the Windows taskbar. Click the button again to restore those elements.

Several status bar buttons, including Snap Mode, Polar Tracking, Object Snap, and Object Snap Tracking, sport right-click menus that offer a speedier way of setting options. With some of the other buttons, such as Grid Display and Dynamic Input, you right-click the button and choose Settings to open the Drafting Settings dialog box to specify options. Chapters 4 and 6 give you specific guidance about when and how to change these settings.

In AutoCAD 2013, primary access to the display commands is via the Navigation bar that appears, by default, at the right edge of the program window. AutoCAD also has a ViewCube that provides an alternative to the

Orbit tool. (Neither the ViewCube nor the Orbit tool are included in AutoCAD LT.) Figure 2-8 shows the differences between the navigation devices in AutoCAD (on the left) and AutoCAD LT. We introduce you to the Navigation bar buttons in the following list, and explain their operation more fully in Chapter 12. We give you the drill on the ViewCube and the Orbit tool in Chapter 21.

Figure 2-8: Navigation tools in AutoCAD (left) and AutoCAD LT (right).

✔ **SteeringWheels:** You were probably wondering when this motoring metaphor was going to pay off, right? Well, believe it or not, there really is an AutoCAD function called the SteeringWheel! (We're still looking for the Gas Pedal . . . oops, we mean GasPedal.) A *SteeringWheel* is described in the online help as a tracking menu — the idea here is that you combine a number of display operations into a single input "device." We mention SteeringWheels in Chapter 12 but point out here that it's of little use in 2D drafting — which, unfortunately, is all that AutoCAD LT users can do with it.

✔ **Pan and Zoom:** These buttons provide access to two commonly used display commands, PAN and ZOOM. PAN moves you around your drawing without changing your viewing distance; ZOOM brings the drawing objects closer so you can see more detail, or farther away so you can see more of the drawing area. These and other display commands are described in Chapter 12.

✔ **Orbit:** The Orbit tool (not available in AutoCAD LT) is an interactive device for viewing your 3D models from any angle. We describe this tool with the other 3D viewing options in Chapter 21.

✔ **ShowMotion:** The ShowMotion tool starts a rudimentary animation program. As the online help describes it, you can generate effects similar to those in TV commercials to dress up motion studies of your designs. ShowMotion isn't included in AutoCAD LT and is beyond — *well* beyond — the scope of this book.

Let your fingers do the talking: The command window

The infamous command window (or command line, or command prompt, or command area, whatever you want to call it), shown in Figure 2-9, is a throwback to the dark ages of AutoCAD. It puzzles newcomers and delights AutoCAD aficionados. Despite the promise of AutoCAD's heads-up Dynamic Input, for now at least, the hard truth is that you have to come to like — or at least tolerate — the command window if you want to become at all comfortable using AutoCAD.

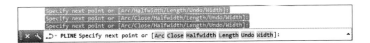

Figure 2-9: You will obey the command window; that is an order.

You should cotton on and cozy up to the command window because it's still AutoCAD's primary communications conduit with you. AutoCAD sometimes displays prompts, warnings, and error messages in the command window that Dynamic Input doesn't show — there simply isn't room in the Dynamic

Input tooltip to show as much information as you get at the command window. True, when using Dynamic Input, you can press the down-arrow key to see more options. But which is less efficient: Moving your eyes down the screen to glance at the command window, or taking your eyes right off the screen to find the down-arrow key on your keyboard? The most common mantra chanted by instructors to students is, "When all else fails, read the command line!"

The command line has gone through a major overhaul in AutoCAD 2013. It is no longer an opaque region at the bottom of the screen. Instead the command line is a semitransparent toolbar that can float anywhere on screen, allowing your drawing to show through it. This recovers some of the drawing window area that was lost to the Ribbon. Hey, Microsoft, screens are getting wider, not taller! By default it displays one command input line plus the last three input prompts, but you can change the number of input prompts that are displayed.

As a command is running, the command line will often display several options that can be invoked during the command. You invoke an option by entering the uppercase letter shown in each option. This is usually the first letter, but not always. For example, you usually enter an upper-case X to eXit from a command.

Starting with AutoCAD 2013, you don't even need to type in the option letter. You can invoke an option by selecting it in the command line.

The key (board) to AutoCAD success

Despite (or is it because of?) AutoCAD's long heritage as the most successful CAD software for personal computers, newcomers are still astonished at the amount of typing they have to do. Modern programs have much less dependency on the keyboard than AutoCAD, but as you get used to it, you'll find that no other input method gives you as much flexibility as pounding the ivories . . . oops, wrong keyboard!

Typing at your computer's keyboard is an efficient way to run some commands, and the *only* way to run a few others. Instead of clicking a button or choosing from a menu, you can start a command by typing the command name and then pressing Enter. Even better, for most common commands, you can type the short form for a command name and press Enter. Most of the short forms (called *aliases*) of command names are just one or two letters — for example, L for the LINE command, C is for CIRCLE, and CP for the COPY command. Most people who discover how to use the aliases for the commands that they run most frequently find that their AutoCAD productivity improves noticeably. If you ever watch high-speed superusers in action, they nearly always run with one hand on the mouse and the other on the keyboard. Even if you're not worried about increasing your productivity with this technique, several everyday commands are nowhere to be found on the Ribbon. If you want to run those commands, you have to type them!

AutoCAD 2013's Autocomplete feature helps you to become a keyboard jockey. Start typing a command name, and a list appears at the cursor showing all commands and options that start with the letters so far. You can continue until only your command appears, or you can scroll down the list and select another command. Aliases are also displayed for those commands that have them, so you soon learn the ones you use most often. Hands up, everyone who'd rather type APPLY than APPLYGLOBALCAPACITIES!

Not all command aliases are as obvious as L for LINE: For example, CP for COPY or — believe it or not — T for MTEXT. To see a complete list of command aliases, look in the AutoCAD (or the AutoCAD LT) Program Parameters (PGP) file by going to the Manage tab and clicking Edit Aliases on the Customization panel. When Windows Notepad opens with the acad.pgp (or acadlt.pgp) file loaded, scroll down to the Sample Aliases for AutoCAD Commands section. We don't recommend changing anything here, but it's a good idea to print this file and pin up the aliases section over your desk.

After you start a command — whether from a Ribbon panel tool button, or by typing — the Dynamic Input tooltip and the command window are where AutoCAD prompts you with options for that command. You activate one of these options by typing the uppercase letter(s) in the option and then pressing Enter.

In many cases, you can activate a command's options by right-clicking in the drawing area and choosing the desired option from the menu that appears, instead of by typing the letter(s) for the option and pressing Enter.

We like Dynamic Input. Really, we do. But sometimes it fights with normal command input, and that can make things really confusing. In the following chapters, we tell you when to be wary.

The following sequence demonstrates how you use the keyboard to run commands and view and select options. If you have Dynamic Input toggled on, your results are going to be different from what we say, so we suggest you click Dynamic Input on the status bar to turn it off, temporarily at least. In the following steps, watch the command window, and pay attention to messages from AutoCAD:

1. **Type L and then press Enter.**

 AutoCAD starts the LINE command and displays the following prompt in the command window:

   ```
   LINE Specify first point:
   ```

2. **Click a point anywhere in the drawing area.**

 The command window prompt changes to

   ```
   Specify next point or [Undo]:
   ```

3. **Click another point anywhere in the drawing area.**

 AutoCAD draws the first line segment.

4. **Click a third point anywhere in the drawing area.**

 AutoCAD draws the second line segment and prompts

   ```
   Specify next point or [Close/Undo]:
   ```

 The command line now displays two options: Close and Undo enclosed in square brackets. To activate an option, type the blue letter(s) shown in uppercase and then press Enter. You can type the option letter(s) in lowercase or uppercase.

 New in AutoCAD 2013, you can also simply click the desired option in the command line.

5. **Type** U **and then press Enter.**

 AutoCAD undoes the second line segment.

6. **Type** 3,2 **(without any spaces) and then press Enter.**

 AutoCAD draws a new line segment to the point whose X coordinate is 3 and Y coordinate is 2.

7. **Click several more points anywhere in the drawing area.**

 AutoCAD draws additional line segments.

8. **Type** X **and then press Enter.**

 X isn't a valid option of the LINE command, so AutoCAD displays an error message and prompts you again for another point:

   ```
   Point or option keyword required.
   Specify next point or [Close/Undo]:
   ```

 Option keyword is programmer jargon for the letter(s) shown in upper-case that activate a command option. This error message is AutoCAD's way of saying, "Huh? I don't understand what you mean by typing **X**. Either specify a point, or type a letter that I do understand."

9. **Type** C **and then press Enter.**

 AutoCAD draws a final line segment, which creates a closed figure and ends the LINE command. A blank command line returns, indicating that AutoCAD is ready for the next command:

   ```
   Command:
   ```

10. **Press F2.**

 AutoCAD displays the AutoCAD Text Window, which is simply an enlarged, scrollable version of the command window, as shown in the left half of Figure 2-10.

The normal three-line command window usually shows you what you need to see, but occasionally you want to review a larger chunk of command-line history. ("What was AutoCAD trying to tell me a minute ago?!")

Figure 2-10: My, how you've grown: F2 (left side) or Ctrl-F2 (right side) expands the command line to a command text window.

11. Press F2 again.

AutoCAD closes the AutoCAD Text Window.

AutoCAD 2013 added a new variation. Pressing F2 produces the scrollable text screen shown in the left half of Figure 2-10, while pressing Ctrl+F2 produces the version shown in the right half of Figure 2-10. The contents of both variants are the same. The difference is that the Ctrl+F2 version includes an Edit button. Selecting it brings up additional functions, including a fly-out list of recent commands, as shown in the right half of Figure 2-10. Selecting a previous command from the list runs it again. It doesn't matter if you opened the text window by pressing F2 or Ctrl+2; it closes when you press F2.

Here are a few other tips and tricks for effective keyboarding:

✔ **Use the Esc key to bail out of the current operation.** Sometimes you might get confused about what you're doing in AutoCAD and/or what you're seeing in the command window or the Dynamic Input tooltip. If you need to bail out of the current operation, just press Esc one or more times until you see a blank command line — Command: at the bottom of the command window, with nothing after it. As in most other Windows programs, Esc is the cancel key. Unlike many other Windows programs, AutoCAD keeps you well informed of whether an operation is in progress. The blank command line indicates that AutoCAD is resting, waiting for your next command.

✔ **Press Enter to accept the default action.** Some command prompts include a default action in angled brackets. For example, the first prompt of the POLYGON command is

```
Enter number of sides <4>:
```

The default here is four sides, and you can accept it simply by pressing Enter. (That is, you don't have to type **4** first.)

AutoCAD uses two kinds of brackets when it prompts.

- *Command options* appear in regular square brackets: [Close Undo].

 To activate a command option, type the letter(s) that appear in uppercase and then press Enter. The Dynamic Input tooltip doesn't display options in brackets; instead, you press the down-arrow key to display additional command options in rows next to the crosshairs.

- A *default value or option* appears in angled brackets: <4>.

 To choose the default value or option, simply press Enter. Default values in angled brackets appear in both the Dynamic Input tooltip and the command-line prompts.

You don't always have to press Enter to forward your input to AutoCAD. Depending on what you're doing, you can often right-click and choose Enter from the top of the right-click menu. And most efficient of all, even for the most inept typists, you can use the spacebar as an Enter key — as long as you're not entering text. That's why we said in Step 6 in the first exercise to type the entry without spaces.

✔ **Watch the command line.** You can discover a lot about how to use the command line simply by watching it after each action that you take. When you click a toolbar button or menu choice, AutoCAD displays the name of the command in the Dynamic Input tooltip and at the command line. If you're watching the command line, you'll absorb the command names more or less naturally.

When AutoCAD echoes commands automatically in response to your toolbar and menu clicks, it usually adds one or two extra characters to the front of the command name:

- AutoCAD usually puts an underscore in front of the command name: for example, _LINE instead of LINE. The underscore is an Autodesk programmers' trick that enables non-English language versions of AutoCAD to understand the English command names that are embedded in the menus.

- AutoCAD sometimes puts an apostrophe in front of the command name and any underscore (for example, '_ZOOM instead of ZOOM). The apostrophe indicates a *transparent* command; you can run a transparent command in the middle of another command without

canceling the first command. For example, you can start the LINE command, run the ZOOM command transparently, and then pick up where you left off with the LINE command.

✔ **Leave the command line in the default configuration.** The command window, like most other parts of the AutoCAD screen, is resizable and movable. The default location (docked at the bottom of the AutoCAD screen) and size (one line in the command window and three semitransparent lines extending up into the drawing area) work well for most people. Resist the temptation to mess with the command window's appearance — at least until you're comfortable with using the command line. AutoCAD 2013 adds many more configuration and display options for the command prompt, but as the popular Canadian comedian Red Green says, "If it ain't broke, you ain't tryin' hard enough."

✔ **Right-click in the command window for options.** If you right-click in the command window, you see a menu with some useful choices, including Recent Commands — the last six commands that you ran.

✔ **Press the up- and down-arrow keys to cycle through the stack of commands that you've used recently.** This is another handy way to recall and rerun a command. Press the left- and right-arrow keys to edit the command-line text that you've typed or recalled.

Most Windows users are familiar with Alt-key shortcuts. Press the Alt key in traditional Windows programs, and your menu bar lights up with one character of each menu item underlined. You type the underlined letter to open the menu or execute the command. AutoCAD's implementation of Microsoft's Fluent User Interface has an equivalent — *KeyTips* — which works in much the same way. In Figure 2-11, I just pressed the Alt key and AutoCAD displayed boxed letter icons that are equivalent to the underlining in traditional Windows programs. If I now enter AN, the Annotate tab will open with a new set of KeyTips, and I can keep entering the keys to execute a specific command.

Figure 2-11: Hold down the Alt key to display a kazillion KeyTips.

Keeping tabs on palettes

Palettes are refined (well-mannered) versions of dialog boxes. Unlike regular dialog boxes, which insist on your undivided attention as long as they're open, palettes stay discreetly in the background as you carry on with other tasks. AutoCAD still has many dialog boxes, but over the past several releases, palettes have replaced quite a few former dialog boxes.

AutoCAD 2013 contains more than a dozen palettes (less than a dozen in AutoCAD LT). Unless noted otherwise, you can open any of these palettes from the Palettes panel of the View tab. The more commonly used palettes are

- **Properties, DesignCenter, and Content Explorer:** These palettes are used to control object properties, and to find and display named objects (layers, blocks, and so on) for copying them between drawings. We cover the first two in Chapter 6.

- **Tool Palettes:** Instead of paint colors, each tool palette holds *content* (drawing symbols and hatch patterns) and/or *commands* (not regular AutoCAD commands — what would be the point? — but macros that make commands do specific things). You can create your own tool palettes, but the ones that come with AutoCAD contain dozens of symbols you can drag into your drawing — check 'em out! When you get a little more proficient in AutoCAD, tool palettes are the second easiest way of customizing AutoCAD to improve productivity and help ensure compliance with CAD standards. The easiest way is to set up custom templates for new drawings as we discuss in Chapter 4. For best results, you should use both methods.

- **Sheet Set Manager:** Provides tools for managing all of a project's drawings as a *sheet set*. We don't cover sheet sets in *AutoCAD 2013 For Dummies*.

- **External References:** Used to attach external files to the current drawing; file types include raster images, Drawing Web Format (DWF or DWFx) files, PDF files, MicroStation DGN files, and other drawing files. We discuss attaching external reference files in Chapter 18.

- **Markup Set Manager:** Displays design and drafting review comments from users of Autodesk Design Review. For more information on markup sets, see the online help.

- **QuickCalc:** A handy pushbutton scientific calculator that hides out on the Home tab's Utilities panel. You'll know if you need this.

- **Layer Properties Manager:** The main control center for managing the layers on your drawing. The palettized Layer Properties Manager not only stays open while you're doing other things, but also applies any changes you make *instantly* in the drawing. The Layer Properties Manager can be found on the Layers panel of the Home tab.

 Using the View and Home tabs is one way of opening palettes. Alternatively, several palettes have keyboard shortcuts. You can toggle these by pressing Ctrl+1 (Properties), Ctrl+2 (DesignCenter), Ctrl+3 (Tool Palettes), Ctrl+4 (Sheet Set Manager), Ctrl+7 (Markup Set Manager), or Ctrl+8 (QuickCalc).

Down the main stretch: The drawing area

After all these warm-up laps, you're probably itching for the main event — the AutoCAD drawing area. This is where you do your drawing, of course. In the course of creating drawings, you click points to specify locations and distances, click objects to select them for editing, and zoom and pan to get a better view of what you're working on.

Most of this book shows you how to interact with the drawing area, but you should know a few things upfront.

Model space and paper space layouts

One of the initially disorienting things about AutoCAD is that finished drawings can be composed of objects drawn in different *spaces,* which AutoCAD indicates with either two status bar buttons, or two or more tabs at the bottom left of the drawing area:

- ✔ **Model space:** Where you create and modify the objects that represent things in the real world — walls, widgets, waterways, or whatever.

- ✔ **Paper space:** Where you create particular views of these objects for plotting, usually with a title block around them. Paper space comprises one or more *layouts,* each of which can contain a different arrangement of model space views and different title block information.

When you click the Model button on the status bar or the Model tab, you see pure, unadulterated model space, as shown in Figure 2-12. When you click the Layout button, you see a paper space layout, as shown in Figure 2-13. A completed layout usually includes one or more *viewports,* which are windows that display all or part of model space at a particular scale. A layout also usually includes a title block or other objects that exist only in the layout and don't appear when you click the Model tab. (Think of the viewport as a window looking into model space and the title block as a frame around the window.) Thus, a layout displays model space and paper space objects together, and AutoCAD lets you draw and edit objects in either space. See Chapter 5 for information about creating paper space layouts and Chapter 16 for the lowdown on plotting them.

Figure 2-12: A building model ready for editing in model space.

Figure 2-13: Freshly laid out in paper space.

When a layout is current, you can move the crosshairs back and forth between model space and paper space while remaining in the layout. You can't be in both spaces at the same time, however; if paper space is current, you can click directly on top of a model space object, but it won't be

selected. Similarly, if model space is current, you can't select anything in paper space. To move between the two spaces, double-click inside a viewport to switch to model space or outside a viewport to switch to paper space.

This back-and-forth double-clicking is necessary only when you're drawing things while viewing one of the paper space layouts or adjusting the view of the drawing objects within the viewport. In practice, you probably won't draw very much using this method. Instead, you'll do most of your drawing on the Model tab and, after you've set up a paper space layout, click its layout tab only when you want to plot.

Drawing on the drawing area

Here are a few other things to know about the AutoCAD drawing area:

- ✓ Efficient, confident use of AutoCAD requires that you continually glance from the drawing area to the command window (to see those all-important prompts!) and then back up to the drawing area. This sequence isn't a natural reflex for most people, and that's why the Dynamic Input tooltip at the crosshairs was introduced. But you still get information from the command line that you don't get anywhere else. Get in the habit of looking at the command line after each action that you take.

- ✓ Clicking at random in the drawing area isn't quite as harmless in AutoCAD as it is in many other Windows programs. When you click in the AutoCAD drawing area, you're almost always performing some action — usually specifying a point or selecting objects for editing. Feel free to experiment, but look at the command line after each click. If you get confused, press Esc a couple of times to clear the current operation and return to the naked command prompt.

- ✓ In most cases, you can right-click in the drawing area to display a menu with some options for the current situation.

Fun with F1

AutoCAD 2013's rather limited Help menu is accessible only as a drop-down list on the program title bar. (As always, pressing F1 at any time opens the online help window.) Click the down arrow beside the question mark to open the menu.

The main AutoCAD 2013 Help system, shown in Figure 2-14, is one of the major components of the Autodesk Exchange for AutoCAD application. AutoCAD LT's setup is similar except that there's no Apps page — just the Home page and the Help system.

Figure 2-14: Help is at your F1 fingertip.

As is the case with most Windows programs, AutoCAD help is context-sensitive; for example, if you start the LINE command and just don't know what to do next, Help will, er, help. You can browse through the online Product Documentation from the AutoCAD 2013 Help page, or type in the Search box to look for specific words. In this book, we sometimes direct you to the AutoCAD online help system for information about advanced topics.

AutoCAD is one program where you really need to take advantage of the online help resources. AutoCAD contains many commands, options, and quirks. (Alas, the quirks aren't listed in the online help.) Everyone from the greenest beginner to the most seasoned expert can find out something by using the AutoCAD online help. Take a moment to peruse the home page of the main help system so that you know what's available. Throughout this book, we direct you to pages in the help system that we think are particularly useful, but don't be afraid to explore on your own when you get stuck or feel curious.

The good news is that the online help is always being monitored and updated to reflect how people are using it and to update any errors or omissions. The bad news is that if you don't have a current Internet connection, all you get is the local *Reader's Digest* version of help. The good news is that you can go to www.autodesk.com, where you can download and install the latest version of the full-meal deal. Having done so, AutoCAD will always look for an Internet connection first so you get the latest help, but if it can't connect, it falls back to the downloaded version you installed.

A Lap around the CAD Track

In This Chapter

▶ Setting up a simple drawing

▶ Drawing some objects

▶ Zooming and panning in your drawing

▶ Editing some objects

▶ Plotting your drawing

The previous two chapters introduce you to the AutoCAD world and the AutoCAD 2013 interface. The chapters that follow present the techniques that underlie good drafting practice. By now, you're probably eager to start moving the crosshairs around and *draw* something! This chapter takes you on a gentle tour of the most common CAD drafting functions:

✓ **Setting up a new drawing**

✓ **Drawing some objects**

✓ **Editing those objects**

✓ **Zooming and panning so you can view those objects better**

✓ **Plotting (printing) the drawing**

Much of the stuff in this chapter may be mysterious to you. Don't worry — we tell you where to look for more information on specific topics. In this chapter, you're simply taking AutoCAD out for a test drive to get a feel for what it can do. Go ahead and kick the tires — and don't worry about putting a dent in the fender!

In this chapter, you create a drawing of an architectural detail — a base plate and column, as shown in Figure 3-1. Even if you don't work in architecture or building construction, this exercise gives you some simple shapes to work with and demonstrates commands you can use in most drafting disciplines.

Throughout this book, we show AutoCAD running in the Ribbon-based Drafting & Annotation workspace that is present in both AutoCAD 2013 and AutoCAD LT 2013. Likewise, we tell you where to find commands and what to select by using the Ribbon.

If you're familiar with earlier versions of AutoCAD and the post-AutoCAD 2008 user interface looks just too weird, you can strap on some training wheels while you're getting used to it. Just click the down arrow at the right end of the Quick Access Toolbar (by default, it appears to the right of the Workspace drop-down list) and choose Show Menu Bar. If you're really and truly a Luddite where the Ribbon is concerned, you can revert to the "classic" way of doing things by either opening the Workspace drop-down on the Quick Access Toolbar or by clicking the Workspace Switching button on the status bar and choosing AutoCAD Classic (AutoCAD LT Classic in that version). *Presto change-o* — suddenly, it's 2008! Don't you sometimes wish you could turn back the real world that easily?

Figure 3-1: How base is my plate.

Although the drafting example in this chapter is simple, the procedures that it demonstrates are real, honest-to-CAD-ness, proper drafting practice. We emphasize from the beginning the importance of proper drawing setup, putting objects on appropriate layers, and drawing and editing with due concern for precision. Some of the steps in this chapter may seem a bit complicated at first, but they reflect the way that experienced AutoCAD users work. My goal is to help you develop good CAD habits and do things the right way from the very start.

The step-by-step procedures in this chapter, unlike those in most chapters of this book, form a sequence. You must do the steps in order. Figuring out how to use AutoCAD is a little like figuring out how to drive, except that with AutoCAD, you're free to stop in the middle of the street and take a break.

If you find that object selection or editing functions work differently from how we describe them in this chapter, you (or someone else) probably changed the configuration settings on the Option dialog box's Selection tab. Chapter 10 describes these settings and how to restore the AutoCAD defaults.

A Simple Setup

In this chapter, we walk you through creating, editing, viewing, and plotting a new drawing — refer to Figure 3-1 if you want to get an idea of what the finished product looks like. You can follow these steps using either imperial or metric units; we show metric values in brackets after the imperial ones, like this: Type **1.5 [38]** and press Enter.

You can find the files we use in this sequence of steps at this book's companion website. Go to www.dummies.com/go/autocad2013fd and download afd03.zip. The Zip file contains imperial and metric versions of the base plate exercise at various stages — the Read Me file on the downloads tab has a detailed description of the files.

Pay attention to AutoCAD's feedback. Glance at the messages AutoCAD sends after each step via the command window at the bottom of the screen or the Dynamic Input tooltip near the crosshairs so that you begin to get familiar with the names of commands and their options. (If you don't see any messages next to the crosshairs as you use the program, click the Dynamic Input button on the status bar — if your status bar displays button icons rather than text labels, click the button with the tooltip that reads "Dynamic Input.") As we describe in Chapter 4, drawing setup sometimes isn't a simple task in AutoCAD. Nonetheless, drawing setup is an important part of the job, and if you don't get in the habit of doing it right, you run into endless problems later on — especially when you try to plot. (See Chapter 16 for the lowdown on plotting your drawings.)

In this first set of steps, you create a new drawing from a template, change some settings to establish a 1:10 scale (that is, 1 inch or 1 millimeter on the drawing is equivalent to 10 inches or 10 millimeters on the real object), and save the drawing:

1. **Start AutoCAD by double-clicking its shortcut on the Windows desktop.**

 If you don't have an AutoCAD shortcut on your desktop, choose Start➪[All] Programs➪Autodesk➪AutoCAD 2013➪AutoCAD 2013. (The last two will be AutoCAD LT 2013, if that's your version.)

The workspaces in AutoCAD 2013 look very similar to one another. To make sure that you're in the same workspace that we are, look at the Workspace label at the left side of the AutoCAD window's title bar (if you're running at a very low screen resolution, you may have to click the little arrow at the right of the Quick Access Toolbar). If it *doesn't* say Drafting & Annotation, click the little black arrow on the button and then select Drafting & Annotation from the menu.

2. **Click the Application button — that's the big red A at the top left of the screen — to display the Application Menu. Then click New, or hover the mouse pointer over New and select Drawing.**

 (Don't click the New button on the Quick Access Toolbar — use the menu. We explain why in Chapter 4, but just humor us for now.) The Select Template dialog box appears with a list of drawing templates (DWT files), which you can use as the starting point for new drawings. *Templates* in AutoCAD are like templates in Word and other programs. Chapter 4 describes how to create and use drawing templates.

3. **Select** `acad.dwt` [`acadiso.dwt`]**, shown in Figure 3-2, and click Open. (For AutoCAD LT, select** `acadlt.dwt` [`acadltiso.dwt`]**.)**

 AutoCAD creates a new, blank drawing that uses the settings in `acad.dwt` or `acadiso.dwt`. The `acad.dwt` template (`acadlt.dwt` in AutoCAD LT) is AutoCAD's default, plain-Jane template for drawings in *imperial units* (units expressed in inches and/or feet). The `acadiso.dwt` (`acadltiso.dwt` in AutoCAD LT) template is the corresponding version for drawings created in metric units. Chapter 4 contains additional information about these and other templates.

Figure 3-2: Starting a new drawing from a template.

4. **Click all the buttons on the left half of the status bar except Dynamic Input until they look dimmed (they'll be gray instead of light blue). If your status bar displays button icons rather than text labels, click the button with the Dynamic Input tooltip.**

 Some of these settings can make selecting points difficult. It's best to start with them all turned off and then toggle them on and off as needed. We tell you which ones to use in the steps that follow.

 If your status-bar buttons show icons instead of text, right-click *any* button and click Use Icons to *de*select the option and display text labels. You can leave them that way or right-click and select Use Icons again to toggle the icon display back on.

5. **Type** LIMITS **and press Enter.**

 Drawing limits define your working area. AutoCAD prompts you to reset the model space limits. For now, ignore the Dynamic Input tooltip next to the crosshairs and look at the command window. The command line reads

   ```
   Specify lower left corner or [ON/OFF] <0.0000,0.0000>:
   ```

6. **Press Enter to keep 0,0 as the lower-left-corner value.**

 AutoCAD prompts for the upper-right corner. The command line reads

   ```
   Specify upper right corner <12.0000,9.0000>
           or[<420.0000,297.0000>]if you started from the
           acadaiso.dwt template.:
   ```

7. **Type** 100,50 or [2750,1250] **(no spaces) and press Enter.**

 AutoCAD echoes the values you enter at the command line.

 100 x 50 corresponds to 10 inches by 5 inches (a little smaller than an 8.5-x-11-inch piece of paper turned on its long side) times a drawing scale factor of 10 (because you're eventually going to plot at 1:10 scale). If you're a metric maven, 2750 x 1250 corresponds to 275mm by 125mm (slightly smaller than an ISO A4 sheet turned lengthways) times a drawing scale factor of 10 (because you, too, will eventually plot at 1:10 scale). See Chapter 4 for more information about drawing scales.

 To be honest, setting limits isn't very important in AutoCAD anymore — modern computers can process much more data than they could in the 1980s when AutoCAD first appeared — but it does make it easier to plot a drawing from model space as you do in this chapter.

8. **Right-click the Snap Mode button on the status bar and choose Settings. If your status bar displays button icons rather than text labels, right-click the button with the Snap Mode tooltip.**

 The Snap and Grid tab of the Drafting Settings dialog box appears, as shown in Figure 3-3. (Note that AutoCAD LT lacks some options that are present in the full version of AutoCAD.)

Figure 3-3: Snap and Grid settings.

9. **Change the values in the dialog box so it looks like Figure 3-3:**

 • *Snap On:* Selected

 Snap constrains your crosshairs to moving in an invisible grid of equally spaced points (0.5 [10] units apart in this case).

 • *Grid On:* Selected

 Grid displays a visible grid of little dots or grid lines on the screen (5 [100] units apart in this case), which you can use as reference points. The grid doesn't appear on printed drawings.

 • *Snap X Spacing:* 0.5 [10]

 • *Snap Y Spacing:* 0.5 [10]

 • *Grid X Spacing:* 5 [100]

 • *Grid Y Spacing:* 5 [100]

10. **Click OK.**

 You see a network of grid lines, 5 [100] units apart, in the drawing area. If you move your mouse pointer around and watch the coordinate display area at the left side of the status bar, you notice that the values still change in very small increments just as they did before. We have more on this in a moment.

11. **Click the tiny down arrow below the Zoom button (the one with the magnifying glass) on the Navigation bar (at the right edge of the drawing area in Figure 3-1), and then choose Zoom All from the menu.**

 AutoCAD zooms out so that the entire area defined by the limits is visible.

12. **Click the Save button on the Quick Access Toolbar or press Ctrl+S.**

 Because you haven't saved the drawing yet, AutoCAD opens the Save Drawing As dialog box.

13. **Navigate to a suitable folder by choosing from the Save In drop-down list and/or double-clicking folders in the list of folders below it.**

 Remember where you save the file so you can go back to it later.

14. **Type a name in the File Name text box and click Save.**

 For example, type **Detail** or **My Plate is Base**.

 Depending on your Windows Explorer settings, you may or may not see the .dwg extension in the File Name text box. In any case, you don't need to type it. AutoCAD adds it for you.

 AutoCAD saves the new DWG file to the folder you specified in Step 13.

Whew — that was more work than digging a post-hole — and all just to set up a simple drawing! Chapter 4 goes into more detail about drawing setup and describes why all these gyrations are necessary, and how to avoid doing them more than once by defining your own template files.

Drawing a (Base) Plate

With a properly set up drawing, you're ready to draw some objects. In this example, you use the RECTANG command to draw a steel base plate and column, the CIRCLE command to draw an anchor bolt, and the POLYGON command to draw a hexagonal nut. (Both the RECTANG and POLYGON commands create *polylines* — objects that contain a series of straight-line segments and/or arc segments.) We describe these drawing commands in more detail in Chapters 8 and 9.

AutoCAD, like most CAD programs, uses layers as an organizing principle for all the objects that you draw. Chapter 6 describes layers and other object properties in detail. In this example, you create separate layers for the base plate, column, anchor bolts, and nuts. This might seem like layer madness, but when you're doing complex drawings, you need to use a lot of layers just to keep things organized.

Drawing rectangles on the right layers

The following steps demonstrate how to create and use layers, as well as how to draw rectangles. You also see how to apply fillets to objects and offset them. (Chapter 6 describes layers in detail, and Chapter 8 covers the RECTANG command. Chapter 11 explains the FILLET and OFFSET commands.)

Start by creating a Column layer and a Plate layer and then drawing a rectangular column on the Column layer and a square base plate on the Plate layer:

1. **Make sure that you complete the drawing set up in the previous section of this chapter and have the drawing open in AutoCAD.**

2. **Click the Home tab on the Ribbon.**

 You'll find the most frequently used commands for 2D drafting tasks on the Ribbon's Home tab. (For a refresher on the contents of the other tabs, refer to the "Unraveling the Ribbon" section in Chapter 2.) Unless we direct you otherwise, look on the Home tab for the panels and buttons we specify in the following steps.

3. **On the Layers panel, click the Layer Properties button.**

 The Layer Properties button is at the upper-left corner of the Layers panel. The LAYER command starts, and AutoCAD displays the Layer Properties Manager palette.

4. **Click the New Layer button.**

 AutoCAD adds a new layer to the list and gives it the default name Layer1 (see Figure 3-4).

Figure 3-4: Creating a new layer.

5. **Type a more suitable name for the layer on which you'll draw the column and press Enter.**

 For this example, type **Column**.

6. **Click the color swatch or name (white) in the Column layer row.**

 The Select Color dialog box appears (see Figure 3-5).

Figure 3-5: Blue is the color — select it from the standard color tiles.

7. **Click color 5 (blue) in the single, separate row to the left of the ByLayer and ByBlock buttons, and then click OK.**

 The Select Color dialog box closes, and AutoCAD changes the color of the Column layer to blue.

8. **With the Layer Properties Manager still open, repeat Steps 4 through 7 to create a new layer named Plate and set its color to 4 (cyan, or light blue).**

9. **With layer Plate still highlighted, click the Set Current button (the green check mark).**

 Plate becomes the current layer, and everything you draw is placed on that layer until you set a different layer current.

10. **Click Close (the "X" at the top-left corner of the palette in Figure 3-4) to close the Layer Properties Manager palette.**

 The Layer drop-down list on the Home tab's Layers panel displays Plate as the current layer. Now you can draw a rectangular plate on the Plate layer.

 You probably already know that the RECTANG command will draw a rectangular plate for you, but for the next step, pretend that you don't.

If you want to cheat a bit, you can start from this point with drawing `afd03a-i.dwg` [`afd03a-m.dwg`] available in the `afd03.zip` download at `www.dummies.com/go/autocad2013fd`. Download it to a suitable location and then click the Application button and then Open. Browse to the file.

11. Start typing RECT . . .

As you type, AutoCAD guesses what you might be looking for. When you type enough letters, the command you're probably looking for appears at or near the top of the list that appears.

12. When "Rectangle" appears in the list, simply click it. In our case, it happens to be the first item in the list, so we can press Enter or the spacebar instead of clicking it.

The RECTANG command starts, and AutoCAD prompts you to specify the first corner point. The command line shows

```
Specify first corner point or [Chamfer/Elevation/
          Fillet/Thickness/Width]:
```

13. Click in the drawing area at the point 32,7 [800,175].

By watching the coordinate display on the Dynamic Input tooltip, you can see the coordinates of the current crosshairs location. Because Snap Mode is set to 0.5 [10] units, you can land right on the point 32,7 [800,175]. Picking the first corner in this location gives you enough room to work.

In previous releases, the cursor jumps to the snap spacing whenever Snap mode is active, but this can cause other inconveniences. In AutoCAD 2013, it jumps to the snap interval only when a command is active that is asking for a point or a distance.

AutoCAD prompts at the command line

```
Specify other corner point or [Area/Dimensions/Rotation]:
```

14. Type 36,36 [900,900] **(without any spaces) and press Enter.**

Make sure that the Dynamic Input button is on for this step. If it's not, AutoCAD treats an input of 36,36 as *absolute coordinates* — that is, 36 units above and 36 units to the right *of the origin*. When Dynamic Input is on, an input of 36,36 is treated as 36 units above and 36 units to the right *of the last point* — in other words, as *relative* to the last point. See Chapter 7 for more information about typing absolute and relative coordinates.

AutoCAD draws the 36 x 36 [900 x 900] rectangle, as shown in Figure 3-6. It's on the Plate layer and inherits that layer's cyan color.

You draw the column next, but first you have to change layers.

Figure 3-6: Your (base) plate is empty.

15. **On the Layers panel of the Home tab, click the Layer drop-down list to display the list of layers. Click Column to set it as the current layer.**

 Using the Layer drop-down list saves you from having to open the Layer Properties Manager, select the layer, and click the Set Current button. Becoming an AutoCAD master is *all* about efficiency!

16. **Right-click in an empty area of the screen to display the shortcut menu. Choose Repeat RECTANG to draw another rectangle.**

 In the next steps, you create a hollow steel column.

17. **At the Specify First Corner Point prompt, type** 44,16 [1100,400] **and press Enter. Be sure to keep your cursor in the drawing area during this step and the next one.**

18. **At the Specify Other Corner Point prompt, type** 12,18 [300,450] **and press Enter.**

 A second rectangle is drawn in the middle of the base plate.

 Next, you round the corners of the column with the FILLET command and then use OFFSET to give it some thickness.

19. **On the Home tab's Modify panel, click the Fillet button.**

The FILLET command starts, and AutoCAD prompts you to select the first object. Look at the command line to see the options for this command. In the next step, you specify a 2-inch [50mm] radius fillet to all four corners.

20. Type R **and press Enter to set a new fillet radius. Type** 2 [50] **and press Enter.**

AutoCAD again prompts you to select the first object. You could pick each of the lines at each corner that need to be filleted (that's eight picks), but because the column is a continuous polyline, in this case a more efficient method is to use the FILLET command's Polyline option to fillet all four corners in one fell swoop.

21. Type P **to choose the Polyline option, and then press Enter.**

AutoCAD prompts you to select a 2D polyline. As you move your mouse pointer over the rectangle, AutoCAD shows you a preview of what the fillet will look like.

22. Select the rectangle you drew in Steps 16 to 18.

All four corners of the column are rounded with a 2-inch [50mm] radius fillet.

Next, offset the polyline to create a ¾-inch [19mm] thick steel column.

23. On the Modify panel, click the Offset button.

24. At the Specify Offset Distance prompt, type .75 [19] **and press Enter.**

Make sure that your Object Snap status bar button is toggled off for the next step, or AutoCAD may offset your object back on top of itself.

25. At the Select Object to Offset prompt, click the rounded rectangle. At the Specify Point on Side to Offset prompt, click anywhere *inside* **the rounded rectangle. Press Enter to complete the command.**

AutoCAD offsets the selected object toward the inside of the rounded rectangle (see Figure 3-7).

26. Click the Dynamic Input button on the status bar so the button looks dimmed.

Now that you've given Dynamic Input a test drive, turn it off for the rest of this chapter. You know how to turn it off and on, and if you like it, by all means, turn it on again for the remainder of the book. Personally, we think that it gets in the way too much to be truly useful, so we rarely use it.

27. Press Ctrl+S to save the drawing.

AutoCAD saves the drawing and renames the previously saved version *drawingname*.bak — for example, My Plate is Base.bak. .bak is AutoCAD's extension for a backup file. When (not "if") things get out of hand, you can always rename the .bak file to .dwg to go back to the earlier version.

Selected object here.

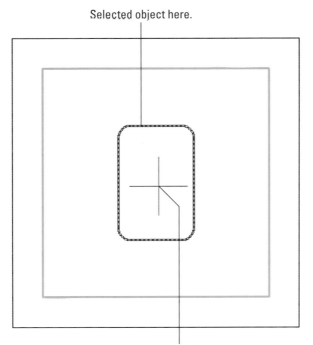

Pick here to show offset directions.

Figure 3-7: Give it some thickness with OFFSET.

Circling your plate

You can use the CIRCLE command to draw a 1½-inch [38mm] diameter anchor bolt on an Anchor Bolts layer by following these steps:

1. **Repeat Steps 2 through 7 in the preceding section to create a new layer for the anchor bolts. Give the layer the name** Anchor Bolts, **assign it the color 3 (green), set it as the current layer, and then close the Layer Properties Manager.**

 The Layer drop-down on the Layers panel displays Anchor Bolts as the current layer.

2. **On the Home tab's Draw panel, click the Circle button.**

 The CIRCLE command starts, and AutoCAD prompts you to specify the center point. The command line shows

   ```
   Specify center point for circle or [3P/2P/Ttr
           (tan tan radius)]:
   ```

3. **Click in the drawing area at point 38,13 [950,325].**

 AutoCAD asks you to specify the size of the circle. The command line shows

   ```
   Specify radius of circle or [Diameter]:
   ```

 You decide that you want 1½-inch [38mm] diameter anchor bolts. AutoCAD is asking for a radius. Although you can probably figure out the radius of a 1½-inch [38mm] diameter circle, specify the Diameter option and let AutoCAD do the hard work.

4. **Type D and press Enter to select the Diameter option.**

 AutoCAD prompts you:

   ```
   Specify diameter of circle:
   ```

5. **Type 1.5 [38] and press Enter.**

 AutoCAD draws the 1½-inch [38mm] diameter circle. It's on the Anchor Bolts layer and inherits that layer's green color (see Figure 3-8).

6. **Press Ctrl+S to save the drawing.**

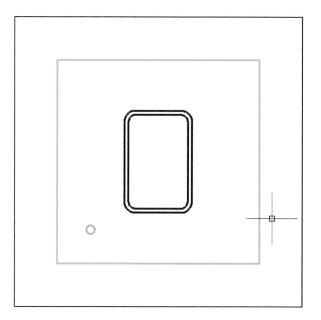

Figure 3-8: Anchor it with CIRCLE.

Nuts to you

Every good bolt deserves a nut. Use the POLYGON command to draw a hexagonal shape on a Nuts layer (well, what else would you call it?). Besides showing you how to draw polygons, these steps introduce you to a couple of AutoCAD's more useful precision techniques: object snaps and Ortho mode.

1. **Repeat Steps 2 through 7 in the "Drawing rectangles on the right layers" section, earlier in this chapter, to create a new layer for the nuts and set the new layer current. Give the layer the name** Nuts **and assign it the color 1 (red).**

 The Layer drop-down list displays Nuts as the current layer.

 You don't have to create a separate layer for every type of object that you draw. For example, you could draw both the anchor bolts and nuts on a layer called Hardware. Layer names and usage depend on industry and office practices, in addition to a certain amount of individual judgment. Having too many layers is better than having too few because lumping two or more layers together is much easier than dividing the objects on one layer into two or more layers.

 The Ribbon's standard panels aren't big enough to contain a button for every command, so AutoCAD hides the ones that don't fit in drop-down buttons or slideout panels that you open by clicking the panel label. A small down-pointing triangle beside the panel name means that there's a slideout with more commands available.

2. **On the Home tab's Draw panel, click the Polygon button — the one that looks like a plan of the Pentagon.**

 If this is the first time you've drawn a polygon in this editing session, its button is hiding under the Rectangle tool button. Look for the button showing a rectangle with little circles at two corners. Click the down arrow beside that button, and then click Polygon.

 If a Ribbon panel has an item with a slideout list, AutoCAD remembers the last one that was used in the current session. When you close AutoCAD and restart it, all the defaults return.

 The POLYGON command starts, and AutoCAD prompts you as follows:

   ```
   Enter number of sides <4>:
   ```

 Peek ahead to Figure 3-9 to get an idea of how the nut will look after you draw it. Four-sided nuts can be a little difficult to adjust in the real world, so we stick with the conventional hexagonal sort.

3. **Type** 6 **and press Enter.**

 AutoCAD next prompts you for the center of the polygon:

   ```
   Specify center of polygon or [Edge]:
   ```

In the next steps, you use one of AutoCAD's precision drafting modes: Object Snap. We explain object snaps in detail in Chapter 7, but for now, just follow along here.

4. **Click the Object Snap button on the status bar to turn on Object Snap mode. When Object Snap is enabled, the button appears light blue and the command prompt shows** `<Osnap on>`.

As you move the crosshairs around near the anchor bolt, notice that AutoCAD tends to pull the crosshairs to certain points on existing objects.

5. **Move the crosshairs over the anchor bolt you just drew.**

A tooltip should show *Center* and pull the crosshairs to the center of the anchor-bolt circle. If you don't see a Center object snap marker or tooltip, then right-click the Object Snap button and click Center. You may also see tracking vectors across the screen from this point — you can ignore those.

6. **Click when the tooltip reads *Center* — not *Center-Intersection* or something similar — just *Center*.**

The POLYGON command draws regular closed polygons based on an imaginary circle; the center of this imaginary circle is the point you just picked.

AutoCAD prompts you:

```
Enter an option [Inscribed in circle/Circumscribed
        about circle] <I>:
```

7. **Press Enter to accept the default Inscribed in Circle option.**

The Inscribed option draws a polygon whose corners touch the circumference of the imaginary circle. The Circumscribed option draws a polygon whose sides are tangent to the circumference of the circle. Circumscribed has nothing to do with being a Jewish male.

AutoCAD then asks you to

```
Specify radius of circle:
```

8. **Turn on Ortho mode by clicking the Ortho Mode button on the status bar until you see** `<Ortho on>` **on the command line.**

Ortho mode forces the crosshairs to move *orthogonally* — that is, in a precise horizontal or vertical direction. (We describe Ortho mode more fully in Chapter 7.)

9. **Move the mouse pointer to the right so the top and bottom sides of the polygon are horizontal, *but don't click yet*!**

10. **Type** 1.5 [38] **and press Enter.**

AutoCAD draws the nut, as shown in Figure 3-9. It's on the Nuts layer and inherits that layer's red color.

I'll

The drawing `afd03b-i.dwg` [`afd03b-m.dwg`] contained in the `afd03.zip` download includes the base plate, column, and one anchor bolt.

Figure 3-9: Bolts and nuts . . . ready to anchor.

If your nut and bolt looks just like Figure 3-9, way to go — you did it right! If, by chance, your bolt is completely inside the circle, you probably missed Step 4 of the "Circling your plate" section, earlier in this chapter, where we tell you to use the CIRCLE command's Diameter option.

11. **Turn off Ortho mode and Object Snap by clicking the Ortho Mode and Object Snap buttons on the status bar until they look dimmed and you see** `<Ortho off>` **and** `<Osnap off>` **on the command line.**

 Occasionally, Ortho Mode and object snaps interfere with drafting in AutoCAD. Disabling them (as you do in this step) keeps them from being a problem.

12. **Press Ctrl+S to save the drawing.**

Not much of a base plate yet, is it? But don't worry — we cover creating more nuts and bolts with editing commands in the section "Modifying to Make It Merrier," later in this chapter. If your brain is feeling full, now is a good time to take a break and go look out the window. If you exit AutoCAD, just restart the program and reopen your drawing when you're ready to continue.

Getting a Closer Look with Zoom and Pan

The example drawing in this chapter is pretty uncluttered and small, but most real CAD drawings are neither of those. Technical drawings are usually jam-packed with lines, text, and dimensions. CAD drawings often get plotted

on sheets of paper that measure 2 to 3 feet on a side — that's in the hundreds of millimeters, if you're a metric maven. Anyone who owns a monitor that large probably can afford to hire a whole room full of drafters (and therefore isn't reading this book). You need to zoom and pan in your drawings — a lot. We cover zooming and panning in detail in Chapter 12. Quick definitions should suffice for now:

- ✔ **Zoom** means changing the magnification of the display. When you zoom in, you move closer to the drawing objects so you can see detail, and when you zoom out, you move farther away so you can see more of the drawing area. This does <u>not</u> change the actual size of the objects in the file.

- ✔ **Pan** means moving from one area to another without changing the magnification. If you've used the scroll bars in any application, you've panned the display.

Zooming and panning frequently lets you see the details better, draw more confidently (because you can see what you're doing), and edit more quickly (because object selection is easier when a zillion objects aren't on the screen).

Fortunately, zooming and panning in AutoCAD is as simple as it is necessary. The following steps describe how to use AutoCAD's Zoom and Pan Realtime feature, which is pretty easy to operate and provides a lot of flexibility. Chapter 12 covers additional zoom and pan options.

To zoom and pan in your drawing, follow these steps:

1. **Right-click in a blank area of the drawing and choose Zoom from the shortcut (right-click) menu.**

 The Realtime option of the ZOOM command starts. The crosshairs change to a magnifying glass, and AutoCAD prompts you at the command line as follows:

   ```
   Press ESC or ENTER to exit, or right-click to display
        shortcut menu.
   ```

2. **Move the crosshairs near the middle of the screen, press and hold the left mouse button, and drag the mouse pointer up and down until the base plate almost fills the screen.**

 As you can see, dragging up increases the zoom magnification, and dragging down decreases it.

3. **Right-click in the drawing area to display the Zoom/Pan Realtime menu (shown in Figure 3-10), and choose Pan from the menu.**

 The magnifying-glass pointer changes to a hand.

| Exit |
| Pan |
| ✓ Zoom |
| 3D Orbit |
| Zoom Window |
| Zoom Original |
| Zoom Extents |

Figure 3-10: The Zoom/Pan Realtime right-click menu.

4. Click and drag to pan the drawing until the plate is more or less centered in the drawing area.

You're not moving the plate, although it may look like it. You're moving your viewing position while the plate stays put. Never move drawing objects if you just want to view them from a different position.

You can use the right-click menu to toggle back and forth between Zoom and Pan as many times as you like. If you get lost, choose Zoom Original or Zoom Extents to return to a recognizable view.

5. Right-click in the drawing area and choose Exit from the Zoom/Pan Realtime menu.

The hand pointer returns to the normal AutoCAD crosshairs.

If you have a wheel mouse, you can zoom simply by rolling the wheel back and forth. To pan, press and hold the wheel (yes, the wheel is also a button) and drag the view around. These actions can be performed even when another command is active.

Modifying to Make It Merrier

When you have a better view of your base plate (which we talk about in the preceding section), you can edit the objects on it more easily. In the following sections, you use the ARRAY command to add more anchor bolts, the STRETCH command to change the shape of the plate, and the HATCH command to add crosshatching to the column. (As always, we cover these commands in detail later in the book.)

Hip-hip-array!

Using the ARRAY command is a great way to generate a bunch of new objects from existing objects at regular angles or spacing. The array pattern can be *rectangular* (that is, columns and rows of objects), *polar* (in a circle around a center point, like the spokes of a wheel around its hub), or it can follow a *path*.

AutoCAD 2012 introduced a sophisticated new method of arraying objects, and AutoCAD 2013 improved on it. We explain it in detail in Chapter 18. In this chapter, we introduce the simpler, old-style array feature. The newer version is more powerful, but the older version is simpler. For our purposes now, the simpler one is adequate.

In this example, you use a rectangular array to create three additional anchor bolts:

1. **Type –ARRAY and press Enter (don't omit the hyphen!).**

 Typing a hyphen in front of a command name tells AutoCAD you want to use the command line rather than a dialog box to specify values for the array.

 The old-style ARRAY command starts at the command line, and AutoCAD prompts you to select the objects you want to array.

2. **Click the anchor bolt and then click the nut.**

 If you encounter any problems while trying to select objects, press the Esc key a couple of times to cancel the command; then restart the –ARRAY command and try again.

 AutoCAD continues to prompt you at the command line:

   ```
   Select objects: 1 found, 2 total
   ```

3. **Press Enter or right-click to end object selection.**

 You specify the parameters of an array by first telling AutoCAD whether you want a rectangular or polar (circular) array. A rectangular array creates regularly spaced rows and columns. Next, you specify the number of rows and the number of columns, and then the spacing between rows and the spacing between columns.

 AutoCAD prompts:

   ```
   Enter the type of array [Rectangular/Polar] <R>:
   ```

4. **Type R and press Enter to accept a rectangular array.**

 AutoCAD prompts:

   ```
   Enter the number of rows (---) <1>:
   ```

AutoCAD wants to know how many rows and columns you want. Because the source object is included in AutoCAD arrays, you must specify two rows and two columns of bolts.

5. **Type 2 and press Enter. At the next prompt for the number of columns, type 2 and press Enter again.**

AutoCAD prompts:

```
Enter the distance between rows or specify unit cell (---):
```

Almost done! To complete the array you tell AutoCAD the spacing between rows and columns.

6. **Type 24 [600] and press Enter. At the Enter distance between columns prompt, type 24 [600] and press Enter again.**

AutoCAD adds the additional objects to the drawing, as shown in Figure 3-11.

7. **If anything looks wrong, type U or click Undo to delete the array and start again.**

Unfortunately, the command line is not as forgiving as a dialog box!

8. **Press Ctrl+S to save the drawing.**

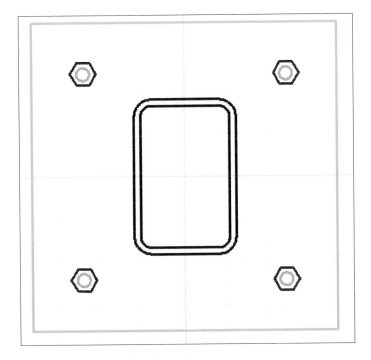

Figure 3-11: Buttoned-down base plate.

Perfect! Except that nutbar engineer (hey, we resemble that remark!) has decided the column needs to be 18 x 18 inches [450 x 450mm] rather than 12 x 18 inches [300 x 450mm — unfortunately, there are just as many metric nutbars as imperial ones]. And that means the base plate is too small, and the anchor bolts are in the wrong place, too. If you were working on the drawing board, you'd be getting out an eraser right about now and rubbing out all your efforts. If you were lucky, you'd have an electric eraser. At some point, you simply tore up the paper and started over. AutoCAD to the rescue!

The drawing `afd03c-i.dwg` [`afd03c-m.dwg`] contained in the `afd03.zip` download adds the remaining anchor bolts.

Stretching out

The STRETCH command is powerful but a little complicated — it can stretch or move objects, depending on how you select them. The key to using STRETCH is specifying a *crossing selection box* properly. (Chapter 10 gives you more details about crossing boxes and how to use them with the STRETCH command.)

Follow these steps to stretch the column and base plate:

1. **On the Modify panel, click the Stretch button — the one with the corner of a rectangle being stretched.**

 The STRETCH command starts, and AutoCAD prompts you to select objects. This is one of those times (and one of those commands) that really does require you to look at the command line:

   ```
   Select objects to stretch by crossing-window or
           crossing-polygon...
   Select objects:
   ```

2. **Click a point above and to the right of the upper-right corner of the plate (Point 1 in Figure 3-12).**

3. **Move the crosshairs down and to the left.**

 The pointer changes to a dashed rectangle enclosing a rectangular green area, which indicates that you're specifying a crossing box. AutoCAD prompts you at the command line as follows:

   ```
   Select objects: Specify opposite corner:
   ```

4. **Click a point below the plate, roughly under the center of the column (Point 2 in Figure 3-12).**

 The crossing box must cut through the plate and column in order for the STRETCH command to work (refer to Figure 3-12).

Figure 3-12: Specifying a crossing box for the STRETCH command.

AutoCAD prompts you at the command line:

```
Select objects: Specify opposite corner: 7 found
Select objects:
```

5. **Press Enter to end object selection.**

 AutoCAD prompts you to specify the base point.

6. **If they're not already on, turn on Snap mode, Ortho mode, and Object Snap by clicking their respective buttons on the status bar until they appear highlighted.**

7. **Move your mouse pointer over the lower-right corner of the plate, and click when you see a square box with an Endpoint tooltip.**

This point serves as the base point for the stretch operation. Chapter 11 describes *base points* and *displacements* in greater detail. As before, if you can't get it to snap to the endpoint, right-click the Object Snap button and select Endpoint.

AutoCAD prompts you at the command line:

```
Specify second point or <use first point as displacement>:
```

8. **Move the crosshairs to the right until the tooltip shows a displacement of 6 [150] units to the right, and then click in the drawing space (see Figure 3-13).**

 AutoCAD stretches the column and plate by the distance that you indicate and moves the anchor bolts that were completely inside the crossing window rectangle, as shown in Figure 3-13.

Figure 3-13: Stretching the base plate.

If your first stretch didn't work right, press Ctrl+Z and try again. STRETCH is an immensely useful command — one that makes you wonder how drafters used to do it all with erasers and pencils — but it does take some practice to get the hang of those crossing boxes.

9. **Press Ctrl+S to save the drawing.**

 The drawing afd03d-i.dwg [afd03d-m.dwg] contained in the afd03.zip download is the stretched version of the base plate.

Crossing your hatches

Your final editing task is to add some crosshatching to the space between the inside and outside edges of the column. The hatch lines indicate that the drawing shows a cross section of the column. To do so, follow these steps:

1. **Turn off Snap, Ortho, and Object Snap modes by clicking their respective buttons on the status bar until they look dimmed.**

2. **Repeat Steps 2 through 7 from the "Drawing rectangles on the right layers" section (earlier in this chapter) to create a new layer named Hatch. Set its color to 6 (magenta) and make it the current layer.**

3. **On the Home tab's Draw panel, click the Hatch button — the one that shows the fine crosshatching inside a square.**

 The Hatch Creation tab appears on the Ribbon. For more information on this tab, and hatching in general, see Chapter 15. Note how the Ribbon has changed to have a light green bar at the bottom, and all the panels now show actions related to creating and editing hatch patterns.

4. **In the Hatch Creation tab's Pattern panel, click the Hatch Pattern button and select ANSI31.**

 Depending on your screen resolution, the panels may show more or less information. You may see an ANSI31 swatch without having to click the Hatch Pattern button.

 As you move your crosshairs over the drawing objects, a live preview shows you the result if you click at the current crosshair position. AutoCAD prompts

   ```
   Pick internal point or [Select objects/seTtings]:
   ```

5. **Move the crosshairs so they're between the inside and outside edges of the column. Zoom in if you need to get closer.**

 The live preview shows the ANSI31 hatch pattern filling the space between the two filleted rectangles. Live preview not only shows you the pattern, it also lets you adjust hatch angle and scale. In this case, it looks like the hatch pattern may be too fine.

6. **In the Scale box of the Hatch Creation tab's Properties panel, change the value to 5 and press the Tab key to confirm it.**

7. **Move your crosshairs back to the space between the two filleted rectangles to preview the hatch again. If it looks okay, click within the hatched area to confirm the hatch object, and then press Enter to finish the command.**

 Your finished column and base plate looks like Figure 3-14.

Figure 3-14: Your column is hatched.

8. **Click the tiny arrow below the Zoom button on the Navigation bar and choose Zoom All from the menu.**

 AutoCAD zooms out so that the entire area defined by the limits is visible.

9. **Press Ctrl+S to save the drawing.**

After some drawing and editing, you may wonder how you're supposed to know when to turn off or on the various status bar modes (Snap, Grid, Ortho, Object Snap, and so on). You'll start to get an instinctive sense of when each mode is useful and when it gets in the way. If one of the modes gets in the way — or you find you need a mode — you can click the buttons at any time during editing and drawing commands. In subsequent chapters of this book, we give you some more specific guidelines.

Drawing `afd03e-i.dwg` [`afd03e-m.dwg`] available in the `afd03.zip` download is the completed base plate. How does it compare with your version?

Following the Plot

Looking at drawings on a computer screen and exchanging them with others via e-mail or websites is all well and good, but sooner or later, someone — maybe you! — will want to see a printed version. Printing drawings — or *plotting,* as CAD geeks like to call it — is much more complicated than

printing a word-processing document or a spreadsheet. That's because you have to worry about things such as drawing scale, lineweights, title blocks, and weird paper sizes. We go deeper into plotting in Chapter 16, but this section gives you an abbreviated procedure that can help you generate a recognizable printed drawing.

The following steps show you how to plot the *model space* portion of the drawing. As Chapter 5 describes, AutoCAD includes a sophisticated feature — *paper space layouts* — for creating arrangements of your drawing that you plot. These arrangements usually include a title block. Because we promised you a *gentle* tour of AutoCAD drafting functions, we save the discussion of paper space layout and title blocks for a bit later. When you're ready for the whole plotting enchilada, turn to Chapter 5 for information about how to set up paper space layouts; see Chapter 16 for full plotting instructions.

Follow these steps to plot a drawing:

1. **Click the Plot button on the Quick Access Toolbar.**

 The Quick Access Toolbar is at the left end of the program's title bar, just to the right of the Application button. The Plot icon looks like an ordinary desktop printer.

 AutoCAD opens the Plot-Model dialog box, with the title bar showing what you're plotting (model space, in this case).

2. **Click the More Options button (in the bottom-right corner of the dialog box, next to the Help button).**

 The Plot dialog box reveals additional settings, as shown in Figure 3-15.

3. **In the Printer/Plotter area, select a printer from the Name drop-down list.**

 If in doubt, the Default Windows System Printer usually works.

4. **In the Paper Size area, use the drop-down list to select a paper size that's loaded in your printer or plotter.**

 Anything Letter size (8½ x 11 inches) [A4 (210 x 297mm)] or larger works for this example.

5. **In the Plot Area, select Limits from the drop-down list.**

 This is the entire drawing area, which you specified when you set up the drawing in the section "A Simple Setup," earlier in this chapter.

6. **In the Plot Offset area, select the Center the Plot check box.**

 Alternatively, you can specify offsets of 0 or other amounts in order to position the plot at a specific location on the paper.

Figure 3-15: The Plot dialog box with the More Options area visible.

7. **In the Plot Scale area, deselect the Fit to Paper check box and choose 1:10 from the Scale drop-down list.**

 1:10 is the scale used to set up the drawing (which we explain in the section "A Simple Setup," earlier in this chapter). No prizes for guessing the metric equivalent of 1:10!

8. **In the Plot Style Table (Pen Assignments) area, click the drop-down list and choose** `monochrome.ctb`**.**

 The `monochrome.ctb` plot style table ensures that all your lines appear solid black, rather than as different colors or weird shades of gray. See Chapter 16 for information about plot style tables and monochrome and color plotting.

9. **Click Yes when a question dialog box appears, asking Assign This Plot Style Table to All Layouts?**

 You can leave the remaining settings at their default values (refer to Figure 3-15).

Some printers let you print closer to the edges of the sheet than do others. To find out the actual printable area of your own printer, move the mouse pointer to the postage-stamp-size partial preview in the middle of the Plot dialog box and pause. A tooltip appears, listing the Paper Size and Printable Area for the printer and the paper size that you selected.

10. Click the Preview button.

If the plot scale you entered in the Plot dialog box is out of sync with the drawing's annotation scale, a Plot Scale Confirm dialog box appears, advising you that the annotation scale isn't equal to the plot scale. This drawing doesn't contain any text or dimensions, and we didn't bother making the hatch annotative, so it's fine to click Continue and generate the plot.

Annotative scaling controls the printed size of text, dimensions, hatching, and other types of annotation objects at plot time — as long as the drawing's annotation scale matches the plot scale. We explain annotative objects in Chapter 13.

The Plot dialog box disappears temporarily, and AutoCAD shows how the plot will look on paper. In addition, AutoCAD prompts you on the status bar as follows:

```
Press pick button and drag vertically to zoom, ESC
        or ENTER to exit, or right-click to display
        shortcut menu.
```

11. Right-click in the preview area and choose Exit.

12. If the preview doesn't look right, adjust the settings in the Plot dialog box and look at the preview again until it looks right.

13. Click OK.

The Plot Scale Confirm dialog box pops up again. You may be tempted to click Always Continue Under These Conditions, but we recommend against that until you've gained a little familiarity with annotative objects.

The Plot dialog box closes. AutoCAD generates the plot and sends it to the printer. After generating the plot, AutoCAD displays a Plot and Publish Job Complete balloon notification from the right end of the status bar. (A Click to View Plot and Publish Details link displays more information about the plot job.)

14. Click the X (Close) button in the Plot and Publish Job Complete balloon notification.

The balloon notification disappears.

If you're not happy with the lineweights of the lines on your plot at this point, fear not. You can use the lineweights feature (Chapter 6) or plot styles (Chapter 16) to control plotted lineweights.

15. Press Ctrl+S to save the drawing.

Congratulations! You successfully executed your first plot in AutoCAD. Chapter 16 tells you more — much more — about AutoCAD's highly flexible (but occasionally perplexing) plotting system.

Setup for Success

*S*urprisingly, drawing setup is one of the trickier aspects of using AutoCAD. It's an easy thing to do incompletely or incorrectly, and AutoCAD 2013 doesn't provide a simple, one-click tool to help you do all of it right. And yet, drawing setup is a crucial thing to get right. Setup steps that you omit or don't do right may come back to bite you later. The good news is that if you do things properly, you need to do them only once.

The really good news is that AutoCAD is extremely versatile and flexible. As a general rule, the easier something is to use, the less able you are to bend, fold, staple, and mutilate to get it to work in some perverse way that's unique to you and your needs.

Sloppy setup really becomes apparent when you try to *plot* (print) your drawing. Things that seemed more or less okay as you zoomed around on the screen are suddenly the wrong size or scale on paper. And nothing brands someone as a naïve AutoCAD wannabe as quickly as the inability to plot a drawing at the right size and scale. Chapter 5 covers plotting setup procedures, but the information in this chapter is a necessary prerequisite to successful plotting and sheet setup. If you don't get this stuff right, there's a good chance you'll find that . . . the plot sickens.

This chapter describes the decisions you need to make before you set up a new drawing, shows the steps for doing a complete and correct setup, and demonstrates how to save setup settings for reuse.

Don't assume that you can just create a new blank DWG file and start drawing things. *Do* read this chapter before you get too deep into the later chapters in this book. Many AutoCAD drawing commands and concepts depend on proper drawing setup, so you'll have a much easier time drawing and editing things if you've done your setup homework. A few minutes invested in setting up a drawing well can save hours of thrashing around later on.

After you've digested the detailed drawing setup procedures described in this and the following chapter, use the AutoCAD Drawing Setup Roadmap on the Cheat Sheet (which you can find at this book's companion website at www.dummies.com/cheatsheet/autocad2013) as a quick reference to guide you through the process.

A Setup Roadmap

You have to set up AutoCAD correctly, partly because AutoCAD is so flexible and partly because, well, you're doing *CAD* — computer-aided drafting (or design). The computer can't aid your drafting (or design) if you don't clue it in on things like system of measure, drawing scale, paper size, and units. In this context, the following facts help explain why AutoCAD drawing setup is important:

✔ **Electronic paper:** The most important thing you can do to make using AutoCAD fun is to work on a correctly set up drawing so that your screen acts like paper, only smarter. When drawing on real paper, you constantly have to translate between units on the paper and the real-life units of the object you're drawing. But when drawing in AutoCAD's smarter paper, you draw directly in real-life units — feet and inches, millimeters, or whatever you typically use on your projects. AutoCAD can then calculate distances and dimensions for you and add them to the drawing. You can make the mouse pointer jump directly to preset intervals onscreen, and a visible, resizable grid gives you a better sense of the scale of your drawing. However, this smart-paper function works well only if you first tell AutoCAD some crucial parameters for your specific drawing. AutoCAD can't really do its job until you tell it how to work.

✔ **Dead-trees paper:** Creating a great drawing onscreen that doesn't fit well on paper is all too easy. After you finish creating your drawing on the smart paper that AutoCAD provides onscreen, you usually have to plot it on the good old-fashioned, real-world paper that people have used for thousands of years. At that point, you must deal with the fact that people like to use certain standard paper sizes and drawing scales. (Most people also like everything to fit neatly on one sheet of paper.) If you set up AutoCAD correctly, good plotting is the automatic result; if not, plotting time can become one colossal hassle.

✔ **It ain't easy:** Hey, if it were easy, then any dummy could do it, right? AutoCAD provides templates and Setup Wizards for you, but the templates don't work well unless you understand them, and some of the wizards don't work well even if you *do* understand them. This deficiency is one of the major weaknesses in AutoCAD. You must figure out on your own (with the help of this book, of course) how to make the program work right. If you just plunge in without carefully setting up, your drawing and printing efforts are likely to wind up a real mess.

Fortunately, setting up AutoCAD correctly is a bit like following a road map to a new destination. Although the directions for performing your setup are complex, you can master them with attention and practice. Even more fortunately, this chapter provides a detailed and field-tested route. And soon, you'll know the route like the back of your hand.

While you're working in AutoCAD, always keep in mind what your final output should look like on real paper. Even your first printed drawings should look just like hand-drawn ones — only without all those eraser smudges and coffee-cup rings. They need to be added manually in AutoCAD.

Before you start the drawing-setup process, you need to make decisions about your new drawing. The following four questions are absolutely critical; if you don't answer them or your answers are wrong, you'll probably need to rework the drawing later:

✔ **What system of measure — metric or imperial — will you use?**

✔ **What drawing units will you use?**

✔ **At what scale — or scales — will you plot it?**

✔ **On what size paper does it need to fit?**

In some cases, you can defer answering one additional question, but it's usually better to deal with it upfront:

What kind of border or title block does your drawing require?

If you're in a hurry, it's tempting to find an existing drawing that was set up for the drawing scale and paper size that you want to use, make a copy of that DWG file, erase the objects, and start drawing. Use this approach with care, though. When you start from another drawing, you inherit any setup mistakes that may lurk in that drawing. Also, drawings that were created in much older versions of AutoCAD may not take advantage of current program features and CAD practices. If you can find a suitable drawing that was set up in a recent version of AutoCAD by an experienced person who was conscientious about doing setup right, then consider using it. Otherwise, you're better off setting up a new drawing from scratch.

Enter the metric system

. . . or, "Let's forget everything we learned about measuring stuff and start over again!" All (well, nearly all) the world is metric. Instead of a system of linear measure based on twelves, of volume measure based on sixteens, and of temperature measure based on who knows *what* (legend has it that Fahrenheit set his first thermometer outside on a cold day to establish zero, and in his mouth one day when he must have been running a slight fever to define 100), metric bases all types of measure on tens and to repeatable physical standards. (Of course, *For Dummies* books are in the metric vanguard because every single *For Dummies* title includes a Part of Tens. Check out Part VI.)

The metric system first gained a toehold (ten toes, of course) in France during the Revolution.

Over time, it became apparent that some standardization was called for, and a mere century and a half later, SI Metric became that standard. SI is short for *Systeme International d'Unites*. (That's International System of Units in English. Isn't it great to speak more than one language?)

The United States may be late coming to the party, but the U.S. federal government *has* made a commitment to adopt SI Metric. For more information, point your browser to the National Institute of Standards and Technology's Special Publication 814 (`http://ts.nist. gov/weightsandmeasures/metric/ pub814.cfm`).

Choosing your units

AutoCAD is extremely flexible about drawing units; it lets you have them *your* way. Usually, you choose the type of units that you normally use to talk about whatever you're drawing: feet and inches for a building in the United States, millimeters for a metric screw, and so on.

Speaking of millimeters, there's another choice you have to make even before you choose your *units* of measure, and that's your *system* of measure.

Most of the world abandoned local systems of measure generations ago. Even widely adopted ones like the imperial system have mostly fallen by the wayside, just like their driving force, the British Empire. Except, of course, in the United States, where feet, inches, pounds, gallons, and degrees Fahrenheit still rule.

During drawing setup, you choose settings for *length* units (for measuring linear objects and distances) and *angle* units (for measuring angles between nonparallel objects or points on arcs or circles) in the Drawing Units dialog box, as shown in Figure 4-1. (We show you how to specify these settings in the section "Setting your units," later in this chapter.) AutoCAD's length unit types are as follows:

✔ **Architectural** units are based in feet and inches and use *fractions* to represent partial inches.

- **Decimal** units are *unitless* — that is, they're not based on any particular real-world unit. With decimal units, each unit in the drawing could represent an inch, a millimeter, a cubit (if you're into building arks in case that rainy day should come), or any other unit of measure you deem suitable.

- **Engineering** units are based in feet and inches and use *decimals* to represent partial inches.

- **Fractional** units, like decimal units, are unitless and show values as fractions rather than decimal numbers.

- **Scientific** units are also unitless and show values as exponents, used for drawing really tiny or really large things. If you design molecules or galaxies, this is the unit type for you.

AutoCAD's angle unit types are as follows:

- **Decimal Degrees** show angles as decimal numbers and are by far the easiest to work with — if your type of work allows it!

- **Deg/Min/Sec** is based on the old style of dividing a degree into minutes and minutes into seconds. But seconds aren't fine enough to display AutoCAD's precision capabilities, so seconds can be further divided into decimals. One nautical mile (6,076 feet) is approximately one minute of arc of longitude on the equator. David Letterman once said that the equator is so long that it would reach once around the world.

- **Grads and Radians** are mathematically beautiful (so I'm told) but are not widely used in drafting. Apparently the French artillery uses grads, but as long as we're friends with them, we shouldn't have to worry.

- **Surveyor's Units** type is similar to Deg/Min/Sec, but uses quadrants (quarter circles), rather than a whole circle, where an angle in Deg/Min/Sec might measure 300°0'0.00", the same angle in Surveyor's Units would be represented as S 30°0'0.00" E.

For the great majority of AutoCAD users, the unit types to know and use are *Decimal, Architectural,* and *Decimal Degree.* You'll know or be told if you need to use one of the other types!

After you specify a type of unit, you draw things onscreen at full size in those units just as though you were laying them out on the construction site or in the machine shop. You draw an 8-foot-high line, for example, to indicate the height of a wall and an 8-inch-high line to indicate the cutout for a doggie door (for a dachshund, naturally). The onscreen line may actually be only 2 inches long at a particular zoom magnification, but AutoCAD stores the length as 8 feet. This way of working is easy and natural for most people for whom CAD is their first drafting experience, but it seems weird to people who've done a lot of manual drafting. If you're in the latter category, don't worry; you'll soon get the hang of it.

Figure 4-1: The Drawing Units dialog box.

When you use dash-dot linetypes (Chapter 6) and hatching (Chapter 15) in a drawing, it matters to AutoCAD whether the drawing uses an imperial (inches, feet, miles, and so on) or metric (millimeters, meters, kilometers, and so on) system of measure. The MEASUREMENT system variable controls whether the linetype and hatch patterns that AutoCAD lists for you to choose from are scaled with inches or millimeters in mind as the plotting units. MEASUREMENT=0 means inches (that is, an imperial-units drawing), whereas MEASUREMENT=1 means millimeters (that is, a metric-units drawing). If you start from an appropriate template drawing (as described in the section "A Template for Success," later in this chapter), the MEASUREMENT system variable will be set correctly, and you won't ever have to think about it. (For an explanation of system variables and how to set them, see Chapter 26.)

Weighing up your scales

The next decision you should make before setting up a new drawing is choosing the scale at which you'll eventually plot the drawing. This decision gives you the *drawing scale* and *drawing scale factor* — two ways of expressing the same relationship between the objects in the real world and the objects plotted on paper.

"Okay," you're saying, "I understand that I need to print my drawings at a *scale* acceptable to the discipline I work in. But if I'm drawing stuff full size, why do I need to worry about the *scale factor?*" Grab yourself a nice mug of cocoa and settle down 'round the fire, because I'm going to tell you. By now you know (because I've told you so) that you draw real things full size, but

drawings contain other things that are *not* real, such as text, dimensions, hatch patterns, title blocks, dash-dot linetypes, and so forth. And those non-real things need to be legible on your plotted drawing.

Say, for example, you want to draw a plan of your garage. You need it to fit on an 11-x-17-inch sheet of paper, and you want to add a title like (if you're really original like me) "My Garage." Typically, text annotations are ³⁄₃₂" or ⅛" high. Now, if you draw your 6"-wide wall full size, put a ⅛"-high title beside it, and then print the drawing at a scale of, say, 1:24 (that's 1 drawing inch equals 24 real inches, usually expressed as ½" = 1'-0"), the 6" wall itself will measure ¼" on the sheet, and the note will be an illegible little speck beside it. You fix it with the help of the drawing scale factor; the "Drawing scale versus drawing scale factor" sidebar explains how you arrive at the scale factor, and Table 4-1, in the following section, presents a list of acceptable standard scales with their corresponding scale factors for both imperial and metric systems of measure.

Thinking annotatively

A few years back, AutoCAD introduced a new way of setting some types of annotation objects to the appropriate plotted size. *Annotative objects* possess a special property so that when you change the annotation scale of a layout's viewport or of the model tab, all the annotative objects — including text, dimensions, dash-dot linetypes, hatch patterns, and symbol blocks — change automatically to their correct size for the chosen scale. We take a closer look at annotative objects in Chapter 13, but in the meantime, it's still worthwhile getting familiar with using drawing scale factors because they're useful in a few other ways and because millions of drawings exist that were created this way.

Drawing scale versus drawing scale factor

CAD users employ two different ways of talking about a drawing's intended plot scale: drawing scale and drawing scale factor.

Drawing scale is the traditional way of describing a scale — traditional because it existed long before CAD came to be. Drawing scales are expressed with an equal sign or colon — for example, ⅛" = 1'-0", 1:20, or 2:1. You can translate the equal sign or colon as "corresponds to." In all cases, the measurement to the left of the equal sign or colon indicates a paper measurement, and the number to the right indicates a real-world measurement. In other words, the imperial drawing scale ⅛" = 1'-0" means that

⅛" on the plotted drawing corresponds to 1'-0" in the CAD drawing in the real world, assuming that the plot was made at the proper scale. A metric drawing scale is usually expressed without units, as a simple ratio. Thus, a scale of 1:20 means 1 unit on the plotted drawing corresponds to 20 units in the real world. In architectural and engineering drawings, the numbers usually refer to millimeters.

Drawing scale factor is a single number that represents a multiplier, such as 96, 20, or 0.5. The drawing scale factor for a drawing is the conversion factor between a measurement on the plot and a measurement in the real world.

You shouldn't just invent some arbitrary scale based on what looks okay on whatever size paper you happen to have handy. Most industries work with a small set of approved drawing scales that are related to one another by factors of 2 or 10. If you use other scales, at best you'll be branded a clue-less newbie — and at worst you'll have to redo all your drawings at an accepted scale.

Table 4-1 lists some common architectural drawing scales, using both imperial and metric systems of measure. The table also lists the drawing scale factor corresponding to each drawing scale and the common uses for each scale. If you work in industries other than those listed here, ask drafters or co-workers what the common drawing scales are and for what kinds of drawings they're used.

Table 4-1	Common Architectural Drawing Scales	
Drawing Scale	*Drawing Scale Factor*	*Common Uses*
$\frac{1}{16}$" = 1'–0"	192	Large-building plans
$\frac{1}{8}$" = 1'–0"	96	Medium-sized building plans
$\frac{1}{4}$" = 1'–0"	48	House plans
$\frac{1}{2}$" = 1'–0"	24	Small-building plans
1" = 1'–0"	12	Details
1:200	200	Large building plans
1:100	100	Medium-sized building plans
1:50	50	House plans
1:20	20	Small building plans
1:10	10	Details

After you choose a drawing scale, engrave the corresponding drawing scale factor on your desk, write it on your hand (don't mix those two up, okay?), and put it on a sticky note on your monitor. You need to know the drawing scale factor for many drawing tasks, as well as for some plotting. You should be able to recite the drawing scale factor of any drawing you're working on in AutoCAD without even thinking about it.

Even if you're going to use the Plot dialog box's Fit to Paper option (rather than a specific scale factor) to plot the drawing, you still need to choose a scale to make the nonreal things (such as text, dash-dot linetypes, hatch patterns, and so on) appear at a useful size. Choose a scale that's in the neighborhood of the Fit to Paper plotting factor, which AutoCAD displays in the Plot Scale area of the Plot dialog box. For example, if you determine that you need to squeeze your drawing down about 90 times to fit on the desired sheet size, choose a drawing scale of $\frac{1}{8}$" = 1'–0" (drawing scale factor = 96) if

you're using architectural units or 1:100 (drawing scale factor – 100) for other kinds of units.

Thinking about paper

With knowledge of your industry's common drawing scales, you can choose a provisional scale based on what you're depicting. But you won't know for sure whether that scale works until you compare it with the size of the paper that you want to use for plotting your drawing. Here again, most industries use a small range of standard sheet sizes. Three common sets of sizes exist, as shown in Figure 4-2 and Table 4-2:

✔ ANSI (American National Standards Institute)

✔ Architectural

✔ ISO (International Organization for Standardization)

Figure 4-2: Relationships among standard paper sizes.

Table 4-2	Common Plot Sheet Sizes	
Sheet Size	*Dimensions*	*Comment*
ANSI *E*	34 x 44"	
ANSI *D*	22 x 34"	*E* sheet folded in half
ANSI *C*	17 x 22"	*D* sheet folded in half
ANSI *B*	11 x 17"	*C* sheet folded in half
ANSI *A*	8½ x 11"	*B* sheet folded in half = letter size
Architectural Large *E*	36 x 48"	
Architectural *E*	30 x 42"	
Architectural *D*	24 x 36"	Large *E* sheet folded in half
Architectural *C*	18 x 24"	*D* sheet folded in half
Architectural *B*	12 x 18"	*C* sheet folded in half

(continued)

Table 4-2 (continued)

Sheet Size	Dimensions	Comment
Architectural *A*	9 x 12"	*B* sheet folded in half
ISO *A0*	841 x 1189 mm	
ISO *A1*	594 x 841 mm	*A0* sheet folded in half
ISO *A2*	420 x 594 mm	*A1* sheet folded in half
ISO *A3*	297 x 420 mm	*A2* sheet folded in half
ISO *A4*	210 x 297 mm	*A3* sheet folded in half

You select a particular set of sheet sizes based on the common practices in your industry. You then narrow down your choice based on the area required by what you're going to draw. For example, most imperial-units architectural plans are plotted on Architectural or ANSI D- or E-size sheets, and most metric architectural plans go on ISO A1 or A0 sheets.

If you know the desired sheet size and drawing scale factor, you can calculate the available drawing area easily. Simply multiply each of the sheet's dimensions by the drawing scale factor. For example, if you choose an 11-x-17-inch sheet and a drawing scale factor of 96 (corresponding to a plot scale of ⅛" = 1'–0"), you multiply 17 times 96, and 11 times 96, to get an available drawing area of 1,632 x 1,056 inches (or 136 x 88 feet). If your sheet size is in inches but your drawing scale is in millimeters, you need to multiply by an additional 25.4 to convert from inches to millimeters. For example, with an 11-x-17-inch sheet and a scale of 1:200 (drawing scale factor = 200), you multiply 17 times 200 times 25.4, and 11 times 200 times 25.4, to get 86,360 x 55,880mm or 86.36 x 55.88mm — not quite big enough for a football field (American *or* European football).

Conversely, if you know the sheet size that you're going to use and the real-world size of what you're going to draw, and you want to find out the largest plot scale you can use, you have to divide, not multiply. Divide the needed real-world drawing area's length and width by the sheet's dimensions. Take the larger number — either the length result or the width result — and round up to the nearest real drawing scale factor (that is, one that's commonly used in your industry). For example, suppose you want to draw a 60-x-40-foot (or 720-x-480-inch) floor plan and print it on 11-x-17-inch paper. You divide 720 by 17, and 480 by 11, to get 42.35 and 43.64, respectively. The larger number, 43.64, corresponds in this example to the short dimension of the house and the paper. The nearest larger common architectural drawing scale factor is 48 (corresponding to ¼" = 1'–0"), which leaves a little room for the plotting margin and title block.

The Cheat Sheet at this book's companion website (www.dummies.com/ cheatsheet/autocad2013) includes two tables that list the available drawing areas for a range of sheet sizes and drawing scales. Those tables can help you decide on an appropriate paper size and drawing scale; revert to the calculation method for situations that the tables don't cover. If you don't keep a favorite old calculator on your physical desktop, don't despair: AutoCAD 2013 has one lurking on the Ribbon. You'll find it on the Home tab's Utilities panel. (Hint: It looks like a calculator.) You speed demons can toggle QuickCalc off and on with the Ctrl+8 key combo!

When you select a sheet size and drawing scale, always leave some extra room, for the following three reasons:

- **Margin allowance:** Most plotters and printers can't print all the way to the edge of the sheet — they require a small margin. For example, my trusty old Hewlett-Packard LaserJet 4050 has a printable area of about 8.0 x 10.7 inches on an 8.5-x-11-inch ANSI A-size (letter-size) sheet. (You can find this information in the Plot dialog box, as described in Chapter 16.) If you're a stickler for precision, you can use the printable area instead of the physical sheet area in the calculations described earlier in this section.

- **Annotations:** Most drawings require some annotations — text, dimensions, grid bubbles, and so on — outside the objects you're drawing, plus a title block surrounding the objects and annotations. If you don't leave some room for the annotations and title block, you'll end up having to cram things together too much or change to a different sheet size. Either way, you'll be slowed down later in the project, when you can least afford it.

- **Multiple views:** Many objects require multiple orthographic views, and details at other scales.

Some industries deal with the sheet-is-too-small/drawing-scale-is-too-large problem by breaking up drawings onto multiple plotted sheets. You might consider doing the same.

Don't be afraid to start with *real* paper. Experienced drafters often make a quick, throwaway pencil-and-paper sketch indicating the dimensions of the sheet of paper they intend to plot on, a sketch of the title block, and a very rough, schematic sketch of the thing they're going to draw. By sketching on paper first, you'll often catch scale or sheet-size problems before you set up a drawing, when repairs take only a few minutes — not after you've created the drawing, when fixing the problem can take hours.

Defending your border

The next decision to make is what kind of border your drawing needs. The options include a full-blown title block, a simple rectangle, or nothing at all around your drawing. If you need a title block, do you have one, can you borrow an existing one, or will you need to draw one from scratch? Although you can draw title block geometry in an individual drawing, you'll save time by reusing the same title block for multiple drawings. Your company may already have a standard title-block drawing ready to use, or someone else who's working on your project may have created one for the project.

The most efficient way of creating a title block is as a separate DWG file, drawn at its normal plotted size (for example, 36 inches long by 24 inches high for an architectural D-size title block, or 841mm long by 594mm high for an ISO A1-size version). You then *insert* or *xref* the title block drawing into each sheet drawing. We explain inserting drawings into other drawings, or attaching drawings as external reference files in Chapters 17 and 18.

A Template for Success

When you start in either the Drafting & Annotation workspace (as we do throughout this book) or the old AutoCAD Classic workspace, AutoCAD creates a new, blank drawing configured for 2D drafting. Depending on where you live (your country, not your street address!) and the dominant system of measure used there, AutoCAD will base this new drawing on one of two default drawing templates: `acad.dwt` for the imperial system of measure, as used in the United States, or `acadiso.dwt` for the metric system, used throughout the rest of the galaxy. (In AutoCAD LT, the two default templates are `acadlt.dwt` and `acadltiso.dwt`.) When you explicitly create a new drawing from within AutoCAD, the Select Template dialog box, shown in Figure 4-3, appears by default so you can choose a template on which to base your new drawing.

You may be familiar with Microsoft Word or Excel template files, and AutoCAD drawing templates work pretty much the same way — because Autodesk stole the idea from them (encouraged, of course, by Microsoft) although one could argue that it was the other way around.

A *template* is simply a drawing whose name ends in the letters *DWT,* which you use as the starting point for another drawing. When you create a new drawing from a template, AutoCAD makes a copy of the template file and opens the copy in a new drawing editor window. The first time you save the file, you're prompted for a new filename to save to; the original template file stays unchanged.

Figure 4-3: A toolbox of templates.

Using a suitable template can save you time and worry because many of the setup options are already set correctly for you. You know the drawing will print correctly; you just have to worry about getting the geometry and text right. Of course, all this optimism assumes that the persons who set up the template knew what they were doing.

The stock templates that come with AutoCAD are okay as a starting point, but you'll need to modify them to suit your purposes or create your own from scratch. In particular, the stock AutoCAD templates are probably not set up for the scales you'll want to use. The instructions in the rest of this chapter tell you how to specify scale-dependent setup information.

So, the only problems with templates are creating good ones and then later finding the right one to use when you need it. Later in this chapter, in the "Making Templates Your Own" section, we show you how to create templates from your own setup drawings. Here we show you how to use an already-created template — say, one of the templates that comes with AutoCAD 2013 or one you get from a CAD-savvy colleague. If you're lucky, someone in your office has created suitable templates that you can use to get going quickly.

Follow these steps to create a new drawing from a template drawing:

1. **Run the NEW command by pressing Ctrl+N or clicking the Application button and choosing New.**

 The Select Template dialog box appears.

The first button on the Quick Access Toolbar runs the QNEW (Quick NEW) command instead of the ordinary NEW command. If you or someone else has changed the Default Template File Name for QNEW in the Options dialog box, QNEW will *not* open the Select Template dialog box; instead, it simply presents you with a new, blank drawing — possibly not the one you wanted. You *can* take advantage of QNEW, though — for information about how, see the "Making Templates Your Own" section, later in this chapter.

2. **Click the name of the template you want to use as the starting point for your new drawing and then click the Open button.**

 A new drawing window with a temporary name, such as `Drawing2.dwg`, appears. (The template you opened remains unchanged on your hard drive.)

 Depending on which template you choose, your new drawing may open in a paper space layout, not in model space. If that's the case, click the Model button on the status bar before changing the settings described in the next section. (We describe how to set up and take advantage of paper space layouts in Chapter 5.)

3. **Press Ctrl+S or click the Application button and choose Save to save the file under a new name.**

 Take the time to save the drawing to the appropriate name and location now.

4. **Make needed changes.**

 With most of the templates that come with AutoCAD, consider changing the units, limits, grid and snap settings, linetype scale, and dimension scale. See the next section for instructions.

5. **Save the drawing again.**

 If you'll need other drawings in the future similar to the current one, consider saving your modified template as a template in its own right. See the section "Making Templates Your Own," later in this chapter, for the lowdown on saving templates.

A few of the remaining templates that come with AutoCAD include title blocks for various sizes of sheets. In addition, most templates come in two versions — one for people who use color-dependent plot styles and one for people who use named plot styles. You probably want the color-dependent versions. (Chapter 16 describes the two kinds of plot styles and why you probably want the color-dependent variety.) We warned you that this drawing setup stuff would be complicated!

Making the Most of Model Space

After you decide on drawing scale and sheet size, you're ready to set up your drawing. Most drawings require a two-part setup:

1. Set up model space, where you'll create most of your drawing.

2. Create one or more paper space layouts for plotting.

As we explain in Chapter 2, model space is the infinitely large, three-dimensional environment in which you create the "real" objects you're drawing. You can set up your model space as described in this section; Chapter 5 introduces you to setting up your paper space layouts.

Setting your units

First, set the linear and angular units that you want to use in your new drawing. The following procedure describes how:

1. **Click the Application button and then choose Units from the Drawing Utilities group.**

 The Drawing Units dialog box appears, as shown in Figure 4-4.

Figure 4-4: Set your units here.

2. **Choose a linear unit type from the Length Type drop-down list.**

 Choose the type of unit representation that's appropriate for your work. Engineering and Architectural units are displayed in feet and inches; the other types of units aren't tied to any particular unit of measurement. You decide whether each unit represents a millimeter, centimeter, meter, inch, foot, or something else. Your choice is much simpler if you're working in metric: Choose Decimal units.

 AutoCAD *can* think in inches! If you're using Engineering or Architectural units (feet and inches), AutoCAD interprets any distance or coordinate you enter as that many *inches*. You must use the ' (apostrophe) character on your keyboard to indicate a number in feet instead of inches.

3. **From the Length Precision drop-down list, choose the level of precision you want when AutoCAD displays coordinates and linear measurements.**

 The Length Precision setting controls how precisely AutoCAD displays coordinates, distances, and prompts in some dialog boxes. For example, the Coordinates section of the status bar displays the current coordinates of the crosshairs, using the current precision.

 The linear and angular precision settings affect only AutoCAD's *display* of coordinates, distances, and angles on the status bar, in dialog boxes, and in the command window and Dynamic Input tooltip areas. For drawings stored as DWG files, AutoCAD *always* uses maximum precision to store the locations and sizes of all objects that you draw, regardless of how many decimal places you choose to display in the Drawing Units dialog box. In addition, AutoCAD provides separate settings for controlling the precision of dimension text — see Chapter 14 for details.

4. **Choose an angular unit type from the Angle Type drop-down list.**

 Decimal Degrees and Deg/Min/Sec are the most common choices.

 The Clockwise check box and the Direction button provide additional angle measurement options, but you'll rarely need to change the default settings: Unless you're a land surveyor, measure angles counterclockwise and use east as the 0-degree direction.

5. **From the Angle Precision drop-down list, choose the degree of precision you want when AutoCAD displays angular measurements.**

6. **In the Insertion Scale area, choose the units of measurement for this drawing.**

 Choose your *base unit* for this drawing — that is, the real-world distance represented by one AutoCAD unit.

 The AutoCAD (but not the AutoCAD LT) Drawing Units dialog box includes a Lighting area where you specify the unit type to be used to measure the intensity of photometric lights. We introduce lighting as part of rendering 3D models in Chapter 23.

7. **Click OK to exit the dialog box and save your settings.**

Making the drawing area snap-py (and grid-dy)

For the last three decades, AutoCAD's *grid* consisted of a set of evenly spaced dots that served as a visual distance reference. You can still configure a dot grid in AutoCAD 2013, but starting with AutoCAD 2011, the default is a snazzy graph-paperlike grid made up of a network of lines.

AutoCAD's *snap* feature creates a set of evenly spaced, invisible *hot spots,* which make the crosshairs move in nice, even increments as you specify points in the drawing. Both Grid mode and Snap mode are like the intersection points of the lines on a piece of grid paper, but the grid is simply a visual reference — it never prints — whereas Snap constrains the points that you can pick with the mouse. You can — and usually will — set grid and snap spacing to different values.

Prior to AutoCAD 2012, when Snap mode was enabled, it was on full time. This could be distracting as you moved your crosshairs around the screen — and downright annoying when you were trying to select an object that didn't happen to fall on a snap point. You no longer have to keep toggling Snap mode on and off. It's now engaged only when you're using a command that asks you to specify a point. For example, when Snap is on, you can move your crosshairs freely around the screen, but when you start the LINE command, Snap mode kicks in, and your crosshairs jump to the closest snap point.

Set the grid and the snap intervals in the Drafting Settings dialog box by following these steps:

1. **Right-click the Snap Mode or Grid Display button on the status bar and choose Settings.**

 The Drafting Settings dialog box appears with the Snap and Grid tab selected, as shown in Figure 4-5.

Figure 4-5: Get your drafting settings here!

The Snap and Grid tab has six sections, but the Snap Spacing and Grid Spacing areas within that tab are all you need to worry about for most 2D drafting work.

2. Select the Snap On check box to turn on Snap mode.

This action enables default snaps half a unit apart (ten units apart if you're working with the default metric template).

AutoCAD usually has several ways of doing things. You can also click the Snap Mode button on the status bar to toggle snap on and off; the same goes for the Grid Display button and the grid setting. Or you could use the function keys: F7 toggles the grid off and on, and F9 does the same for Snap mode.

3. Enter the snap interval you want in the Snap X Spacing box.

Use the information in the sections preceding this procedure to decide on a reasonable snap spacing.

If the Equal X and Y Spacing check box is selected, the Y spacing changes automatically to equal the X spacing, which is almost always what you want. Deselect the check box if you want to specify unequal snap spacing.

4. Select the Grid On check box to turn on the grid.

5. Enter the desired grid spacing in the Grid X Spacing box.

Use the information in the sections preceding this procedure to decide on a reasonable grid spacing.

As with snap spacing, if the Equal X and Y Spacing check box is selected, the Y spacing automatically changes to equal the X spacing. Again, you usually want to leave it that way.

X measures horizontal distance; Y measures vertical distance. The AutoCAD drawing area normally shows an X and Y icon in case you forget.

If you're an old AutoCAD hand and find the graph-paper grid too obtrusive, select the Display Dotted Grid In 2D Model Space check box in the Grid Style area to switch to the old-style rows and columns of dots.

6. Specify additional grid display options in the Grid Behavior area.

If you select the Adaptive Grid check box, AutoCAD changes the density or spacing of the grid lines or dots as you zoom in and out. If you also select Allow Subdivision Below Grid Spacing, the spacing can go lower than what you've set, and it may go higher if you're zoomed a long way out of your drawing. (If it didn't, you couldn't see your drawing for the grid!)

Selecting the Display Grid Beyond Limits check box allows the grid to display over the entire drawing area, no matter how far you're zoomed out. Clearing this check box makes AutoCAD behave the way it's always behaved — that is, the grid is displayed only in the area defined by the drawing limits.

The Follow Dynamic UCS option (not available in AutoCAD LT) is a 3D-specific feature that changes your drawing plane as you mouse over 3D objects. We cover this feature in Chapter 22.

7. Click OK to close the Drafting Settings dialog box.

Setting linetype and dimension scales

Even though you've engraved the drawing scale factor on your desk and written it on your hand — not vice versa — AutoCAD doesn't know the drawing scale until you enter it. Keeping AutoCAD in the dark is fine as long as you're just drawing continuous lines and curves representing real-world geometry because you draw these objects at their real-world size, without worrying about plot scale.

However . . . as soon as you start using noncontinuous dash-dot linetypes (line patterns that contain gaps in them), you need to tell AutoCAD how to scale the gaps in the linetypes based on the plot scale. If you forget this, the dash-dot linetype patterns can look waaaay too big or too small. Figure 4-6 shows what we mean.

Too Small... Too Big... Just Right!

Figure 4-6: . . . and this little center line looks juuuust right!

The scale factor that controls dash-dot linetypes is found in a system variable called LTSCALE (as in LineType SCALE). You can change this setting at any time, but it's best to set it correctly when you're setting up the drawing.

The following sequence includes directions for typing system variable and command names. To set the linetype scale at the keyboard, follow these steps:

1. **Type** LTSCALE **(or** LTS**) and press Enter.**

 AutoCAD responds with a prompt, asking you for the scale factor. The value at the end of the prompt is the current linetype scale setting, as shown in the following command line example:

   ```
   Enter new linetype scale factor <1.0000>:
   ```

2. **Type the value you want for the linetype scale and press Enter.**

 The easiest choice is to set the linetype scale to the drawing scale factor. Some people, however, find that the dashes and gaps in dash-dot linetypes get a bit too long when they use the drawing scale factor. If you're one of those people, set LTSCALE to one-half of the drawing scale factor. (Feel free to experiment with this value; some people prefer a linetype scale of three-quarters the scale factor. If you're working in metric, try 0.75 times the scale factor instead — just ask your calculator if you don't believe me.)

 Alternatively, you can specify linetype scale in the Linetype Manager dialog box: Click the Linetype drop-down on the Properties panel of the Ribbon's Home tab and select Other. Then in the Linetype Manager dialog box, click the Show Details button, and type your desired linetype scale in the Global Scale Factor text box.

Besides LTSCALE, there are three other similarly named system variables you can use to control the display of dash-dot linetypes:

- **PSLTSCALE:** Makes linetype spacing look the same in paper space viewports, regardless of the viewport scale.

- **CELTSCALE:** Changes the effective linetype scale factor for new objects.

- **MSLTSCALE:** Visually displays dash-dot linetypes in the model tab based on the annotative scale setting.

If any of these sound useful — and we highly recommend you enable PSLTSCALE — check them out in the online help index.

The procedure described here for setting linetype scale assumes that you're starting a new drawing from one of the plain-jane templates (acad.dwt or acadiso.dwt in the full version, acadlt.dwt or acadltiso.dwt in AutoCAD LT) and using the default linetype scale. Don't change LTSCALE in existing drawings without knowing exactly why you're doing it and what values to set them to, in case someone before you set their values for good reasons.

Entering drawing properties

We recommend one last bit of housekeeping before you're finished with model space drawing setup: Enter summary information in the Drawing Properties dialog box, as shown in Figure 4-7. Click the Application button; in

the Drawing Utilities section, choose Drawing Properties to open the Drawing Properties dialog box; then click the Summary tab. Enter the drawing scale and the drawing scale factor you're using in the Comments area, plus any other information you think useful.

Don't confuse *drawing* properties (which are really file properties) with your drawing's *object* properties — they're different things. The properties you enter here can help you or someone you love when she opens your drawing and wonders how you set it up. *Object* properties are a big enough topic to merit their own chapter — see Chapter 6.

Figure 4-7: Surveying your drawing's properties.

Making Templates Your Own

You can create a template from any DWG file by using the Save Drawing As dialog box. Follow these steps to save your drawing as a template:

1. **Click Save As on the Quick Access Toolbar.**

 The Save Drawing As dialog box appears, as shown in Figure 4-8.

2. **From the Files of Type drop-down list, choose AutoCAD Drawing Template (*.dwt) or AutoCAD LT Drawing Template (*.dwt).**

3. **Navigate to the folder where you want to store the drawing template.**

Figure 4-8: Saving a drawing as a template and applying options.

The AutoCAD 2013 default folder for drawing templates is buried deep in the bowels of your Windows user profile, which by default isn't visible in Windows Explorer. Hey, we never said this made any sense! Save your templates there if you want them to appear in AutoCAD's Select Template list. You can save your templates in another folder, but if you want to use them later, you have to navigate to that folder every time you want to use them. See the Technical Stuff paragraph that follows this procedure for additional suggestions.

4. **Enter a name for the drawing template in the File Name text box and click Save.**

 A dialog box for the template description and units appears.

5. **Specify the template's measurement units (English or Metric) in the drop-down list.**

 Enter the key info now — you can't do it later unless you save the template to a different name. Don't bother filling in the Description field; AutoCAD doesn't display it in the Select Template dialog box. Don't worry about the New Layer Notification area shown in Figure 4-8 for now; we tell you all about drawing layers in Chapter 6.

6. **Click OK to save the file.**

 The Template Options dialog box closes, and the template is saved to your hard drive.

7. **To save your drawing as a regular drawing, click Save As on the Quick Access Toolbar.**

 The Save Drawing As dialog box appears again.

8. **From the Files of Type drop-down list, choose AutoCAD 2013 Drawing (*.dwg).**

Choose the AutoCAD LT equivalent, if that's your version. AutoCAD 2013 uses a new file format that can't be opened by earlier releases. Choose a previous DWG file format if you want to be able to open your drawing in AutoCAD 2012 or earlier, but note that some features introduced in later releases may not translate properly to earlier ones, and probably won't survive a round trip back into 2013.

9. **Navigate to the folder where you want to store the drawing.**

 Use a different folder from the one with your template drawings.

10. **Enter the name of the drawing in the File Name text box and click Save.**

 The file is saved. Now, when you save it in the future, the regular file — not the template file — is updated.

The QNEW (Quick NEW) command, when properly configured, can bypass the Select Template dialog box and create a new drawing from your favorite template. The first button on the Quick Access Toolbar — the button with the plain white sheet of paper — runs the newer QNEW command instead of the older NEW command.

To put the Quick into QNEW, though, you have to tell AutoCAD which default template to use:

1. **Click the Application button, and then click the Options button at the lower-right corner of the Application Menu.**

2. **On the Files tab, choose Template Settings⇨Default Template File Name for QNEW.**

 The QNEW default file name setting is None, which causes QNEW to act just like NEW (that is, QNEW opens the Select Template dialog box). Specify the name of your favorite template here, and you get a new drawing file based on it every time you click QNEW.

AutoCAD 2013 stores drawing templates and many other support files under your Windows user folder. To discover where your template folder is hiding, open the Options dialog box. On the Files tab, choose Template Settings⇨Drawing Template File Location, as shown in Figure 4-9.

You don't have to keep your template files where that bossy Mister Gates tells you. Create a folder that you can find easily (for example, `C:\Acad-templates` or `F:\Acad-custom\templates` on a network drive), put the templates that you actually use there, and change the Drawing Template File Location setting so that it points to your new template folder.

Figure 4-9: Seek and you shall find your template folder.

Planning for Paper

In This Chapter

▶ Setting up paper space layouts

▶ Buttons or tabs for layout fashionistas

▶ Looking into viewports

▶ Working in paper space

M ost of what the earlier chapters look at revolves around setting up the *model space environment* — that infinitely large, three-dimensional realm wherein you create your gleaming towers, your wondrous electronic gadgetry, . . . or your garden shed or your angle bracket. However, you may have picked up a hint here or there that AutoCAD has a whole different environment known as *paper space.*

The final product of all this setup, remember, is a printed drawing on a piece of paper. In most industries, paper drawings are legal contract documents, so it's pretty important that they're understandable and easily read. The first part of that process is configuring the sheet layout in paper space, which we explain in this chapter. For the actual process of outputting either model space or layouts to printer or plotter, see Chapter 16.

This wizard provides you the ability to de
layout.

You can choose a plot device and plot
insert a title block and specify a viewpo

When you have completed the wizard,
will be saved with the drawing.

To modify these settings, you can use th
Setup dialog from within the layout.

Enter a name for the new layout you are

D-Size Sheet

:k

Viewports

ocation

Chapter 2 introduces you to the two spaces — model and paper — and Chapter 4 explains how to configure model space for efficient drawing. Before you plunge into paper space, a quick recap of model space is in order.

Model space is the drawing environment that's current when the Model tab (not the Model button) on the status bar is active. Model space is where you create the "real" objects that you're drawing, so these objects are referred to as *model geometry* whether they're 2D or 3D entities. When the Model tab is active, you see objects in model space only — anything in paper space is invisible.

In AutoCAD 2013, it's still possible to ignore paper space layouts entirely and do all your drawing *and* plotting in model space. But you owe it to yourself to give layouts a try. You'll probably find that they make plotting more consistent and predictable. They'll give you more plotting flexibility when you need it. And you'll certainly encounter drawings from other people that make extensive use of paper space, so you need to understand it if you plan to exchange drawings with anyone else.

Setting Up a Layout in Paper Space

A *paper space layout* is a representation of a drawing sheet. Although the model geometry — the real stuff — goes in model space, the "not-real" drawing objects (for example, a drawing border, title block, general notes, perhaps view labels, and symbols like North arrows) all go in paper space on the layout. In essence, model space is like the world, infinitely large and three dimensional; paper space is finite — the size of a drawing sheet, in fact — and two dimensional, just like a drawing sheet.

Aside from just an arrangement of your drawing sheet, layouts also store plot information. AutoCAD can save a separate plot setting with each layout, as well as model space, so that you can plot each one differently. In practice, you'll probably need to use only one of the paper space layout tabs, especially when you're getting started with AutoCAD. Theory and practice are the same in theory, but seldom in practice.

Rather than just reading about it, you may also want to open a few of the AutoCAD 2013 sample drawings and click the Model and Layout buttons or tabs to witness the variety of ways in which paper space is used.

Specialized sample drawings are installed in the \Samples folder. The generic AutoCAD and AutoCAD LT sample drawings are no longer installed with the program, but they're still available — online. Download them from www. autodesk.com/autocad-samples or www.autodesk.com/autocadlt-samples. The upside of the change is that users of either program now have access to the other's sample files.

Will that be tabs or buttons?

The Autodesk documentation sometimes refers to the *Model tab* or to *layout tabs,* and sometimes (like just a second ago) we do here as well. In its out-of-the-box condition, AutoCAD does display actual, selectable tabs at the lower-left edge of the drawing window, clearly labeled Model, Layout1, and Layout2 (you can see this later in the chapter in Figure 5-4). You can gain a fraction more screen space if you hide the tabs, but even when they're hidden, they're still referred to as tabs. Here's how to toggle the way that tabs are displayed:

✔ **To hide layout tabs:** Right-click the visible Model tab or any layout tab, and choose Hide Layout and Model Tabs from the pop-up menu.

✔ **To show layout tabs:** Right-click the Model button (the one with the icon and the Model tooltip, not the Model or Paper Space button, which is sometimes confusingly labeled MODEL) — or the Layout button right next door — and choose Display Layout and Model Tabs. Huh? Right-click the Model button but not the Model button? Correct. The one on the left end of the set of three switches between paper space or letting you reach into model space through a hole cut in the layout, while the one immediately to the right of it switches you completely over to model space.

Hiding the tabs does give you a bit more drawing area, but there's a drawback — the Layout button can control only a single layout (whichever layout happens to be current). You have to use the Quick View Layouts feature (described in the next section) to switch between layouts, but if your drawing has only one layout, hiding the tabs is well worthwhile.

You can rename layout tabs — but not the Model tab — by double-clicking the layout name and typing a new one.

The state of your tabs is stored — but not automatically saved — in your current workspace. For example, if you're working in the Drafting & Annotation workspace, then switch to the AutoCAD Classic workspace, and then switch back to Drafting & Annotation, the change you made from tabs to buttons (or vice versa) will not be retained. For information on saving your own custom workspace, look up **workspace** in the online help system.

View layouts Quick (View)ly

Quick View Layouts is the second of two features that use the Quick View image strip to display preview images of drawings or layouts. We introduce Quick View Drawings — which previews all your open drawings in the Quick View strip — in Chapter 2.

The following steps explain how to change between model space and a layout or switch between layouts:

1. **Click the Quick View Layouts button on the status bar.**

 The Quick View image strip appears above the status bar and displays resizable image panels for model space and all layouts. Right below the row of images is the Quick View toolbar. Figure 5-1 shows a typical arrangement in a multilayout drawing.

Quick View Layouts preview images

Quick View toolbar

Model or Paper space toggle

Quick View Layouts button

Figure 5-1: View those layouts, and make it Quick!

Don't confuse the Quick *View* toolbar with the Quick *Access* Toolbar that lives up top, next to the Application Menu button. (AutoCAD is getting so quick, it's hard to keep up with it!)

AutoCAD 2013 adds an improvement. To simplify things when you have several drawings open and/or the open drawing(s) have several layouts, the Quick View panels have green borders to show which drawing and which view in that drawing are currently visible onscreen.

The Quick View toolbar contains four buttons that perform the following tasks (buttons are listed from left to right):

- *Pin Quick View Layouts:* Normally the images disappear as soon as you select a layout or click outside it. Clicking this button reorients the side view of the pushpin so it looks like it's poking a hole in your screen (you should be aware that neither Autodesk nor we are responsible for punctures in your monitor) and forces the image panels to remain open.

- *New Layout:* Click this button to create a new layout with a single viewport. The new layout appears as a new image at the end of the strip.

- *Publish:* Click this button to open the Publish dialog box. You use the PUBLISH command if you have a whole set of drawings you want to output and package at one time. We explain the AutoCAD version of publishing in Chapter 20.

- *Close Quick View Layouts:* Use this button to close the Quick View Layouts image strip if you pinned it open. Simply clicking outside the image strip closes the image strip if it's unpinned.

2. **Move your mouse pointer over each image in the Quick View panel.**

 The image background highlights to indicate which layout the pointer's focus is on.

 When a panel is highlighted, two icons appear at the top corners of the panel. The Publish button at top right does the same thing as Batch Plot on the Application Menu. If you want to print the individual layout without going through all the Publish rigmarole, click the Plot icon at the top left.

3. **Click the preview image of model space or the layout you want to make current.**

 The selected layout is activated and fills the drawing window; the preview image strip closes.

If you have a wheel mouse, you can move between previews by scrolling the wheel in either direction. You can also resize the previews by mousing over an image and then pressing the Ctrl key while scrolling the wheel back and forth.

Creating a layout

Creating a simple paper space layout is straightforward, thanks to the Create Layout Wizard, as shown in Figure 5-2. (Yes! Finally, a useful AutoCAD wizard.) The command name is LAYOUTWIZARD, but the bad news is that it's missing in action from AutoCAD 2013's default user interface. To get to it, type LAYOUTWIZARD at the keyboard (or, if you're using the AutoCAD Classic workspace, open the Insert menu and choose Layout, and then Create Layout Wizard).

Create Layout - Begin

▶ Begin
 Printer
 Paper Size
 Orientation
 Title Block
 Define Viewports
 Pick Location
 Finish

This wizard provides you the ability to design a new layout.

You can choose a plot device and plot settings, insert a title block and specify a viewport setup.

When you have completed the wizard, the settings will be saved with the drawing.

To modify these settings, you can use the Page Setup dialog from within the layout.

Enter a name for the new layout you are creating.

D-Size Sheet

< Back Next > Cancel

Figure 5-2: The Create Layout Wizard.

Although the Create Layout Wizard guides you, step by step, through the process of creating a paper space layout from scratch, it doesn't eliminate the necessity of coming up with a sensible set of layout parameters. The sheet size and plot scale that you choose provide a certain amount of space for showing your model (see the "Thinking about paper" section in Chapter 4), and wizards aren't allowed to bend the laws of arithmetic to escape that fact. For example, a map of Australia at a scale of 1 inch = 1 foot won't fit on an 8½- x-11-inch sheet, no way, no how. In other words, garbage in, garbage (lay) out. Fortunately, the Create Layout Wizard lends itself to experimentation, and you can easily delete layouts that don't work.

Follow these steps to create a layout:

1. **Type** LAYOUTWIZARD **and press Enter.**

 The Create Layout Wizard displays its first page and prompts you to enter a name for the new layout.

2. **Give the new layout a name and click Next.**

 In place of the default name, Layout3, we recommend something more descriptive — for example, *D-Size Sheet.* Or you can call it *A1-Size Sheet* if you're of the metric persuasion.

3. **Choose a printer or plotter to use when plotting this layout and then click Next.**

 Think of your choice as the *default* plotter for this layout. You can change to a different plotter later — or create page setups that plot the same layout on different plotters. (We explain page setups in Chapter 16.)

 Many of the names in the configured plotter list should look familiar because they're your Windows printers (*system printers,* in AutoCAD lingo). Names with a .pc3 extension represent nonsystem printer drivers. See Chapter 16 for details.

4. **Choose a paper size, specify whether to use inches or millimeters to represent paper units, and click Next.**

 The available paper sizes depend on the printer or plotter that you selected in Step 3.

5. **Specify the orientation of the drawing on the paper and click Next.**

 The icon displaying the letter *A* on the piece of paper shows you which orientation is which.

6. **On the Create Layout – Title Block page, select None and click Next.**

 We don't recommend selecting one of the two available title blocks, as odds are slim that either of those will fit on the paper size you selected in Step 4. Here's why

Earlier AutoCAD releases included a handy set of predrawn title blocks for a range of both imperial and metric paper sizes. Sad to say, all but two of them have disappeared, and those two are still the only ones available in AutoCAD 2013's Layout Wizard. Unfortunately, neither of them is likely to work out for you. If, in Step 4, you chose inches as your units and any paper size _other than_ ARCH D (36.00 x 24.00 inches) — or chose millimeters as your units and _any paper size at all_ — the title block will not fit the sheet.

When you know your way around the program a bit, you can always draw, insert, or xref a title block later. (See Chapters 17 and 18 for information about inserting or xrefing a title block.) You can also add custom title block drawings to your AutoCAD Template folder. If you want to know where to put them, see the section on making templates in Chapter 4.

7. **Define the arrangement of viewports that AutoCAD should create and select the viewport scale for them all from the drop-down list. Then click Next.**

 A _viewport_ is a window from paper space into model space. You must create at least one viewport to display the model in your new layout. We tell you more about viewports in the section "A view(port) for drawing in," later in this chapter.

 The default Viewport scale, Scaled to Fit, ensures that all your model drawing objects appear in the viewport, but it results in an arbitrary scale factor. Most technical drawings require a specific scale, such as 1:100 or 1/8" = 1'–0".

8. **Click Select Location to specify the location of the viewport(s) on the layout; then pick the viewport's corners.**

 After you click the Select Location button, the Create Layout Wizard displays the preliminary layout with any title block that you've chosen. Pick two points to define a rectangle that falls within the drawing area of your title block (or within the plottable area of the sheet, if you chose no title block in Step 6). AutoCAD then redisplays the Finish page of the Create Layout Wizard.

 AutoCAD represents the plottable area of the sheet with a dashed rectangle near the edge of the sheet. If you don't select a location for the viewport(s), the Create Layout Wizard creates a viewport that fills the plottable area of the sheet.

9. **Click Finish.**

 AutoCAD creates the new layout.

 Like the other wizards, the Create Layout Wizard is aimed at new users or old-timers who have somehow overlooked the introduction of paper space layouts. You won't need to run this wizard every time you start a new drawing, but you should run it once and then save the resulting file as a template for future drawings (see Chapter 4 for more about templates).

Copying and changing layouts

After you create a layout, you can delete, copy, rename, and otherwise manipulate it by clicking Quick View Layouts on the status bar and right-clicking a preview image. If you're using layout tabs rather than buttons, right-click a tab to display the menu or simply drag the tab to a new position. Figure 5-3 shows the menu options when you right-click a layout tab.

New layout

From template...

Delete

Rename

Move or Copy...

Select All Layouts

Activate Previous Layout

Page Setup Manager...
Plot...

Import Layout as Sheet...
Export Layout to Model...

Hide Layout and Model tabs

Figure 5-3: The Quick View Layouts right-click menu.

The From Template option refers to layout templates. After you create layouts in a template (DWT) or a drawing (DWG) file, you can use the From Template option to import these layouts into the current drawing. For details, see the LAYOUT command's Template option in the Command Reference section of online help.

Many drawings require only one paper space layout. If you always plot the same view of the model and always plot to the same device and on the same size paper, a single paper space layout should suffice. If you want to plot your model in different ways (for example, at different scales, with different layers visible, with different areas visible, or with different plotted line characteristics), you may want to create additional paper space layouts.

Lost in paper space

After you create a paper space layout, you suddenly have two views of the same drawing geometry: the view in your original model space and the new layout's view (perhaps decorated with a handsome title block and other accoutrements of plotting nobility). It's important to realize that both views are of the *same* geometry. If you change the model geometry on one view, you're changing it everywhere because all layouts display the same model space objects.

When you make a layout current, you can switch the active space between paper space (that is, drawing and zooming on the sheet of paper) and model space (drawing and zooming on the model, inside the viewport) in several ways, including the following:

- ✔ In the drawing area, double-click inside a viewport boundary to move the crosshairs into model space in that viewport. Alternatively, you can double-click outside all viewports (for example, in the gray area outside the sheet) to move the crosshairs into paper space.

- ✔ Click the Maximize/Minimize Viewport button on the status bar. (For more information, see Chapter 2.)

- ✔ Type **MSPACE** (the command alias is **MS**) or **PSPACE** (**PS**) at the keyboard.

- ✔ Click the MODEL/PAPER button on the status bar.

MODEL

PAPER When the crosshairs are in model space, anything you draw or edit changes the model in model space and therefore, through the viewports, on all paper space layouts. When the crosshairs are in paper space, anything you draw appears only on that one layout. It's as though you were drawing on an acetate sheet over the top of that sheet of plotter paper — the model beneath remains unaffected.

This behavior can make your brain hurt until you get used to it. To avoid confusion, stick with the following approach (at least until you're more familiar with paper space):

- ✔ **If you want to edit the model:** Do so in full-screen model space. Click the Model tab if tabs are displayed, or click the Model button if tabs are hidden. (The Model button is the one with the little black icon; don't confuse it with the MODEL/PAPER button, which switches between model and paper space within the same layout.) Don't try to edit the model in a paper space viewport — it's a very inefficient use of your screen space.

- ✔ **If you want to edit a particular layout without affecting the model:** Use one of the methods we describe to make that layout current, and make sure that the crosshairs are in paper space.

Spaced out

When you start working in layouts, it may not always be crystal clear whether you're in model space or paper space. The status bar button will help — it will say PAPER if you're in paper space or MODEL if you're in the other place. Here are a few other ways to tell your layout spaces apart:

- **Check the crosshairs.** If you're in paper space, you can move the crosshairs over the entire drawing area. If you're in model space, you can move the crosshairs only within the currently active viewport; if you try to move the crosshairs outside the viewport, they turn into a Windows selection arrow.

- **Select some model geometry.** Try clicking some objects that you know are in model space. If you can select them and they highlight, then you're in model space. If nothing happens when you click them, they're inaccessible because you're in paper space.

- **Check the UCS icon.** The UCS (for User Coordinate System) icon is the symbol at the lower-left corner of the drawing area. The model space icon takes the shape of two lines at right angles to each other, with the letters indicating the direction of the X-axis and the Y-axis. (If you've configured AutoCAD to use the 2D UCS icon, the *W* stands for the World Coordinate System.) The paper space icon is triangular, and the closed, three-sided shape represents a flat plane. If you don't see such a symbol, type **UCSICON** and press Enter; then type either **ON** to display the UCS icon in the lower-left corner of the display, or **OR** to display it at the drawings origin (that is, 0,0 coordinates), as shown in Figure 5-4. We explain more about user coordinate systems in Chapter 7.

Figure 5-4 shows the 2D UCS icon. By default, AutoCAD displays the 3D UCS icon, even when you're working in the Drafting & Annotation workspace. You can switch to the 2D style, adjust the icon size, and tell AutoCAD to display the icon in three colors by entering the UCSICON command and then clicking Properties.

```
Y
|
|w ___ X

|◄ ◄ ► ►|\ Model / Layout1 / Layout2 /
Command: UCSICON
Enter an option [ON/OFF/All/Noorigin/ORigin/Selectable/Properties] <ON>:
Command:
32.0184, 14.3262, 0.0000
```

Figure 5-4: Displaying the 2D style UCS icon.

A view (port) for drawing in

A *viewport* is a paper space object — a window into your drawing sheet — through which you view model space objects from paper space. By default, when you create a new layout, a large single viewport is created.

The viewports we talk about in this chapter are paper space viewports. You can also create viewports in model space, but they're completely different animals. Model space viewports are also known as *tiled* viewports because (like bathroom tiles) they can't have any space between them. You can use tiled viewports to look closely at widely separated areas of your screen. What's potentially confusing is that AutoCAD uses the same command name, and even the same dialog box, for creating the two different types of viewports. For this chapter, make sure that you're in paper space when you create viewports.

Paper space viewports are assigned drawing scales, and you can have multiple viewports with different scales on the same layout. For example, one viewport can show the floor plan of an exhibit space at ¼" to one foot, and another viewport can show an enlarged view of a display cabinet at 1"=1'. Because the individual viewports are scaled, the entire layout can be plotted at 1:1.

The Create Layout Wizard is fine when you're starting out, but most real drawings have unique, *nonstandardized* arrangements of viewports. When creating layouts, it's often easiest to create viewports from scratch. The following procedure explains how:

1. **Using one of the techniques described in the "Creating a layout" section, earlier in this chapter, create a new layout in your drawing.**

 For example, click Quick View Layouts to display the preview images, and then right-click any of the images and choose New Layout. A new layout is added to the end of the image strip.

2. **Click the image for the new layout to open it.**

 A new layout appears in the drawing window, showing the default sheet area and a single rectangular viewport centered on the sheet. You aren't going to use this viewport.

3. **Move the crosshairs over the viewport boundary and click to select it. Press the Delete key.**

 Although they don't behave like other drawing objects, viewports *are* objects, just like lines or circles. And like any other drawing objects, they can be selected and moved, copied, resized, arrayed — or deleted.

4. **On the Ribbon, click the Layout tab; then in the Layout Viewports panel, choose Rectangular.**

 AutoCAD prompts you to pick the first corner for the new viewport.

 You must be in paper space for these steps to work as described. If the Rectangular button (we know; they're *all* rectangular — we mean the one that says "Rectangular") is grayed out, you're still in model space.

5. **Pick a point somewhere on the blank page to locate the first corner of the new viewport.**

 AutoCAD prompts you to pick the second corner.

6. **Pick another point to place the second corner of the new viewport.**

 AutoCAD draws the viewport, and the model space geometry appears inside it. Next, specify a drawing scale for your viewport(s).

 Specifying the correct viewport scale sooner rather than later bestows a couple of important benefits:

 - Correctly scaling viewports allows you to use annotative documentation objects such as text, dimensions, hatch patterns, blocks, and noncontinuous (dash-dot) linetypes. We introduce you to annotative objects in Chapter 13.

 - Correctly scaling all your viewports allows you to easily plot the completed layout at a scale of 1:1, while retaining individual, true-to-scale viewports.

7. **Double-click inside the viewport you want to apply a scale to.**

 Model space becomes active, as it must, because that's the space you have to scale. The Viewport Scale button appears toward the right side of the status bar when model space is activated in a layout.

8. **Click the Viewport Scale button on the status bar.**

 Clicking the Viewport Scale button opens a pop-up list of every drawing scale registered in the scales list — including metric scales even if you're working in an English-units drawing, and vice versa.

 Most of the time, for most people, there are way too many scales in the lists you see in the Viewport Scale button and the Plot dialog box. AutoCAD has a handy-dandy Edit Drawing Scales dialog box that lets you remove those imperial scales if you never work in feet and inches and vice versa, if you work only in metric. To run through your scales, choose Scale List from the Annotation Scaling panel on the Annotate tab, or type **SCALELISTEDIT** and press Enter to open the Edit Drawing Scales dialog box. If (more likely "when") you make a mistake, the Reset button in the Edit Drawing Scales dialog box will restore all the default scales.

9. **Find the scale you want to apply to the active viewport and select it from the list.**

 The display zooms in or out to adjust to the chosen viewport scale.

Reread that last sentence and then think about how often you have to pan and zoom in your drawing. If you zoom inside a viewport whose scale you've set — *kaboom!* — you just blew the scale off the map. Luckily, you can prevent yourself or anyone else from inadvertently destroying your beautifully arranged and scaled viewport by completing the final steps of viewport setup:

10. **Make sure that you're in paper space (check the UCS Icon or move the crosshairs).**

11. **Select the boundary of the viewport whose arrangement you want to protect.**

 With the viewport selected, the Viewport Scale button reappears with its selectable list of scales, and right beside it is another button with a yellow unlocked padlock icon. As its tooltip indicates, its function is to lock and unlock viewports.

12. **Click the Lock/Unlock Viewport button to lock the viewport scale.**

 The yellow unlocked padlock changes to a blue locked padlock, and the Viewport Scale button now becomes unselectable. Locking the display sets AutoCAD up for some nifty zooming . . . if you're in paper space, a normal zoom is executed. If you're in model space inside a viewport, a normal zoom would wreck the scale, so when you try to zoom, AutoCAD near-instantaneously switches to paper space, zooms you in, and then switches back to model space. Sheer prestidigitation!

Sometimes the perfect viewport arrangement requires that a smaller viewport be completely surrounded by a larger one. Easy enough to create, yes, and easy to select — as long as you're in paper space. However, if you're in model space and you want to click from one viewport to the next to make it current, it's impossible to make model space current in a completely surrounded viewport by clicking inside it. Let your fingers come to the rescue: The Ctrl+R key combination cycles through model space in all drawing viewports, even if they're completely surrounded by other viewports.

And there you have your 12-step program to layout bliss! All that setup had a purpose, of course: to enable you to print perfect paper plots (or plot-perfect paper prints, if you prefer to see it that way). We cover plotting in depth in Chapter 16, but a short introductory word here might be useful.

About Paper Space Layouts and Plotting

As this chapter describes, you can use AutoCAD's paper space feature to compose one or more *layouts* for plotting your drawing in particular ways. Each layout lives on a separate tab, which you click at the bottom of the drawing area — or in a secret hiding place if you've hidden the Model and Layout tabs. AutoCAD saves plot settings (plot device, paper size, plot scale, and so on) separately for each of the layouts, as well as model space.

Whether to plot model space or a layout in a drawing depends entirely on how the drawing was set up. If you or someone else went through a layout-setup procedure similar to the one in this chapter, you probably should plot the layout. If not, plot model space.

Viewport boundaries will print if you don't pay attention to where you create them. What that means is that each drawing view has a nice rectangular border around it. Nice, but a definite no-no in every drafting office. In Chapter 6, we introduce you to object properties, including probably the most important one, *layers.* You can define a layer so that objects on it do not plot, and that's where you should create your viewports.

If you don't have any paper space drawings handy, you can use one of the AutoCAD sample drawings. Refer to the tip near the beginning of the "Setting Up a Layout in Paper Space" section, earlier in the chapter, for where to find the sample drawings.

Some different ways of plotting the same model can be handled in a single paper space layout with different page setups. See Chapter 16 for more details. If your projects require lots of drawings, you can parlay layouts into *sheet sets* — a feature that makes for more sophisticated creation, management, plotting, and electronic transfer of multisheet drawing sets.

Part II
Let There Be Lines

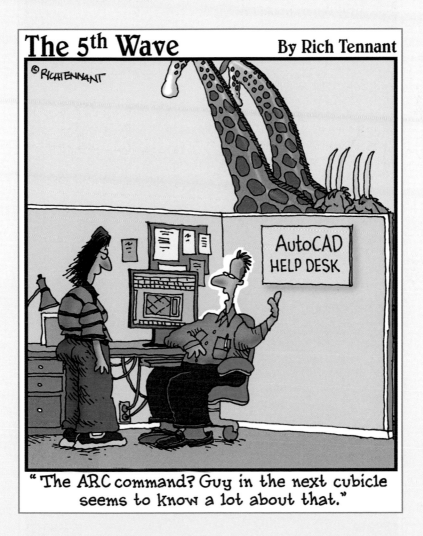

The 5th Wave — By Rich Tennant

AutoCAD HELP DESK

"The ARC command? Guy in the next cubicle seems to know a lot about that."

*L*ines, circles, and other elements of geometry make up the heart of your drawing. AutoCAD offers many different drawing commands, many ways to use them to draw objects precisely, and many properties for controlling the on-screen and plotted appearance of objects. After you draw your geometry, you'll probably spend at least as much time editing it as your design and drawings evolve. And in the process, you'll need to zoom in and out and pan all around to see how the entire drawing is coming together.

Drawing geometry, editing it, and changing the displayed view are the foundation of the drawing process; this part shows you how to make that foundation solid.

Manage Your Properties

*C*AD programs are different from other drawing programs. You have to pay attention to little details, like object properties and the precision of the points that you specify when you draw and edit objects. If you ignore these details and just start drawing, you'll end up with a mess of sloppy geometry that's hard to edit, view, and plot.

This chapter introduces you to *object properties,* one set of AutoCAD tools and techniques that helps you prevent CAD messes. Chapter 7 explains the most important precision drawing techniques that you need to observe to create usable AutoCAD drawings. The information in these two chapters is essential to understand before you start drawing and editing objects, procedures that we describe in Chapters 8 through 11.

When you first start using AutoCAD, one of its most overwhelming aspects is the number of property settings and precision controls that you need to pay attention to — even when you draw a simple line. Unlike many other programs, it's not enough to draw a line in a more-or-less-adequate location and then slap some color on it. But all those settings and controls can inspire the feeling that you have to learn how to drive a Formula 1 car to make a trip down the street. (The advantage is that after you *are* comfortable in the driver's seat, AutoCAD takes you on the long-haul trips and gets you there faster.)

Following are the three keys to good CAD drawing practice:

✔ **Properties:** Pay attention to and manage the properties of every drawing object that you create — especially the layer that each drawing object is on. We explain layers and other object properties in the next section.

✔ **Named objects:** Pay attention to and use the named objects in every drawing — the layers, text styles, block definitions, and other *nongraphical* objects that serve to define the look of all the *graphical* objects in the drawing. We enlighten you in the "Using Named Objects" section, later in this chapter.

✔ **Precision:** Pay attention to and control the precision of every point and distance that you use to draw and edit each object. We fill you in on AutoCAD's precision drawing techniques in Chapter 7.

These can seem like daunting tasks at first, but the following sections help you cut them down to size.

Managing Your Properties

All the objects that you draw in AutoCAD are like good Monopoly players: They own *properties.* In AutoCAD, these properties aren't physical things; they're the object's characteristics, such as layer, color, linetype, lineweight, transparency, and plot style. You use properties to communicate information about the characteristics of the objects you draw, such as the kinds of real-world objects they represent, their materials, their relative location in space, or their relative importance. In AutoCAD, you also use properties to organize objects for editing and plotting purposes.

You can view — and change — *all* properties of an object in the Properties palette, and many of them in the Quick Properties palette. In Figure 6-1, the Properties palette at the left and the Quick Properties palette at the right show properties for the selected line object.

The Properties palette was joined in AutoCAD 2009 by its more streamlined little sibling, Quick Properties. When Quick Properties is turned on in the status bar, selecting an object opens a floating palette that displays a customizable selection of that object's properties. (If your status bar buttons show text rather than icons, look for the QP button.)

Handy as it is, the Quick Properties palette has a knack of popping up on top of drawing objects that you need to see. In AutoCAD, you can keep Quick Properties mode turned off at the status bar, and instead use the QUICKPROPERTIES command. Type its alias **QP** and then select an object to display the Quick Properties panel. You can also double-click most objects to display their quick properties.

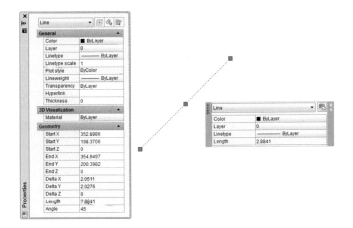

Figure 6-1: Comprehensive or quick? Sometimes you need lots of information, and sometimes you don't.

To toggle the full Properties palette on and off, click the Properties button on the View tab of the Ribbon or use the Ctrl+1 key combination. Before you select an object, the Properties palette displays the *current properties* — properties that AutoCAD applies to new objects when you draw them. After you select an object, the Properties palette displays the properties for that object. If you select more than one object, the Properties palette displays the properties that they have in common.

Layer one on me!

Every object has a layer as one of its properties. You may be familiar with *layers* — independent drawing spaces that stack on top of each other to create an overall image — from using drawing programs. AutoCAD, like most CAD programs, uses layers as the primary organizing principle for all the objects that you draw. You use layers to organize objects into logical groups of things that belong together; for example, walls, furniture, and text notes usually belong on three separate layers, for a couple of reasons:

- ✔ Layers give you a way to turn groups of objects on and off — both on the screen and on the plot.
- ✔ Layers provide the most efficient way of controlling object color, line-type, lineweight, transparency, and plot style.

So, to work in AutoCAD efficiently, you create as many layers as the drawing needs, and then assign them names and properties, such as colors and line-types. Then you draw objects on specific layers. When you draw an object, AutoCAD automatically puts it on the *current layer* — the layer that you see in the Layer drop-down list on the Home tab's Layers panel when no objects are selected. If a layer already exists in your drawing, you can make it the current layer by choosing it in the Layer drop-down list, as shown in Figure 6-2.

It's not absolutely necessary to create *all* your layers before you draw any-thing, but it will save you some time if you start as many layers as you think you need, and then only add more layers as needed. You can save even more time by creating all the layers you need in a new drawing and then saving it as a template file (covered in Chapter 4). Now each drawing you start from that template has all the layers you need. If you are unsure of which layers your drawing might need, no worries: Some experienced AutoCAD users draw things first, and then create appropriate layers and change the objects to them. You can easily change an object's layer by selecting the object and then choosing the desired layer name from the Layer drop-down list.

Figure 6-2: Setting an existing layer as the current layer.

Make sure that no objects are selected before you use the Layer drop-down list to change the name of the current layer. (Press the Esc key twice to be sure.) If objects *are* selected, selecting another name from the Layer drop-down list changes those objects' layers. When no objects are selected, the Layer drop-down list displays (and lets you change) only the current layer.

Stacking up your layers

How do you decide what to call your layers and which objects to put on them? Some industries have developed layer guidelines, and many offices have created documented layer standards. Some projects even impose specific layer requirements. (But be careful; if someone says, "You need a brick layer for this project," that can mean a couple of different things.) Ask experienced CAD drafters in your office or industry how they use layers in AutoCAD. If you can't find any definitive answer, create a chart of layers for yourself. Each row in the chart should list the layer name, default color, default linetype, default lineweight, default transparency, and what kinds of objects belong on that layer. If you use named plot styles to control your plotted output, add a default plot style to the list — that's not necessary for traditional color-based plotting.

Accumulating properties

Besides layers, the remaining object properties that you're likely to want to use often are color, linetype, lineweight, transparency, and possibly plot style. Table 6-1 summarizes these five properties.

Table 6-1	Useful Object Properties
Property	*What It Controls*
Color	Displayed colors and plotted colors or line widths
Linetype	Displayed and plotted dash-dot line patterns
Lineweight	Displayed and plotted line widths
Transparency	Displayed and plotted opacity of objects
Plot style	Plotted characteristics (See Chapter 16.)

Long before AutoCAD could display lineweights on the screen and print those same lineweights on paper, object *colors* controlled the printed lineweight of objects. AutoCAD 2000 introduced a more logical system, where you could assign an actual plotted thickness to *objects*. As logical as that method seems, the older method, in which the color of objects determines their plotted lineweight, continues to dominate. You may find yourself working this way even in AutoCAD 2013, for compatibility with drawings (and co-workers) that use the old way. Figure 6-3 shows you the idea. The model space view at the left shows objects in different colors, but with the same default lineweight. The paper space view at the right (what your plotted drawing will actually look like) shows that, although the lines are all black, their thicknesses vary, determined by the model space colors. For example, blue is very thick, and black is very thin.

Figure 6-3: Change my line thickness but color me black.

AutoCAD gives you two different ways of controlling object properties:

- **By layer:** Each layer has a default color, linetype, lineweight, transparency, and plot style property. Unless you tell AutoCAD otherwise, objects inherit the properties of the layers on which they're created. When objects are selected in a drawing created by using this system, the object properties are listed as *ByLayer*.

- **By object:** AutoCAD also enables you to override an object's layer's property setting and give the object a specific color, linetype, lineweight, transparency, or plot style that differs from the layer's.

If you've worked with other graphics programs, you may be used to assigning properties, such as color, to specific objects. If so, you may be tempted to do the same in AutoCAD. Resist the temptation. Did you catch that? One more time: *Resist the temptation.*

In almost all cases, it's better to create layers, assign properties to each layer, and let the objects on each layer inherit that layer's properties. Here are some benefits to using the ByLayer approach:

- You can easily change the properties of a group of related objects that you put on one layer. You simply change the properties for the layer, not for a bunch of separate objects.

 Here's a worst-case scenario: You receive an architectural drawing from someone else. You now want to plot it without any dimensions showing, so you freeze the dimension layer. Oh, poop! (Or words to that effect.) Only half the dimensions disappear, but so do some of the center lines, a couple of walls, the toilet, . . .

✔ Experienced drafters use the ByLayer approach, so if you work with drawings from other people, you'll be much more compatible with them if you do it the same way. You'll also avoid getting yelled at by irate CAD managers, whose job duties include haranguing any hapless newbie who assigns properties to individual objects.

If you take my advice and assign properties ByLayer, all you have to do is set layer properties in the Layer Properties Manager palette (we tell you how in this section), as shown in Figure 6-4. Before you draw any objects, make sure that the Color Control, Linetype Control, and Lineweight Control drop-down lists, *and* the Transparency button on the Ribbon's Home tab's Properties panel are all set to ByLayer, as shown in Figure 6-5. (Remember that the configuration of panels and drop-down lists may vary according to the resolution of your display.) If the drawing is set to use color-based plot styles instead of named plot styles (see Chapter 16), the Plot Style Control drop-down list will be inactive and will display ByColor.

Figure 6-4: Use layer properties to control object properties.

If the drawing is set to use named plot styles instead of color-based plot styles (see Chapter 16), the Plot Style control drop-down list should also display ByLayer.

WARNING!

If you want to avoid doing things the wrong way and getting yelled at by CAD managers, don't assign properties to objects in either of these ways:

✔ Don't make the *very* common beginner's mistake of choosing a specific color, linetype, lineweight, transparency, or plot style from the appropriate drop-down list on the Properties panel of the Ribbon's Home tab, or from the Properties palette, and then drawing the objects.

✔ Don't make the also-very-common beginner's mistake of drawing the objects, selecting them, and then choosing a property from the same drop-down lists.

Color control

Lineweight control

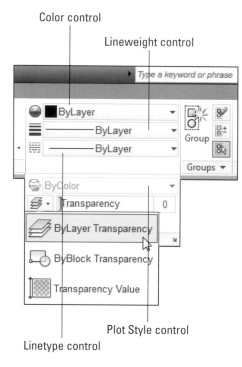

Plot Style control

Linetype control

Figure 6-5: ByLayer (nearly) all the way.

If you prefer to do things the right way (that is, *our* way!), assign these properties ByLayer, as we describe in the following section.

 AutoCAD's SETBYLAYER command lets you correct those non-ByLayer properties — on the Ribbon's Home tab, click the Modify panel label to open the panel slideout, and then click Set to ByLayer. Answer the prompts at the command line to finish modifying objects. For more information, refer to SETBYLAYER in the online help.

Creating new layers

If a suitable layer doesn't exist, you need to create one in the Layer Properties Manager palette. Follow these steps:

 1. **Click the Layer Properties button on the Layers panel of the Ribbon's Home tab, or type LAYER (or LA) at the command line and press Enter.**

 The Layer Properties Manager palette appears. A new drawing has only one layer: Layer 0. You need to add the layers necessary for your drawing.

2. **Click the New Layer button (it looks like a sheet of paper with a little sunburst on one corner) to create a new layer.**

A new layer appears. AutoCAD names it Layer1 but highlights the name in an edit box so you can type a new name to replace it easily, as shown in Figure 6-6.

Figure 6-6: Adding a new layer in the Layer Properties Manager palette.

3. Type a name for the new layer.

Type the layer name with *initial caps* (only the first letter of each word in uppercase). Layer names written completely in uppercase are much wider, which means that they often get truncated in the Layer Control drop-down list.

Layer names should be descriptive and organized so they're easily identifiable and sort logically. For example, names like *Floor 01 plan, Floor 01 walls, Floor 01 electrical, Floor 02 plan*, and so on are better than a drawing we saw recently that had 132 layers named with this sequence: *001, 002, 003, 004, . . .*

4. On the same line as the new layer, click the color block or color name (White by default) of the new layer.

The Select Color dialog box appears, as shown in Figure 6-7.

The normal AutoCAD color scheme — AutoCAD Color Index (ACI) — provides 255 colors. So many choices are overkill for ordinary drafting.

For now, stick with the first nine colors — the ones that appear in a single, separate row to the left of the ByLayer and ByBlock buttons on the Index Color tab of the Select Color dialog box — for the following reasons:

- These colors are easy to distinguish from one another.
- Using a small number of colors makes configuring your plot parameters easier. (We describe that procedure in Chapter 16.)

Figure 6-7: The Select Color dialog box. Magenta is selected from the Standard Colors list.

In the Select Color dialog box, the True Color tab offers a choice of more than 16 million colors, which you can specify by using HSL (hue, saturation, and luminance) or RGB (red, green, and blue) numbers. The Color Books tab enables you to use PANTONE, DIC, and RAL color schemes, which are popular in publishing. If your work requires tons of colors or close color matching between the computer screen and printed output, you're probably familiar with the relevant color palette and how to use it. If you're using AutoCAD for ordinary drafting or design, stick with the AutoCAD Color Index palette.

5. **Click a color to select it as the color for this layer and click OK.**

 The Select Color dialog box closes, and focus returns to the Layer Properties Manager palette. In the Color column, the new layer color changes to either the name or the number of the color that you selected.

AutoCAD's first seven colors have both numbers and standard names: 1 = red, 2 = yellow, 3 = green, 4 = cyan, 5 = blue, 6 = magenta, and 7 = white (which appears black when displayed on a white background). The remaining 248 colors have numbers only.

6. **On the same line as the new layer, click the Linetype name of the new layer.**

 The Select Linetype dialog box appears, as shown in Figure 6-8.

 The default AutoCAD linetype is Continuous, which means no gaps in the line.

Select Linetype

Loaded linetypes

Linetype	Appearance	Description
Continuous	————————	Solid line

OK Cancel Load... Help

Figure 6-8: The Select Linetype dialog box.

If you already loaded the linetypes you need for your drawing, or if the template file you started from has some linetypes loaded, the Select Linetype dialog box displays them in the Loaded Linetypes list. If not, click the Load button to open the Load or Reload Linetypes dialog box. By default, AutoCAD displays linetypes from the standard AutoCAD or AutoCAD LT linetype definition file — `acad.lin` for imperial-units drawings or `acadiso.lin` for metric-units drawings (`acadlt.lin` and `acadltiso.lin` in AutoCAD LT). Load the desired linetype by selecting its name and clicking OK.

Unless you have a really good reason (for example, your boss tells you so), avoid loading or using any linetypes labeled ACAD_ISO. These linetypes are normally used only in metric drawings — and rarely even then. They overrule everything we're trying to show you about printed lineweight in what follows, so if at all possible, just say NO to ACAD_ISO. We promise you'll find it easier to use the linetypes with the more descriptive names: CENTER, DASHED, and so on.

7. **Click the desired linetype in the Loaded Linetypes list to select it as the linetype for the layer; say that really fast five times and then click OK.**

 The Select Linetype dialog box disappears, returning you to the Layer Properties Manager palette. In the Name list, the linetype for the selected layer changes to the linetype you just chose.

8. **On the same line as the new layer, click the new layer's lineweight.**

 The Lineweight dialog box appears, as shown in Figure 6-9.

Figure 6-9: The Lineweight dialog box.

9. **Select the lineweight you want from the list and click OK.**

 Using the lineweight property is a two-step process. After you've assigned a lineweight to a layer, you must click the Show/Hide Lineweight (LWT) button on the status bar to see the effect. You can turn the feature off and on with this button.

 The lineweight 0.00mm tells AutoCAD to use the thinnest possible lineweight on the screen and on the plot. We recommend that for now, you leave lineweight set to Default, and instead later map screen colors to plotted lineweights, as described in greater detail in Chapter 16.

10. **In the same line as the new layer, click the value in the Transparency column.**

 AutoCAD's transparency property will probably be most appreciated by people preparing drawings for presentation. Clicking in the Transparency column opens the Layer Transparency dialog box; type a numeric value between 0 and 90 or use the drop-down list to set a value. Transparency = 0 is the default, and means no transparency at all — objects drawn on a layer set to Transparency = 0 are completely opaque. Set the value to greater than 0 and you start seeing things through the objects you draw.

 Similar to the Lineweight property, you have to turn on the Transparency (TPY) button on the status bar to see through your objects.

11. **Set the plot style for the new layer.**

 The Plot Style column's contents depend on whether the drawing uses named plot styles or the traditional color-based plotting. Drawings set up to use color-based plotting display an unchangeable plot style name based on the layer's color property. The grayed-out style name changes only when the layer color changes. If, on the other hand, your drawing uses named plot styles, you can assign a named plot style to the layer in this column. (Chapter 16 explains why you might not want to.)

12. **Turn plotting on and off.**

 The setting in the Plot column controls whether the layer's objects appear on plots. Click the little printer icon to turn off this setting (the little printer gets a red bar through it) for any layer whose objects you want to see on the screen but hide on plots. Layout viewports, covered in Chapter 5, are a good use for this feature.

13. **(Optional) If you want to add a description to the layer, scroll the layer list to the right to see the Description column, click in the Description box corresponding to your new layer, and type a description.**

 As indicated in Step 2, our advice is to name your layers so you can tell what's on them. If you do choose to use layer descriptions, stretch the Layer Properties Manager palette to the right so that you can see the descriptions without having to scroll the layer list.

14. **Repeat Steps 1 through 13 to create any other layers that you want.**

15. **Select the new layer that you want to make current and click the Set Current button (the green check mark).**

 Changes you make in the Layer Properties Manager palette are instantaneous, unlike a dialog box in which you have to click OK to close the dialog box and apply the change.

 Don't forget to toggle on the Lineweight and Transparency buttons on the status bar to see the effect of assigning these properties. Unlike color and linetype, lineweight and transparency can be switched off and on.

 The Layer Control drop-down list now displays your new layer as the current layer — the one on which AutoCAD places new objects that you draw.

After you create layers, you can set any one of them to be the current layer: Make sure that no objects are selected, and then choose the layer name from the Layer Control drop-down list on the Layers panel in the Ribbon or the Layers toolbar.

A load of linetypes

When you load a linetype, AutoCAD copies its *linetype definition* — a formula for how to create the dashes, dots, and gaps in that particular linetype — from the `acad.lin` (imperial units) or `acadiso.lin` (metric units) file into the drawing. (The files are `acadlt.lin` and `acadltiso.lin`, respectively, in AutoCAD LT.) The definition doesn't automatically appear in other drawings; you have to load each linetype that you want to use into each drawing in which you want to use it. If you find yourself loading the same linetypes repeatedly into different drawings, consider adding them to your template drawings instead. (See Chapter 4 for information about templates and how to create them.) After you add linetypes to a template drawing, all new drawings that you create from that template will start with those linetypes loaded automatically.

Don't go overboard on loading linetypes. For example, you don't need to load *all* the linetypes in the `acad.lin` file on the off chance that you might use them all someday. The resulting linetype list would be long and unwieldy. Most drawings require only a few linetypes, and most industries and companies settle on a half dozen or so linetypes for common use. Your industry, office, or project manager may have guidelines about which linetypes to use for which purposes.

If you're the technodweeb type and don't mind editing a text file that contains linetype definitions, you can define your own linetypes or weed out the ones you'll never use. Press F1 to open the online help window. Then choose Customization Guide➪Custom Linetypes.

As with all palettes in AutoCAD, you can leave the Layer Properties Manager open while you do other things in the drawing — unlike the dialog box method of stopping what you're doing, opening the dialog box, making adjustments, closing the dialog box, and then resuming what you were doing. Also like other palettes, the Layer Properties Manager can be set to auto-hide itself to its title bar, to be either floating or docked, or to be anchored (do you get the sense that there are some AutoCAD programmers who'd rather be sailing?) to either side of the screen. If your computer has two monitors, you can drag the palettes to the second monitor.

Manipulating layers

After you create layers and draw objects on them, you can turn a layer off or on to hide or show the objects on that layer. In the Layer Properties Manager palette, the first three icons to the right of the layer name control AutoCAD's layer visibility modes:

- **Off/On:** Click the lightbulb icon to toggle visibility of all objects on the selected layer. AutoCAD doesn't regenerate the drawing when you turn layers back on. On the other hand, frozen layers don't regenerate while you're working on the drawing. (We give you the lowdown on regenerations in Chapter 12.)

✔ **Freeze/Thaw:** Click the sun icon to toggle off visibility of all objects on the selected layer. Click the snowflake icon to toggle visibility on. AutoCAD regenerates the drawing when you thaw layers.

✔ **Lock/Unlock:** Click the padlock icon to lock and unlock layers. When a layer is locked, you can see but not edit objects on that layer.

You can rearrange column order by simply dragging and dropping the column label to a new place. And you can right-click any column label to display a menu from which you can turn columns off and on.

Off/On and Freeze/Thaw do almost the same thing — both settings let you make objects visible or invisible by layer. You'll probably find it makes no appreciable difference whether you freeze and thaw layers or turn them off and on.

You can turn layers off and on, freeze and thaw them, and lock and unlock them by clicking the appropriate icons in the Layer Control drop-down list on the Ribbon.

The state of your layers

Say you have a floor plan of a house that includes a layer showing the framing and another layer showing the wiring. You'd probably never show both of those elements on the same drawing, so you'd need to do some layer management when you showed your drawing to the framers or the electricians. Rather than turning a dozen layers off and a different dozen layers on when you want a different view into your drawing, you can save groups of layer settings as a named *layer state*. You can manage your layer states in the appropriately named Layer States Manager dialog box by clicking the Layer States Manager button in the Layer Properties Manager. You can also access the Layer States Manager directly by entering **LAYERSTATES** at the command line or choosing Manage Layer States from the Layer State drop-down list in the Layers panel.

AutoCAD fades objects on locked layers, giving you a really effective visual reference without confusing you about which layers might be locked or not. You can control the amount of fading by setting a nonzero value for the system variable LAYLOCKFADECTL. (See Chapter 26 for an explanation of system variables and check out the online help for specific info on this one.) You can turn off fading but retain the current setting for future use by adding a minus sign (–) in front of the fade value, or you can turn off the fading altogether by setting this value to 0.

If you find yourself using lots of layers, you can create *layer filters* to make viewing and managing the layer list easier. A *group filter* is simply a subset of layers that you choose (by dragging layer names into the group filter name or by selecting objects in the drawing). A *property filter* is a subset of layers that AutoCAD creates and updates automatically according to layer property

criteria that you define (for example, all layers whose names contain *Wall* or whose color is green). To find out more, move your mouse pointer into the Layer Properties Manager palette, press F1, and click the New Property Filter hyperlink.

In both AutoCAD and AutoCAD LT, you can access a set of layer tools through the Layers panel of the Ribbon's Home tab — see Figure 6-10. (You may have to open the panel slideout to see them all.) Layer Isolate and Layer Off are especially useful — you simply click an object to specify the layer to *isolate* (that is, fade all layers except the chosen one) or turn off altogether. For more information on layers, open the online help system and choose User's Guide⇨Create and Modify Objects⇨Control the Properties of Objects⇨Work with Layers⇨Use Layers to Manage Complexity.

Figure 6-10: Tooling through the layer tools.

The LAYISO command incorporates the same layer-fading feature described in the preceding tip for locked layers — and it locks the layers as well. Set it up the way you want by typing **S** (for Settings) and pressing Enter; then type the option letter for the specific settings you want. Look up LAYISO in the online help Index for more information.

Instead of turning off a layer when there are only a few things in the way, you can hide or isolate individual objects with the ISOLATEOBJECTS and HIDEOBJECTS commands while keeping normal visibility for other objects on the layer. We discuss these commands in Chapter 10.

Using Named Objects

One of the things that can make AutoCAD a tough nut to crack is the somewhat cavalier naming conventions used in the program's documentation. For years, things like lines, arcs, and other *graphical* items were called *entities,* but then more recently, they started being called *objects.* Fair enough, but *object* has also long been used to define certain *nongraphical* components of a drawing — things that you'd hardly consider to be objects at all — and *those* are the kind of "named objects" we describe in what follows.

Hidden in the innards of every AutoCAD drawing file is a set of *named objects,* which are organized into *symbol tables,* and the properties that are common to all AutoCAD objects are defined in these tables. For example, all the line objects in a drawing are stored on one or more layers, so a layer property is common to all lines and is defined in the layer table. But the coordinates that define the start and end points of a given line are unique to that line (or they should be!) — so the coordinate properties are *not* common to all lines.

A layer is one example of a named object. The layer table in a given drawing contains a list of the layers in the current drawing, along with the settings for each layer (including color, linetype, on/off setting, and so on).

Named objects don't appear as graphical objects in your drawing. They're like the hardworking pit crew that keeps the race cars running smoothly behind the scenes. The named objects you're likely to use the most include the following:

- ✔ Layers (covered in the section "Layer one on me!," earlier in this chapter)
- ✔ Linetypes (covered in the section "Accumulating properties," earlier in this chapter)
- ✔ Text styles (See Chapter 13.)
- ✔ Table styles (See Chapter 13.)
- ✔ Multileader styles (See Chapter 13.)
- ✔ Multiline styles (not covered in this book; see the online help)
- ✔ Dimension styles (See Chapter 14.)
- ✔ Block definitions and xrefs (See Chapters 17 and 18.)
- ✔ Layouts (See Chapter 5.)

When you use commands such as LAYER, LINETYPE, and DIMSTYLE you're creating and editing named objects. After you've created named objects in a drawing, AutoCAD DesignCenter or Content Explorer give you the tools to copy them between drawings.

Donald Trump might think otherwise, but you *can* have too many properties (at least in AutoCAD). You may have created layers or loaded linetypes, text, or dimension styles that you end up not using. If you think that you may have some of these superfluous named objects in your drawing, the PURGE command helps you get rid of them. Click the Application button to display the Application Menu. Choose Drawing Utilities, and then Purge to open the Purge dialog box. You can click the plus sign (+) beside each category to purge individual items, or you can click Purge All and get rid of tons of stuff at once. Visit the online help for more about purging.

Using AutoCAD DesignCenter

DesignCenter is a dumb name for a useful, if somewhat busy, palette. (At least they didn't call it DesignCenter Manager!) The DesignCenter palette is handy for borrowing data from other drawings. Whereas the Properties palette (described in the section "Managing Your Properties," earlier in this chapter) is concerned with properties of graphical objects, the DesignCenter palette deals primarily with named objects: layers, linetypes, block definitions, text styles, and other organizational objects in drawings.

The DesignCenter palette (shown in Figure 6-11) consists of a toolbar at the top, a set of three tabs below that, a tree view pane on the left, and a content pane on the right. The tree view pane displays a Windows Explorer–like navigation panel, showing drawing files and the symbol tables contained in each drawing. The content pane usually displays the contents of the selected drawing or symbol table.

Tabs

Tree view pane

Content pane

Figure 6-11: The AutoCAD DesignCenter palette.

The three tabs just below the DesignCenter toolbar control what you see in the tree view and content panes:

 ✓ **Folders:** This tab shows the folders on your local and network drives, just like the Windows Explorer Folders pane does. Use this tab if the drawing you want to copy from isn't currently open in AutoCAD.

✔ **Open Drawings:** This tab (current in Figure 6-11) shows the drawings that are currently open in AutoCAD. Use this tab to copy named objects between open drawings.

✔ **History:** This tab shows drawings that you've recently browsed in DesignCenter. Use this tab to jump quickly to drawings that you've used recently on the Folders tab.

The Autodesk Seek Design Content button on DesignCenter's toolbar links to parts libraries that are available on Autodesk's website. (Seek is also accessible through the Content Explorer, which we introduce you to in Chapters 1 and 2.) Autodesk Seek is essentially an online catalog of drawings of building products, like doors and bolts. Browse the offerings to see whether any of the online libraries can be useful in your work.

The toolbar buttons further refine what you see in the tree view and content panes. A few of these buttons toggle different parts of the panes.

The following steps outline the procedure for using DesignCenter to copy named objects from one drawing to another. See the next section for a specific example.

1. **If it isn't already open, switch to the Ribbon's View tab, find the Palettes panel, and click DesignCenter to open the DesignCenter palette.**

 You can also press Ctrl+2 to open this palette.

2. **Select or load the drawing(s) whose content you want to view or use into the navigation pane on the left.**

 If the source drawing is already open, you can access its content from the Open Drawings tab. If the source drawing isn't open but is stored on your hard drive or network, click Load on the DesignCenter toolbar and navigate to the file's location in the Folders tab.

3. **In the Open Drawings tab (if the source drawing is currently open) or the Folders tab (if the source drawing isn't open) of the tree view pane, click the plus sign (+) beside the source file to expand the list of named object categories.**

 The named object categories appear in a list in the tree view pane on the left and as icons in the content pane on the right.

4. **In the tree view pane, select the category of named object you want to copy.**

 The content pane now displays the individual named objects within the named object category. For example, in Figure 6-11 (shown previously), the Layers category is selected in the tree view pane, and icons for each named layer are shown in the content pane.

5. **In the content pane, select the items you want to copy. Right-click and choose Add [Symbol] (or Insert Block if you're copying block definitions) or simply drag and drop them into the drawing area.**

Use Shift or Ctrl to select multiple named objects.

Copying layers between drawings

The preceding set of steps outlines the general procedure for copying named objects from one drawing to another by using DesignCenter. The following steps show a specific example: copying layers from one drawing to another. You can use the same technique to copy dimension styles, layouts, linetypes, table styles, text styles, or any of the named objects shown in the tree view pane in Figure 6-11.

1. **Open the drawing that contains the layers you want to copy (the *source* drawing).**

2. **Open the drawing to which you want to copy the layers (the *destination* drawing).**

If you already had both drawings open, make sure that you can see the destination drawing. If you can't, click Switch Windows in the View tab's User Interface panel and choose the destination drawing in order to bring it to the foreground, or tile the windows, shown in Figure 6-12, by clicking Tile Vertically in the same Windows panel.

3. **Click the DesignCenter button on the Palettes panel of the Ribbon's View tab or press Ctrl+2.**

Figure 6-12: Copying a layer from one drawing to another.

4. **In the DesignCenter palette, click the Open Drawings tab.**

 The DesignCenter tree view pane on the left side of the palette displays a list of drawings that you currently have open in AutoCAD.

 You can also use the Folders tab, the Load button, or the Search button to load a drawing into DesignCenter without opening it in AutoCAD.

5. **In the tree view pane of the DesignCenter palette, click the plus sign (+) next to the name of the source drawing that you opened in Step 1.**

 A list of symbol categories that you can copy, including layers, appears in the tree view pane.

6. **Click Layers in the list in the tree view pane.**

 The display in the content pane at the right changes to show the individual layers that are stored in the source drawing.

7. **Click and drag the desired layer or layers from the content pane of the DesignCenter palette into the window containing the destination drawing that you opened in Step 2; refer to Figure 6-12.**

If the current drawing contains a layer whose name matches the name of one of the layers you're copying, AutoCAD doesn't change the current drawing's layer definition. For example, if you add a layer named Doors whose color is red into a drawing that already includes a Doors layer whose color is green, the destination drawing's Doors layer remains green. Named objects from DesignCenter never overwrite objects with the same name in the destination drawing. AutoCAD always displays the message `Duplicate definitions will be ignored` even if there aren't any duplicates.

If you're repeatedly copying named objects from the same drawings or folders, add them to your DesignCenter favorites list. On the Folders tab, right-click the drawing or folder, and choose Add to Favorites from the menu. This procedure adds another shortcut to your list of favorites.

 ✔ **To see your favorites:** Click the DesignCenter toolbar's Favorites button.

 ✔ **To return to a favorite:** Double-click its shortcut in the content pane.

Preciseliness Is Next to CADliness

*D*rawing precision is vital to good CAD drafting practice, even more than for manual drafting. (Accuracy, of course, is vital to both types of drafting — if you're sketchy on the difference between accuracy and precision, look ahead to the "CAD precision versus accuracy" sidebar in this chapter.) If you think CAD managers get a little tense when you assign properties directly to objects instead of ByLayer, wait until you see them lay into someone (we sincerely hope it's not you!) who doesn't use precision techniques when creating drawings in AutoCAD.

Controlling Your Precision

In AutoCAD, lack of precision makes later editing, hatching, and dimensioning tasks much more difficult and time consuming. Keep these facts in mind:

- Small errors in precision in the early stages of creating or editing a drawing often have a big effect on productivity and precision later.

- CAD drawings are often used for much more than just giving a picture to someone. If they've been properly created, they can also be queried for things like sizes, areas, and quantities.

- Drawings may guide manufacturing and construction projects; drawing data may drive automatic manufacturing machinery. Huge amounts of money and even lives can ride on a drawing's precision.

CAD precision versus accuracy

You often hear the words *precision* and *accuracy* used interchangeably, but it's useful to understand the difference. In this book, we use *precision* to mean controlling the placement of objects so they lie exactly where you want them to lie in the drawing. For example, lines whose endpoints meet must meet *exactly,* and a circle that's supposed to be centered on the coordinates 0,0 must be drawn with its center *exactly* at 0,0. We use *accuracy* to refer to the degree to which your drawing matches its real-world counterpart. An accurate floor plan is one in which the dimensions of the CAD objects equal the dimensions of the as-built house. In a sense,

then, it's not the drawing that should be accurate — it's the house!

CAD precision usually helps produce accurate drawings, but that's not always the case. You can produce a precise CAD drawing that's inaccurate because you started from inaccurate information (for example, the contractor gave you a wrong field measurement). Or you might deliberately exaggerate certain distances to convey the relationship between objects more clearly on the plotted drawing. Even where you must sacrifice accuracy, aim for precision.

In recognition of these facts, a passion for precision permeates the profession. Precision is one of the characteristics that separates CAD from ordinary illustration-type drawing work. The sooner you get fussy about precision in AutoCAD, the happier everyone is.

When we talk about drawing things precisely, we mean using precision techniques and tools to specify points and distances with as much exactness as the program allows. Luckily, AutoCAD provides a comprehensive package of tools for doing just that. Table 7-1 lists the more important AutoCAD precision techniques, along with visual cues to the status bar buttons that you click to toggle some of the features.

As we describe in Chapter 2, you can switch the display on status bar buttons between text and icons by right-clicking any of those buttons and selecting or deselecting Use Icons. Table 7-1 shows the icons and lists the text for both alternatives.

Precision is especially important when you're drawing or editing *geometry* — the lines, arcs, and so on that make up whatever you're representing in the CAD drawing. Precision placement usually is less important with notes, leaders, and other *annotations* that describe, not show.

Table 7-1			**Precision Tools and Techniques**
Technique	*Status Bar Button Label*	*Status Bar Button Icon*	*Description*
Infer Constraints	INFER		Applies geometric constraints at specific pick points (not in AutoCAD LT); see Chapter 19.
Snap mode	SNAP		Forces the crosshairs to move on an imaginary grid of equally spaced *hot spots*.
Polar snap	—	—	Forces the crosshairs to move specific distances along polar tracking angles.
Grid display	GRID		Displays a nonprinting reference grid of lines or dots arranged in rows or columns.
Ortho mode	ORTHO		Forces the crosshairs to move horizontally or vertically from the previous point.
Polar tracking	POLAR		Causes the crosshairs to jump to specified angles.
Object snap	OSNAP		Enables picking specific points on existing drawing objects multiple times.
3D Object snap	3DOSNAP		Enables picking specific points on existing 3D objects multiple times (not in AutoCAD LT).
Object snap tracking	OTRACK		Causes the crosshairs to locate new points based on multiple object snap points.
Object snap overrides	—	—	Enables picking specific points on existing drawing objects one time only.
Coordinate input	—	—	Enables you to type exact X,Y or polar coordinates.
Direct distance entry	—	—	Enables you to locate a point by typing a distance and moving the crosshairs to show the direction.

Before you draw objects, always check the status bar buttons and set them according to your precision needs.

✔ A button that looks lit (that is, just a little brighter than its neighbors — typically, a light blue) indicates that the feature is on.

✔ A button that looks dimmed (typically, dark gray) indicates that the feature is off.

Keyboard capers: Coordinate input

The most direct way to enter points precisely is to type numbers at the keyboard. AutoCAD uses these keyboard coordinate entry formats:

✔ Absolute Cartesian (X,Y) coordinates in the form *X,Y* (for example, 7,4)

✔ Relative X,Y coordinates in the form @*X,Y* (for example, @3,2)

✔ Relative polar coordinates in the form @*distance<angle* (for example, @6<45)

Understanding AutoCAD's coordinate systems

AutoCAD stores locational data for every object in a drawing based on a centuries-old system of Cartesian, or X,Y, coordinates.

Cartesian coordinates are named for French philosopher René "I think, therefore I am" Descartes. In his *Discourse on Method,* Descartes came up with the idea of locating any point on a planar surface by measuring its distance from the intersection of a pair of axes (that's *axes* as in more than one axis, not the tool for chopping wood). By convention, the intersection of those axes (called, also by convention, the X-axis and the Y-axis) are perpendicular to one another, and their intersection point is identified as 0,0. The logical next step in this system of X,Y coordinates is to introduce a third axis (called, what else, the Z-axis), perpendicular to the plane defined by the X- and Y-axes. This one shares the X,Y intersection point of 0,0 and so its coordinates are identified as 0,0,0.

Theoretically, any point in three-dimensional space can be located by a set of X,Y,Z coordinates. And by extension, every point in an AutoCAD drawing file can be identified by its X,Y,Z coordinates (in most 2D drawings, the Z-coordinate is 0). This system of coordinates is referred to in AutoCAD as the World Coordinate System, or WCS.

Introducing User Coordinate Systems

Many times, it's convenient to define additional coordinate systems to make drawing things a little easier, so AutoCAD lets you roll your own. These non–World Coordinate Systems are called *User Coordinate Systems* (UCS for short),

and they're so widely used that UCS now refers to every coordinate system in AutoCAD.

Why would you want to diverge from the standard WCS? Well, the most common reason is that you might be working in 3D, and it's way easier to calculate and enter coordinates if they're based on the plane you want to work on. For example, say you're modeling one of those old-fashioned wedge-shaped rubber doorstops, and you want to add the manufacturer's logo to the sloping surface of the wedge. That's not easy if you stay in the WCS, but AutoCAD lets you set a new UCS based on that sloping surface. After that UCS is made current, you draw in it just as you draw in the WCS. (We have more to say about UCSs in 3D in Chapter 21.)

Think of the real world. A specific latitude and longitude (WCS) always identi-fies the same point, but the actual location for a description like "the corner of 33rd and Main" depends on which city you're in (UCS).

UCSs can be useful on two dimensions as well as three. The WCS assumes the north direction is straight up — 90 degrees, according to AutoCAD's defaults — but your drawing might work better on a sheet where north pointed to the left. Easy enough — create a UCS with north pointing left (we'll leave you to look up this process in the online help — we only have so many pages!)

It's generally easier to create a UCS by typing options at the command line, but after they're created, they're easier to manage through the UCS dialog box. Type **UCSMAN** and press Enter to display this dialog box.

AutoCAD's UCS icon shows you clearly whether you're in paper space or model space, and almost as clearly whether you're in the WCS or a UCS if you're in model space. Figure 7-1 shows AutoCAD 2013's variations on the theme.

You can use the UCS command in paper space as well as model space, but it's almost always a bad idea. Leave paper space in the WCS to make your plotting a whole lot easier.

The UCS icon is selectable; click it, and grips appear at the origin and the ends of the axis indicators. You can drag the icon by its grips to set a new UCS. We cover this feature more fully in Chapter 21.

Drawing by numbers

AutoCAD locates *absolute* X,Y coordinates with respect to the 0,0 point (oth-erwise known as the *origin*) of the drawing — usually its lower-left corner. AutoCAD locates *relative* X,Y coordinates and *relative* polar coordinates with respect to the previous point that you picked or typed. Figure 7-2 dem-onstrates how to use all three coordinate formats to draw a pair of line seg-ments that start at absolute coordinates 2,1; then go 3 units to the right and 2 units up relative to the first point; then relative to that point, go 4 units at an angle of 60 degrees.

Icon indicates World Coordinate System.

Icon indicates User Coordinate System.

Icon indicates paper space.

Figure 7-1: The UCS icon shows you your current coordinate system.

In case you're wondering, AutoCAD also understands *absolute polar coordinates* in the form *distance<angle,* but this format is almost never useful.

Relative polar coordinates

Relative X, Y coordinates

Absolute X, Y coordinates

Figure 7-2: Coordinating from the keyboard.

You can find out the X,Y location of your crosshairs by moving them around in the drawing area and reading the coordinate values at the left end of the status bar. The X,Y coordinates should change as you move the crosshairs. If the coordinates don't change, click the drawing coordinates area until you see <Coords on> in the command window.

Astute observers of the full version of AutoCAD will have noticed that there are *three* numbers at the left end of the status bar (AutoCAD LT is numerically challenged). AutoCAD is actually showing you the X,Y coordinates of the crosshairs and the current elevation (the Z value). However, in 2D drafting, the Z value is (or should be) 0, so you can continue calling them X,Y coordinates.

Although it's not apparent at first, there are, in fact, four coordinate display modes. Clicking the coordinates readout cycles through them, as follows:

- **Off** (<Coords off>)**:** The status bar coordinate readout is dimmed, and the coordinate values don't update until you pick a point.

- **On, showing X,Y coordinates** (<Coords on>)**:** The coordinate readout appears black, and the absolute X,Y coordinates update continuously as you move the crosshairs. If no command is active, clicking the coordinates readout alternates between this mode and <Coords off>.

- **On, showing polar coordinates** (<Coords on>)**:** This mode, which displays distance and angle relative to the last point picked rather than absolute X,Y values, appears if a command is active and AutoCAD is waiting for you to pick a point.

- **On, showing geographic coordinates** (<Coords on>)**:** This mode displays coordinates as the latitude and longitude values, but can be used only after you set the drawing's geographic location with the, what else, GeographicLocation command.

If you start a command such as LINE, pick a point, and then click the Coordinates area a few times, the display changes from coordinates off to live absolute coordinates (X,Y position) to live polar coordinates (distance and angle from the previous point). Displaying live polar coordinates is the most informative mode most of the time.

When you type coordinates at the command line, do *not* add any spaces because AutoCAD interprets a space as though you've pressed Enter. This "Spacebar = Enter" weirdness is a productivity feature that's been in AutoCAD forever. It's easier to find the spacebar than the Enter key when you're entering lots of commands and coordinates in a hurry — and it's especially handy for touch typists who are all thumbs.

If you're working in AutoCAD's Architectural or Engineering units, the default unit of entry is *inches,* not feet. Here are some things to consider about entering numeric values when you work in feet and inches:

✔ To specify feet, you must enter the ' symbol for feet after the number. For example:

> **6'** for 6 feet.

✔ You can enter a dash to separate feet from inches, as architects often do:

> **6'–6"** is 6 feet, 6 inches.

✔ Both the dash and the inch mark are optional when you're entering coordinates and distances:

> **6'6"** and **6'6** are the same as **6'–6"**.

✔ If you're typing a coordinate or distance that contains fractional inches, you *must* enter a dash -– not a space — between the whole number of inches and the fraction:

> **6'6–1/2** (or **6'–6–1/2**) represents 6 feet, 6 1/2 inches.

✔ If all this dashing about confuses you, enter partial inches by using decimals instead:

> **6'6.5** is the same as **6'6–1/2"** to AutoCAD, whether you're working in Architectural or Engineering units.

Have you ever wanted to check the accuracy (or precision!) of something that's already drawn? The MEASUREGEOM command is a one-stop shop where you can query drawing objects for distances, angles, areas, and other geometric or locational information about drawing objects. You can find it on the Utilities panel of the Home tab — look for an icon with a yellow ruler.

Grab an object and make it snappy

After you've drawn a few objects precisely in a new drawing, the most efficient way to draw more objects with equal precision is to grab specific, geometrically precise points, such as endpoints, midpoints, or quadrants, on the existing objects. Every object type in AutoCAD has at least one of these points, and you can "snap" to them precisely as you draw by using *object snaps* (*osnaps* for short by those in the know).

AutoCAD provides two ways of using object snaps:

✔ **Object snap *overrides:*** An object snap override is active for a single pick.

✔ ***Running* object snaps:** A running object snap stays in effect until you turn it off.

AutoCAD (but not LT) has a suite of object snaps specifically for working in 3D. We cover them fully in Chapter 21, but point them out here because the new 3DOSNAP status bar button is right next to the regular old OSNAP button, and not so easy to distinguish from it. In this section, you use the

regular Object Snap button that shows the square with the sunburst at the top-left corner, not the 3D-looking box with the sunburst at the bottom-left corner.

Grabbing points with object snap overrides

Here's how you draw precise lines by using object snap overrides:

1. **Open a drawing containing some geometry.**

2. **Turn off running object snap mode by clicking the Object Snap button on the status bar until the button appears to be dimmed and** <Osnap off> **appears in the command window.**

 Although you *can* use object snap overrides while running object snaps are enabled, we recommend that you turn off any running object snaps while you're getting familiar with object snap overrides. After you've gotten the hang of each feature separately, you can use them together.

3. **Start the LINE command by clicking the Line button on the Ribbon's Draw panel or typing** LINE **(or** L**) and pressing Enter.**

 AutoCAD prompts you to select the starting point of the line:

    ```
    Specify first point:
    ```

4. **Hold down the Shift key, right-click anywhere in the drawing area, and release the Shift key.**

 The Object Snap menu appears, as shown in Figure 7-3.

5. **Choose an Object Snap mode, such as Endpoint, from the object snap menu.**

 The Object Snap menu disappears, and the command window displays an additional prompt to indicate that you've directed AutoCAD to seek out, for example, the endpoints of existing objects:

    ```
    _endp of:
    ```

6. **Move the crosshairs slowly around the drawing, pausing over various lines and other objects without clicking yet.**

 When you move the crosshairs near an object with an endpoint, a colored square icon appears at the endpoint, indicating that AutoCAD can snap to that point. If you stop moving the crosshairs for a moment, a tooltip displaying the Object Snap mode (for example, Endpoint) appears, to reinforce the idea.

7. **Click when the Endpoint object snap square appears on the point you want to snap to.**

 AutoCAD snaps to the endpoint, which becomes the first point of the new line segment that you're about to draw. The command line prompts you to select the other endpoint of the new line segment:

    ```
    Specify next point or [Undo]:
    ```

Figure 7-3: The Object Snap right-click menu.

When you move the crosshairs around the drawing, AutoCAD no longer seeks out endpoints because object snap overrides last for only a single pick. You can use the Object Snap right-click menu again to snap the other end of your new line segment to another point on an existing object.

8. **Use the Shift+right-click sequence described in Step 4 to display the Object Snap menu again. Then choose another Object Snap mode, such as Midpoint, from the Object Snap menu.**

The command line displays an additional prompt indicating that you've directed AutoCAD to seek, for example, midpoints of existing objects:

```
_mid of:
```

When you move the crosshairs near the midpoint of an object, a colored triangle appears at the snap point. Each object snap type (Endpoint, Midpoint, Intersection, and so on) displays a different symbol. If you stop moving the crosshairs, the tooltip text reminds you what the symbol means. Figure 7-4 shows what the screen looks like during this step.

Already object-snapped to endpoint

Newline segment

About to object-snap
to midpoint

Figure 7-4: A snappy line.

9. **Draw additional line segments by picking additional points. Use the Object Snap right-click menu to specify a single object snap type before you pick each point.**

Try the Intersection, Perpendicular, and Nearest object snaps. If your drawing contains arcs or circles, try Center and Quadrant.

10. **When you're finished experimenting with object snap overrides, right-click anywhere in the drawing area and choose Enter from the menu to end the LINE command.**

There's a difference between right-clicking and Shift+right-clicking in the drawing area:

- *Right-clicking:* Displays menu options for the current command (or common commands and settings when no command is active).

- *Shift+right-clicking:* Always displays the same Object Snap menu.

Running with object snaps

Often, you use an object snap setting (such as Endpoint) repeatedly. Use running object snaps to address this need.

The following steps set a running object snap:

1. **Right-click the OSNAP button on the status bar.**

 The Object Snap menu appears, as shown in Figure 7-5.

 Many status bar buttons display shortcut menus when you right-click, as shown in Figure 7-5. (Object Snap and Object Snap Tracking both display the menu of running object snaps.) Many settings, including all running Object Snap types, can be set by clicking a menu item — you no longer need to open the Drafting Settings dialog box, make your settings, and then click OK to close the dialog box.

2. **Click in the menu to select one or more Object Snap settings.**

 Active running Object Snap settings show a highlighted square around the icon (see Figure 7-5).

You click the Object Snap button on the status bar to toggle Running Object Snap mode. After you turn on Running Object Snap, AutoCAD hunts for points that correspond to the object snaps you checked on the Object Snap button's right-click menu. As with object snap overrides, AutoCAD displays a special symbol — such as a square for an Endpoint object snap — to indicate that it has found an object snap point. If you keep the crosshairs still, AutoCAD also displays a tooltip that lists the *kind* of object snap point.

Use object snap overrides or running object snaps to enforce precision by making sure that new points you pick coincide *exactly* with points on existing objects. In AutoCAD, it's not good enough for points to *almost* coincide or to look like they coincide. You lose points, both figuratively and literally, if you don't use object snaps or one of the other precision techniques covered in this chapter to enforce precision.

Active Object Snap mode

✎	Endpoint
✎	Midpoint
◎	Center
○	Node
✦	Quadrant
✕	Intersection
----	Extension
⊡	Insertion
⊥	Perpendicular
○	Tangent
⁄∘	Nearest
⋈	Apparent Intersection
∕∕	Parallel
✓	Enabled
✓	Use Icons
	Settings...
	Display ▸

Inactive Object Snap mode

Figure 7-5: Grabbing multiple object features is an osnap.

For example, applying crosshatching rapidly becomes impossible if the boundary of the area you are hatching has even microscopic leaks.

Most, but not all, object snap overrides have Running Object Snap equivalents. For example, Endpoint, Midpoint, and Center work as either overrides or running object snaps, but Mid Between 2 Points works only in Override mode.

Other Practical Precision Procedures

The following are some other AutoCAD precision techniques (refer to Table 7-1):

✔ **Snap:** If you turn on Snap mode, AutoCAD constrains the crosshairs to an imaginary rectangular grid of points at the spacing that you've specified when AutoCAD prompts you to specify a point.

When you enable Snap mode, at first it seems to be broken because the cursor doesn't snap to the imaginary grid but travels freely. It becomes active only when the program asks you to pick a point.

Follow these steps to turn on Snap mode:

1. *Right-click the Snap Mode button on the status bar.*

2. *Choose Settings.*

 The Snap and Grid tab on the Drafting Settings dialog box appears.

3. *Enter a snap spacing in the Snap X Spacing field and click OK.*

Click the Snap Mode button on the status bar (labeled SNAP if your status bar buttons show text) or press F9 to toggle Snap mode off and on. To use Snap effectively, change the snap spacing frequently — changing to a smaller spacing as you zoom in and work on smaller areas.

You can switch between *Grid Snap* (that is, snap points in rows and columns) and *PolarSnap* (snap points based on distances and angles) by using the Snap Mode button's shortcut menu. See the PolarSnap item later in this list for more info.

✔ **Ortho:** Ortho mode forces the crosshairs to move horizontally or vertically relative to the current coordinate system's X- and Y-axes. Click the Ortho Mode button (ORTHO for text buttons) on the status bar or press F8 to toggle Ortho mode. Because technical drawings often include lots of orthogonal lines, you may use Ortho mode a lot — but take a close look at polar tracking as well.

✔ **Direct distance entry (DDE):** This point-and-type technique is an easy and efficient way to draw with precision. You simply point the crosshairs in a particular direction, type a distance value at the command line, and press Enter. You can use DDE any time the crosshairs are anchored to a point, and the command line or Dynamic Input tooltip prompts you for another point or a distance.

You'll usually use DDE with Polar Tracking turned on to specify distances in particular directions (for example, in angle increments of 45 degrees). You can also combine DDE with Ortho mode to specify a distance in an orthogonal direction (0, 90, 180, or 270 degrees).

✔ **Object Snap Tracking:** This feature extends running object snaps so that you can locate points based on more than one object snap point.

For example, you can define a point at the center of a square by tracking to the midpoints of two perpendicular sides. Click Object Snap Tracking on the status bar (if you're showing text instead of icons, this button is labeled OTRACK — which has nothing at all to do with the Irish railway system) or press F11 to toggle Object Snap Tracking.

✔ **Polar Tracking:** When you turn on Polar Tracking, the crosshairs jump to increments of the angle you specified in the Drafting Settings dialog box or chose on the right-click menu. When the crosshairs jump, a tooltip label starting with *Polar:* appears. Right-click the Polar Tracking button on the status bar (POLAR on buttons that show text labels) and choose the Settings option to display the Polar Tracking tab on the Drafting Settings dialog box. Select an angle from the Increment Angle drop-down list and then click OK. Click the Polar Tracking button on the status bar or press F10 to toggle Polar Tracking mode.

Remember, you can set a predefined Polar Tracking angle by right-clicking the Polar Tracking button and choosing it from the menu. If you want to add an angle that's not on the list, you have to click Settings to open the Drafting Settings dialog box.

✔ **PolarSnap:** You can force polar tracking to jump to specific incremental distances along the tracking angles by changing the snap type from Grid snap to PolarSnap. For example, if you turn on polar tracking and set it to 45 degrees, and then turn on PolarSnap and set it to 2 units, polar tracking jumps to points that are at angle increments of 45 degrees and distance increments of 2 units from the previous point. PolarSnap has a similar effect on Object Snap tracking.

To activate PolarSnap, right-click the Snap Mode button and choose PolarSnap from the menu. To specify a PolarSnap distance, follow these steps:

 1. *Right-click the SNAP button on the status bar.*

 2. *Choose Settings.*

 The Snap and Grid tab on the Drafting Settings dialog box appears.

 3. *Click the PolarSnap radio button, type a distance in the Polar Distance text box, and then click OK.*

When you want to return to ordinary rectangular snap, as described at the beginning of this list, right-click the Snap Mode button and choose Grid Snap from the menu.

✔ **Temporary overrides:** Settings such as SNAP, ORTHO, and POLAR remain on until you turn them off. You can also use *temporary overrides,* which last only as long as you hold down their key or key combination. For example, with Ortho turned off, holding down the Shift key puts AutoCAD into a temporary Ortho mode for as long as you press Shift. For additional information, visit the online help system.

If you're new to AutoCAD, its wide range of precision tools probably seems overwhelming at this point. Rest assured that there's more than one way to skin a cat precisely (with cats, accuracy is unimportant), and not everyone needs to understand all the ways. You can make perfectly precise drawings without using every single implement in AutoCAD's precision toolkit. We recommend these steps:

1. **Get comfortable with typing coordinates, Ortho mode, direct distance entry, and Object Snap overrides.**

2. **Become familiar with running object snaps and try Snap mode.**

3. **After you have all these precision features under your belt, feel free to experiment with Polar Tracking, PolarSnap, and Object Snap Tracking.**

It's easy to confuse the names of the snap and object snap (osnap) features. Remember that *snap* constrains the crosshairs to locations whose coordinates are multiples of the current snap spacing. Snap works whether or not there are objects in the drawing. *Object snap (osnap)* enables you to grab points on existing objects, whether or not those points happen to correspond with the snap spacing.

So what happens if some of your drawing-with-precision choices seem to contradict each other? Simple. AutoCAD goes with the one that took you the most effort to initiate. That is, Snap is overridden by Osnap, which is overridden by snap overrides, which is overridden by keyboard entry of points or distances.

8

Along the Straight and Narrow

In This Chapter

▶ Drawing linear things with the AutoCAD drawing commands

▶ Lining up for lines and polylines

▶ Closing up with rectangles and polygons

*A*s you probably remember from your crayon-and-coloring-book days, drawing stuff is *fun*. CAD imposes a little more discipline, but drawing stuff with AutoCAD is still fun (trust me on this one). In computer-aided drafting, you usually start by drawing *geometry* — shapes such as lines, circles, rectangles, and so on — that represents the real-world object that you're documenting. This chapter shows you how to draw *linear* geometry — objects that proceed in a straightforward manner from one point to the next. In Chapter 9, we throw some curves at you.

After you've created some straight or curvy geometry, you'll probably need to add some dimensions, text, and hatching, but those elements come later (in Part III of this book). Or you may want to use that geometry as the basis for some cool 3D modeling (we introduce you to that topic in Part V). Your first task is to get the geometry right; then you can worry about labeling things.

Drawing geometry properly in AutoCAD depends on paying attention to object properties and the precision of the points that you specify to create the objects. We cover these matters in Chapters 6 and 7, so if you eagerly jumped to this chapter to get right to the fun stuff, take a moment to review those chapters first.

Introducing the AutoCAD Drawing Commands

For descriptive purposes, we're dividing the drawing commands into three groups:

- **Straight lines,** and objects composed of straight lines (covered in this chapter)
- **Curves** (which we explain in Chapter 9)
- **Points** (See Chapter 9 if you're wondering what the point is.)

Table 8-1 presents the most important commands for drawing 2D linear objects in AutoCAD. It lists each command by name, with its short form, or *alias* (when one exists), in parentheses. The table also displays each command's graphical icon, as found on the Draw panel of the Ribbon's Home tab, and in identical form on toolbar buttons and pull-down menus in the AutoCAD Classic workspace.

Table 8-1	AutoCAD Drawing Commands for Linear Objects			
Button	*Command*	*Draw Panel*	*Draw Toolbar*	*Draw Menu*
	LINE (L)	Line	Line	Line
	RAY	Ray (on slide-out)	Not available	Ray
	XLINE (XL)	Construction Line (on slide-out)	Construction Line	Construction Line
	PLINE (PL)	Polyline	Polyline	Polyline
	RECTANG (REC)	Rectangle	Rectangle	Rectangle
	POLYGON (POL)	Polygon (on the Rectangle drop-down menu)	Polygon	Polygon

If you're coming from AutoCAD 2008 or earlier, or even if you've been resisting the Ribbon in more recent releases, AutoCAD 2013's Ribbon is obviously very different from what you're used to; it's even a little different from the Ribbon in previous releases. Like many Ribbon panels, the Draw panel has additional tool buttons on a slideout you can use once or pin so it stays open — refer to Chapter 2 for a refresher on Ribbon panels and slideouts. Similarly, many of the choices on the AutoCAD Draw menu open submenus containing several variations on each drawing command.

AutoCAD's drawing commands are highly interactive. You need to read and respond to the prompts in the command window (or at the Dynamic Input tooltip next to the crosshairs if Dynamic Input mode is turned on). You can also access many of the command options that you see in command window prompts by pressing the up- and down-arrow keys to display the options at the Dynamic Input tooltip. You can even right-click and select command options from the context-specific shortcut menu.

AutoCAD's Dynamic Input system displays a lot of the information that you used to have to look down to the command window to see. To use Dynamic Input, make sure that the Dynamic Input button on the status bar is turned on (that is, it looks highlighted). You can also press the F12 function key to toggle Dynamic Input on and off. Don't turn the command window off just yet, though — especially if you're new to AutoCAD.

So what's the best course: to enter drawing commands from the command line, which you can do in any workspace? Or to choose commands from the Ribbon in the Drafting & Annotation workspace, or the AutoCAD Classic workspace's menus or toolbars? Well . . . it all depends:

 ✔ **If you've never used AutoCAD in your life:** Use the Ribbon (that is, the default Drafting & Annotation workspace) rather than the toolbars and menus of the traditional AutoCAD Classic workspace. Thanks to Microsoft's clout in the user-interface world, we don't think the Ribbon is going away anytime soon, or at least until Microsoft comes up with something else.

 ✔ **If you're an experienced AutoCAD user who's been away for a release or two:** Give the Ribbon a decent test-drive before you switch to the AutoCAD Classic workspace. To ease your transition, you can display the classic menu bar above the Ribbon. Simply click the down arrow at the right end of the Quick Access Toolbar and choose Show Menu Bar (see Figure 8-1).

Whichever kind of user you are and regardless of the workspace you choose, it's a truth universally acknowledged that the most efficient way of working with AutoCAD is to use the keyboard to enter command aliases or open and close palettes. No matter how many times the graphical user interface changes, just remember that you can *always* use the system that's been part of AutoCAD since version 1.0 in 1982: Use the keyboard, and let your fingers do the talking.

Figure 8-1: You can display the classic menu bar if you want to.

The Straight and Narrow: Lines, Polylines, and Polygons

As we harp on a bunch of times elsewhere in this book, CAD programs are for precision drawing, so you'll spend a lot of your AutoCAD time drawing objects composed of straight-line segments. The rest of this chapter covers these commands:

- **LINE (L):** Draws a series of straight-line segments; each segment is a separate object.

- **PLINE (PL):** Draws a *polyline* — a series of straight- and/or curved-line segments. (Yes, I'm cheating a bit here — curvy things are covered in Chapter 9 — but we don't want you to have to read about one command in two different places!) All the segments remain connected to each other as a single object.

- **RECTANG (REC):** Draws a polyline in the shape of a rectangle.

- **POLYGON (POL):** Draws a polyline in the shape of a *regular polygon* (that is, a closed shape with all sides equal and all angles equal).

The following additional straight-line drawing commands are also available in AutoCAD:

- **RAY:** Draws a line that starts at a point and just keeps on going; a *ray* therefore is a line that extends infinitely in one direction.

- **XLINE (XL):** Draws a line that passes through a point and extends infinitely in both directions. The question of the day is, which of these two lines is longer?

The RAY and XLINE commands are used to draw *construction lines* that guide the construction of additional geometry. Drawing construction lines is less common in AutoCAD than in some other CAD programs. AutoCAD's many precision techniques often provide more efficient methods for creating new geometry than adding construction lines to your drawing does. In particular, object snap tracking (discussed in Chapter 7) and parametrics (discussed in Chapter 19) usually eliminate all need for construction geometry or even for a mitre line when creating orthographic views.

Toeing the line

The LINE command in AutoCAD draws a series of one or more visually connected line segments. Although the lines appear to be physically connected, in fact, each *segment,* or piece of a line with endpoints, is a separate object. This construction doesn't seem like a big deal until you try to move (or otherwise edit) a series of segments that you drew with the LINE command; you must select every piece separately. To avoid such a hassle, use polylines (described in the following section), not lines (or lines and arcs), when you want the connected segments to act as a single object.

If you're used to drawing lines in other programs, you may find it confusing at first that AutoCAD's LINE command doesn't stop after you draw a single segment. AutoCAD keeps prompting you to specify additional points so that you can draw a series of (apparently) connected segments. When you're finished drawing segments, just press Enter to finish the LINE command.

Unlike a lot of the AutoCAD drawing commands, LINE doesn't offer a bunch of potentially confusing options. It has a Close option to create a closed polygonal shape and an Undo option to remove the most recent segment that you drew.

Like all drawing commands, LINE puts the line segments that it draws on the current layer and uses the current color, linetype, lineweight, transparency, and plot-style properties. When you're doing real drafting, as opposed to just experimenting, make sure of the following:

- ✓ **Think about setting these properties before you start drawing.** Although you can easily change an object's layer or other object properties, it's often more efficient to set properties first. (We recommend that you set color, linetype, lineweight, transparency, and, if you're using named plot styles, plot style to ByLayer.) See Chapter 6 for information on setting the current properties with the tools on the Home tab's Properties panel.

- ✓ **Use the right precision tools.** Make sure that you use one of AutoCAD's precision tools, such as object snaps, typed coordinates, or tracking, to ensure that you specify each object point precisely. Chapter 7 describes these tools.

Follow these steps to draw a series of line segments by using the LINE command:

1. **Set an appropriate layer to be current.**

2. **Click the Home tab on the Ribbon.**

 The panels on the Home tab contain the most commonly used commands in AutoCAD.

3. **Click the Line button on the Draw panel of the Ribbon's Home tab, or type** L **and press Enter.**

 AutoCAD starts the LINE command and prompts you to select the first point.

4. **Specify the starting point by clicking a point or typing coordinates.**

 Remember to use one of the precision techniques we describe in Chapter 7 if you're doing real drafting. For the first point, you can type coordinates, pick a precise point if snap is turned on, or use object snap if other objects already exist in the drawing. AutoCAD prompts you to specify the other endpoint of the first line segment. The command window prompt shows

   ```
   Specify next point or [Undo]:
   ```

 You can also see command prompts at the Dynamic Input tooltip beside the crosshairs by pressing the down-arrow key (press F12 or click the Dynamic Input status bar button to enable Dynamic Input mode). The arrow icon on the Dynamic Input tooltip is your indicator that there are options available.

5. **Specify additional points by clicking or typing.**

 Again, use one of the AutoCAD precision techniques if you're doing real drafting. For the second and subsequent points, all the techniques mentioned in Step 4 work well, as do ortho, polar, object snap tracking, and direct distance entry.

 After you specify the third point, AutoCAD adds the Close option. The command prompt shows

   ```
   Specify next point or [Close/Undo]:
   ```

6. **When you're finished drawing segments, end with one of these steps:**

 • *Keep the figure open.* Either press Enter, or right-click anywhere in the drawing area and choose Enter from the right-click menu to leave the figure open.

 • *Close the figure.* Type **C** and press Enter, or press the down arrow on your keyboard and choose Close from the menu (shown in Figure 8-2) to close the figure.

In either case, the blank command prompt indicates that the LINE command is finished:

```
Command:
```

Figure 8-2: Line it up — drawing line segments with the LINE command.

Connecting the lines with polyline

The LINE command is fine for many drawing tasks, but the PLINE command is better for others. Experience will help you to choose. The PLINE command draws a special kind of object called a *polyline*. You may hear CAD drafters refer to a polyline as a *pline* (rhymes with *beeline*) because of the command name. This has nothing to do with the queue at a busy restroom.

The most important differences between the LINE and PLINE commands are these:

- ✓ **The LINE command draws a series of separate line segments.** Even though they appear to be connected on the screen, each segment is a separate object. If you move one line segment, the other segments that you drew at the same time don't move with it.

- ✓ **The PLINE command draws a single, connected, multisegment object.** If you select any segment for editing, your changes affect the entire polyline. Figure 8-3 shows how the same sketch drawn with the LINE and the PLINE commands responds when you select one of the objects.

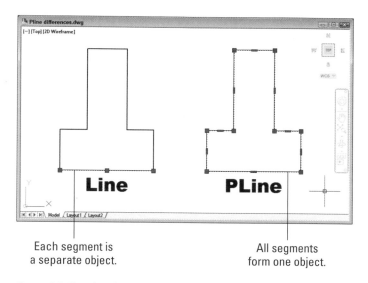

Each segment is a separate object.

All segments form one object.

Figure 8-3: Results of drawing with the LINE and PLINE commands.

Use PLINE rather than LINE in most cases where you need to draw a series of connected line segments. If you're drawing a series of end-to-end segments, there's a good chance that those segments are logically connected — for example, they might represent the outline of a single object or a continuous pathway. If the segments are connected logically, it makes sense to keep them connected in AutoCAD. The most obvious practical benefit of grouping segments together into a polyline is that many editing operations are more efficient when you use polylines. When you select any segment in a polyline for editing, the entire polyline is selected.

As covered in Chapter 19, using parametrics on line segments can often produce the same results as using a PLINE.

✔ **The PLINE command can draw curved segments as well as straight ones.** If you want a combination of separate linear and curved segments, you must switch back and forth between the LINE and ARC commands (we cover arcs in Chapter 9). With PLINE, you can switch between linear or circular-curve sections by choosing the command options described in the steps that come after this list.

✔ **Polylines can have width.** Polyline segment width is visually similar to AutoCAD's lineweight object property, except that polyline width can vary from segment to segment, and individual segments can be tapered. But wait! There's more! After drawing a polyline, you can have it automatically reshape itself into a smooth, flowing curve based on the vertex points you selected.

After you create a polyline, you can adjust its segments by grip editing any of the vertex points. (The little squares on the vertices in Figure 8-3 are called *grips;* see Chapter 10 for details on grip editing.) For more complicated polyline-editing tasks, you can use the PEDIT command to edit the polyline, or you can convert the polyline to a collection of line and arc segments by using the EXPLODE command — although you lose any width defined for each segment when you explode a polyline. For more information on these two commands, look them up in the index of the online help.

Drawing polylines composed of straight segments is pretty much like drawing with the LINE command, as demonstrated in the following procedure. The PLINE command has lots of options, so watch the prompts! If Dynamic Input is on, use the down-arrow key to see the options listed near the crosshairs, or right-click to display the PLINE right-click menu, or simply read the command line.

To draw a polyline composed of straight segments, follow these steps:

1. **Set an appropriate layer to be current.**

2. **Click the Polyline button on the Ribbon's Draw panel or type** PL **and press Enter.**

 AutoCAD starts the PLINE command and prompts you to specify a start point.

3. **Specify the starting point by clicking a point or typing coordinates.**

 AutoCAD displays the current polyline segment line width at the command line and prompts you to specify the other endpoint of the first polyline segment:

   ```
   Current line-width is 0.0000
   Specify next point or [Arc/Halfwidth/Length/Undo/
           Width]:
   ```

4. **If the current line width isn't zero, change it to zero by typing** W **to select the Width option, and then entering** 0 **as the starting and ending widths, as shown in the following command-line sequence:**

   ```
   Specify next point or [Arc/Halfwidth/Length/Undo/Width]: W
   Specify starting width <0.0000>: 0
   Specify ending width <0.0000>: 0
   Specify next point or [Arc/Halfwidth/Length/Undo/
           Width]:
   ```

 Despite what you may think, a zero-width polyline segment isn't the AutoCAD equivalent of drawing with invisible ink. *Zero width* means "display this segment using the normal, single-pixel width on the screen and plot as thin as possible."

5. **Specify additional points by clicking or typing.**

After you specify the second point, AutoCAD adds the Close option to the prompt. The command line shows

```
Specify next point or [Arc/Close/Halfwidth/Length/
          Undo/Width]:
```

In addition, you can view and choose options from the Dynamic Input options list, shown in Figure 8-4, by pressing the down arrow on your keyboard.

Figure 8-4: Making a PLINE.

6. **After you finish drawing segments, either press Enter (to leave the figure open) or type C and press Enter (to close it).**

 AutoCAD draws the final segment. The blank command line indicates that the PLINE command is finished.

In the following procedure, we spice things up a bit and give you a preview of coming (curvy) attractions (in Chapter 9) by adding an arc segment to a polyline.

Just so you know, curved segments in polylines are *circular arcs* — pieces of circles with center points that you can draw with AutoCAD's ARC command. AutoCAD can draw other kinds of curves, including ellipses and splines, but not within the PLINE command.

To draw a polyline that includes curved segments, follow these steps:

1. **Repeat Steps 1 through 5 of the previous procedure.**

2. **When you're ready to add one or more arc segments, type** A **and press Enter to select the Arc option.**

 The prompt changes to show arc segment options. Most of these options correspond to the many ways of drawing circular arcs in AutoCAD; see the section on arcs in Chapter 9. The command line shows

   ```
   Specify endpoint of arc or [Angle/CEnter/CLose/
        Direction/Halfwidth/Line/Radius/Second
        pt/Undo/Width]:
   ```

3. **Specify the endpoint of the arc by clicking a point or typing coordinates.**

 AutoCAD draws the curved segment of the polyline. The prompts continue to show arc segment options.

 Your options at this point include

 - Specifying additional points to draw more arc segments
 - Choosing another arc-drawing method (such as Center or Second pt)
 - Returning to drawing straight-line segments with the Line option

 In this example, you return to drawing straight-line segments.

 Perhaps the most useful of the alternative arc-drawing methods is Second pt. That gives you more control over the direction of the arc, but at the cost of losing tangency of adjacent segments. Sometimes it's best not to go off on a tangent, anyway.

4. **Type** L **and press Enter to select the Line option.**

   ```
   Specify endpoint of arc or [Angle/CEnter/CLose/
           Direction/Halfwidth/Line/Radius/Second pt/
           Undo/Width]: L
   ```

 The prompt changes back to showing straight-line segment options.

   ```
   Specify next point or [Arc/Close/Halfwidth/Length/
           Undo/Width]:
   ```

5. **Specify additional points by clicking or typing.**

6. **After you're finished drawing segments, either press Enter, or type** C **and press Enter.**

Figure 8-5 shows some of the things that you can draw with the PLINE command by using straight segments, arc segments, varying-width segments, or a combination of all of them.

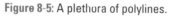

Figure 8-5: A plethora of polylines.

The LINE and PLINE commands work well for drawing a series of end-to-end single lines, but what if you want to draw a series of double lines to represent, for example, the edges of a wall or roadway? Here are some options:

- Use the AutoCAD MLINE command to draw *multilines* — series of two or more parallel straight lines. The AutoCAD multiline feature was full of limitations when it debuted way back in 1994 (in the notorious Release 13), and despite some minor tweaks in AutoCAD 2006, it hasn't improved significantly since then. It exists mostly for compatibility with MicroStation files. Look up the MLINE and MLSTYLE commands in AutoCAD's online help system if you'd like to tangle with this feature, but be prepared to spend time experimenting and struggling.

- Use the PLINE command to draw a single set of connected line and/or arc segments, and then use the OFFSET command to create one or more sets of parallel segments. Chapter 11 covers the OFFSET command.

- In AutoCAD LT only, use the DLINE (DL), or Double Line, command to draw pairs of parallel line and/or arc segments. AutoCAD LT doesn't include the MLINE command, which, given MLINE's problems, is more of a blessing than a limitation. AutoCAD, on the other hand, doesn't include the DLINE command. (Score one for the little brother!)

Squaring off with rectangles

You can use the PLINE or LINE command to draw a rectangle, segment by segment. In most cases, though, you'll find it easier to use the special-purpose RECTANG command. The following procedure demonstrates how:

1. **Set an appropriate layer to be current.**

2. **Click the Rectangle button on the Home tab's Draw panel, or type** REC **and press Enter.**

AutoCAD starts the RECTANG command and prompts you to specify a point for one corner of the rectangle. The command line shows

```
Specify first corner point or [Chamfer/Elevation/
       Fillet/Thickness/Width]:
```

You can add fancy effects with the additional command options. The default options work best for most purposes. Look up RECTANG in the AutoCAD help system if you want to know more about the options.

3. **Specify the first corner by clicking a point or typing coordinates.**

 AutoCAD prompts you to specify the other corner of the rectangle — the one that's diagonally opposite from the first corner.

```
Specify other corner point or [Area/Dimensions/
       Rotation]:
```

4. **Specify the other corner by clicking a point or typing coordinates.**

 If you know the size of the rectangle that you want to draw (for example, 100 units long by 75 units high), type relative coordinates to specify the dimensions — for example, **@100,75**, or just **100,75** if Dynamic Input is enabled. (Chapter 7 describes how to type coordinates.)

 AutoCAD draws the rectangle.

Unlike the neglected MLINE command, the RECTANG command has improved considerably since its debut. You can specify a rotation angle and — very handy for space planners — you can provide one dimension and an area. RECTANG will calculate the length of the other side and draw the rectangle.

Choosing your sides with polygon

Rectangles and other closed polylines are types of *polygons,* or closed figures with three or more sides. The AutoCAD POLYGON command provides a quick way of drawing *regular polygons* — polygons in which all sides and angles are equal. This is different from an escaped parrot.

The following procedure demonstrates the POLYGON command:

1. **Set an appropriate layer to be current.**

2. **Click Polygon on the Home tab's Draw panel's Rectangle drop-down button, or type POL and press Enter.**

 AutoCAD starts the POLYGON command and prompts you to enter the number of sides for the polygon.

```
Enter number of sides <4>:
```

3. **Type the number of sides for the polygon that you want to draw and press Enter.**

 Your polygon can have between 3 and 1,024 sides.

AutoCAD prompts you to specify the center point of the polygon.

```
Specify center of polygon or [Edge]:
```

You can use the Edge option to draw a polygon by specifying the length of one side instead of the center and then the radius of an imaginary inscribed or circumscribed circle. The imaginary circle method is much more common.

4. **Specify the center point by clicking a point or typing coordinates.**

 AutoCAD prompts you to specify whether the polygon will be *inscribed in* (that is, the corners touch the circumference of the circle) or *circumscribed about* (that is, the sides are tangent to the circle) an imaginary circle whose radius you will specify in Step 6. Note that circumscribed has nothing to do with being Jewish.

   ```
   Enter an option [Inscribed in circle/Circumscribed
             about circle] <I>:
   ```

5. **Type I (for inscribed) or C (for circumscribed), and press Enter.**

 The command line prompts you to specify the radius of an imaginary circle.

   ```
   Specify radius of circle:
   ```

6. **Specify the radius by typing a distance or clicking a point.**

 AutoCAD draws the polygon.

 If you type a distance or you click a point with ortho turned on, the polygon will be aligned orthogonally, as shown in Figure 8-6.

Rectangles and polygons aren't special object types. They are simply regular polylines that have been constructed by special command macros.

Figure 8-6 shows the results of drawing plenty of polygons — a practice known as *polygony,* which, as far as we know, is legal nearly everywhere.

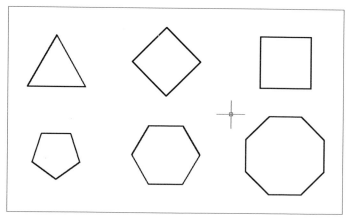

Figure 8-6: A polygonal part.

9

Dangerous Curves Ahead

In This Chapter

▶ Rounding the curves with circles, arcs, splines, and clouds

▶ Eccentric ellipses

▶ Dunking for donuts

▶ Making your points

Although straight-line segments predominate in many CAD drawings, even the most humdrum, rectilinear design is likely to have a few curves. And if you're drawing Audi car bodies or Gaudí buildings, your drawings are going to contain a *lot* of curves! Your drawings should also have a point; in fact, they may have several points, so at the end of this chapter, we fill you in on creating point objects in AutoCAD. But to begin, we show you how to use the following AutoCAD curve-drawing commands:

▶ **CIRCLE:** Draws circles. (You were expecting hyperbolic paraboloids, maybe?)

▶ **ARC:** Draws *circular* arcs — arcs with center points and fixed radii, not arcs cut from ellipses, parabolas, or some other complex curve.

▶ **ELLIPSE:** Draws ellipses and elliptical arcs.

▶ **SPLINE:** Draws smoothly flowing curves of a variety of shapes.

▶ **DONUT:** Draws filled-in rings and circles. Unfortunately, the filling isn't jelly.

▶ **REVCLOUD:** Draws freeform "clouds," the most common application of which is to indicate revised areas in the drawing.

5.0000

(Throwing) Curves

Table 9-1 lists the AutoCAD commands for drawing curvy things. It shows you the tool icons found on the Ribbon, toolbars, and menus, and gives the command name with its alias (where one exists) if you like to type. It also tells you where to find or how to enter the commands, using both the Ribbon in the Drafting & Annotation workspace and the Draw toolbar and Draw menu in the AutoCAD Classic environment.

Table 9-1	AutoCAD Drawing Commands for Curved Objects			
Button	Command	Draw Panel	Draw Toolbar	Draw Menu
	CIRCLE (C)	Circle	Circle	Circle + submenu
	ARC (A)	Arc	Arc	Arc + submenu
	ELLIPSE (EL)	Ellipse	Ellipse	Ellipse + submenu
	ELLIPSE (EL), A	Ellipse Arc (on button menu)	Ellipse Arc	Ellipse + submenu
	SPLINE (SPL)	Spline Fit & Spline CV (on panel slideout)	Spline	Spline + submenu
	DONUT (DO)	Donut (on panel slideout)	Not available	Donut
	REVCLOUD	Revision Cloud (on panel slideout)	Revision Cloud	Revision Cloud

Slideout panels are part of the Ribbon interface in AutoCAD 2013's Drafting & Annotation, 3D Basics, and 3D Modeling workspaces. Slideouts are present in panels that show a small down-pointing triangle next to the panel title. To open a slideout, click the panel title bar (for example, Draw on the Home tab). The panel expands downward, and a pushpin icon appears at the left end of the

panel title bar. After you click a tool button, the slideout panel closes. Click the pushpin in the title bar to *pin* the panel — that is, force it to stay open.

If you're familiar with earlier AutoCAD releases, you may suspect that the Draw panel in AutoCAD 2013's Ribbon interface is also missing some commands. Well, as they used to say in the '90s, the paradigm has shifted! Those commands are still there, they've just been shifted around a bit to make the Ribbon organization more task based.

Going full circle

AutoCAD offers an easy and intuitive way to draw circles, and it also offers . . . *other* ways. The easy way is to define the center point of the circle and then to specify the radius (the default option) or the diameter. You can also define a circle by choosing one of the following options of the command (for those other ways):

- **2-Point (2P):** Draws a circle where the distance between two specified points is equal to the diameter of the circle. If you're keyboarding, enter **2P** at the command prompt to choose this option; it's spelled out as *2-Point* on tooltips.

- **3-Point (3P):** Draws a circle through any three specified points.

- **Tangent-Tangent-Radius (Ttr):** Draws a circle tangent to two existing drawing objects and a specified radius.

- **Tangent-Tangent-Tangent:** Draws a circle tangent to three *valid* existing drawing objects. (By *valid,* we mean it's mathematically possible to construct a circle tangent to the three selected objects.) Note that you can't create this kind of circle by typing a command option at the command line because there *is* no such command option. This method is actually a macro, and you run it by choosing Tan, Tan, Tan from the Circle button menu on the Home tab's Draw panel.

Figure 9-1 illustrates these six different ways of drawing circles. Whether these additional methods are useful or not depends on the kinds of drawings that you make and how geometry is defined in your industry. Get familiar with the default center point/radius method and then try the other methods to see whether they may be helpful to you. If you find yourself going around in circles, you can always draw them the default way and move them into position with other geometry.

Follow these steps to use the CIRCLE command:

1. **Click the Home tab on the Ribbon.**

 The most frequently used commands in AutoCAD are found on the Ribbon's Home tab.

2. **Set an appropriate layer to be current.**

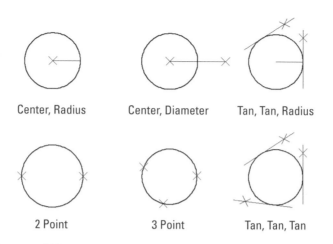

Center, Radius Center, Diameter Tan, Tan, Radius

2 Point 3 Point Tan, Tan, Tan

Figure 9-1: Pi R squared; circles R round, pizzas are flat and round.

3. **Click the Circle button on the Ribbon's Draw panel, or type** C **and press Enter.**

 AutoCAD starts the CIRCLE command and prompts you to specify the center point of the circle. If Dynamic Input is toggled on, press the down arrow on your keyboard to see the options at the crosshairs. The command line shows

   ```
   Specify center point for circle or [3P/2P/Ttr (tan tan
           radius)]:
   ```

 The prompts show the methods other than "center point plus radius" that you can use to draw circles in AutoCAD. (No, tan tan radius is not a mathematician's dance.) Look up *CIRCLE command* in the online help if you think you may have a use for these less-common circle-drawing techniques.

4. **Specify the center point by clicking a point or typing coordinates.**

 Use one of the precision techniques described in Chapter 7 if you're doing real drafting. Object snap, snap, and typing coordinates all work well for specifying the center point.

 AutoCAD then prompts you to specify the circle's radius.

   ```
   Specify radius of circle or [Diameter]:
   ```

 Type **D** and press Enter if you prefer to enter the diameter rather than the radius and you've forgotten your two-times tables — or, more seriously, if the diameter is easier to type exactly than the radius is.

5. Specify the radius by typing a distance or clicking a point.

AutoCAD draws your circle and returns to a blank command prompt. The first point you picked is the center. The command prompt doesn't tell you so, but if you pick a second point instead of entering a number (or typing **D** to invoke the Diameter option), AutoCAD interprets the distance between the first and second points as the radius value.

Arc-y-ology

Arcs in AutoCAD are, quite simply, pieces of circles. As with circles, AutoCAD offers you an easy way to define arcs. Just specify three points onscreen to define the arc, easy as one-two-three. These points tell AutoCAD where to start the arc, how much to curve it, and where to end it.

Sounds pretty easy, right? So, where's the problem? The trouble is that you nearly always have to specify arcs more exactly than is possible by using this method. AutoCAD helps you specify such arcs, too — but the procedure ain't easy.

You can start your arc by specifying the center of the arc or the start point. If you choose the Center option, AutoCAD prompts you for the center point first and the start point second. AutoCAD draws arcs in a counterclockwise direction, so pick a start point in a clockwise direction from the endpoint. After you specify the center and start point, AutoCAD presents several options you can choose, including the following:

- **Angle:** Specifies the included angle that the arc sweeps out. A 180-degree angle, for example, is a semicircle.
- **Length of Chord:** Specifies the length of an imaginary straight line connecting the endpoints of the arc. Most people seldom or never use this option.
- **Endpoint:** Specifies where the arc ends. It's the default option and often the easiest to use.

If you specify the start point as the first option, you can choose among the following three command options as well:

- **Center:** Prompts you for the arc's center point and then finishes with the three options listed previously.
- **End:** Specifies the endpoint of the arc. You then need to define the angle that the arc covers, its direction, its radius, or its center point.
- **Second Point:** The default option. The second point you choose isn't the endpoint; instead, it's a point on the arc that, along with the start point and endpoint, defines how much the arc curves. After you enter the second point, you must enter an endpoint to complete the arc.

To get a feel for how these permutations can be strung together to create different arc-drawing methods, click the down arrow beside the Arc tool button on the Ribbon's Draw panel and look at the drop-down menu that unfurls, as shown in Figure 9-2. Using the Ribbon is also the most direct way of actually using any of these options — at least until you're really familiar with the program and are adept at entering keyboard shortcuts.

Most problems that beginners (and even many experienced users) have with the ARC command is that they forget that when using many of its options it draws *counterclockwise* from the start point.

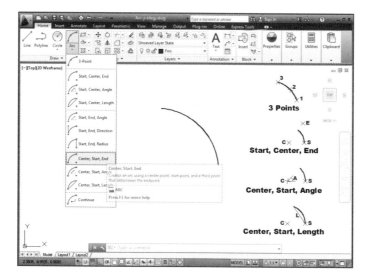

Figure 9-2: A deluge of Arc options, with the results of using some of those options.

The following example shows how you draw an arc with the default start point/second point/endpoint method:

1. **Set an appropriate layer to be current.**

2. **Click the Arc button on the Home tab's Draw panel, or type A and press Enter.**

 AutoCAD starts the ARC command and prompts you to specify the start point of the arc. The command line shows

   ```
   Specify start point of arc or [Center]:
   ```

3. **Specify the start point by clicking a point or typing coordinates.**

 AutoCAD prompts you to specify a second point on the arc.

4. **Specify a second point on the arc by clicking a point or typing coordinates.**

The second point lies somewhere along the curve of the arc. AutoCAD determines the exact curvature of the arc after you choose the final endpoint in the following step. To align the second point with an existing object, use an Object Snap mode.

AutoCAD prompts you to specify the endpoint of the arc; as you move the crosshairs around, AutoCAD shows how the arc will look.

5. **Specify the endpoint of the arc by clicking a point or typing coordinates.**

AutoCAD draws the arc, as shown previously in Figure 9-2.

As you may recall, pressing Enter repeats the last command. What often throws new AutoCAD users is that Enter doesn't repeat the *options* of the last command. If you draw an arc by using the Center, Start, End option, for example, pressing Enter isn't going to repeat that method — it's going to repeat the ARC command in its default form, and the three points you pick probably won't give you the arc you meant to draw. Bottom line: Watch the command line!

Solar ellipses

In case you've forgotten your ninth-grade math, an *ellipse* is like a squished circle (please excuse the technical jargon). Mathematically, an ellipse is defined by a *major* (long) axis and a *minor* (short) axis. These axes determine the ellipse's length, width, and degree of curvature. An *elliptical arc* is an arc cut from an ellipse.

The AutoCAD ELLIPSE command provides a straightforward way of drawing an ellipse: You specify the two endpoints of one of its axes and then specify an endpoint on the other axis. But like the ARC command, the ELLIPSE command offers a bunch of other options:

- ✓ **Arc:** Generates an elliptical arc, not a full ellipse. You define an elliptical arc just as you do a full ellipse. The methods that we discuss in this section for creating an ellipse apply to either.

- ✓ **Center:** This option requires that you define the center of the ellipse and then the endpoint of an axis. You can then either enter the distance of the other axis or specify that a rotation around the major axis defines the ellipse. If you choose the latter, you can enter (or drag the ellipse to) a specific rotation angle for the second axis that, in turn, completely defines the ellipse.

✔ **Rotation:** With this option, you specify an angle which defines the curvature of the ellipse — small angles make fat ellipses (0 degrees creates a circle, in fact), and large angles make skinny ellipses. After dinner tonight, if you've eaten everything including the vegetables, pick up your dinner plate and hold it up vertically in front of you and look straight on at it. It will look like a circle. Now slowly rotate it about its vertical axis until you are looking edge-on. In between, you will have seen every possible ellipse as defined by the rotation angle.

The following command line example creates an ellipse by using the default endpoints of the axes method. Figure 9-3 shows an ellipse and an elliptical arc.

```
Command: ELLIPSE
Specify axis endpoint of ellipse or [Arc/Center]: pick or
         type the first endpoint of one axis
Specify other endpoint of axis: pick or type the other
         endpoint of one axis
Specify distance to other axis or [Rotation]: pick or type
         the endpoint of the other axis
```

You can create *elliptical* arcs (as opposed to the circular arcs that the AutoCAD ARC command draws) by using the Arc option of the ELLIPSE command; it can draw a pretty good representation of a snowball trajectory, neglecting air resistance. Alternatively, you can draw a full ellipse and use the TRIM or BREAK command to cut a piece out of it.

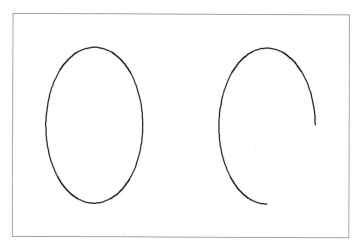

Figure 9-3: To make an omelet, sometimes you have to break a few ellipses.

Splines: The sketchy, sinuous curves

Most people use CAD programs for precision drawing tasks: straight lines, carefully defined curves, precisely specified points, and so on. AutoCAD is not the program to free your inner artist — unless your inner artist is Mondrian. Nonetheless, even meticulously created CAD drawings sometimes need free-form curves. The AutoCAD *spline object* is just the thing for the job.

You can use AutoCAD splines in two ways:

✔ **Wing it.** Eyeball the location and shape of the curve and don't worry too much about getting it just so. That's the free-form, sketchy, not-too-precise approach that we describe in this section.

✔ **Specify their control points and curvature characteristics precisely.**

Beneath their easygoing, informal exterior, AutoCAD splines are really highly precise, mathematically defined entities called *NURBS curves* (NonUniform Rational B-Spline curves). Mathematicians and some mechanical and industrial designers care a lot about the precise characteristics of the curves they work with. For those people, the AutoCAD SPLINE and SPLINEDIT commands include a number of advanced options. Look up *spline curves* in the AutoCAD online help if you need precision in your splines.

Drawing splines is straightforward, if you ignore the advanced options. The following procedure draws a free-form curve with the SPLINE command:

1. **Set an appropriate layer as current.**

2. **Click the Spline Fit button on the Home tab's Draw panel slideout, or type SPL and press Enter.**

 AutoCAD starts the SPLINE command and prompts you to specify the start point of the spline. The command line shows

   ```
   Current settings: Method=Fit Knots=Chord

   Specify first point or [Method/Knots/Object]:
   ```

3. **Specify the start point by clicking a point or typing coordinates.**

 AutoCAD prompts you to specify additional points:

   ```
   Enter next point or [start Tangency/toLerance]:
   ```

4. **Specify additional points by clicking or typing coordinates.**

 After you pick the second point, press the down-arrow key to display additional options at the Dynamic Input tooltip. (Enable Dynamic Input at the status bar if you need to.) The command line shows

   ```
   Enter next point or [end Tangency/toLerance/Undo/
          Close]:
   ```

Because you're drawing a free-form curve, you usually don't need to use object snaps or other precision techniques when picking spline points.

5. Press Enter after you've chosen the endpoint of your spline.

AutoCAD draws the spline.

You can specify the start and end tangency of the spline to control the curvature of the start points and endpoints of the spline. If all you're after is a swoopy free-form curve, just picking points as in this example works fine.

Figure 9-4 shows some examples of splines.

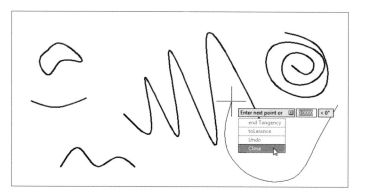

Figure 9-4: A slew of splines.

After you've drawn a spline, you can grip edit it to adjust its shape. See Chapter 10 for information about grip editing. If you need finer control over spline editing, look up the SPLINEDIT command in the AutoCAD online help.

Donuts: The circles with a difference

A *donut* in AutoCAD is another special type of polyline object that you create with (what else?) the DONUT command. (The rectangles and regular polygons we show you in Chapter 8 are also polyline objects.) Creating a *donut* is a simple way to define a single object that consists of two concentric circles with the space between them filled.

When you start the DONUT command, AutoCAD prompts you for the inside diameter and the outside diameter — the size of the hole and the size of the donut — as measured across their widest points. After you've entered these values, AutoCAD prompts you for the center point of the donut. But one donut is rarely enough, so AutoCAD keeps prompting you for additional center points until you press Enter (the AutoCAD equivalent of saying, "No, really, I'm full now!").

The following example draws a regulation-size donut, with a 1.5-inch hole and 3.5-inch outside diameter.

```
Command: DONUT
Specify inside diameter of donut <0.5000>: 1.5
Specify outside diameter of donut <1.0000>: 3.5
Specify center of donut or <exit>: pick or type the center
                point of one or more donuts
```

TIP

You can use the DONUT command to create a filled circle — also known as a jelly-filled donut. Just specify an inside diameter of 0. Figure 9-5 shows both kinds of donuts.

TIP

If you are Canadian, the DOUGHNUT command also works, but *TimHorton's* doesn't.

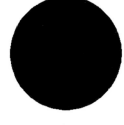

Inside Diameter = 1.5 Inside Diameter – 0
Outside Diameter = 3.5 Outside Diameter = 3.5

Figure 9-5: Donuts, plain and jelly-filled.

Revision clouds on the horizon

It's customary in many industries to submit a set of drawings at different project milestones or stages of completion and then submit them again later with *revisions* — corrections, clarifications, and requested changes. Usually, the recipients like to locate changed stuff easily, and a common drafting convention is to call attention to revised items by drawing free-form clouds around them. The REVCLOUD command makes quick work of drawing such clouds.

Drawing revision clouds is easy, after you understand that you click only once in the drawing area. That one click defines the starting point for the cloud's perimeter. After that, you simply move the crosshairs around, and the cloud takes shape. When you return to near the point that you clicked in the beginning, AutoCAD automatically closes the cloud.

The following command line example shows you how to draw a revision cloud. Figure 9-6 shows what revision clouds look like.

```
Command: REVCLOUD
Minimum arc length: 0.5000 Maximum arc length: 0.5000 Style:
          Normal
Specify start point or [Arc length/Object/Style] <Object>:
          pick a point along the perimeter of your future
          cloud
Guide crosshairs along cloud path... sweep the crosshairs
          around to define the cloud's perimeter
```

You don't need to click again. Simply move the crosshairs around without clicking. AutoCAD draws the next arc segment of the cloud when your crosshairs reach the minimum arc length distance from the end of the previous arc segment.

Continue moving the crosshairs around until you return to the point where you clicked first.

Min. arc length = 0.5 Min. arc length = 0.5 Min. arc length = 1.0
Max. arc length = 0.5 Max. arc length = 1.0 Max. arc length = 1.0

Figure 9-6: Today's forecast: revision cloudy.

Here are a few tips for using revision clouds:

- ✔ **Create a cloud layer.** It's a good idea to put revision clouds on their own layer so you can choose to plot with or without the clouds visible. In paper-and-pencil days, revision clouds were sketched on the back of the drafting vellum so they could easily be erased.

- ✔ **Turn off Ortho mode.** You'll probably find it easier to control the shape of revision clouds if you turn off Ortho mode before you start the command.

✔ **Include the revision number.** You may need to add a triangle and number, shown in Figure 9-6, to indicate the revision number. A block with an attribute is a good way to handle this requirement: Chapter 17 covers blocks and attributes.

If the revision cloud's arcs are too small or too large, erase the cloud, restart the REVCLOUD command, and use the command's Arc Length option to change the minimum and maximum arc lengths. The default minimum and maximum lengths are 0.5 (or 15 in metric drawings). If you make the minimum and maximum lengths equal (which is the default), the lobes will be approximately equal in size. If you make them unequal, there will be more variation in lobe size — you'll get fluffier clouds. Fortunately, all these options are more than most nonmeteorologists will need.

Scoring Points

We thought about not covering points in this book, but we didn't want you complaining that *AutoCAD 2013 For Dummies* is pointless.

The word *point* describes two different things in AutoCAD:

✔ A **location** in the drawing that you specify (by typing coordinates or clicking with the mouse)

✔ An **object** that you draw with the POINT command

Throughout this chapter and most of the book, we tell you to specify points — that's the location meaning. This section tells you how to draw point objects.

A *point object* in AutoCAD can serve two purposes:

✔ **Points often identify specific locations in your drawing to other people who look at the drawing.** A point can be something that displays on the screen, either as a tiny dot or as another symbol, such as a cross with a circle around it.

✔ **You can use points as precise object snap locations.** Think of them as construction points. For example, when you're laying out a new building, you might draw point objects at some of the engineering survey points and then snap to those points as you sketch the building's shape with the PLINE command. You use the *Node* Object Snap mode to snap to AutoCAD point objects.

What makes AutoCAD point objects complicated is their almost limitless range of display options, provided to accommodate the two different kinds of purposes just described (and possibly some others that we haven't figured out yet). You use the Point Style dialog box, shown in Figure 9-7, to specify how points should look in the current drawing.

Figure 9-7: The Point Style dialog box controls the way point objects appear onscreen.

The Point Style dialog box can be found on the Home tab's Utilities panel slideout, or by typing its command name — which happens to be about the least intuitive command name in all of AutoCAD: **DDPTYPE** (pronounced *dee dee pee type*). The top portion of the dialog box shows the available point display styles. Most of the choices do pretty much the same thing. Just click one of the squares that says, "Hey, that's a good point!" to you.

The first choice, a single-pixel dot, is hard to see on the screen, and the second choice, invisible (a stealth point?), is impossible to see. Avoid these choices if you want your point objects to show up on the screen and on plots. The single-pixel dot, which is the default display style, works well if you use point objects as object snap locations and don't want obtrusive points on your plots.

The remaining settings in the Point Style dialog box control the size at which points appear on the screen at different zoom magnifications. The default settings often work fine, but if you're not satisfied with them, click the Help button in the dialog box to find out how to change them.

 After you specify the point style, placing points onscreen is easy. The following example shows you how; just type **POINT** and press Enter.

```
Command: POINT
Current point modes: PDMODE=0 PDSIZE=0.0000
Specify a point: pick or type the coordinates of a location
          in the drawing
```

The PDMODE and PDSIZE items listed in the command window are system variables that correspond to the point display mode and display size options in the Point Style dialog box. If you want to know exactly how the system variables correspond to the dialog box choices, you have all the makings of a successful CAD nerd. Click the Help button in the Point Style dialog box to find out more (about the system variables — not about yourself).

10

Get a Grip on Object Selection

In This Chapter

▶ Using command-first editing

▶ Selecting objects with maximum flexibility

▶ Editing with grips

*E*diting objects is the flip side of creating them, and in AutoCAD, you spend a lot of time editing — far more than drawing objects from scratch. That's partly because the design and drafting process is, by its nature, repetitive, and also because AutoCAD makes it easy to edit objects cleanly. Creating an object and then editing it can also be faster than doing it right the first time. In particular, placing a circle and then breaking or trimming it is often faster than fighting your way through all the ARC command's options.

When you edit objects in AutoCAD, you need to be just as concerned about specifying precise locations and distances as you are when you originally create the objects. Make sure that you're familiar with the precision techniques described in Chapter 7 before you apply the editing techniques from this chapter to real drawings.

Commanding and Selecting

AutoCAD offers three styles of editing:

▶ **Command-first editing**

▶ **Selection-first editing**

▶ **Direct object manipulation** (grip editing)

AutoCAD refers to command-first editing as *verb-noun editing* and to selection-first editing as *noun-verb editing*. When you see this terminology — for example, in the Options dialog box or the online help system — don't worry; you haven't dropped back into your fifth-grade English class!

Command-first editing

With *command-first editing,* you start a command and then select the objects on which the command works. This style of editing may seem backward to you at first unless you're a longtime AutoCAD user. Command-first editing works well for power users who are in a hurry and willing to memorize most of the commands they need to do their work. It's also the *only* way to use some of the editing commands (such as FILLET and BREAK). It's no surprise that command-first editing is the traditional editing style in AutoCAD, and the one method with which you need to be most comfortable.

Selection-first editing

In *selection-first editing,* you perform the same steps — in the same order — as in most Windows applications: Select the object first, and then choose the command. Selection-first editing tends to be easier to master and makes AutoCAD more approachable for new and occasional users.

Direct object manipulation

With *direct object manipulation,* you perform common editing operations by using the mouse to grab the selected object and perform an action on it, such as moving all or part of it to a different place in the drawing. No named command is involved; the act of moving the mouse and clicking the mouse buttons in certain ways causes the editing changes to happen. AutoCAD supports direct object manipulation through a powerful technique called *grip editing. Grips* are the little square, rectangular, or triangular handles that appear on an object when you select it. You can use the grips to stretch, move, copy, rotate, scale, or otherwise edit the object.

Choosing an editing style

This book emphasizes command-first editing, but we also discuss grip editing in the section "Get a Grip," later in this chapter. AutoCAD, in its heart of hearts, is a command-first program. In fact, it started out offering *only* command-first editing and later added selection-first methods; AutoCAD 2013 inherits this ancestral trait. We stress command-first editing for the following reasons:

 ✓ It's the editing style that's been in AutoCAD the longest, and the one with which experienced AutoCAD users are most familiar.

 ✓ It works consistently with *all* editing commands — some editing commands remain command-first only.

 ✓ It provides added object selection flexibility, which is useful when you work on complicated, busy drawings.

After you know how to do command-first editing, you can simply reverse the order of many editing operations to do them selection-first style, instead. But if you don't get familiar with command-first editing in the beginning, you'll be bewildered by a few useful AutoCAD commands that work only in the command-first style; commands such as these ignore any already-selected objects and prompt you to select objects before you can continue.

Much of the information in the rest of this book assumes that you're using the default AutoCAD selection settings. If you find that object selection or grip editing are working differently from the way we describe them in this chapter, click the Application button, choose Options from the bottom of the Application Menu to open the Options dialog box, and then check the settings on the Selection tab. The 11 check box settings listed next should be selected, as shown in Figure 10-1. (All other check box settings should be deselected.)

✔ Noun/Verb Selection

✔ Object Grouping

✔ Implied Windowing

✔ Selection Preview When a Command Is Active

✔ Selection Preview When No Command Is Active

✔ Show Grips

✔ Show Grip Tips

✔ Show Dynamic Grip Menu

Figure 10-1: Setting selection options in the Options dialog box.

- ✔ Allow Ctrl+Cycling Behavior
- ✔ Show Single Grip on Groups
- ✔ Show Bounding Box on Groups

For information on what these options do, hover the mouse pointer over an option to display a tooltip with information from the online help.

Grab It

Part of AutoCAD's editing flexibility comes from its object-selection flexibility. For example, command-first editing offers 16 selection modes! (We describe the most useful ones in this chapter.) Don't worry, though; you can get by most of the time with three selection modes, each of which we describe in this section:

- ✔ **Selecting a single object by picking it**
- ✔ **Selecting multiple objects by enclosing them in a *window* selection box or polygon**
- ✔ **Selecting multiple objects by enclosing them in a *crossing* selection box or polygon**

One-by-one selection

The most obvious way to select objects is to pick (by clicking) them one at a time. One or more objects that are selected and ready for editing are called a *selection set.* You can build a selection set cumulatively with this pick-one-object-at-a-time selection mode, but this cumulative convention may be different from what you're used to. In most Windows programs, if you select one object and then another, the first object is *deselected,* and the second one selected; only the object you select last remains selected. In AutoCAD, *all* the objects you select, one at a time, remain selected and are added to the selection set, no matter how many objects you pick. (You can change this behavior to make AutoCAD work like other Windows programs by turning on the Use Shift to Add to Selection option on the Option dialog box's Selection tab, but we suggest that you don't change it.) Most editing commands affect the entire group of selected objects.

Use the SELECTSIMILAR command to automatically select similar objects based on their properties. Select an object, right-click, and choose Select Similar from the shortcut menu, and AutoCAD selects *all* similar objects. You can filter the properties used for selection by typing **SELECTSIMILAR** at the command prompt, and then entering **SE** to display the Select Similar Settings dialog box (see Figure 10-2).

Figure 10-2: Choose your similarity-selection settings here.

Selection boxes left and right

Selecting objects one at a time works great when you want to edit a small number of objects, but many CAD editing tasks involve editing lots of objects. Do you really want to pick 132 lines, arcs, and circles, one at a time?

Like most Windows graphics programs, AutoCAD provides a *selection window* feature for grabbing a bunch of objects in a rectangular area. As you may guess by now, the AutoCAD version of this feature is a bit more powerful than the similar feature in other Windows graphics programs. AutoCAD calls its version *implied windowing.* Here's how you use it.

- ✓ **Window object selection:** If you click a blank area of the drawing — that is, not on an object — you're *implying* to AutoCAD that you want to specify a selection by dragging a window around the objects. If you move the crosshairs to the <u>right</u> before picking the next corner of the selection area, you're further implying that you want to select all objects that reside *completely* within the selection area.

- ✓ **Crossing object selection:** If you click a blank area of the drawing — that is, not on an object — you're *implying* to AutoCAD that you want to specify a selection by dragging a window around and through the objects. If you move the crosshairs to the <u>left</u> before picking the next corner of the selection area, you're implying that you want to select all objects that reside completely within *or touch or cross* the selection area boundary.

Fortunately, AutoCAD gives you visual cues that there's a difference. As you move to the right, the window area appears as a rectangular or polygonal area with a blue fill and a solid border. As you move to the left, the crossing area appears as a rectangle or polygon with green fill and a dashed border.

If your editing method of preference is selection-first, AutoCAD gives you the option of dragging a polygonal window or crossing area, or simply dragging a series of lines through the objects you want to select. You simply click a point and drag to the left or right to get rectangular selection boxes as described above, or you can choose the WPolygon, CPolygon, or Fence options by typing the appropriate letter at the command line.

Figures 10-3 and 10-4 show a window box and a crossing box, respectively, in action.

Figure 10-3: A window selection box, drawn left to right, selects only the two objects that are completely within the box.

You can mix and match, selecting individual objects, specifying a window box, and specifying a crossing box. Each selection adds to the current selection set, allowing you to build an enormously complicated selection of objects and then operate on them with one or more editing commands.

You can press the Shift key in combination with any of the three standard selection modes — single object, window area, and crossing area — to *remove* already-selected objects from the selection set. This feature is especially useful when you're building a selection set in a crowded drawing; you can select a big batch of objects by using Window or Crossing, and then hold

down the Shift key while selecting to remove the objects that you want to exclude from the editing operation.

Pick point 2

Closet #1 Closet #2

Select objects:

Selection box

Pick point 1

Figure 10-4: A crossing selection box, drawn right to left, selects 11 objects that are completely or partially within the box.

Perfecting Selecting

When you edit in command-first mode, you have all the selection options described in the previous section — single object, window box, window polygon, crossing polygon, and crossing box — plus a slew of others. If you type **?** and press Enter at any `Select objects` prompt, AutoCAD lists all the selection options at the command line:

```
Window/Last/Crossing/BOX/ALL/Fence/WPolygon/CPolygon/
    Group/Add/Remove/Multiple/Previous/Undo/AUto/
    SIngle/SUbobject/Object
```

Table 10-1 summarizes the most useful command-first selection options.

Table 10-1	Some Useful Command-First Selection Options
Option	*Description*
Window	All objects completely within a rectangular area that you specify by picking two points
Crossing	All objects within, crossing, or touching a rectangular area that you specify by picking two points
WPolygon	All objects completely within a polygonal area whose corners you specify by picking points
CPolygon	All objects within, crossing, or touching a polygonal area whose corners you specify by picking points
Fence	All objects touching an imaginary polyline whose vertices you specify by picking points
Last	The last object you drew (whether or not it's visible in the display)
Previous	The previous selection set that you specified
ALL	All objects on layers that aren't frozen or locked and that are in the current space (model space or paper space), including objects that aren't currently displayed because you are zoomed in

To use any of the command-first selection options at the `Select objects` prompt, type the uppercase letters indicated in Table 10-1 that correspond to the desired option and press Enter. After you're finished selecting objects, you must press Enter again to tell AutoCAD that you've finished selecting objects and want to start the editing operation.

After you're finished selecting objects, you must press Enter again to tell AutoCAD that you've finished selecting objects and want to start the editing operation. Say . . . is there an echo in here? As a matter of fact, we *are* repeating ourselves. One of the things that most new AutoCAD users find hardest to remember is the necessity of pressing Enter after you finish selecting objects.

AutoCAD's *selection preview* features remove a lot of doubt about which objects you're selecting. *Rollover highlighting* displays individual objects with a thick, dashed lineweight as you move the crosshairs over them. *Area selection* displays a transparent, colored highlight over multiple selections when you use Window and Crossing options. You can enable and disable both features on the Selection tab of the Options dialog box (refer to Figure 10-1).

The following example demonstrates how to use the ERASE command in command-first mode with several different selection options. The selection techniques used in this example apply to most AutoCAD editing commands.

1. **Open a drawing that contains some objects, or start a new drawing and create some lincs, arcs, or circles.**

 You needn't be too particular drawing these because you're going to blow them away in the following steps.

2. **Press Esc to make sure that no command is active and no objects are selected.**

 If any objects are selected when you start an editing command, the command, in most cases, will operate on those objects (selection-first editing) instead of prompting you to select objects (command-first editing). For the reasons that we describe in the section "Commanding and Selecting," earlier in this chapter, we recommend that you use command-first editing style until you're thoroughly familiar with it. Later, you can experiment with selection-first editing if you like. (Just reverse the sequence of commanding and selecting that we describe in this chapter.)

3. **Click the Erase button on the Home tab's Modify panel.**

 AutoCAD displays the `Select objects` prompt at the command line and, if Dynamic Input is enabled on the status bar, the Dynamic Input tooltip.

4. **Select two or three individual objects by clicking each one.**

 AutoCAD adds each object to the selection set. All the objects you select remain highlighted, and AutoCAD continues to display the `Select objects` prompt.

5. **Specify a window selection box that completely encloses several objects.**

 Move the crosshairs to a point below and to the left of the objects, click, release the mouse button, move the crosshairs above and to the right of the objects, and click again.

 All objects that are completely within the box are selected.

6. **Specify a crossing selection box that completely encloses a few objects and cuts through several others.**

 Move the crosshairs to a point below and to the right of some of the objects, click, release the mouse button, move the crosshairs above and to the left of some of the objects, and click and release again.

 All objects that are completely within, cross through, or touch the box are selected. AutoCAD continues to display the `Select objects` prompt.

7. **Type WP and press Enter to activate the WPolygon selection option.**

 AutoCAD prompts you to pick points that define the selection polygon.

8. Pick a series of points and press Enter.

Figure 10-5 shows an example. After you press Enter, AutoCAD selects all objects that are completely within the polygon. AutoCAD continues to display the `Select objects` prompt until you press Enter.

Figure 10-5: Lassoing objects with a WPolygon selects the concentric circles and their center lines.

9. Press Enter to end object selection.

AutoCAD erases all the selected objects and returns to an empty command prompt.

Notice how you could use a combination of object selection methods to build a selection set and then press Enter to execute the command on the selected objects. Most AutoCAD editing commands work this way in command-first mode.

 If, after erasing a selection set, you immediately realize that you didn't really mean to do away with so many objects, you can use the Undo button on the Quick Access Toolbar to restore them all. But AutoCAD has one additional unerase trick up its sleeve — the aptly named OOPS command. When you type **OOPS** and press Enter, AutoCAD restores the last selection set that you erased — even if you've run other commands after ERASE.

 The ERASE command isn't the only way to remove unwanted objects from your drawing. Easiest of all in any workspace is to simply select an item and press the Delete key on your keyboard.

It's all too easy to draw objects on top of other objects, and after they're there, pretty well impossible to recognize that there *are* multiples so you can weed out the ones you don't want. For some earlier releases, holding down the Shift key and the spacebar together while clicking suspected multiple objects will highlight them, one after the other; when the one you're after lights up, you press Enter to select it. AutoCAD 2011 introduced a more powerful selection cycling method. With Selection Cycling enabled on the status bar, AutoCAD displays a blue overlapping rectangles icon if it detects multiple objects under your crosshairs. When you pick an object with this icon displayed, AutoCAD opens a Selection dialog box where you can choose the object you actually want.

Duplicate overlapping objects can be a real nuisance, but fortunately AutoCAD can find those duplicates and blow them away for you! Click the Delete Duplicate Objects tool (look for the broom on the Modify panel slide-out on the Home tab) to run the aptly named OVERKILL command.

OVERKILL can delete all but one of any number of identical overlapping objects, it can join overlapping collinear line segments into a single line, and it can join concentric overlapping arc segments into a single arc. Better yet, if the combined arc segments cover a range equal to or greater than 360 degrees, it turns them into a circle.

You can clean up an entire drawing at one fell swoop by entering **ALL** at the Select Objects prompt.

When you complete the object selection process, the Delete Duplicate Objects dialog box appears; there you can set a number of properties and options (see Figure 10-6). Check the online help for more about this command.

For some strange reason, the tool button we describe in the preceding paragraph may not have made it onto LT's Modify panel. However, you do have access to the command — you just need to type **OVERKILL** at the command prompt to call up the Delete Duplicate Objects dialog box.

AutoCAD Groupies

AutoCAD lets you select a bunch of objects and gather them into a group, so that when you click one object, everything in the group is selected. You simply select your objects and click Group on the Groups panel of the Home tab. If you want, you can name your group as you create it. The buttons on the main Groups panel let you create new groups, toggle group selection off and on, edit groups by adding or removing individual objects, or permanently ungroup a selected group.

Figure 10-6: Weed out those duplicate objects.

Object Selection: Now You See It . . .

The many object-selection modes we describe in previous sections — and some we don't describe at all, such as the FILTER command (check out the online help system for more on that) — are useful as far as they go.

AutoCAD lets you control the visibility of individual objects. This may or may not sound like a big deal, but believe me, it is. Before AutoCAD 2011, the only way to control the display of objects was to turn off or freeze the layer on which they resided. If there were other objects on that layer that you *did* want to see . . . too bad! Three commands turn that limitation into ancient history:

- **HIDEOBJECTS:** Prompts you to select those objects you want to make temporarily disappear.

- **ISOLATEOBJECTS:** Prompts you to select those objects you want to see while temporarily making everything else disappear.

- **UNISOLATEOBJECTS:** Ends the hiding and isolating of objects.

The primary method of invoking these commands is via the right-click menu. Using either command-first or selection-first editing (as described in the section "Commanding and Selecting," earlier in this chapter), simply right-click

and you see the Isolate item shown in Figure 10-7. A status bar icon — a light bulb at the lower-right corner of the display — is dimmed when objects are either hidden or isolated. Click this icon to open a menu that lets you turn off the hiding or isolating.

If you're worried about the possible implications of this ("Hmm. . . I was sure I added those center lines . . . do I need to add them again?"), relax. Hiding and isolating objects is temporary — it only lasts as long as your current drawing session. If you end a drawing with objects isolated or hidden, they reappear when you reopen the file.

Rumor has it that the Autodesk programmers stole this cloaking and uncloaking concept from the Romulans.

Figure 10-7: Make those selected objects go away (but only temporarily!).

Get a Grip

Although command-first editing is the most flexible and widespread editing style in AutoCAD, it's not the only way. Grip editing is a useful adjunct to command-first editing, especially when you want to modify just one or two objects. You may have encountered grip editing when using other kinds of graphics programs. But even if you're an experienced user of other graphics programs, you've never seen grips used in quite the way that AutoCAD uses them.

Anything that you can do with grip editing can be done with command-first editing as well. In some situations, grip editing is a little more efficient or convenient than command-first editing, but command-first editing always gets the job done. If you master only one style of editing, make it command-first style. In other words, feel free to skip this section — at least until you're comfortable with command-first editing.

About grips

Grips are those little square, rectangular, or triangular handles that appear on an object after you select it.

In their simplest guise, AutoCAD grips work similarly to the little squares on graphical objects in other Windows programs. But in AutoCAD, instead of clicking and dragging a grip, you must click, release the mouse button, move the crosshairs, and click again at the new location. (By separating the selection of beginning and ending points into two different operations, AutoCAD allows you to use different techniques — such as different object snaps — to select each point.)

AutoCAD grips are, for sophisticated users, better than the grips found in most other programs because you can do so much more with them. You can, for example, use AutoCAD grips to move, stretch, or copy an object. You also can use them to rotate an object, scale it to a different size, or *mirror* an object — that is, create one or more reversed copies. Grips also act as *visible object snaps,* or little magnets that attract the crosshairs.

Starting with AutoCAD 2012, grips on lines, arcs, and elliptical arcs have become multifunctional. Hovering over an endpoint grip displays a pop-up menu that offers you a choice of lengthening or stretching the object. Hovering over the midpoint grip on an arc offers the choice of stretching the arc by its midpoint (that is, keeping the same endpoints) or changing its radius. Elliptical arcs display triangular grips that let you increase the length of the arc without changing its other parameters. Hovering over a grip on the midpoint of a polyline segment offers the choice of *stretching* (that is, moving the current segment while maintaining its connections to its siblings), adding a new vertex (that is, split the current segment into two), or turning a line segment into an arc or vice versa.

A gripping example

The following sections cover in detail the five grip editing modes: STRETCH, MOVE, ROTATE, SCALE, and MIRROR. Follow these steps to explore the grip editing modes:

1. **Draw some simple geometry, such as the object shown in Figure 10-8.**

 Here's a great place to practice some of the straight-line object creation tools we describe in Chapter 8!

2. **Press Esc to make sure that no command is active and no objects are selected, and then click Quick Properties on the status bar to turn off the Quick Properties palette.**

The Quick Properties palette is pretty useful for editing the properties of objects, but more often than not, it gets in the way when you want to edit the objects themselves. Besides, properties should normally be set ByLayer rather than by object overrides. Property overrides are covered in Chapter 6.

AutoCAD displays a blank command prompt — that is, no command is currently active.

3. **Click an object onscreen to select it and display its grips.**

 Grips — solid blue squares on the selected object — appear at various points on the object. Note that the AutoCAD command prompt remains blank; you haven't started a command or grip editing operation yet.

4. **Click another object.**

 Both the newly selected object and the previously selected object display grips.

5. **Click one of the grips on either object.**

 If a pop-up menu appears when you get close to a grip, ignore it for now and go ahead and click the grip. The blue square turns to a red square. This grip is now *hot,* or selected and ready for a grip editing operation. Grip editing options now appear on the command line. The first option to appear is STRETCH.

6. **Press the spacebar repeatedly to cycle through the five grip editing options on the command line.**

   ```
   ** STRETCH **
   Specify stretch point or [Base point/Copy/Undo/eXit]:
   ** MOVE **
   Specify move point or [Base point/Copy/Undo/eXit]:
   ** ROTATE **
   Specify rotation angle or [Base point/Copy/Undo/Reference/eXit]:
   ** SCALE **
   Specify scale factor or [Base point/Copy/Undo/Reference/eXit]:
   ** MIRROR **
   Specify second point or [Base point/Copy/Undo/eXit]:
   ```

 The grip editing option displayed on the command line and the Dynamic Input tooltip (if Dynamic Input is enabled) changes as you press the spacebar. If you move the crosshairs (without picking) in between each press of the spacebar, the appearance of your selected object changes as you display each option. Choosing STRETCH, for example, causes a stretched version of the object to appear onscreen.

Pressing the spacebar a bunch of times is a good way to become familiar with the grip editing modes, but there's a more direct way to choose a particular mode. After you click a grip to make it hot, right-click to display the grip editing menu. That menu contains all the grip editing options plus some other choices, as shown in Figure 10-8.

Figure 10-8: The grip editiwng right-click menu.

TIP

If Dynamic Input is enabled, pressing the down-arrow key while cycling through the grip editing options displays a dynamic menu at the cross-hairs from which you can choose options specific to the current grip editing function.

7. **Press the spacebar until STRETCH (or the option you want) reappears as the grip editing option.**

8. **Move the hot grip in the direction in which you want to stretch (or otherwise manipulate) your object.**

 AutoCAD dynamically updates the image of the object to show you what the modified object will look like before you click the final location.

9. **Click again to finish the grip editing operation.**

 The selected object with the hot grip updates.

10. **Click the same grip that you chose in Step 5 (now in a different location) to make it hot.**

11. **This time, move the crosshairs near one of the grips on the other object. When you see the magnetic pull of the grip on the other object, click again to connect the hot grip with the other grip.**

 The object point represented by the hot grip now coincides exactly with the grip on the other object.

12. **Press Esc to deselect all objects and remove all grips.**

Figure 10-9 shows a hot (red) endpoint grip of a line being connected to the endpoint grip of another line. The angled line shows the original position of the line being edited, and the thin vertical line shows the new position. Using

a grip in this way as a visible object snap offers the same advantage as using Object Snap overrides, as described in Chapter 7: It ensures precision by making sure that objects meet exactly.

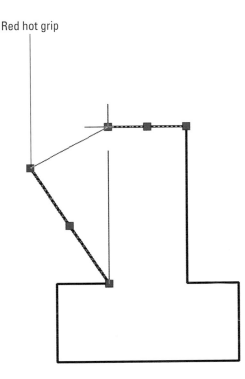

Figure 10-9: Using grips to connect two objects.

You can experiment with all the grip editing options to find out how they affect a selected object. Because MOVE and STRETCH are the most useful grip editing modes, we cover them in more detail.

Move it!

Back in the days of manual drafting, moving objects was a big pain in the eraser. You had to erase the stuff you wanted to move and redraw the objects in their new location. In the process, you usually ended up erasing parts of other stuff that you didn't want to move and left smudged lines and piles of eraser dust everywhere. CAD does away with all the fuss and muss of moving objects, and AutoCAD grip editing is a great way to make it happen. The following steps describe how to move objects:

1. **Select one or more objects.**

 Use any combination of the three object selection modes — single object, window selection, and crossing selection — described in the "Grab It" section, earlier in this chapter.

2. **Click one of the grips to make it hot.**

 At this point in your editing career, it doesn't matter which grip you click. As you become more familiar with grip editing, you'll discover that certain grips serve as better reference points than others for particular editing operations.

3. **Right-click anywhere in the drawing area and choose Move from the crosshairs menu.**

4. **Move the crosshairs to a different location and click.**

 As you move the crosshairs around, AutoCAD displays the tentative new positions for all the objects, just as it does for the regular MOVE command, as shown previously in Figure 10-9. After you click, the objects assume their new positions.

5. **Press Esc to deselect all objects and remove all grips.**

Copy, or a kinder, gentler Move

If you were paying attention during the section "A gripping example," earlier in the chapter, you may have noticed while pressing the spacebar that *copy* was not among the five grip editing modes. Why not? Because *every* grip mode includes a copy option (as the command-line prompts show in the "A gripping example" section). In other words, you can STRETCH with copy, MOVE with copy, ROTATE with copy, SCALE with copy, and MIRROR with copy.

The copy option leaves the selected objects in place and does the editing operation on a new copy of the objects.

By far the most common use for the copy option is with the MOVE grip editing mode. If you think about "MOVE with copy" for about two seconds, you'll realize that it's just a complicated way of saying "copy." The following steps show how to copy objects quickly by using grip editing:

1. **Select one or more objects.**

2. **Click any one of the grips to make it hot.**

3. **Right-click anywhere in the drawing area and choose Move from the menu.**

4. **Right-click again and choose Copy from the menu.**

5. **Move the crosshairs to a different location and click.**

 After you click, new objects appear in the new location.

6. **Move the crosshairs to additional locations and click there if you want to make additional copies.**

7. **Press Esc twice — once to end the copying operation and once to deselect all objects and remove all grips.**

A warm-up stretch

The STRETCH grip editing mode works differently from the other modes. By default, it affects only the object with the hot grip on it, not all objects with grips on them. You can override this default behavior by using the Shift key to pick multiple grips and make them hot. Follow these steps to get acquainted with using the STRETCH grip editing mode to stretch one or more objects:

1. **Make sure that Ortho mode is toggled off on the status bar by clicking the Ortho Mode button until** `<Ortho off>` **appears on the command line.**

 Ortho mode forces stretch displacements to be *orthogonal* — that is, parallel to lines running at 0 and 90 degrees. During real editing tasks, you'll often want to turn on Ortho mode, but while you get acquainted with stretching, leaving Ortho mode off makes things clearer.

2. **Select several objects, including at least one line.**

3. **On one of the lines, click one of the endpoint grips to make it hot.**

 All the objects remain selected, but as you move the crosshairs, only the line with the hot grip changes. Figure 10-10 shows an example.

4. **Click a new point for the hot endpoint grip.**

 The line stretches to accommodate the new endpoint location.

5. **On the same line, click the midpoint grip to make it hot.**

 As you move the crosshairs, the entire line moves. Using the STRETCH grip editing mode with a line's midpoint "stretches" the entire line to a new location.

6. **Click a new point for the hot midpoint grip.**

 The line moves to the new midpoint location.

7. **Hold down the Shift key. On one of the lines, click one of the endpoint grips to make it hot.**

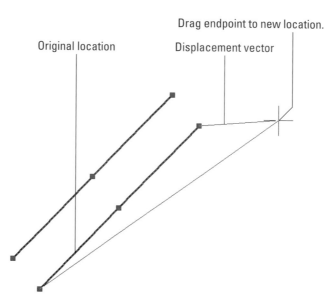

Figure 10-10: Dragging a line's endpoint in the middle of the STRETCH grip editing operation.

8. **Still holding down the Shift key, click one of the endpoint grips on a different line to make it hot.**

 Two grips on two different lines are now hot because you held down the Shift key and then clicked both grips.

 You can create more hot grips by holding down the Shift key and clicking more grips.

9. **Release the Shift key and re-pick any one of the hot grips.**

 Releasing the Shift key signals that you're finished making grips hot. Re-picking one of the hot grips establishes it as the base point for the stretch operation.

10. **Click a new point for the grip.**

 All the objects with hot grips stretch, based on the displacement of the grip that you clicked in Step 9 (see Figure 10-11).

Multiple hot grips

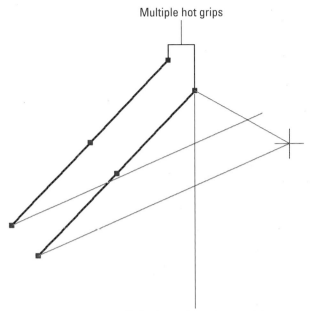

Hot grip used as a base point

Figure 10-11: Stretching multiple objects with multiple hot grips.

11. **Turn on Ortho mode by clicking its status bar button until** <Ortho on> **appears on the command line. Repeat Steps 2 through 10 to see the effect of Ortho mode on stretching.**

Edit for Credit

In This Chapter

▶ Moving, copying, and stretching objects

▶ Manipulating whole objects

▶ Changing pieces of objects

▶ Editing object properties

▶ Fixing your mistakes

*I*n Chapter 10, you discover that AutoCAD has several different methods of modifying drawing objects. You also learn how to select those objects in the first place so you can edit them. Now it's time to roll up your sleeves and get dirty — in this chapter, we introduce the primary edit commands in AutoCAD.

The following sections cover the most important AutoCAD editing commands, using command-first editing mode.

As we explain in Chapter 10, command-first editing — or *verb-noun editing* in AutoCAD-ese — is one of three different approaches to modifying objects in AutoCAD. We concentrate on this method, where you start a command and then pick the objects on which the command will act, because it's the only method that works for all editing commands in AutoCAD.

Your AutoCAD Toolkit

Table 11-1 lists AutoCAD's most frequently used editing commands. It shows the tool icons found on the Ribbon, the classic toolbar, and the classic menu, and it gives the official command name with corresponding alias (where one exists) for the typists in the room. Ribbon buttons are on the Home tab's Modify panel in the Drafting & Annotation workspace. In the AutoCAD Classic workspace, look for these commands on the Modify or Modify II toolbar and Modify menu.

The ARRAY command underwent such a massive revision in AutoCAD 2012 that it hardly qualifies as a Modify command any more. We cover the associative array feature in Chapter 18. However, we think there's still a need for simple arrays — that is, copies of objects in regular patterns — so we explain how to do those (and it's just slightly different from what it used to be) in this chapter. The icons and input locations for the four Array commands shown in Table 11-1 run the new associative array commands that we cover in Chapter 18; we include them here because they're still grouped with the other Modify commands in the Ribbon, the menu, and the toolbars.

Table 11-1		AutoCAD's Modify Commands		
Button	**Command**	**Modify Panel**	**Modify Toolbar**	**Modify Menu**
	ERASE (E)	Erase	Erase	Modify, Erase Edit, Clear
	MOVE (M)	Move	Move	Move
	COPY (CO or CP)	Copy	Copy	Modify, Copy (not Edit, Copy)
	STRETCH (S)	Stretch	Stretch	Stretch
	MIRROR (MI)	Mirror	Mirror	Mirror
	ROTATE (RO)	Rotate	Rotate	Rotate
	SCALE (SC)	Scale	Scale	Scale
	ARRAYRECT	Rectangular Array	Rectangular Array	Modify, Array, Rectangular Array

Button	Command	Modify Panel	Modify Toolbar	Modify Menu
	ARRAYPOLAR	Polar Array	Polar Array	Modify, Array, Polar Array
	ARRAYPATH	Path Array	Path Array	Modify, Array, Path Array
	ARRAYEDIT	Edit Array (on slideout panel)	Edit Array (on the Modify II toolbar)	Modify, Object, Array
	-ARRAY (-AR)	Not available	Not available	Not available
	OFFSET (O)	Offset	Offset	Offset
	TRIM (TR)	Trim (on drop-down button)	Trim	Trim
	EXTEND (EX)	Extend (on drop-down button)	Extend	Extend
	LENGTHEN (LEN)	Lengthen (on slideout panel)	Not available	Lengthen
	BREAK (BR); two points	Break (on slideout panel)	Break	Break
	BREAK (BR); 1 point	Break at point (on slideout panel)	Break at point	Not available
	EXPLODE (X)	Explode	Explode	Explode

(continued)

Table 11-1 *(continued)*

Button	Command	Modify Panel	Modify Toolbar	Modify Menu
	FILLET (F)	Fillet (on drop-down button)	Fillet	Fillet
	CHAMFER (CHA)	Chamfer (on drop-down button)	Chamfer	Chamfer
	BLEND	Blend Curves (on drop-down button)	Blend Curves	Blend Curves
	JOIN (J)	Join (on slideout panel)	Join	Join
	REVERSE	Reverse (on slideout panel)	Not available	Not available
	OVERKILL	Delete Duplicate Objects (on slideout panel)	Delete Duplicate Objects on Modify II toolbar	Delete Duplicate Objects

No matter how you start an editing command, in almost all cases AutoCAD prompts you for object selection, points, distances, and options in the command window. Read the prompts during every step of the command, especially when you're figuring out how to use a new editing command. When all else fails, read the command prompt!

AutoCAD's Dynamic Input system displays command options at the crosshairs. When you see a Dynamic Input tooltip with a down-arrow icon, press the down-arrow key to display the command options. You then can use the mouse to select an option (see Figure 11-1). Pressing the up-arrow key displays previous input.

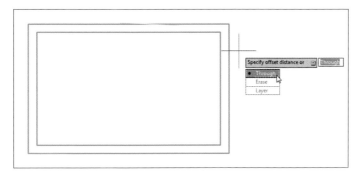

Figure 11-1: Choosing command options from the Dynamic Input menu.

As we describe in Chapter 7, maintaining precision when you draw and edit is crucial to good CAD work. If you've used a drawing program and are accustomed to moving, stretching, and otherwise editing objects by eye, you'll need to suppress that habit when you edit in AutoCAD. Nothing ruins a drawing faster than eyeball editing, in which you shove objects around until they look okay, without worrying about precise distances and points.

Users of Windows Paint and other bitmap drawing programs will be familiar with the concept of "nudging" — selecting some objects and using the arrow keys to move them a certain number of pixels horizontally or vertically. For better or worse, AutoCAD has joined the nudging party. You can move objects a pixel's-worth this way or that by holding down Ctrl and pressing an arrow key. When working with AutoCAD, you should *always* use tried-and-true precision drafting techniques, and moving objects by the pixel instead of by real-world units is the *opposite* of precise. It might be okay to move a piece of text by nudging it, but you should *never* move actual drawing geometry that way.

The Big Three: Move, Copy, and Stretch

Moving, copying, and stretching are, for many drafters, the three most common editing operations. AutoCAD obliges this need with the MOVE, COPY, and STRETCH commands.

Base points and displacements

The MOVE, COPY, and STRETCH commands all require that you specify how far and in what direction you want the objects to be moved, copied, or stretched. After you've started the command and selected the objects to be edited, AutoCAD prompts you for two pieces of information:

```
Specify base point or [Displacement] <Displacement>:
Specify second point or <use first point as displacement>:
```

In a subtle way, these prompts say that two possible methods exist for you to specify how far and in what direction you want the objects copied, moved, or stretched:

- **The most common way is to pick or type the coordinates of two points that define a displacement vector.** AutoCAD calls these points the *base point* and the *second point.* Imagine an arrow pointing from the base point to the second point — that arrow defines how far, and in what direction, the objects are copied, moved, or stretched.

- **The other way is to type an X,Y pair of numbers that represents a distance rather than a point.** This distance is the absolute displacement that you want to copy, move, or stretch the objects.

How does AutoCAD know whether your response to the first prompt is a base point or a displacement? It depends on how you respond to the second prompt. It might seem a little confusing at first, but it's actually quite simple. First, you pick a point onscreen or enter coordinates at the Base point prompt. Next, there are a couple of possibilities:

- If you then pick or type the coordinates of a point at the second point prompt, AutoCAD says to itself, "Aha — displacement vector!," and moves the objects according to the imaginary arrow pointing from the base point to the second point.

- If you press Enter at the second prompt (without having typed anything), AutoCAD says, "Aha — displacement distance," and uses the X,Y pair of numbers that you typed at the first prompt as an absolute displacement distance.

What makes this displacement business interesting is that AutoCAD lets you pick a point at the first prompt *and then* press Enter at the second prompt. AutoCAD still says, "Aha — displacement distance," but now it treats the coordinates *of the point you picked* as an absolute distance relative to the drawing's origin. If the point you picked has relatively large coordinates, the objects can be moved to somewhere northeast of Greenland. You probably won't see where they've gone because you're zoomed into part of your normal drawing area, and so it just seems like the objects have vanished! In short, be careful when you press Enter during the MOVE, COPY, and STRETCH commands. Press Enter in response to the second prompt *only* if you want AutoCAD to use your response to the first prompt as an absolute displacement. If you make a mistake, click Undo or press Ctrl+Z to back up and try again. You can use Zoom Extents (described in Chapter 12) to look for objects that have flown off into space.

Move

The following steps demonstrate command-first editing with the MOVE command, using the base point method of indicating how far and in what

direction to move the selected objects. This procedure also gives detailed recommendations on how to use precision techniques when you edit.

1. **Press Esc to make sure that no command is active and no objects are selected.**

2. **Click the Move button on the Modify panel of the Home tab.**

 The command line displays the `Select objects` prompt.

3. **Select one or more objects.**

 You can use any of the object selection techniques described in the "Perfecting Selecting" section in Chapter 10.

4. **Press Enter when you're finished selecting objects.**

 AutoCAD displays the following prompt:

   ```
   Specify base point or [Displacement] <Displacement>:
   ```

5. **Specify a base point by clicking a point or typing coordinates.**

 This point serves as the tail end of your imaginary arrow that indicates how far and in what direction you want the objects moved. After you pick a base point, it's fairly easy to see what's going on because AutoCAD displays a temporary image of the object that moves around as you move the crosshairs. Figure 11-2 shows what the screen looks like.

Figure 11-2: Dragging objects in the middle of the MOVE command.

Specify a base point somewhere on or near the object(s) that you're moving. You can use an object snap mode to choose a point exactly on one of the objects.

AutoCAD displays the following prompt:

```
Specify second point or <use first point as
       displacement>:
```

6. **Specify the second point by clicking a point or typing coordinates.**

The second point serves as the arrow end of your imaginary displacement arrow. After you specify the second point, AutoCAD moves the objects.

Don't press Enter alone at this prompt! If you do, AutoCAD treats the X,Y coordinates of the first point you picked as an absolute displacement, and the objects fly off unpredictably. *I repeat: Don't press Enter alone at this prompt!* As indicated in the previous warning, pressing Enter without picking a point or typing coordinates at this prompt is one of the most common errors new AutoCAD users make, and it can really pollute your drawing with unwanted objects.

These are the common precision techniques for specifying the second point:

- ✓ Use an object snap mode to pick a second point exactly on another object in the drawing.

- ✓ Type a relative or polar coordinate, as described in Chapter 7. For example, if you type **@6,2**, AutoCAD moves the objects 6 units to the right and 2 units up. If you type **@3<45**, AutoCAD moves the objects 3 units at an angle of 45 degrees.

Use direct distance entry to move objects in an orthogonal or polar-tracking direction. See Chapter 7 for instructions.

Copy

The COPY command works almost identically to the MOVE command, except that AutoCAD leaves the selected objects in place and makes new copies of them in the new location.

The COPY command creates multiple copies by default. If you want only one copy, press Enter after placing it in the drawing. Choosing mOde at the command prompt or the Dynamic Input options list lets you switch between making a single copy and multiple copies. If you mostly make multiple copies or mostly make single copies, you'll appreciate being able to change the default setting.

The COPY command includes an Array option. In addition to plunking copied objects down just anywhere, typing **A** to choose the Array option lets you specify spacing for an evenly laid-out linear array. That's good if you just want a single row of copies, but the ARRAY command (which we describe later in this chapter and in Chapter 18) is required to create rows and columns or circular patterns of copied objects.

The COPY command includes an Undo option with which you can roll back multiple copies within a single COPY operation.

Copy between drawings

You can't copy or move objects from one drawing to another with the COPY command. Instead, you use the COPYCLIP or CUTCLIP commands together with their companion command, PASTECLIP.

COPYCLIP, CUTCLIP, and PASTECLIP use the Windows Clipboard to temporarily store drawing objects from one file so they can be pasted into another file. The Clipboard panel on the Ribbon contains Cut, Copy, and Paste tools, the three standard Clipboard buttons you find in every Windows program.

 As you're figuring out where things are lurking in the AutoCAD 2013 Ribbon, remember that the standard Windows keyboard shortcuts — Ctrl+X (cut), Ctrl+C (copy), and Ctrl+V (paste) — are still available and are often the most efficient way of using the Windows Clipboard — even *after* you've found the Clipboard panel!

Table 11-2 summarizes AutoCAD's most important Clipboard-related commands, along with the equivalent choices on the right-click menu and Ribbon's Clipboard panel. (The Classic Standard toolbar buttons' tooltips display the same names.)

Table 11-2	AutoCAD Clipboard Commands		
Command Name	*Right-Click Menu*	*Clipboard Panel*	*Classic Standard Toolbar*
CUTCLIP (Ctrl+X)	Cut	Cut	Cut
COPYCLIP (Ctrl+C)	Copy	Copy Clip	Copy
COPYBASE (Ctrl+Shift+C)	Copy with Base Point	Not available	Not available
COPYLINK	Not available	Not available	Not available
PASTECLIP (Ctrl+V)	Paste	Paste	Paste
PASTEBLOCK (Ctrl+Shift+V)	Paste as Block	Paste as Block (on Paste flyout)	Not available
PASTEAS HYPERLINK	Not available	Paste as Hyperlink (on Paste flyout)	Not available
PASTEORIG	Paste to Original Coordinates	Paste to Original Coordinates (on Paste flyout)	Not available
PASTESPEC	Not available	Paste Special (on Paste flyout)	Not available

Stretch

The STRETCH command is superficially similar to COPY and MOVE; it has the same interesting base point and displacement prompts, and it shifts objects to other locations in the drawing. But it also has one big important difference: It can move one end of one or more objects, leaving the other end or ends where they are so you can use it to change the length of lines, for example. Here are the things you need to know to make STRETCH your friend:

✏ **Selecting objects to stretch:** To use STRETCH to change the length of objects, you *must* select objects by using a *crossing* selection box (or crossing polygon), as described in Chapter 10. See Figure 11-3 for a visual explanation.

Figure 11-3: Use a crossing selection box to select objects for stretching.

✏ **Defining points:** STRETCH operates on the defining points of objects — endpoints of a line, vertices of a polyline, the center of a circle, and so on — according to the following rule: If a defining point is within the crossing selection box that you specify, AutoCAD moves the defining point and updates the object accordingly.

For example, if your crossing selection box surrounds one endpoint of a line but not the other endpoint, STRETCH moves the selected endpoint and redraws the line in the new position dictated by the selected end-point's new location. It's as though you have a rubber band tacked to the wall with two pins, and you move one of the pins.

✏ **Compressing and stretching:** STRETCH can make lines longer or shorter, depending on your crossing selection box and displacement vector. In other words, the STRETCH command really combines stretching and compressing.

✔ **Getting in the mode:** Depending on what you're trying to accomplish, you may want to turn on Ortho or Polar Tracking mode before stretching. Figure 11-4 shows the results of an Ortho and a non-Ortho stretch.

Figure 11-4: The hazards of stretching without ortho or polar tracking turned on.

The following steps describe how to stretch lines:

1. **Draw some lines in an arrangement similar to the dark lines shown in Figure 11-5.**

 Start your stretching with simple objects. You can work up to more complicated objects — polylines, arcs, and so on — after you've limbered up with lines.

2. **Press Esc to make sure that no command is active and no objects are selected.**

3. **Click the Stretch button on the Modify panel of the Ribbon's Home tab.**

 The command line displays the Select objects prompt with a warning to use the Crossing or CPolygon object-selection mode:

   ```
   Select objects to stretch by crossing-window or crossing-
           polygon...
   Select objects:
   ```

4. **Pick points to specify a crossing selection box that encloses some, but not all, endpoints of the lines.**

 Figure 11-5 shows a sample crossing selection box that completely encloses the two vertical lines on the right side of the figure. This crossing selection box cuts through the four horizontal lines, enclosing only one endpoint of each.

Unselected lines don't move.

Selected lines being dragged to new location

Specify second point or <use first point as displacement>:

Crossing window
pick point 2

Crossing window
pick point 1

Figure 11-5: Dragging objects in the middle of the STRETCH command.

You specify a crossing selection box by picking a point, moving your mouse to the *left,* and picking a second point.

5. **Press Enter to end object selection.**

 AutoCAD displays the following prompt:

   ```
   Specify base point or [Displacement] <Displacement>:
   ```

6. **Specify a base point by object snapping to a point on an existing object or by typing absolute X,Y coordinates.**

 AutoCAD displays the following prompt:

   ```
   Specify second point or <use first point as
           displacement>:
   ```

Toggle Ortho mode on and then off by clicking the Ortho Mode button on the status bar; try moving the crosshairs around first with Ortho on and then with it off to see the difference.

Figure 11-5 shows what the screen looks like as you move the crosshairs around without benefit of ortho or polar tracking.

7. **Toggle Ortho mode on (if it isn't already), and then specify the second point — usually by using direct distance entry.**

 You can also specify the second point by object snapping to a point on an existing object or by typing relative X,Y coordinates.

After you pick the second point, AutoCAD stretches the objects. Notice that the STRETCH command *moved* the two vertical lines because the crossing selection box contained both endpoints of both lines. STRETCH lengthened or shortened the four horizontal lines because the crossing selection box enclosed only one endpoint of each.

The STRETCH command takes some practice, but it's worth the effort. Draw some additional kinds of objects and practice stretching with different crossing selection box locations as well as different base points and second points.

The STRETCH command prompt says `Select objects to stretch by crossing-window or crossing-polygon`, but picking points as in Step 4 doesn't give you the crossing-polygon option. (See Chapter 10 if you need a refresher on crossing-polygon selection.) To use a polygonal crossing selection, type **CP** at the `Select objects` prompt and press Enter.

You can use more than one crossing window within a single run of the STRETCH command, and you can select objects that are outside a crossing window to have them move when other objects that cross the selection window(s) are stretched. The only objects that change size are stretchable objects that are *crossed* by a crossing window or polygon.

More Manipulations

The commands in this section — MIRROR, ROTATE, SCALE, ARRAY, and OFFSET — provide other ways (in addition to MOVE, COPY, and STRETCH) of manipulating objects or creating new versions of them. The procedures for each command assume that you're familiar with the object selection and editing precision techniques presented in the MOVE, COPY, and STRETCH procedures (see Chapter 10 and the previous sections in this chapter).

Mirror

The MIRROR command creates a reverse copy of one or more objects. After you select your objects, AutoCAD prompts you to select two points that define a line about which the objects will be mirrored. You then have the option to retain or delete the source objects. Follow these steps to use the MIRROR command:

1. **Press Esc to make sure that no command is active and no objects are selected.**

2. **Click the Mirror button on the Home tab's Modify panel.**

3. **Select one or more objects, and then press Enter to end object selection.**

AutoCAD prompts you to define the mirror line by picking points:

```
Specify first point of mirror line:
```

4. **Specify the start of the mirror line by clicking a point or typing coordinates.**

 AutoCAD prompts

```
Specify second point of mirror line:
```

5. **Pick a second point.**

 Most of the time, you'll want to have Polar Tracking or Ortho mode enabled so you can mirror your objects precisely. You can also use object snaps on existing objects, including ones being mirrored. The latter case is used when you want to ensure exact symmetry between the source and the mirrored objects. The mirrored copies temporarily disappear, and AutoCAD prompts

```
Erase source objects? [Yes/No] <N>:
```

 If you type **Y** at the final prompt, the source objects disappear, and you're left with the new mirrored copy. Accept the default No option if you want to retain the source objects along with the mirrored copies.

Normally when you mirror text or dimensions, the words come out backward. The system variable MIRRTEXT can handle that little problem. By default, MIRRTEXT is turned off (that is, its value is 0) so the text itself still reads the right way around after the objects are mirrored. If you really want your drawing text to be backward, change the value of MIRRTEXT to 1. (We cover system variables in a little more detail in Chapter 26.)

Rotate

The ROTATE command pivots one or more objects around a point that you specify. Follow these steps to use the ROTATE command:

1. **Press Esc to make sure that no command is active and no objects are selected.**

2. **Click the Rotate button on the Home tab's Modify panel.**

3. **Select one or more objects and then press Enter to end object selection.**

 AutoCAD prompts you for the base point for rotating the selected objects:

```
Specify base point:
```

4. **Specify a base point by clicking a point or typing coordinates.**

The base point becomes the point around which AutoCAD rotates the objects. You also have to specify a rotation angle:

```
Specify rotation angle or [Copy/Reference] <0>:
```

5. **Specify a rotation angle by typing an angle measurement and pressing Enter, or just press Enter to accept the default value shown in angle brackets.**

 Alternatively, you can indicate an angle on the screen by moving the crosshairs until the Coordinates section of the status bar indicates the desired angle and then clicking. If you choose this alternative, you will need to use Ortho mode or Polar Tracking to indicate a precise angle (for example, 90 or 45 degrees) or an object snap to rotate an object so it aligns precisely with other objects.

 Positive angle values rotate things counter-clockwise (counter to what you might expect) and negative values go clockwise. For example, entering 270 degrees or -90 degrees produces the same result.

 After you specify the rotation angle by typing or picking, AutoCAD rotates the objects into their new position. The ROTATE command's Copy option makes a rotated copy while leaving the source object in place.

Scale

If you read all our harping about drawing scales and scale factors in Chapter 4, you may think that the SCALE command performs some magical scale transformation on your entire drawing. No such luck. It also has nothing to do with ladders or fish. It merely uniformly *scales* (enlarges or reduces) one or more objects up or down by a factor that you specify. Here's how it works:

1. **Press Esc to make sure that no command is active and no objects are selected.**

2. **Click the Scale button on the Home tab's Modify panel.**

3. **Select one or more objects and then press Enter to end object selection.**

 AutoCAD prompts you for the base point around which it will scale all the selected objects:

```
Specify base point:
```

4. **Specify a base point by picking a point or typing coordinates.**

 The base point becomes the point around which the objects are scaled. AutoCAD prompts you for the scale factor:

```
Specify scale factor or [Copy/Reference] <1.0000>:
```

Don't assume that AutoCAD will scale the objects but leave them more or less where they are in the drawing. AutoCAD scales the distance *between* objects as well as the objects themselves. For example, if you select a circle to scale, pick a point outside the circle as the base point and then specify a scale factor of 2. AutoCAD not only makes the circle twice as big, but also moves the circle twice as far away from the base point that you specified. If you want to make a circle bigger but leave it where it's currently located, make sure that you use the CEN object snap to select its center point as the base point for the scale operation.

5. **Type a scale factor and press Enter.**

 AutoCAD scales the objects by the factor that you type, using the base point that you specified. Numbers greater than 1 increase the objects' sizes. Numbers smaller than 1 but greater than zero decrease the objects' sizes. Negative scale factors are invalid.

Just like the ROTATE command, SCALE also has a copy option with which you can make enlarged or reduced duplicates of selected objects — without altering the source objects. And both SCALE and ROTATE remember the last scale factor or rotation angle entered throughout the drawing session.

Array

The ARRAY command is like a supercharged COPY: You use it to create a rectangular grid of objects at regular X and Y spacings or a radial arrangement of objects around a center point at a regular angular spacing. For example, you can use rectangular arrays to populate an auditorium with chairs or a polar array to populate a bicycle wheel with spokes.

The kind of array we describe in this chapter is the old-style — but still very useful — non-associative array. (we cover the new-style array in Chapter 18). Non-associative arrays are simply copies of the source object; they dwell on the same layers as their source, and they can be edited individually, even in older releases of AutoCAD.

The following steps describe how to create a rectangular array, which you'll probably do more often than creating a polar array:

1. **Press Esc to make sure that no command is active and no objects are selected.**

2. **Type -ARRAY (don't forget the hyphen) and press Enter.**

 Typing a hyphen in front of an AutoCAD command normally tells the program to run at the command line rather than in a dialog box. Starting with AutoCAD 2012, typing **ARRAY** runs the associative array tool, whereas typing **-ARRAY** runs the non-associative version.

First, AutoCAD prompts you to select the objects you want to array.

3. **Select one or more objects; then press Enter.**

Next, AutoCAD prompts you to choose the type of array you want:

```
Enter the type of array [Rectangular/Polar] <R>:
```

4. **Type R and press Enter to create a rectangular array.**

Next, you specify the number of rows and columns you want, and the distance between each of them. AutoCAD prompts:

```
Enter the number of rows (---) <1>:
```

5. **Enter a value and press Enter.**

AutoCAD next asks the number of columns, the distance between rows, and finally the distance between columns.

The Rows and Columns numbers include the row and column of the original objects themselves. In other words, entries of 1 don't create any new objects in that direction.

6. **Enter values for the number of columns, and the distances between adjacent rows and columns, and then press Enter.**

AutoCAD creates regularly spaced copies of the selected objects in neat rows and columns.

To create regularly arrayed objects in rows and columns or arranged around a center point, you must use the command-line version of ARRAY by typing a hyphen in front of the command name. Typing ARRAY without the hyphen creates new-style associative array objects. Associative arrays, covered in Chapter 18, are more powerful and versatile, but non-associative ones may still be adequate for many applications.

Offset

You use OFFSET to create parallel or concentric copies of lines, polylines, circles, arcs, or splines. Follow these steps to use OFFSET:

1. **Click the Offset button on the Home tab's Modify panel.**

AutoCAD displays the current command settings and prompts you for the *offset distance* — the distance from the original object to the copy you're creating:

```
Current settings: Erase source=No Layer=Source
        OFFSETGAPTYPE=0
Specify offset distance or [Through/Erase/Layer]
        <Through>:
```

2. **Type an offset distance and press Enter.**

 Alternatively, you can indicate an offset distance by picking two points on the screen. If you choose this method, you should normally use object snaps to specify a precise distance from one existing object to another.

 AutoCAD prompts you to select the object from which you want to create an offset copy:

   ```
   Select object to offset or [Exit/Undo] <Exit>:
   ```

3. **Select a single object, such as a line, a polyline, or an arc.**

 Note that you can select only one object at a time with the OFFSET command. AutoCAD asks where you want the offset object:

   ```
   Specify point on side to offset or [Exit/Multiple/
           Undo] <Exit>:
   ```

4. **Point to one side or the other of the object and then click.**

 It doesn't matter how far away from the object the crosshairs are when you click. You're simply indicating a direction.

 AutoCAD repeats the `Select object` prompt, in case you want to offset other objects by the same distance:

   ```
   Select object to offset or [Exit/Undo] <Exit>:
   ```

5. **Go back to Step 3 if you want to offset another object or press Enter if you're finished offsetting objects for now.**

Figure 11-6 shows the OFFSET command in progress. For information on the command options — and Multiple, Erase, and Layer are all useful options — look up **OFFSET** in the online help's Command Reference section.

Object to offset

Point on side of offset

Figure 11-6: Offsetting a polyline.

If you want to offset a series of connected lines (for example, a rectangular house plan outline or one side of a pathway on a map), make sure that you either draw it as a polyline or convert the individual line and/or arc segments into a polyline with the JOIN command. (We cover JOIN later in this chapter.) If you draw a series of line segments with the LINE command and then try to offset it, you have to pick each segment and offset it individually. Even worse, the corners usually aren't finished off in the way that you'd expect because AutoCAD doesn't treat the segments as connected. You avoid all these problems by offsetting a polyline, which AutoCAD does treat as a single object. Figure 11-6 shows an offset polyline. See Chapter 8 for more information about the differences between lines and polylines.

Slicing, Dicing, and Splicing

The commands in this section — TRIM, EXTEND, BREAK, FILLET, CHAMFER, BLEND, and JOIN — are useful for shortening and lengthening objects, for breaking them in two, and for putting them back together again.

Trim and Extend

TRIM and EXTEND are the twin commands for making lines, polylines, and arcs shorter and longer. They're the yin and yang, the Laurel and Hardy, the Jack Sprat and his wife of the AutoCAD editing world. The two commands and their prompts are almost identical, so the following steps cover both. We show the prompts for the TRIM command; the EXTEND prompts are similar.

1. Click the Trim or Extend button on the Home tab's Modify panel.

AutoCAD prompts you to select cutting edges that will do the trimming (or, if you choose the EXTEND command, boundary edges for extending to):

```
Current settings: Projection=UCS, Edge=None
Select cutting edges ...
Select objects or <select all>:
```

2. Press Enter to accept the default option to select all drawing objects, or select individual objects by picking them. Press Enter to end object selection.

The objects you select in this step become the cutting edge of the TRIM command or the boundary to which objects will be extended by the EXTEND command.

Figure 11-7 shows a cutting edge (for TRIM) and a boundary edge (for EXTEND).

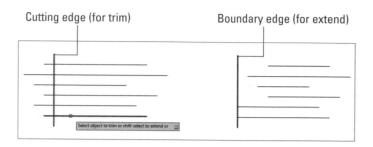

Cutting edge (for trim) Boundary edge (for extend)

Select object to trim or shift-select to extend or

Figure 11-7: Anatomy of the TRIM and EXTEND operations.

AutoCAD prompts you to select objects that you want to trim or extend (EXTEND doesn't have the eRase option):

```
Select object to trim or shift-select to extend or
          [Fence/Crossing/Project/Edge/eRase/Undo]:
```

3. **Select a single object to trim or extend. Choose the portion of the object that you want AutoCAD to trim away or the end of the object that's closer to the extend-to boundary.**

 AutoCAD trims or extends the object to one of the objects that you selected in Step 2. If AutoCAD can't trim or extend the object — for example, if the trimming object and the object to be trimmed are parallel — the command line displays an error message such as `Object does not intersect an edge`.

 You can select multiple objects to trim and extend by typing **F** and pressing Enter to use the Fence object selection mode or by entering **C** to use Crossing selection. Even better, you can use implied windowing and drag a selection box to select multiple objects. Refer to Chapter 10 for more on multiple object selection.

 The command line continues to prompt you to select other objects to trim or extend:

```
Select object to trim or shift-select to extend or
          [Fence/Crossing/Project/Edge/eRase/Undo]:
```

4. **Choose additional objects or press Enter when you're finished trimming or extending.**

 Here's a triple-threat tip: If you accidentally trim or extend the wrong object and you're still in the TRIM or EXTEND command, type **U** and press Enter to undo the most recent trim or extend. You can switch between TRIM and EXTEND without exiting the command by holding down the Shift key. And finally, if you find yourself with a remnant that won't trim because it doesn't cross the cutting edge, type **R** (for eRase) and press Enter to erase it without leaving the TRIM command.

The example in Figure 11-7 shows trimming to a single cutting edge, in which the end of each trimmed line gets lopped off. Another common use of the TRIM command is for trimming out a piece of a line between two cutting edges. In the two-cutting-edges scenario, TRIM cuts a piece out of the middle of the trimmed line. The default option for selecting cutting edges or boundaries is ALL, which works well in this scenario. Pressing Enter to accept the default option selects all objects in the drawing as a cutting edge if you're in the TRIM command, or a boundary if you're in the EXTEND command.

An object being trimmed or extended can also be a cutting edge or extending boundary and vice versa, all in the same run of the command.

The LENGTHEN (LEN) command provides other useful ways to make lines, arcs, and polylines longer (or shorter). You can specify an absolute distance (or *delta*) to lengthen or shorten by, a percentage to lengthen or shorten by, or a new total length. Look up the LENGTHEN command in AutoCAD's help system for more information.

LENGTHEN is an option on the grip pop-up menus on lines and arcs. To display the menu, just hover your mouse pointer over an endpoint grip on either of those object types or over one of the new triangular grips on an elliptical arc and click Lengthen.

Break

The BREAK command isn't what you use before heading out for coffee. (AutoCAD doesn't have a command for that yet, but we keep hoping.) It's for creating gaps in lines, polylines, circles, arcs, or splines. BREAK also comes in handy if you need to split one object into two without actually removing any visible material.

The following example shows how you BREAK an object (don't worry — in AutoCAD, you won't have to pay for it):

1. **On the Ribbon's Home tab, click the label of the Modify panel to open its slideout and then click the Break button.**

 AutoCAD prompts you to select a single object that you want to break.

2. **Select a single object, such as a line, a polyline, or an arc.**

The point you pick when selecting the object serves double duty: It selects the object, of course, but it also becomes the *default first break point* (that is, it defines one side of the gap that you'll create). Thus, you should either use one of the AutoCAD precision techniques, such as an object snap, to pick the object at a precise point or use the First point option (described in the next step) to repick the first break point.

AutoCAD prompts you to specify the second break point or to type **F** and press Enter if you want to respecify the first break point:

```
Specify second break point or [First point]:
```

3. **If the point that you picked in the preceding step doesn't also correspond to a break point (see the preceding Tip), type F and press Enter to respecify the first break point. Then pick the point with an object snap or other precision technique.**

 If you do type **F** and press Enter and then respecify the first break point, AutoCAD prompts you to select the second break point:

```
Specify second break point:
```

4. **Specify the second break point by picking a point or typing coordinates.**

 AutoCAD cuts a section out of the object, using the first and second break points to define the length of the gap.

If you want to cut an object into two pieces without removing anything, click the Break at Point button on the Modify panel's slideout. You first select the object and then choose a point that defines where AutoCAD breaks the object in two. You can then move, copy, or otherwise manipulate each section of the original object as a separate object.

As indicated near the bottom of Table 11-1, AutoCAD has an EXPLODE command. As with all things explosive, approach this command with caution. EXPLODE breaks up complex objects into AutoCAD primitive objects. For example, a multisegment polyline explodes into separate line and arc objects. Most of the time, those complex objects are created that way for a reason. The things you can explode (but shouldn't unless you have a really, *really* good reason) include polylines, blocks, 3D solids, associative arrays, tables, and multiline text. And even though AutoCAD will let you, you should never, *ever* explode dimensions or leaders.

Fillet and Chamfer and Blend

Whereas TRIM, EXTEND, and BREAK alter one object at a time, the FILLET and CHAMFER commands modify a pair of objects. As Figure 11-8 shows, FILLET creates a curved corner between two lines, whereas CHAMFER creates a beveled corner. (In case you wondered, it's pronounced *FILL-et,* not *fill-AY.* Saying that you know how to *fill-AY* may get you a job in a butcher shop, but it will get you strange looks in a design office.)

FILLET and CHAMFER show a preview of the results of the operation as soon as you select the objects to modify. If the fillet radius or the chamfer distances don't look right in the preview, you can change their values before completing the command.

Original lines Filleted lines Chamfered lines Lines filleted with zero radius

Figure 11-8: Cleaning up those corners with FILLET and CHAMFER.

The following steps describe how to use the FILLET command. The CHAMFER command works similarly except that, instead of specifying a fillet radius, you specify either two chamfer distances or a chamfer length and angle.

1. **Click the Fillet button on the Home tab's Modify panel.**

 FILLET and CHAMFER share a flyout button; If you see a straight-line corner instead of a rounded one, click the flyout arrow to select FILLET.

 AutoCAD displays the current fillet settings and prompts you to select the first object for filleting or specify one of three options:

   ```
   Current settings: Mode = TRIM, Radius = 0.0000
   Select first object or [Undo/Polyline/Radius/Trim/
         Multiple]:
   ```

2. **Type R and press Enter to set the fillet radius.**

 AutoCAD prompts you to specify the fillet radius that it uses for future fillet operations:

   ```
   Specify fillet radius <0.0000>:
   ```

3. **Type a fillet radius and press Enter.**

 The number you type will be the radius of the arc that joins the two lines.

 AutoCAD then asks you to select the first object:

   ```
   Select first object or [Undo/Polyline/Radius/Trim/
         Multiple]:
   ```

4. **Select the first line of the pair that you want to fillet.**

 AutoCAD prompts you to select the second object for filleting:

   ```
   Select second object or shift-select to apply corner
         or [Radius]:
   ```

5. **Select the second line of the pair that you want to fillet.**

 AutoCAD fillets the two objects, drawing an arc of the radius that you specified in Step 3.

FILLET has more tricks up its sleeve. You can fillet two lines and specify a radius of zero to make them meet at a point. If you have lots of lines to fillet, whether with a zero or the same nonzero radius, use the FILLET command's Multiple option to speed the process. If you start FILLET and select two parallel lines, you get a nice 180-degree arc joining them. You can add fillets to arcs and splines. And you can fillet all the vertices on a polyline at one time by choosing the Polyline option before you select the object.

Holding down the Shift key before picking the second line automatically gives you a clean intersection, the same as if you'd set the fillet radius to 0. The CHAMFER command has the same Shift-select option.

The BLEND command joins CHAMFER and FILLET, offering yet another method for creating transitions between 2D drawing objects. Where CHAMFER creates beveled corners (that is, straight lines), and FILLET creates round corners (circular arcs), BLEND's corners are spline objects. Figure 11-9 shows the two types of available blend; the feature is connecting the green lines. Choosing the Tangent option produced the red spline, and choosing the Smooth option produced the blue spline. Unlike CHAMFER and FILLET — both of which would modify the source objects in order to make a radiused or beveled transition, BLEND leaves the source objects intact. Blends are going to appeal to industrial designers and other purveyors of swoopy shapes. If you're a mechanical drafter, it's usually best to stick with fillets and chamfers.

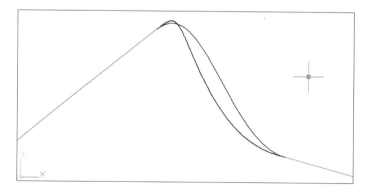

Figure 11-9: Blending smoothly (or tangentially).

Join

Use the JOIN command to fill gaps in lines, arcs, elliptical arcs, splines, and polylines. If the lines are *collinear* (that is, they lie in the same straight line), or the arcs, splines, polylines, or elliptical arcs are on a similarly curved path, JOIN will create a single new entity to replace the existing separate pieces, as shown in Figure 11-10.

Objects to be joined must be collinear or their ends must be coincident. You can't JOIN noncollinear objects that have gaps between them or that cross or overlap.

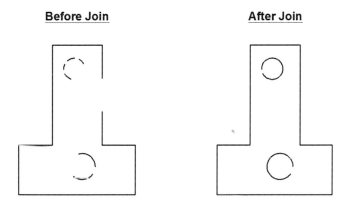

Figure 11-10: Joining sundered pieces.

The following steps describe how to use the JOIN command:

1. **Click the Modify panel title at the bottom edge of the Ribbon's Home tab to open the Modify panel's slideout, and then click the Join button.**

 If you foresee doing a lot of joinery, you can pin the slideout open, as shown in Figure 11-10. AutoCAD prompts you to select the source object.

2. **Select the *source object* — that is, the object you want to join other objects to.**

 AutoCAD prompts according to the object type selected. If you select a line, the command prompt or Dynamic Input tooltip shows

   ```
   Select source object or multiple objects to join at
            once:
   ```

3. **Select valid objects to join to the original source object.**

 For example, if you selected a line as your source object, AutoCAD continues prompting for additional adjoining lines until you press Enter to end object selection.

4. **Press Enter to end the command.**

 AutoCAD joins the selected objects into a single object. The new object will inherit relevant properties such as the layer or linetype of the source object.

Polishing those properties

When you think of editing objects, you probably think first about editing their *geometry:* moving, stretching, making new copies, and so on. That's the kind of editing we cover in this chapter.

Another kind of editing is changing objects' *properties.* As we describe in Chapter 6, every object in an AutoCAD drawing has a set of nongeometrical properties, including layer, color, linetype, lineweight, transparency, and maybe plot style. Sometimes you need to edit those properties — when you accidentally draw something on the wrong layer, for example. Here's a handful of ways of editing an object's properties in AutoCAD:

✓ **The Properties palette:** This is the most flexible way to edit properties. Select any object (or objects), right-click in the drawing area, and choose Properties from the menu. The Properties palette displays the names and values of all properties. Click in the appropriate value cell to change a particular property.

✓ **The Quick Properties palette:** If Quick Properties is enabled by clicking its status bar button, a palette pops up near the crosshairs when you select an object. Like the Properties palette, the Quick Properties palette contains value cells that you can click to change the specific property. You can choose how many lines of information you want Quick Properties to display by right-clicking the Quick Properties status bar button and choosing Settings.

✓ **Layers and Properties control lists:** Another way to change properties is to select objects and then choose from the drop-down lists (Layer, Color, and so on) on the Properties palette. It's fine to change layers this way, but don't be slapdash about changing the other properties — see Chapter 6 for more information.

✓ **Match Properties:** You can use Match Properties to copy the properties from a source object to one or more other objects. You can find the Match Properties button on the Clipboard panel of the Ribbon's Home tab. Match Properties works similarly to the Format Painter button in Microsoft applications. Match Properties works even when the objects reside in different drawings.

 As discussed in Chapter 6, it's almost never correct to set the color, linetype, or lineweight to be anything other than ByLayer. To do so invites chaos.

✓ **Change Space:** We introduce the concepts of model space and paper space in Chapters 4 and 5. Sometimes you add some geometry to paper space and then realize it should have been in model space, or vice versa. The CHSPACE command can come to the rescue — you'll find it on the Modify panel slideout on the Ribbon's Home tab. For more information, look up CHSPACE in the Command Reference of the online help.

 You aren't limited to selecting a single object at the first prompt. If you select multiple objects by using windowing, JOIN will join whatever objects it can and reject those that it can't.

You can turn an arc into a circle or an elliptical arc into a full ellipse with JOIN's cLose option.

The REVERSE command provides an easy way of reversing the direction of lines and polylines. Why does that matter? Well, most of the time it doesn't, but if you happen to be using a complex linetype that uses text or a directional arrow block, you probably want the text to read right-way-up and the arrow to point in the right direction. Lines, polylines, and other entity types have start points and endpoints, and therefore, a direction that runs from the former to the latter. Instead of redrawing your linework so your text or symbols appear the right way up, use the REVERSE command to flip the start and endpoints.

The new system variable PLINEREVERSEWIDTHS controls how REVERSE handles polylines with varying widths. When set to the default of 0 (zero), REVERSE reverses the start and end sequence but doesn't affect the width. When set to 1, the start and end widths of segments are also reversed.

The Delete Duplicate Objects tool (also known as the OVERKILL command) looks for fully or partially overlapping objects, and either combines or deletes them. It's covered in Chapter 10.

When Editing Goes Bad

Analysis of AutoCAD users' actions suggests that one of the most commonly used commands is Undo. It comes in several forms and depth of action, which we now reveal. If you are the impatient type, you can jump ahead to the last two items because they'll probably account for the majority of your undo actions.

- ✔ **OOPS:** As we discuss in Chapter 10, the OOPS command unerases the last set of erased objects, even if other editing or drawing actions have taken place in between. You need to type this command in because there aren't menu or Ribbon picks for it.

- ✔ **UNDO:** This command is quite versatile and powerful, as controlled by several options. Among other things, you can have it undo a specified number of actions, or you can have it drop a marker flag, or you can have it undo back as far as the marker flag. See the help facility for more information. You need to type this command in because the only menu pick (to be discussed in a moment) undoes only one step and doesn't prompt for the other options.

- ✔ **U:** This command is available in two forms. When typed in as a command, it undoes the last thing you did, and you can use it repeatedly to step back through the current editing session. You can also enter it as a prompt during a number of other commands, such as LINE, PLINE, and COPY. In this case, it undoes the last line or polyline segment, or the last objects to be copied — but then the parent command resumes, and you can continue drawing or placing copies.

- **REDO:** This command reverses the last U or UNDO operation and must immediately follow one of them.

- **DOO-DOO:** (Or words to that effect.) This isn't a command, but instead is what you say when you Undo too many steps and then learn to your horror that REDO can only redo one undo step.

- **MREDO:** This command reverses multiple undos, and pretty much eliminates the need for DOO-DOO. It has several advanced options.

- **BAK:** This isn't a command; it's a file type. Whenever you save your work in process, AutoCAD creates a file with the extension .bak that contains how your drawing looked immediately after the previous save. You can go back to this version simply by using Windows Explorer to rename the BAK file to one with the .dwg extension.

- **SV$:** This isn't a command; it's a file type. As you work, AutoCAD automatically saves a copy of your drawing every ten minutes and gives it the .sv$ file extension. You can go back to this version simply by using Windows Explorer to rename the SV$ file to one with the .dwg extension. You'll find your SY$ files in the *c:\Users\<login name>\appdata\local\temp* folder, but you can use the Files tab of the OPTIONS command to have them go to any location you like.

- **Undo button:** The Quick Select menu includes an Undo button, just like many Windows applications. It invokes the UNDO 1 command and option.

- **Redo button:** The Quick Select menu includes a Redo button, just like many Windows applications. It invokes the REDO 1 command and option.

Don't you just wish that the real world had Undo and Redo buttons?

12

A Zoom with a View

In This Chapter

▶ Zooming and panning

▶ Naming and restoring views

▶ Zooming and panning in paper space layouts

▶ Regenerating the display

*O*ne of AutoCAD's advantages over manual drawing is its ability to show you different views of your drawing. You can zoom in close, zoom out to a great distance, and pan around. In fact, not only *can* you zoom and pan in your drawing, but in most kinds of drawings, you *must* also do it frequently to be able to draw and edit effectively.

Technical drawings are jam-packed with lines, text, and dimensions. Zooming and panning frequently enables you to see the details better, draw more confidently (because you can see what you're doing), and edit more quickly (because object selection is easier when there aren't a zillion objects on the screen). This chapter covers AutoCAD's most useful display control features.

Zoom and Pan with Glass and Hand

Moving your viewpoint in to get a closer view of your drawing data is called *zooming in;* moving your viewpoint back to get a more expansive view is called *zooming out.* Moving your viewpoint to another part of your drawing without zooming in or out is called *panning.*

Changing your viewing position lets you do detailed work on tiny objects and then zoom out and move around rooms, houses, or neighborhoods from an Olympian perspective. Early versions of AutoCAD included a sample drawing

of our solar system, drawn to scale with kilometers as units, which proved this. If you zoomed all the way out, you could see Pluto's orbit (yes, kids, Pluto *was* a planet back then), and you could zoom in close enough to Earth's moon to read the inscription on the plaque left by the Apollo 11 astronauts!

In fact, AutoCAD's zoom range is far more impressive than this. AutoCAD can draw a circle with a radius of 10^{98} units, but the radius of the known (so far) universe is "only" about 8.2×10^{21} miles. At the other end of the range, it can draw a circle with a radius of 10^{-98} units, versus the Lorentz or "standard" radius of an electron of about 1.1×10^{-12} inches.

Panning means changing your viewing position without changing the magnification of the view. If you zoom in enough that some of your drawing no longer shows up onscreen, you're going to want to *pan* around — move left, right, up, and down in your drawing — without zooming in and out. AutoCAD makes panning easy with scroll bars and realtime panning. And in case you're wondering what *realtime panning* might be (as opposed to pretendtime panning, maybe?), it simply means you can see the objects moving around the screen as you drag the mouse up and down or back and forth. (Of course, it's your viewpoint that's moving, not the objects!)

Both panning and zooming change the *view* — the current location and magnification of the AutoCAD depiction of your drawing. Each time you zoom or pan, you establish a new view. You can give a name to a specific view to make returning to that view easy, as we demonstrate in the section "A View by Any Other Name . . . ," later in this chapter.

You'll get a better sense of panning and zooming around a drawing if you actually have a drawing to look at. Draw some objects on the screen, open one of your own existing drawings, or launch one of AutoCAD's sample drawings. (If you haven't done so already, you can download the sample files from `www.autodesk.com/autocad-samples`; the AutoCAD LT sample files are also online at `www.autodesk.com/autocadlt-samples`.)

The wheel deal

Later in this chapter, we cover AutoCAD's various commands and options for panning and zooming in more detail. On the other hand, if you have a wheel mouse, you'll rarely need to use other methods, especially when working in 2D drawings. If you don't have a wheel mouse, you should run out and buy one because the slight cost will be more than offset by your increased productivity. The following three actions will usually suffice for almost all your panning and zooming needs.

- **To zoom in and out:** Roll the scroll wheel forward and backward.

- **To pan:** Many people don't know that the scroll wheel is also a button. To pan, hold down the scroll wheel as you move the mouse.

> ✏ **To zoom to the extents of your drawing:** Double-click the scroll wheel. This is particularly useful when you don't heed the warnings in Chapter 11 about when to press Enter during a Move or Copy.

Navigating your drawing

You may think that AutoCAD is all about drawing, and maybe, occasionally, even about erasing. In that case, it may surprise you to learn that two of the most frequently used commands in all of AutoCAD are PAN and ZOOM. These commands and a few others can be found on an interface component called the *Navigation bar*.

The Navigation bar is linked by default to another interface component named the ViewCube. (AutoCAD LT users get the Navigation bar, but not the ViewCube.) Figure 12-1 shows the upper-right corner of the AutoCAD window with the ViewCube and Navigation bar in their default locations.

— ViewCube

Navigation bar

— Pan
— Zoom split button

— Navigation bar menu

Figure 12-1: Belly up to the Navigation bar.

We fill you in on the ViewCube in Chapter 21, since it's a more useful tool in three dimensions than in two. We also cover the SteeringWheels and ShowMotion commands (the latter isn't present in AutoCAD LT) in Part V of this book.

Controlling your cube

Apart from the big chunk of screen space the ViewCube and Navigation bar occupy, the cube itself has some disconcerting behaviors. If you click the Home button, for example, you automatically switch to a preset 3D isometric view — not that helpful if you're doing a 2D drawing. Worse yet, any of the side views just show you the edge of your 2D drawing.

We think the cube-bar combo is worthwhile when you're doing 3D modeling, but more intrusive than useful for 2D drafting. Luckily, AutoCAD offers quite a bit of control over both the ViewCube and the Navigation bar. You can turn off the navigation buttons you don't use, and you can turn off the ViewCube itself, either for the drawing session or permanently.

- **To turn off navigation buttons:** Open the Navigation bar's menu by clicking the down arrow at its bottom-right corner (refer to Figure 12-1) and deselecting SteeringWheels, Orbit, and ShowMotion.

- **To turn off the ViewCube in the current viewport:** Go to the View tab's Windows panel, click User Interface, and deselect ViewCube. Reverse the procedure to turn it on again.

- **To turn off the ViewCube permanently:** Open the Options dialog box, and select the 3D Modeling tab. In the Display Tools in Viewport area, deselect 2D Wireframe Visual Style and All Other Visual Styles under Display the ViewCube.

In addition to the Navigation bar, the Navigate and Navigate 2D panels of the Ribbon's View tab contains a Pan button and a drop-down set of Zoom tool buttons (in our opinion, not a very convenient location for such frequently used commands!).

AutoCAD offers 11 different ways of zooming around in your drawing; a wheel mouse can fulfill most of your needs, but we explain the most important of the other methods in the next section. The following steps describe how to use AutoCAD's Zoom and Pan Realtime feature, which is easy to operate and provides a lot of flexibility:

1. **Click the lower part of the Zoom split button on the Navigation bar and choose Zoom Realtime from the menu.**

The Realtime option of the ZOOM command starts. The crosshairs change to a magnifying glass, and AutoCAD prompts you at the command line:

```
Specify corner of window, enter a scale factor (nX or nXP), or [All/Center/
         Dynamic/Extents/Previous/Scale/Window/Object] <real time>:
Press ESC or ENTER to exit, or right-click to display shortcut menu.
```

2. **Move the magnifying glass cursor near the middle of the screen, press and hold down the left mouse button, and drag the cursor up and down until the objects you want to see almost fill the screen.**

 Dragging up increases the zoom magnification, and dragging down decreases it.

3. **Right-click in the drawing area and choose Pan from the menu that appears (as shown in Figure 12-2).**

Figure 12-2: The Zoom/Pan Realtime right-click menu.

 The magnifying glass cursor changes to a hand.

 (Because AutoCAD LT doesn't do 3D, there's no 3D Orbit choice on LT's right-click menu.)

4. **Click and drag to pan the drawing in any direction.**

 You can use the right-click menu to toggle between Zoom and Pan as many times as you like. If you get lost in your drawing, choose Zoom Original or Zoom Extents to return to a more familiar view.

5. **Right-click in the drawing area and choose Exit.**

 The Zoom or Pan Realtime cursor returns to the normal AutoCAD crosshairs.

In the preceding example, you started with zooming and ended with panning. You also have the option of doing the reverse: Click the Pan button on the Navigation bar, and after you've panned, use the right-click menu to switch to zooming. However you start it, the important thing to realize is that Zoom and Pan Realtime is a single AutoCAD function. At any time, you can switch between panning and zooming (or switch to a related function, such as Zoom Window) by using the right-click menu.

The scroll wheel or middle mouse button zoom and pan operations described in the preceding list depend on an obscure AutoCAD system variable named MBUTTONPAN. When MBUTTONPAN is set to 1 — the default value — you can use the middle button to pan and zoom as we describe earlier. Unless your system has been customized by someone, if you change MBUTTONPAN to 0, clicking the middle mouse button displays an Object Snap menu at the crosshairs, as it did in older AutoCAD releases. If you can't zoom or pan with your middle mouse button, set MBUTTONPAN back to 1. (With MBUTTONPAN set to 1, you use Shift+right-click to display the Object Snap menu at the crosshairs.)

Zooming and panning by using the mouse wheel is the easiest, most interactive way to get around in your drawings. In some situations, though, this method is less efficient or precise than the old-fashioned methods, the most important of which we describe in the next section.

Another way to pan in AutoCAD should be familiar from other Windows programs — the scroll bars in the drawing area. Scrolling is the same in AutoCAD as in any other Windows program; click the arrows in the right and bottom scroll bars on the borders of the drawing window to scroll, or pan, a step at a time; or click and drag the little scroll boxes to pan as little or as much as you want to. To turn scroll bars off or on, choose Options in the Application Menu (or type **OPTIONS** or **OP**) to display the Options dialog box. On the Display tab, select or deselect the Display Scroll Bars in Drawing Window check box. Our own preference is not to use scroll bars and thus regain the screen space they occupy, so that's why you don't see them in most figures in this book.

Time to zoom

Realtime zooming is good as far as it goes, but you get much more control over the display if you use some of ZOOM's alternative methods. Because zooming is such a frequent activity in AutoCAD, it's worth knowing some of those alternative ways of doing it.

In addition to the Navigation bar button we describe earlier, you'll find tool buttons for all the ZOOM options on the View tab's Navigate 2D panel (this panel is called, simply, Navigate in AutoCAD's 3D Modeling workspace). The magnifying-glass button has a menu — click the down arrow beside the magnifying glass, and a menu with the other options opens (see Figure 12-3).

Figure 12-3: A menu for magnifying.

The ZOOM command has 11 different options, the most important of which are the following:

✔ **Extents and All:** Zoom Extents (the button with the four-headed arrow and the magnifying glass) zooms out just far enough to show all the objects in the current drawing. Zoom All (the button showing the sheet with the folded-over corner) does almost the same thing. It zooms to show the rectangular area defined by the limits, or it zooms to show the extents, whichever is larger. These two options are especially useful when you zoom in too close or pan off into empty space and want to see your entire drawing again.

It's a good idea to Zoom All or Zoom Extents and then save the drawing before you close it. By performing these steps, you ensure the following:

• The next person who opens the drawing — whether it's you or someone else — can see the full drawing as soon as they start working.

• If you've accidentally copied some objects way beyond where they should be, Zoom All or Extents will make them show up so you can delete them.

• The drawing preview that appears in the Select File dialog box displays the full drawing, instead of just a tiny, unidentifiable corner of it.

✔ **Window:** This option is great for zooming in quickly and precisely. It zooms to a section of your drawing that you specify by clicking two points. The two points define the diagonal of a window around the area you want to look at.

Note that the ZOOM command's Window option is not a click-and-drag operation — unlike in some other Windows programs and, confusingly, unlike in the Zoom/Pan Realtime Zoom Window option. With the ZOOM command's Window option, you click one corner, release the mouse button, and then click the other corner.

Entering the shortcuts Z A, Z E, and Z W (note the mandatory space between the letters) at the keyboard is usually faster than trying to find them in the various menus or toolbars.

✔ **Realtime:** Realtime zooming, the technique described previously, enables you to zoom in and out by starting a realtime zoom and then dragging the magnifying glass cursor up (to zoom in) or down (to zoom out).

✔ **Previous:** This option undoes the last zoom and/or pan sequence, taking you back to where you started. You can repeat this to step back through previous views, even if you do other object creation or editing in between.

✔ **Object:** This option zooms in close enough to show selected objects as large as they can be displayed onscreen. Using ZOOM Object is like putting the selected objects under AutoCAD's microscope.

AutoCAD provides *smooth view transitions* whenever you use the nonrealtime pan and zoom commands. Sometimes you can get lost if you do a ZOOM All from a small, highly magnified area. It's a bad idea to leave a trail of breadcrumbs across your screen, so these slow-motion pans and zooms may be fine, at least until you do know your way out of the forest . . . or your drawing. If, like us, you find that this feature gets old fast in 2D drawings, there's a View Transitions dialog box (type **VTOPTIONS** to open it) in which you can turn it off. Just deselect the Enable Animation for Pan & Zoom option. On the other hand, it can be most useful in 3D work.

Some of the zoom options take some getting used to. We recommend that you use the mouse wheel for most of your zooming and panning. Supplement it with Zoom Window to move quickly into a precise area, Zoom Previous to go back in zoom/pan time, and Zoom All or Zoom Extents to view your whole drawing.

If you're wondering about those other ZOOM command options — the ones we suggest are less important (Dynamic, Center, Scale, In, and Out), look up **ZOOM** in the online help's Command Reference section. Zoom Dynamic is an old, *old* command option that's been made redundant by the Realtime option. As for the remaining options, you can probably get to the view you want by deft movements with your wheel mouse (you *are* using a wheel mouse, aren't you?).

A View by Any Other Name . . .

If you find yourself repeatedly zooming and panning to the same area, you can probably get there faster with a named view. After you name and save a view of a particular area of your drawing, you can return to that area quickly by restoring the view. You use the VIEW command, which displays the View Manager dialog box, to create and restore named views.

The View Manager manages *shots* as well as views. Views have been a part of AutoCAD from very early days, but shots are a recent addition. While views are static, shots are motion based. (In regular AutoCAD, but not AutoCAD LT, you may have noticed the ShowMotion button on the Navigation bar.) And not only can you create animated scenes, you can even add fancy transitions like jump cuts and fades. We introduce you to shots (the nonpotable kind!) and the ShowMotion feature in Part V of this book.

Follow these steps to create a named view:

1. **Zoom and pan until you find the area of the drawing to which you want to assign a name.**

2. **On the Ribbon's View tab, choose View Manager from the Views panel.**

 The View Manager dialog box appears.

3. **Click New.**

 The New View/Shot Properties dialog box appears, as shown in Figure 12-4.

Figure 12-4: Save a view into your drawing.

4. **Type a name in the View Name text box.**

5. **(Optional) Type a new category in the View Category box or select an existing one from the drop-down list.**

 You create your own View Categories to organize views and certain display characteristics of views. This feature is used mainly in sheet sets. If you aren't using sheet sets, you can leave this box blank.

6. **Make sure that the View Type drop-down is set to Still.**

 Visit the online help if you want to know more about the Cinematic and Recorded Walk options.

 AutoCAD LT doesn't support view types. The New View dialog box in LT is missing the View Type list box, most of the Settings drop-downs, and the Background area shown in Figure 12-4.

7. **In the Boundary area, select the Current Display radio button, if it's not selected already.**

 If you want to save a different view boundary, select the Define Window radio button instead, click the Define View Window button to the right of it, and pick two corners of the region's boundary (as if you were zooming windows).

8. **Confirm or change the choices in the Settings area.**

 If you select the Save Layer Snapshot with View check box, when you later restore the view, AutoCAD also will restore the layer visibility

settings (On/Off and Freeze/Thaw) that were in effect when you created the view. (Chapter 6 describes the layer visibility settings.) The Live Section and Visual Style settings are primarily for 3D drawings; these two settings aren't included in AutoCAD LT.

9. **Click OK.**

 The New View/Shot Properties (New View in AutoCAD LT) dialog box disappears, and you see your new named view in the list in the View Manager dialog box.

10. **Click OK.**

 The View Manager dialog box disappears.

To restore a named view, proceed as follows:

1. **Go back to the Ribbon's View tab and choose View Manager from the View panel.**

 Alternatively, type **VIEW** (or **V**) and press Enter. The View Manager dialog box appears.

2. **In the Views list, expand either Model Views or Layout Views (depending on where you saved your view).**

3. **Click the name of the view that you want to restore, click the Set Current button, and then click OK to close the dialog box.**

You also can plot the area defined by a named view. See Chapter 16 for instructions on plotting views.

AutoCAD (but not AutoCAD LT) has an extremely handy set of model space viewport controls. There are three of these *in-canvas* controls at the top-left corner of the drawing area:

✔ **[-][+]:** Double-click [-] to toggle between a single model space viewport that fills the drawing area and (by default) four equally sized viewports configured for 3D viewing. Click once to display a menu with options to reconfigure the viewport layout, and to toggle the display of the ViewCube, SteeringWheels, and Navigation bar.

✔ **[View name]:** Click the current view name ([Top], for example) to open a menu listing all default and custom views in the drawing. Click a menu item to switch to a different view. You can also open the View Manager, and switch the view projection between parallel and perspective, which is normally only meaningful in 3D.

✔ **[Visual Style]:** Click the current visual style name ([2D Wireframe], for example) to open a menu listing all the visual styles defined in the drawing (visual styles are most useful in 3D modeling, and we discuss them in Chapter 21). Click a menu item to switch to a different visual style, or to open the Visual Styles Manager palette.

In both AutoCAD and AutoCAD LT, you can set named views current without having to open the View Manager dialog box. Just go to the Views panel on the View tab and choose a named view to restore from the list.

Looking Around in Layout Land

All the zoom, pan, and view operations we describe in this chapter work in paper space layouts as well as in model space. (Chapters 4 and 5 describe the differences between model space and paper space and how to navigate between the two.) One little complication exists, though: In a *paper space layout* — that is, any drawing area tab except for the Model tab — it's possible for the crosshairs to be in either paper space or in model space inside a viewport. Zooming and panning produce different effects depending on which space your crosshairs are in at the moment. You switch between the two spaces, using the MSPACE (MS) and PSPACE (PS) commands.

Experiment with the different effects by following these steps:

1. **Open a drawing that contains at least one paper space layout with a title block and one or more viewports.**

 If you don't have any such drawings handy, try using one of the AutoCAD sample drawings that you can download from www.autodesk.com/autocad-samples. For example, have a look at architectural_-_annotation_scaling_and_multileaders.dwg.

2. **Click Quick View Layouts on the status bar and then click one of the layout preview images — that is, any image other than the Model preview image.**

 AutoCAD displays the paper space layout, including any title block and viewports. Click somewhere away from an image to dismiss the Quick View image bar.

3. **Type PSPACE (or PS) and press Enter.**

 AutoCAD either switches to paper space or tells you that you're already there.

 Alternatively, you can double-click in the gray part of the drawing area or anywhere outside the viewport.

 You should see the triangular paper space UCS icon at the lower-left corner of the display. If you don't see an icon, click the View tab on the Ribbon and then click Show UCS Icon or Show UCS Icon at Origin on the Coordinates panel's Show UCS Icon drop-down menu.

Starting with AutoCAD 2012, the Coordinates panel was removed from the View tab in the Drafting & Annotation workspace. The good news is that you can put it back! To do so, with the View tab current, right-click anywhere in the Ribbon and choose Show Panels from the shortcut menu. Select Coordinates to permanently add this panel to the View tab.

Depending on your screen resolution, this might require other tabs to get narrower and some of their icons to move to their panel's drop list.

The crosshairs are now in paper space, so zooming and panning changes the appearance of all the objects in the layout, including the title block.

4. Type Z, press Enter, type A, and then press Enter.

AutoCAD displays the entire layout, as shown in Figure 12-5.

Figure 12-5: The full layout.

As an alternative to typing — or to navigating through Ribbon panels — here's an easier way to choose from a list of all available ZOOM options: Type **Z** and press Enter; then right-click in the drawing area to see the right-click menu, as shown in Figure 12-6.

5. Zoom and pan by using any of the techniques described in this chapter.

While you're in paper space, zooming and panning change the magnification of the whole drawing layout, as shown in Figure 12-7. The effect is similar to moving a plotted sheet in and out and all around in front of your face.

| Enter |
| Cancel |
| All |
| Center |
| Dynamic |
| Extents |
| Previous |
| Scale |
| Window |
| Object |
| Pan |
| Zoom |
| SteeringWheels |
| QuickCalc |

Figure 12-6: All (and Extents, and Window) is revealed when you right-click.

6. **Return to a zoomed-all view by using any of these techniques; or type** Z **and press Enter, then type** A **and press Enter.**

 AutoCAD displays the entire layout again.

7. **Type** MSPACE **(or MS) and press Enter.**

 Alternatively, you can double-click with the crosshairs over a viewport.

Figure 12-7: Zooming in paper space.

You should see the model space UCS icon at the lower-left corner of the display (refer to Step 3 if you don't see an icon). The crosshairs are now in model space, *inside* the viewport, so zooming and panning change only the display of the objects that are visible in the viewport. The display of the title block doesn't change.

8. Zoom and pan by using any of the techniques described in this chapter.

Zooming and panning don't change the appearance of the title block, as shown in Figure 12-8. The result looks as if you're moving a picture of the model space geometry in and out and all around behind a frame.

In real drawings, you usually shouldn't zoom and pan inside viewports after they've been set up (see Chapter 5). Doing so changes the scale of the viewport, which messes up plotting. We're asking you to do it here only to illustrate the difference between zooming in paper space and zooming in a model space viewport.

If the title block changes when you zoom and pan, it means someone has locked the viewport to prevent the kind of mischief that we warn against in the previous paragraph. (You also see the command prompt `Viewport is view-locked. Switching to Paper space.`) Refer to Chapter 5 for information on locking and unlocking viewports.

9. Choose Zoom Previous by using your favorite ZOOM technique one or more times until you've restored the original view.

Figure 12-8: Showing nothing but the kitchen sink in a model space viewport.

10. Type PS **and press Enter.**

Always leave the crosshairs in paper space when you're ready to call a drawing finished.

11. Click the Close window control in the upper-right corner of the drawing area. Click No to close the drawing without saving changes.

In this example, we have you close the drawing without saving changes just in case you did mess up the viewport zoom scale.

In most cases, you set up a paper space layout once (as described in Chapter 5) and then just return to it to plot. You shouldn't be spending a lot of time zooming and panning in paper space layouts. You zoom and pan to get a better view of what you're drawing and editing, and that's what full-screen model space is for. But if you do want to zoom in paper space — to get a better look at part of your title block, for example — make sure that you're doing it with the triangular paper space UCS icon on display at the lower-left corner of the drawing area.

The in-canvas viewport controls we describe earlier in the chapter are for manipulating model space, or tiled, viewports. The VPMAX and VPMIN commands allow you to maximize and minimize a viewport in the current layout. These commands provide an alternative to switching between the Model and Layout buttons without the potential problems of zooming inside of paper

space viewports. The easiest way to run VPMAX or VPMIN is to click the Maximize Viewport/Minimize Viewport button located on the status bar, to the right of the Model and Layout buttons.

Degenerating and Regenerating

As you zoom and pan around your drawing, you may wonder how the image that you see onscreen is related to the DWG file that AutoCAD saves on the hard drive. Well, maybe you don't wonder about that, but we're going to tell you anyway!

When you draw and edit objects, AutoCAD stores all their *geometrical properties* (that is, location and size) in a highly precise form — technically, *double floating-point precision*. The program always maintains that precision when you save the DWG file. For computer performance reasons, however, AutoCAD does *not* use that high precision form of the data to display your drawing onscreen. Instead, AutoCAD converts the highly precise numbers in the DWG file into slightly less precise *integers* in order to create the view that you see onscreen.

The happy consequence of this conversion is that zooming, panning, and other display changes are a lot faster than they would be otherwise. The unhappy consequence is that the conversion can make circles and arcs look like polygons. AutoCAD solves this by *regenerating* the drawing. This is also known as performing a *regen*.

In most cases, AutoCAD performs regenerations automatically when it needs to. You will sometimes see command-line messages like `Regenerating model` or `Regenerating layout`, which indicate that AutoCAD is taking care of regens for you.

If, on the other hand, you see the command-line message `Regen queued`, AutoCAD is warning you that it's *not* performing a regeneration, even though one might be advisable now. In addition, you might see a warning dialog box with the message `About to regen -- proceed?`. These messages are AutoCAD's way of saying, "What your drawing looks like on the screen at the moment may not exactly match the real version of the drawing database that gets stored when you save the drawing. I'll update the display version at the next regeneration." You can control whether regenerations happen automatically with the REGENMODE system variable — see the online help for more information on this variable and refer to Chapter 26 for more information on system variables in general.

The REGENALL (REA) command (once again, only available from the command line) regenerates all viewports in a paper space layout. If you run the REGENALL command in model space, it has the same effect as the ordinary REGEN command.

If you zoom a long way in to a drawing that has small circles and arcs in a large drawing, you may find that they've turned to hexagons. Not to worry; all you really need is a REGEN. You can also minimize this effect in the future by running the VIEWRES command and increasing the value from the default 1,000 up to as high as 20,000, but a very high number can also slow down a very complex drawing. Experiment a bit.

Part III
If Drawings Could Talk

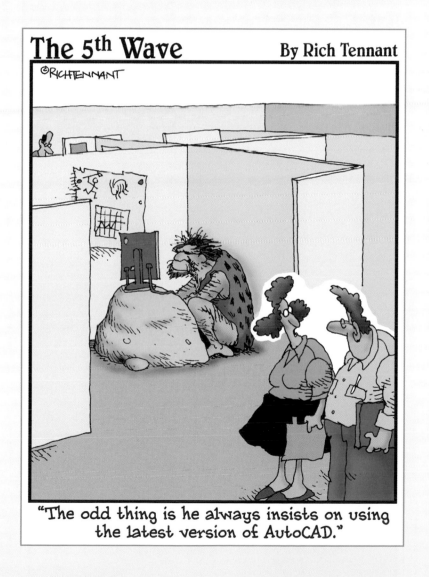

The 5th Wave By Rich Tennant

"The odd thing is he always insists on using the latest version of AutoCAD."

ext, dimensions, and hatching have long been important clarifying elements in drafting. In AutoCAD, these elements are flexible almost to a fault — and you can edit and update them quickly as you change the geometry beneath them. The text, dimension, and hatching annotations that you add "speak" about the geometry so others can understand exactly what, how big, and how far.

After you've made some drawings that talk, you'll probably send the message around by printing — or, as CAD users call it, plotting — them. Chapter 16 is your guidebook to navigating the plot process, understanding how the legacy of AutoCAD plotting still influences current practice, and most of all, getting a good-looking, properly scaled plot onto paper.

13

Text with Character

In This Chapter

▶ Creating annotative text

▶ Using text styles to control text appearance

▶ Creating single-line and multiline text

▶ Using fields and background masks with text

▶ Making numbered and bulleted lists

▶ Working with columns and paragraphs

▶ Editing text contents and properties

▶ Creating tables

▶ Drawing multileaders

*I*t used to be said that "a picture is worth a thousand words," but with the current state of the economy, a picture is now worth only about 628 words — and the bank is about to foreclose on them. On the other hand, the opposite is often true as well: Adding a few words to your drawing can save you from having to draw thousands of lines and arcs. It's a lot easier to write `Simpson A35 framing clip` next to a simple, schematic representation of a clip than to draw one in microscopic detail and hope that the contractor can figure out what it is!

Most CAD drawings include some text in the form of explanatory notes, object labels, and titles. This chapter shows you how to add general drawing text and *leaders* (descriptive notes with arrows that point to specific drawing objects) to your drawings. We show you how to take advantage of AutoCAD's annotative text objects and text styles, as well as how to find specific text and check your drawing for spelling errors. Chapter 14 covers text that's connected with dimensions.

In most cases, adding text, dimensions, and other descriptive symbols is something that you should do later in the drafting process, after you've drawn at least some of the geometry. In CAD drawings, text and other annotations are usually intended to complement the geometry, not to stand alone. Thus, you generally need to have the geometry in place before you annotate it. Many drafters find that it's most efficient to draw as much geometry as possible first, and then to add text annotations and dimensions to all the geometry at the same time. In this way, you develop a rhythm with the text and dimensioning commands instead of bouncing back and forth between drawing geometry and adding annotations.

As we mention in Chapter 4, AutoCAD's *annotative objects* present a stream-lined way of adding notes, dimensions, and other annotations to your draw-ings. This chapter introduces annotative text, and subsequent chapters cover annotative dimensions and hatches. See the "Annotatively yours" sidebar, later in this chapter, for some background.

Getting Ready to Write

In AutoCAD, adding text to a drawing is very similar to adding it to a word-processing document. Here are the basic steps, which we explain in more detail in the sections that follow:

1. **Select an existing AutoCAD text style, or create a new style, that includes the font and other text characteristics you want to use.**

 Just like a word processor, AutoCAD uses *styles* — collections of format-ting properties — to control the appearance of drawing text. We explain text styles in the next section.

2. **Make an appropriate layer current.**

 To make your AutoCAD drawing efficient and easy to edit for both you and others, create text on its own layer. Most drafting offices already have a set of CAD standards that establish specific layers for text and other object types.

3. **Run *one* of these commands to draw text:**

 • *TEXT:* Draws single-line text.

 • *MTEXT:* Draws paragraph (also called *multiline*) text.

4. **Specify the text alignment points, justification, and (if necessary) height.**

5. **Type the text.**

6. **(Optional) For annotative text, assign additional annotation scales to the text you just typed, if desired.**

Annotatively yours

One of the great things about AutoCAD is that it offers multiple ways of accomplishing your drafting tasks. This usually comes about because successive releases of AutoCAD add new or improved methods of performing existing tasks. You're almost always better to adopt the newer methods, but in this book, we try to give you a taste of the older methods because there are literally billions of existing drawings out there that were created by using the older methods — and you're bound to encounter them sooner rather than later in your career. Text and dimensions are prime examples of this. We cover text annotations in this chapter and dimensions in the next.

AutoCAD supports three different methods for annotating your drawings:

✔ **Add text and dimensions in model space, multiplying the drawing scale factor (see Chapter 4 for details) times the desired plotted text height.** For example, assume that someone has drawn a floor plan at a scale of 1/4" = 1'–0" (corresponding to a drawing scale factor of 48), and you want your notes to appear 1/8" high when the drawing is plotted to scale. You need to create text that's 48 times 1/8", or 6", high. And that works fine — until you need to plot your drawing at a different scale, or you want to create a detail at a different scale.

This is particularly cumbersome if you're working with feet, inches, and fractions but is a bit easier when you're using decimals of inches or metric units.

✔ **Add text and dimensions in layouts in paper space.** Because paper space is plotted at 1:1, you create annotations at their actual plotted size. The scale calculations are simple ("What's 1/8" times 1, boss?" "I don't know; my calculator's broken."), but sometimes it's beneficial to have drawing annotations in the same space as the drawing geometry. And you may have to duplicate notes in each layout.

✔ **Add text and dimensions in model space by using annotative text and dimension styles.** This is very similar to the first method, except that AutoCAD automatically does the size calculations for you.

Using annotative objects makes the most sense to us, as they can cover all plot scales. Also, because they're in model space, they don't have to be duplicated on multiple layouts. As you're learning AutoCAD, one of the trickier concepts to grasp is the necessity of scaling text and dimensions to apparently ludicrous sizes (6"-high drawing text, for example) so that they plot correctly. Annotative objects allow you to keep your annotations in model space and specify the paper size; AutoCAD does the scale calculations for you. Better yet, details at different scales are handled almost automatically.

Annotative object types include both single-line and multiline text (covered in the sections "Using the Same Old Line" and "Saying More in Multiline Text," respectively, in this chapter), leaders (covered in the section "Take Me to Your Leader," in this chapter), dimensions (covered in Chapter 14), hatches (see Chapter 15), and blocks and attributes (see Chapter 17). In theory, only annotative objects at the current annotation scale as set on the application or drawing status bar are displayed, but unfortunately, the default setting of a handy toggle beside the Annotation Scale list views all annotative objects at all scales, which confuses the issue more than a little. More on this later.

The annotative workflow might require an additional step compared with the other two methods listed previously. On the other hand, it eliminates the calculation steps, which can get messy when dealing with details at other scales. We describe the process in detail in the steps in this chapter and in the following chapters.

You're probably familiar with most of these steps already — especially if you've ever used a word processor. In the next few sections of this chapter, we review the particularities of AutoCAD text styles, the two kinds of AutoCAD text, and ways of controlling height and justification.

Simply stylish text

AutoCAD assigns text properties to individual lines or paragraphs of text based on *text styles*. These text styles are similar to the paragraph styles in a word processor; they contain font and other settings that determine the look and feel of text. An AutoCAD text style includes

- ✓ The **font**
- ✓ A **text height,** which you can set to a specific value or leave at 0 for later flexibility
- ✓ **Special effects** (where available), such as italic
- ✓ *Really* **special effects,** such as vertical and upside down, which almost nobody uses

Before you add text to a drawing, use the Text Style dialog box to select an existing style or create a new one with settings that are appropriate to your purpose.

You can assign the annotative property to text styles in old drawings by opening the Text Style dialog box in the drawing, selecting the individual text style you want to update, selecting the Annotative check box, and then saving the drawing.

Most drawings require very few text styles. You can create one style for all notes, object labels, and annotations, and another text style for special titles. You may also want to create a unique text style for your dimensions (see Chapter 14 for more on dimension text). A title block may require one or two additional fonts, especially if you want to mimic the font used in a company logo or project logo.

As with layers, your office may have its own standards for text styles. If so, you'll make everyone happy by following those standards. One of the best ways to make your use of text styles efficient and consistent is to create them in a template drawing that you use to start new drawings. (If your office is well organized, it may already have a template drawing with the company-approved styles defined in it.) See Chapter 4 for information about creating and using templates. Another handy technique is to copy existing text styles from one drawing to another by using the DesignCenter palette. See Chapter 6 for instructions.

Font follies

When you create a text style in AutoCAD, you have a choice of a huge number of fonts. AutoCAD can use two different kinds of fonts: native AutoCAD SHX (compiled shape) fonts and Windows TrueType fonts:

- **SHX:** In the Text Style dialog box, SHX font names appear with a drafting compass to the left of the name and display the .shx file extension. SHX fonts usually provide better performance because they're optimized for AutoCAD's use.

- **TrueType:** In the Text Style dialog box, TrueType font names appear with a TT symbol to the left of the name and no file extension. TrueType fonts give you more and fancier font options, but they can slow down AutoCAD when you zoom, pan, or select and snap to objects. TrueType fonts also can cause greater complications when you exchange drawings with other AutoCAD users.

It's okay to use a TrueType font sparingly for something like a title-block logo, but in general, you should stick with standard AutoCAD SHX fonts whenever possible.

The most popular AutoCAD font is Romans.shx (Roman Simplex). (You may also run into Simplex.shx, an older version of Roman Simplex.) Romans. shx is a good, general-purpose font for drafting in AutoCAD and closely resembles traditional hand lettering. Avoid complicated, thick fonts. They can slow down AutoCAD, and they're usually more difficult to read than the simpler fonts. Remember, you're doing CAD here, not fancy graphic design or reproductions of medieval manuscripts! The bad news is that AutoCAD defaults to using Arial, a TrueType font.

Whenever possible, avoid *custom fonts,* which are font files that don't come with AutoCAD or AutoCAD LT (both programs come with the same fonts). AutoCAD installs its standard SHX fonts in the C:\Program Files\Autodesk\ AutoCAD 2013\Fonts folder, (C:\Program Files\Autodesk\AutoCAD LT 2013\Fonts in AutoCAD LT); as long as you haven't added any custom fonts to that folder, you can refer to it for a list of standard fonts. AutoCAD doesn't embed font files in drawings; instead, it must refer to the font files installed locally under either AutoCAD (for SHX fonts) or Windows (for TrueType fonts). If you use a custom font of either type, exchanging your drawings with other people will be more complicated. If you must use a custom font, make a note of it and remember either to send it whenever you send the DWG file (assuming that the font isn't copyrighted, which many custom fonts are) or to warn the recipients that the text will appear different on their systems. It's far less hassle to avoid custom fonts altogether. See Chapter 20 for additional information about how to deal with fonts when you send and receive drawings.

Get in style

The following steps describe how to select an existing text style or create a new one before you enter text into a drawing. If you want to experiment with an existing drawing that contains a variety of text styles, you can download the AutoCAD sample drawings from www.autodesk.com/autocad-samples. Look for architectural_-_annotation_scaling_and_multileaders.dwg.

1. **On the Ribbon's Home tab, click the Annotation panel's label to open the slideout and then click Text Style.**

 The Text Style dialog box appears, as shown in Figure 13-1.

Figure 13-1: Text — with style.

2. **In the Styles list, select each style in turn to examine the properties of the text styles that have been created in this drawing.**

 Note the font name and look at the Preview panel in the lower-left corner of the dialog box to get a feel for what the different fonts look like.

3. **If you find a suitable text style, select it in the Styles list, click Set Current, and then skip to Step 9.**

 What makes a text style suitable depends on industry practices, office standards, and personal preferences about how the text should look. The information in previous sections may help you decide. If not, ask an experienced drafter in your office or look at some printed drawings and try to match the text on those. If you're starting from scratch, we highly recommend that you use annotative styles — look for the triangular symbol beside the style name.

4. **If you don't find a suitable text style or if you prefer to create your own text style, click New.**

Pay attention to the style that's current when you click New. If it's an annotative style, your new style will be annotative; if the current style isn't annotative, the new style won't be, either. It's easy enough to select or deselect the Annotative check box, but you may overlook this action at first.

The New Text Style dialog box appears, with a text box for you to type a name.

5. **Type a name for your new text style and then click OK.**

Your new text style is added to the Styles list and becomes the current style.

6. **Choose a font from the Font Name list.**

Romans.shx is the best all-purpose font for most drafting work. If you want to use a different font, review the font suggestions and warnings in the preceding section.

The font that you choose becomes the font that's assigned to your new text style.

7. **To create an annotative text style, select the Annotative check box. Deselect the check box for non-annotative text.**

Click the *i* icon next to the Annotative label to open AutoCAD's online help and find out more.

8. **Adjust the remaining text style settings.**

The text style shown in Figure 13-1 has the following setup:

- **Paper Text Height** (just Height for non-annotative styles) = 0.0
- **Width Factor** = 1.0
- **Oblique Angle** = 0
- All check boxes other than Annotative are deselected.

A text style height of 0.0 makes the style *variable height,* which means that you have to specify the height separately for each text object as it is created. Assigning a *fixed* (that is, nonzero) height to a text style forces all text that uses the style to be the same height. Variable height styles are more flexible, but fixed height styles usually make it easier to draw text of consistent height. The decision to use styles of variable height versus fixed height is another aspect of text that depends on office practice; if you work with other AutoCAD users, ask around.

Dimensions use text styles to format the appearance of the dimension text. When you create a text style that you think you might use for your dimensions, you *must* set a height of 0. Otherwise, the setting that controls the dimension text won't work, and your dimension text is likely to be either enormous or microscopic. This one should be a double warning because it's one of the most common mistakes made by new AutoCAD drafters!

9. Click Apply and then click Close.

The Text Style dialog box closes, and the text style that you selected or created is now the current style for new text objects.

Taking your text to new heights

On the off chance that you're choosing not to use annotative text styles, this section shows you why you might want to change your mind.

In Chapter 4, we describe the importance of choosing an appropriate drawing scale when you set up a drawing. We warn you that you need to know the drawing scale factor for tasks described in other chapters of this book. This is one of those chapters, and we're about to explain one of those tasks! And when we're done, remember — you can avoid all the arithmetic by using annotative text — it's just a check box away!

Drawing scale is the traditional way of describing a scale with an equal sign or colon — for example 1/4" = 1'–0", 1:20, or 2:1. The *drawing scale factor* represents the same relationship with a single number, such as 48, 20, or 0.5. The drawing scale factor is the multiplier that converts the first number in the drawing scale into the second number.

Make it a point to determine the drawing scale factor of a drawing before you add non-annotative text to it.

Plotted text height

Most industries have plotted text height standards (AutoCAD refers to *paper* text height, which means the same thing). A plotted text height of 1/8" or 3mm is common for notes. Some companies use slightly smaller heights (for example, 3/32" or 2.5mm) to squeeze more text into small spaces.

Calculating non-annotative AutoCAD text height

To calculate non-annotative text height, you need to know the drawing scale factor, the desired plotted text height, and the location of the multiplication button on your calculator. Use the following steps to figure out text height:

1. **Determine the drawing scale factor.**

 If you set up the drawing, you should know its drawing scale, as described in Chapter 4. If someone else set up the drawing, and is still around, ask that person!

 Other methods of figuring out a drawing's scale factor include searching the drawing for a bar scale or a text note that indicates the drawing scale, or if a printout is available, measuring dimensioned distances on the hard copy with an architectural or engineering scale if the drawing was plotted to a specific scale and not "to fit". Finally, if the drawing dimensions are in model space, you can check the value of the DIMSCALE variable (the system variable that controls dimension scale), as described in Chapter 14.

2. **Determine the height that your notes should appear when you plot the drawing to scale.**

 See the preceding "Plotted text height" section for suggestions.

3. **Multiply the numbers that you figured out in Steps 1 and 2.**

 After you know the AutoCAD text height, you can use it to define the height of a text style or of an individual text object.

If you assign a nonzero height to a text style (Step 8 in the "Get in style" section, earlier in this chapter), all text that you create with that style will use the fixed height. If you leave the text style's height set to 0, AutoCAD asks you for the text height when you draw single-line text objects.

This discussion of text height assumes that you're adding non-annotative text in model space. In addition to annotative text in model space, there's a third alternative. You can add annotative or non-annotative text to a paper space layout — for example, when you draw text in a title block or add a set of sheet notes that doesn't directly relate to the model space geometry. When you create text in paper space, you specify the actual, plotted paper height instead of the scaled-up height.

One line or two?

For historical reasons (namely, because the AutoCAD text capabilities used to be much more primitive than they are now), AutoCAD offers two different kinds of text objects and two corresponding text-drawing commands. Table 13-1 explains the two commands, with their aliases shown in parentheses.

Table 13-1		The Two Kinds of AutoCAD Text	
Button Icon	*Text Object*	*Command (with Alias)*	*Comments*
A	Single-line text	TEXT (DT)	Designed for creating single lines. Although you can press Enter to create more than one line of text, each line becomes a separate text object.
A	Paragraph text	MTEXT (T)	Designed for multiple lines, with word-wrapping. AutoCAD keeps the multiple lines together as a single object. Other special formatting, such as numbered or bulleted lists and columns, is possible.

Although you may be inclined to ignore the older single-line text option, it's worth knowing how to use both kinds of text. The TEXT command is quite a bit simpler than the MTEXT command, and it's still useful for entering short, single-line pieces of text such as object labels and one-line notes. And it's the command of choice for CAD comedians who want to document their one-liners!

If you work in an office with people who've been AutoCAD users for more than a few years, you may hear them referring to DTEXT. For the last few releases, TEXT has been an alias for the DTEXT (*D* for *Dynamic*) command. However, lurking up in the dusty back corners of AutoCAD's attic is a *third* text-creation command, also named TEXT (confused yet?); if you want to experience this creaky old command, type -**TEXT**. Unlike the current TEXT (formerly known as DTEXT) command, with -TEXT you get no onscreen feedback at all. In summary, TEXT begat DTEXT which begat TEXT . . . hey, don't shoot the messengers! We just report on what we know!

Your text will be justified

Both the TEXT and MTEXT commands offer a bewildering array of text *justification* options — in other words, which way the text flows from the point or points that you pick in the drawing to locate it. For most purposes, the default Left justification for single-line text or Top Left justification for paragraph text works fine. Occasionally, you may want to use a different justification, such as Center for labels or titles. Both commands provide options for changing text justification. We point out these options when we demonstrate the commands later in this chapter.

Using the Same Old Line

Despite its limitations, the TEXT command is useful for labels and other short notes for which MTEXT would be overkill. The following procedure shows you how to add text to your drawing by using AutoCAD's TEXT command.

You *can* use TEXT for multiple lines of text: Just keep pressing Enter after you type each line of text, and TEXT puts the new line below the previous one. The problem with this approach is that TEXT creates each line of text as a separate object. If you want to add or remove words in those multiple lines later on, AutoCAD can't do any word-wrapping for you; you have to edit each line separately, cutting words from one line and adding them to the adjacent line.

The TEXT command doesn't use a dialog box, a fancy formatting toolbar, or a contextual Ribbon tab like the MTEXT command's In-Place Text Editor. You set options by typing them into the command line or the Dynamic Input tooltip.

Here's how you add text with the TEXT command:

1. **Set an appropriate text style current, as described in the section "Simply stylish text," earlier in this chapter.**

 It's possible to set an already created text style current at the TEXT command prompt, but it's usually more straightforward to set the style before starting the command.

 An alternative to opening the Text Style dialog box to make an existing style current is to click the Text Style drop-down list and choose the style there. Look for the Text Style drop-down list on the Annotation panel's slideout (Home tab) or the Text panel of the Annotate tab.

2. **(Optional) Use the Object Snap button on the status bar to enable or disable running object snaps.**

 You may or may not want to snap text to existing objects. For example, you'd want to use a Center object snap to locate a letter or number precisely at the center of a circle. Make sure that you specify *middle-center* (MC) justification for the text to ensure that this works perfectly.

3. **On the Home tab's Annotation panel, click the lower part of the big button labeled Text, and then choose Single Line from the drop-down menu to start the TEXT command.**

 Don't click the upper part of the Text button — that starts the multiline text command, MTEXT, which we cover in the next section.

 If your text style is annotative and this is the first annotative object you're creating in this drawing session, AutoCAD usually displays a Select Annotation Scale dialog box, which advises you that you are

indeed creating an annotative object and asks you to set the scale at which you want the annotation to appear; click OK to continue. Later, we explain how and why to turn this annoying dialog box off.

AutoCAD tells you the current text style and height settings and prompts you to select a starting point for the text or to choose an option for changing the text justification or current text style first:

```
Current text style: "Standard" Text height: 0.2000
         Annotative: No
Specify start point of text or [Justify/Style]:
```

If the text style is annotative, the text height displayed in the prompt is the model space height, not the ultimate plotted text height. For example, if the text style is created with a fixed paper text height of 0.2000, and the annotation scale is set to 1:2, the AutoCAD prompt will read `Text height: 0.4000`.

4. **If you want a different justification from the default (Left), type** J, **press Enter, and choose one of the other justification options.**

 Look up *create single-line text* in the online help system if you need help with the justification options.

5. **Specify the insertion point for the first text character.**

 You can enter the point's coordinates from the keyboard, use the mouse to click a point onscreen, or press Enter to locate new text immediately below the most recent single-line text object that you created.

 AutoCAD prompts you for the text height (or the paper height if the text style is annotative):

   ```
   Specify height <0.2000>:
   ```

6. **Specify the height for the text.**

 This prompt doesn't appear if you're using a text style with a *fixed* (that is, nonzero) height. See the "Simply stylish text" section, earlier in this chapter, for information about fixed versus variable text heights.

 AutoCAD prompts you for the text rotation angle:

   ```
   Specify rotation angle of text <0>:
   ```

7. **Specify the text rotation angle by typing the rotation angle and pressing Enter or by rotating the line onscreen with the mouse.**

 AutoCAD prompts you to type the text.

8. **Type the first line of text and press Enter.**

9. **Type additional lines of text, pressing Enter at the end of each line.**

 Figure 13-2 shows text appearing onscreen as you type it (or it would if this book had animated pages).

Figure 13-2: Single-line text appears letter by letter.

10. **To stop entering text and return to the command prompt, press Enter at the start of a blank line.**

 AutoCAD adds the new single-line text object — or objects, if you typed more than one line — to the drawing.

To align lines of text exactly, make sure that you type all the lines in one instance of the TEXT command, pressing Enter after each line to make the next line appear just after it. Otherwise, aligning different lines of text precisely is harder to do (unless you set your snap just right or use a complicated combination of object snaps and point filters). To edit single-line text after you've created it, select the text, right-click, and choose Edit (or double-click the text) to open the In-Place Text Editor. (*In-place* simply means that you edit text at its exact size and location in the drawing.) We tell you more about in-place text editing in the section "Making it with Mtext," later in this chapter.

An in-place editing box highlights the selected text object, enabling you to edit the contents of the text string. If you want to edit other text properties such as text height, select the text, right-click, and choose Properties to display the Properties palette. Use the Properties palette to change parameters as needed.

If the Quick Properties button on your application status bar is enabled, clicking a single-line text object opens the Quick Properties panel, allowing you to change some (but not all) of the same properties as the Properties palette.

Turning On Your Annotative Objects

Annotative objects were introduced in AutoCAD 2008, ending 25 years of calculating agony, but a quick show of hands at Autodesk University and AUGI CAD Camp classes reveals that on average only about 20 percent have ever tried them — and most of them gave up and went back to the old way because they thought they weren't working. There's a very simple explanation for this, which we come to in a moment.

Here's a quick example that shows how things are supposed to work. Make sure that you are in model space.

1. **Set the annotation controls.**

 In the lower-right corner of the AutoCAD screen, you'll find three buttons with variants of a triangular symbol. They represent the end view of an engineer's triangular scale; an old-timer in your office should be able to show you one and how they worked. Click the center and right-hand buttons, the ones without the numbers beside them, until they are grayed out and don't show a small yellow splash in them. If the left-hand button doesn't display the numbers *1:1*, click it and select 1:1 from the drop-down list.

2. **Select an annotative text style.**

 Use the STYLE command as described previously in the "Get in style" section and set the Annotative style to be current. Set its Paper Text Height to 0.125.

3. **Create some text.**

 Use the TEXT command and create a line of text that says *Scale 1:1*.

 The first time you place annotative text, you're asked to select a drawing scale, and it defaults to the current scale, which is probably what you want anyway. Eventually this becomes a nuisance, so the check box lets you turn it off.

4. **Change the drawing scale.**

 Click the left-hand annotative control button and select 1:2 from the drop-down list. This sets the current drawing scale to 1:2. Hey, the first piece of text disappears! Not to worry; that's what it's supposed to do.

5. **Create some text.**

 Use the TEXT command again and create a line of text that says *Scale 1:2*, and another one that says *Both scales*. Note that they are twice as tall as the now-invisible Scale 1:1 text.

6. **Change the drawing scale.**

 Click the left-hand annotative control button and select 1:1 from the drop-down list. Interesting! The first piece of text reappears, but the other two disappear!

7. **Add another scale to an object.**

 Click the left-hand annotative control button and select 1:2 from the drop-down list. Now click the *Both scales* text and then right-click. Select Annotative Object Scale, and then select Add/Delete Scales. When the dialog box appears, click the Add button in the upper-right corner and then select 1:1 from the list. Click OK, and then OK again, to return to the drawing screen.

8. **Change the drawing scale.**

 Click the left-hand annotative control button and select 1:1 from the drop-down list. Interesting! The *Scale 1:1* text reappears, *Scale 1:2* disappears, and *Both scales* changes size to match the height of *Scale 1:1* text!

9. **Change the drawing scale again.**

 Click the left-hand annotative control button and select 1:5 from the drop-down list. All three text items disappear!

As indicated earlier, that's how annotative objects, including text, dimensions (discussed Chapter 14), hatch patterns (Chapter 15), and blocks (Chapter 17) are supposed to work. Upon creation, they automatically size themselves to suit the current drawing scale, they're visible only when their annotation scales match the current drawing scale, and they can have more than one scale attached, so they're visible in more than one drawing scale setting.

Better yet, they exhibit this same behavior in paper space viewports. It thus becomes trivially easy to set up drawings with details at other scales. We cover this in more detail in Chapter 14.

If an annotative object has multiple scales attached and you edit its location at one scale, this doesn't affect its location at the other scales.

But wait! There's more! When viewing an object with multiple scales, you aren't looking at a copy of the object but instead you see a different configuration of the same object. To see this, edit the contents of your *Both scales* text object to say something else. The new contents automatically appear at all scale representations of that object.

Now we reveal the dirty, dark secret as to why most people gave up on them. It all gets back to Step 1 in the preceding instructions. By default, the middle- and right-hand buttons are both turned on, but we had you turn them off. Turn the middle button back on and observe that now all annotative objects at all scales

are always visible, no matter what the value of the current drawing scale, even if none of the objects has a scale that matches the current drawing scale.

But wait! It gets worse! If you turn on the right-hand button and then change the drawing scale, every annotation object retroactively gets the current scale added to it.

It's easy to see how the last two statements would easily confuse people into not understanding how annotative objects work. We can think of only one situation where you would want all objects to retroactively receive the new drawing scale, and that would be where you have created a drawing with the intention of printing it at a specific scale, and then you decide that you need to change the scale to suit a different printer or paper size.

Most of the time, for most people, there are way too many scales listed in the Add Scales to Object dialog box. AutoCAD has a handy-dandy Edit Drawing Scales dialog box that lets you remove those imperial scales from your current drawing if you never work in feet and inches. (And vice versa, for the metrically challenged.) To run through your scales, choose Scale List on the Annotation Scaling panel of the Ribbon's Annotate tab. If you make a mistake, the Reset button will restore all the default scales. You can remove those extra scales for *all* your drawing in the Default Scale List dialog box, accessible on the User Preferences tab of the Options dialog box.

You can display the drawing status bar (shown in Figures 13-2 and 13-3) by clicking the down arrow near the right end of the application status bar to open the application status bar menu, and then choosing Drawing Status Bar.

Figure 13-3 shows two versions of the same drawing, with the same text objects (the bulleted notes and windows sizes) and wall hatching displaying at the different annotation scales specified in the two status bars. The non-annotative text (the room label) remains unchanged. (we cover hatching your drawings in Chapter 15.)

Figure 13-3: Annotative objects resize automatically as the annotation scale changes.

Saying More in Multiline Text

When you just can't shoehorn your creative genius into one or more one-line pieces of text, AutoCAD's multiline text object gives you room to go on and on and on. The following procedure shows you how to create multiline text with the MTEXT command.

Making it with Mtext

The first part of the MTEXT command prompts you for various points and options. Read these steps and the prompts carefully to avoid confusion.

Here's how you use the MTEXT command:

1. **Set an appropriate text style current and (optionally) turn off running object snaps, as described in Steps 1 and 2 in the "Using the Same Old Line" section, earlier in this chapter.**

 If you're doing real drafting, you should also set an appropriate layer to be current.

2. **On the Home tab's Annotation panel, click the upper part of the split button labeled Text to start the MTEXT command.**

 The command line displays the current text style and height settings, and prompts you to select the first corner of an imaginary rectangle that will determine the word-wrapping width for the text object:

   ```
   Current text style: "Standard" Text height: 0.2000
           Annotative: No
   Specify first corner:
   ```

3. **Pick a point in the drawing.**

 The command line prompts you for the opposite corner of a rectangle that will determine the word-wrapping width; it also gives you the option of changing settings first:

   ```
   Specify opposite corner or [Height/Justify/Line
           spacing/Rotation/Style/Width/Columns]:
   ```

4. **Type H and press Enter to change the default text height.**

 The command line prompts you for a new default text height if your current text style has a height of 0.0:

   ```
   Specify height <0.2000>:
   ```

5. **If applicable, type an appropriate text height.**

 See the "Taking your text to new heights" section, earlier in this chapter, for information. If you're adding text in model space, we highly recommend that you use annotative text.

The prompt for the opposite corner of the Mtext rectangle reappears. The command line shows

```
Specify opposite corner or [Height/Justify/Line
        spacing/Rotation/Style/Width/Columns]:
```

6. **If you want a different justification from the default (top left), type** J, **press Enter, and choose one of the other justification options.**

 Enter **justify multiline text** in the search box of the online help system if you want an explanation of the other justification options.

7. **Pick another point in the drawing.**

 Don't worry about the *height* of the rectangle that you create by choosing the second point; the width of the rectangle is all that matters. AutoCAD adjusts the height of the text rectangle to accommodate the number of lines of word-wrapped text. Don't worry too much about the width, either; you can adjust it later.

 The In-Place Text Editor frameless window appears with the tab and indent ruler above it, and a previously hidden Text Editor contextual tab appears on the Ribbon, as shown in Figure 13-4. (If you don't see the tab and indent ruler at the top of your Text Editor window, right-click inside the window and choose Editor Settings, and then Show Ruler from the right-click menu.)

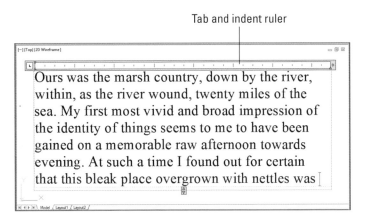

Figure 13-4: Adding immortal multiline text.

New isn't *always* better; you may prefer the classic Text Formatting toolbar over the Ribbon's Text Editor contextual tab. If you want to give the classic version a test-drive, change the value of the system variable MTEXTTOOLBAR. The default value (2) displays the Text Editor tab only; setting it to 1 displays both the tab and the toolbar. We don't recommend

setting this variable to 0 — that turns off the Text Formatting toolbar in all workspaces. For more about system variables, see Chapter 26.

When you create multiline text in either AutoCAD or AutoCAD LT, your text objects default to Dynamic Column mode. You can tell that's what you're going to get if the In-Place Text Editor displays a double-headed-arrow symbol in the center of the bottom border of the rectangle you define (refer to Figure 13-4). As indicated earlier, the initial selection window primarily sets the width. By default, if you enter enough text so that it fills the window, MTEXT defaults to splitting the text into two columns like a newspaper. If you don't like this, you can dynamically stretch the text window to be wider or longer.

If you never want to use columns in the current drawing, click Columns on the Insert panel of the Text Editor tab, which only appears when you're editing text. This sets the MTEXTCOLUMN system variable to 0. It affects only the current drawing, so if you <u>never</u> want columns, set this up in your template drawings. We cover templates in Chapter 4.

8. Verify the text font and height.

The text font and height should be right if you correctly performed Steps 1, 4, and 5. If not, you can change these settings in the Font drop-down list and the Text Height text box on the Text Editor tab (or the classic Text Formatting toolbar).

9. Type text into the text area of the In-Place Text Editor.

AutoCAD word-wraps multiline text automatically. If you want to force a line break at a particular location, press Enter.

10. If you want other formatting options, select text, right-click, and make an appropriate choice from the menu (as shown in Figure 13-5).

By convention in most industries, text in drawings is always uppercase. How many times have you forgotten to press the Caps Lock key before entering drawing text? How many times have you forgotten to turn Caps Lock off again when it's time to type your e-mail? To save yourself some agony, right-click in the In-Place Text Editor and choose AutoCAPS from the menu.

11. Click Close Text Editor (or OK in the classic Text Formatting toolbar).

The In-Place Text Editor window closes, and AutoCAD adds your text to the drawing.

You can close the text editor much more easily by simply clicking outside its window. But if you like clicking buttons instead, AutoCAD has amply provided for you.

Select All	Ctrl+A
Cut	Ctrl+X
Copy	Ctrl+C
Paste	Ctrl+V
Paste Special	▶
Insert Field...	Ctrl+F
Symbol	▶
Import Text...	
Paragraph Alignment	▶
Paragraph...	
Bullets and Lists	▶
Columns	▶
Find and Replace...	Ctrl+R
Change Case	▶
AutoCAPS	
Character Set	▶
Combine Paragraphs	
Remove Formatting	▶
Background Mask...	
Editor Settings	▶
Help	F1
Cancel	

Columns submenu:
- No Columns
- Dynamic Columns ▶
- Static Columns ▶
- Insert Column Break Alt+Enter
- Column Settings...

Dynamic Columns submenu:
- Auto height
- Manual height

Figure 13-5: Right-click your way to textual excellence.

12. Use annotation scales with multiline text objects.

The steps are the same for multiline text as for single-line text. Refer to the "Turning On Your Annotative Objects" section, earlier in this chapter, if you need a refresher.

As you can tell by looking at the Text Editor tab (or the Text Formatting toolbar) and multiline text right-click menu, the MTEXT command gives you plenty of other options. You can show or hide the toolbar, the ruler, or the Options buttons, and you can give the In-Place Text Editor an opaque background. Other tool buttons give you access to columns and numbered or bulleted lists (both are covered in the section "Doing a number on your Mtext lists," later in this chapter).

Between them, the Text Editor tab (or the Text Formatting toolbar) and the right-click menu also include a Stack/Unstack feature for fractions, a Find and Replace utility, tools for changing between lowercase and uppercase, options for applying background masks and inserting fields, a special Symbol submenu, and an Import Text option for importing text from a TXT (ASCII text) file or RTF (Rich Text Format) file. We discuss background masks and fields in the next section. If you think you may have a use for any of these other features, choose Command Reference➪Commands➪M Commands➪MTEXT in AutoCAD's online help browser to find out more about them.

It slices; it dices . . .

Two more useful options on the multiline text right-click menu are
Background Mask and Insert Field.

Mtext dons a mask

When you turn on background masking, AutoCAD hides the portions of any
objects that lie underneath the multiline text. This feature is used primarily
when adding text to an area that has already been cross-hatched. (We cover
hatching in Chapter 15.) Use these steps to turn on and control this feature:

1. **Right-click in the In-Place Text Editor and choose Background Mask
 from the menu.**

 The Background Mask dialog box appears.

2. **Click the Use Background Mask check box so that this option is
 turned on.**

3. **Either click Use Drawing Background Color (to make the mask the
 same color as the drawing area's background color) or choose a color
 from the drop-down list (to make the text appear in a solid rectangle
 of the specified color).**

4. **Click OK to return to the In-Place Text Editor.**

If you've turned on background masking but it isn't having the desired effect,
use the TEXTTOFRONT command to move the text on top of other objects.
Click the Bring to Front drop-down button on the Home tab's Modify panel
slideout and choose Bring Text to Front. Mtext plays the field.

The Insert Field option on the In-Line Text Editor's right-click menu creates
a *text field* that updates automatically every time you open, save, plot, or
regenerate the drawing. Fields can contain data such as the date, filename,
or author. Fields draw information from the operating-system settings,
Drawing Properties dialog box, sheet sets feature (not covered in this book),
AutoCAD system variables (for more information about system variables,
see Chapter 26), and information about specific drawing objects such as the
circumference of a circle or the area enclosed by a closed polyline. Use the
following procedure to add a field while you're creating multiline text:

1. **Right-click in the In-Place Text Editor and choose Insert Field from the
 menu.**

 The Field dialog box appears.

2. **Choose a Field Name in the left column.**

3. **Choose a Format in the right column, or for date fields, type a format in the Date Format box.**

4. **Click OK.**

AutoCAD adds the field to the Mtext object that you're creating or editing.

Doing a number on your Mtext lists

Mtext supports bulleted and numbered lists. This feature is especially useful for creating general drawing notes, as shown in Figure 13-6. AutoCAD automates the process of creating numbered lists almost completely. Here's how:

1. **Follow Steps 1 through 8 in the earlier section, "Making it with Mtext," to open the In-Place Text Editor.**

2. **Type a title — for example,** DESIGN CRITERIA.

 If you want your title underlined, click Underline on the Formatting panel (or the Text Formatting toolbar) before you type the title; click Underline again to turn it off. Press Enter to go to the next line, and press Enter again to leave a little more space.

3. **On the Paragraph panel of the Text Editor tab, click the Bullets and Numbering drop-down button; verify that Allow Auto-List, Use Tab Delimiter Only, and Allow Bullets and Lists are selected; then click Numbered, as shown in Figure 13-6.**

 The number 1 followed by a period appears on the current line, and the cursor jumps to the tab stop visible in the ruler at the top of the In-Place Text Editor window.

 Enabling the Numbered option places numerals followed by periods in front of items in a list. (Bulleted places bullet characters in front of items in a list.) Allow Auto-List enables automatic numbering — each time you press Enter to move to a new line, AutoCAD increments the number.

4. **Type the text corresponding to the current number or bullet.**

 As AutoCAD wraps the text, the second and subsequent lines align with the tab stop, and the text is indented automatically.

5. **Press Enter at the end of the paragraph to move to the next line.**

 Just like creating numbered lists in your favorite word processor, AutoCAD automatically inserts the next number at the beginning of the new paragraph, with everything perfectly aligned.

To create nested numbered or bulleted items as shown in Figure 13-6, simply press Tab at the start of the line. If you change your mind, you can bump a nested text item up a level by selecting the item in the In-Place Text Editor and pressing Shift+Tab.

Indentation of second and subsequent lines

Indentation of first line

Tab

In-Place Text Editor right-click

Figure 13-6: Tabs, indents, and automatic numbering are set to create numbered lists.

6. **Repeat Steps 4 and 5 for each subsequent numbered or bulleted item.**

For legibility, you sometimes want to add spaces between the notes. If you press Enter twice to give yourself a blank line, AutoCAD — like every good word processor — thinks you're finished with your list and turns numbering off. AutoCAD is smart, so you need to be smarter. If you put the cursor at the end of the first note and press Enter, you get a blank line. The problem is, the blank line is now numbered, and your intended Note 2 is now Note 3. Just press the Backspace key. The number on the blank line disappears, and Note 2 is back to being Note 2 again. When you delete a numbered item, the remaining numbers adjust automatically.

If you don't like the horizontal spacing of the numbers or the alignment of subsequent lines, you can adjust them easily by manipulating the tab and indent markers in the In-Place Text Editor's ruler.

7. **In the ruler, drag the upper slider (the triangle pointing down) to the right a short distance. Drag the lower slider (the triangle pointing up) a slightly greater distance to the right.**

The upper slider controls the indentation of the first line in each paragraph. The lower slider controls the indentation of the second and subsequent lines. An indent of one to two of the short, vertical tick marks usually works well for the first line. An indent of two to four tick marks works well for the second and subsequent lines.

8. **Click in the ruler just above the lower slider.**

 A small *L* appears above the lower slider. The *L* shows the tab stop.

 Make sure that the corner of the *L* aligns horizontally with the point of the lower slider triangle. If not, click and drag the *L* until it aligns.

If you prefer to type tab and indent distances, not adjust them with the cursor, open the Paragraph dialog box by either

- Clicking the little arrow at the right end of the Paragraph panel label (in AutoCADese, it's called a Panel Dialog Box Launcher).
- Right-clicking inside the In-Place Text Editor and choosing Paragraph.

Whichever way you do it, if you select text first, the tab and indent changes apply to the selected text. If you don't select text first, the changes apply to new text from that point forward in the multiline text object.

Line up in columns — now!

The text functionality of AutoCAD is getting more and more word processor–like. A few releases back, it was simple indents; then came numbered and bulleted lists. The most recent addition is columns in multiline text.

Columns come in two flavors: *static* and *dynamic*.

- **Static:** You specify the number of columns into which you want to flow your text. Columns are always the same height, and text is allowed to overflow the final column if there's too much of it.
- **Dynamic:** As you might expect, these columns are friendlier, more flexible, and the life of any party. You can individually adjust column heights, and new columns are added automatically to accommodate the text.

Selecting either column type also offers you a Column Settings dialog box where you can specify values numerically instead of by dragging grips.

Figure 13-7 shows a block of multiline text imported as an RTF file from a word processor and then formatted in dynamic columns with the Manual Height option.

Figure 13-7: Dynamically columnizing your text.

Setting up columns is pretty straightforward — the following steps explain how:

1. **Open a drawing that contains a large multiline text object or create a large multiline text object in a new drawing.**

 If you already have drawing specifications or general notes in a word-processor document, or even a text file, you can right-click inside the MTEXT command's In-Place Text Editor and choose Import Text. The Select File dialog box opens, giving you the choice of Rich Text Format (RTF) or ASCII text (TXT) files.

2. **If the In-Place Text Editor isn't already open, double-click the text, or select it, and then right-click and choose Mtext Edit.**

3. **Click Columns in the Insert panel and choose either Dynamic Columns or Static Columns.**

 If you choose Dynamic Columns, select either Auto Height or Manual Height. Selecting Manual Height puts grips on each column so you can adjust their height individually (refer to Figure 13-7). Auto Height displays a single grip — so the heights of all columns remain the same, but new columns are still added as required by the amount of text.

 If you choose Static Columns, select the number of columns you want from the menu. Clicking 2, for example, creates two columns regardless of the length of your text — you may end up with overflowing text or empty columns.

4. **Click Close Text Editor (or OK in the Text Formatting toolbar) when you're satisfied with the column arrangement.**

 You can revert to a noncolumnar arrangement by clicking the Columns button in the Insert panel and choosing No Columns.

Modifying Mtext

After you create a multiline text object, you can edit it in the same ways as a single-line text object: Select the object, right-click, and choose Mtext Edit or Properties.

- ✔ **Mtext Edit:** Selecting this option opens the In-Place Text Editor window so that you can change the text contents and formatting.

- ✔ **Properties:** Selecting this option opens the Properties palette, where you can change overall properties for the text object.

- ✔ **Quick Properties:** Enable this setting on the status bar to make simply selecting a multiline text object open the Quick Properties palette, in which you can modify a subset of the Mtext object's properties.

The easiest way to change the word-wrapping width of a paragraph text object is to *grip edit* it. Select the text object, click one of the corner grips, release the mouse button, move the crosshairs, and click again. Chapter 10 describes grip editing in detail.

Just like any good word processor or text editor, AutoCAD includes both spell checker and a find-and-replace tool for text or dimensions. To check the spelling of selected objects or the entire drawing, click the Annotate tab on the Ribbon and choose Check Spelling from the Text panel to display the Check Spelling dialog box. On the same panel, clicking Find Text, or typing FIND and pressing Enter, displays the Find and Replace dialog box. Handily, Find and Replace and Spell Check are both also accessible from the Text Editor tab's Spell Check and Tools panels — in case you just want to replace text or check spelling within a single multiline text object. Look up *SPELL* or *FIND* in the online help if you need more information on either command.

Gather Round the Tables

You don't know the meaning of the word *tedious* unless you've tried to create a column-and-row data table in older versions of AutoCAD by using the LINE and TEXT commands. AutoCAD's table object and the TABLESTYLE and TABLE commands for creating it make the job almost fun.

Table objects in AutoCAD 2013 are *not* annotative, so you have just two methods of adding them to drawings: You can create them in model space, scaling them up by the drawing scale factor (see Chapter 4 for a refresher), or — and this seems more sensible to us — you can create them in a layout, in paper space, defining them by their actual plotted (paper) dimensions.

Tables have style, too

You control the appearance of tables — both the text and the gridlines — with *table styles* (just as you control the appearance of stand-alone text with text styles). Use the TABLESTYLE command to create and modify table styles. Follow these steps to create a table:

1. **On the Home tab, click the Annotation panel's label to open its slide-out and then choose Table Style.**

 The Table Style dialog box appears.

2. **In the Styles list, select the existing table style whose settings you want to use as the starting point for the settings of your new style.**

 For example, select the default table style named Standard.

3. **Click the New button to create a new table style that's a copy of the existing style.**

 The Create New Table Style dialog box appears.

4. **Enter a New Style Name and click Continue.**

 The New Table Style dialog box appears, as shown in Figure 13-8.

Figure 13-8: Setting the table.

5. **In the Cell Styles area, with Data showing in the list box, specify settings for the data alignment, margins, text, and borders.**

The settings you're likely to want to change are Text Style, Text Height, and perhaps either Text Color (all three are on the Text tab) or Grid Color (on the Borders tab). If you leave colors set to ByBlock, the text and grid lines will inherit the color that's current when you create the table. That color will be the current layer's color, if you follow my advice in Chapter 6.

6. **In the Cell Styles area, open the drop-down list and repeat Step 5 for the Headers (that is, the column headings) and the Title.**

7. **Click OK to close the New Table Style dialog box.**

 The Table Style dialog box reappears.

8. **Click Close.**

 Your new table style becomes the current table style that AutoCAD uses for future tables in this drawing, and the Table Style dialog box closes. Now you're ready to create a table, as described in the next section.

You can access the Manage Cell Styles dialog box directly from the Cell Styles drop-down list of the New Table Style dialog box. The Table Cell Format (on the General tab, Format row, click the ellipsis button) dialog box provides a number of additional options for formatting cells by data type.

AutoCAD stores table styles in the DWG file, so a style that you create in one drawing isn't immediately available in others. You can copy a table style from one drawing to another with DesignCenter. (Use the procedure for copying layers between drawings outlined in Chapter 6, but substitute Tablestyles for Layers.) Table styles can also be defined in your template files (see Chapter 4).

Creating and editing tables

After you create a suitable table style, adding a table to your drawing is easy with the TABLE command. Here's how:

1. **Set an appropriate layer current.**

 Assuming that you leave the current color, linetype, and lineweight set to ByLayer, as we recommend in Chapter 6, the current layer's properties will control the properties of any parts of the table that you left set to ByBlock when you defined the table style. (See Step 5 in the preceding section, "Tables have style, too.")

2. **On the Home tab's Annotation panel, choose Table.**

 The Insert Table dialog box appears.

3. **Choose a table style from the Table Style drop-down list.**

4. **Choose an Insertion Behavior:**

 - *Specify Insertion Point:* The easiest method. You pick the location of the table's upper-left corner (or lower-left corner if you set Table Direction to Up in the table style). When you use this method, you specify the default column width and number of rows in the Insert Table dialog box.

 - *Specify Window:* You pick the upper-left corner and then the lower-right corner. When you use this method, AutoCAD automatically scales the column widths and determines how many rows to include.

5. **Specify Column & Row Settings.**

 If you chose Specify Window in Step 4, AutoCAD sets the Column Width and number of Data Rows to Auto, which means that AutoCAD will figure them out, basing those values on the overall size of the table that you specify in Steps 7 and 8.

6. **Click OK.**

 AutoCAD prompts you to specify the insertion point of the table.

7. **Click a point or type coordinates.**

 If you chose Specify Insertion Point in Step 4, AutoCAD draws the table grid lines, places the cursor in the title cell, and displays the Text Editor tab on the Ribbon.

8. **If you chose Specify Window in Step 4, specify the diagonally opposite corner of the table.**

 AutoCAD draws the table based on the table size you indicated and chooses the column width and number of rows.

9. **Type a title for the table.**

10. **Type values in each cell, using the arrow keys or Tab key to move among cells.**

 The cell right-click menu offers many other options, including copying contents from one cell to another, merging cells, inserting rows and columns, changing formatting, and inserting a *block* (that is, a graphical symbol — see Chapter 17 for information about blocks).

The fields feature described earlier in this chapter works for table text, too — you can insert a field into a table cell. For example, you might use this feature to create part of a title block, with fields serving as the "date" and "drawn by" data.

You can also insert blocks into table cells. We cover blocks in Chapter 17.

11. **Click Close Text Editor on the Ribbon (or click OK on the Text Formatting toolbar).**

Figure 13-9 shows a completed table, along with the Insert Table dialog box.

Figure 13-9: The Insert Table dialog box and one result of using it.

You can edit cell values later, simply by double-clicking in a cell. To change column width or row height, click the table grid and then click and move the blue grips. (To change the width of one column without altering the overall width of the table, hold down the Ctrl key while you move the grip.) If you want to change other aspects of a table or individual cells in it, select the table or cell and use the Quick Properties palette or the Properties palette to make changes.

TIP

The DATAEXTRACTION and DATALINK commands are very powerful tools in AutoCAD. Between them they can be used to link all or part of an Excel spreadsheet into a table in a drawing, or interrogate a drawing and produce a great variety of information from it such as sizes, areas, perimeters, and quantities of drawing objects and then create a linked table of the data, or write the data out to an Excel spreadsheet, or all three options at once. A detailed description of these functionalities is beyond the scope of this book, but there are several online references available that cover them. Here are two that can get you started:

www.cadalyst.com/cad/autocad/tell-me-all-you-know-
attribute-extraction-part-1-learning-curve-autocad-
tutorial-6271

www.cadalyst.com/cad/autocad/tell-me-all-you-know-
and-even-more-advanced-attribute-extraction-part-
2-learning-curve-a

Take Me to Your Leader

Don't worry; we're not space aliens, popular opinion to the contrary. No, we're talking about those notes with arrows that point to drawing objects that you need to embellish with some verbiage.

Multileaders — *mleaders* for short — are a vast improvement over old-style leaders available prior to AutoCAD 2008. In fact, they're so good, they should be running the United Nations! Mleaders, unlike the old-style leaders, are single objects. They are also able to point in multiple directions at once (just don't ask them which way is the bus station). Finally, multileaders — just like text, dimensions, hatching, and other objects you use to document your drawing — can be annotative.

There are two older-style leaders stored in AutoCAD's attic (Autodesk hates to throw anything away, because sure as blazes someone will complain that they still need it for a custom menu macro they created twenty years ago and use all the time). These semiretired leaders are no longer accessible on menus or toolbars, but they're still lurking up there waiting to . . . er, lead you astray. If you've become attached to typing commands, you may be inclined to type either **LEADER** or **LE** to create those pointy-headed thingies. If you do, be aware that LEADER runs the positively ancient command for creating notes-with-arrows. There are no options, so only straight leader lines and infinitely long text strings are what you get. LE (the alias for the QLEADER command) runs the merely elderly command for creating notes-with-arrows; this one has a Settings dialog box where you can set some options, and it does ask you to specify a width for your Mtext note. However, unlike multileaders, both LEADER and LE create the leader lines and the text as two separate objects. The main reason for mentioning them here is that you'll probably run into them in older drawings.

Electing a leader

You can draw multileader objects that consist of leader lines and multiline text at the same time by using the MLEADER command, as described in the following steps:

1. **Set a multileader style — one that's appropriate for your needs — current.**

 Choose an existing style from the Multileader Style drop-down list on the Home tab's Annotation panel slideout, or create a new style by clicking the Multileader Style button on the Annotation slideout. Visit the online help for tips on creating new multileader styles.

2. **Choose Multileader from the Annotation panel.**

 The command line prompts you to select the location for the pointy end of the leader arrowhead:

   ```
   Specify leader arrowhead location or [leader Landing
   first/Content first/Options] <Options>:
   ```

 The initial default method is to locate the arrowhead followed by the *leader landing* (that is, the short horizontal line between the leader line and the text), at which point AutoCAD displays the In-Place Text Editor, and you enter the text of your note. If you'd rather place the leader landing first, type **L** and press Enter. If you'd rather type the content first, type **C** and press Enter.

 If you want to draw spline-curved rather than straight leader lines, specify the number of pick points for the leader lines and press Enter to display multileader options at the command line or the Dynamic Input tooltip. Refer to the online help for more information on the command options.

3. **Pick a location in the drawing that you want the leader to point to.**

 If you use an object snap mode, such as Nearest or Midpoint, to pick a point on an object, AutoCAD associates the leader with the object. If you later move the object, AutoCAD updates the leader so that it points to the new location.

 The command line prompts you for the next point.

4. **Pick a second point.**

 AutoCAD draws a shaft from the arrowhead to this point.

 If you pick a second point that's too close to the arrowhead point and AutoCAD doesn't have enough room to draw the arrowhead, it omits the arrowhead.

 By default, AutoCAD lets you pick two points for the leader line: The first point locates the arrowhead, and the second point locates the start of the short horizontal leader landing. If you need more points than that, restart the command and choose Options, Maxpoints and set a new value.

 After you pick the point for the leader landing, AutoCAD opens the In-Place Text Editor.

5. **Type your text.**

 You're now in the same In-Place Text Editor we describe earlier in this chapter, with the same Text Editor tab and options.

6. **Click Close.**

 The In-Place Text Editor window closes and adds your text to the drawing, next to the leader.

Figure 13-10 shows several different leaders with notes.

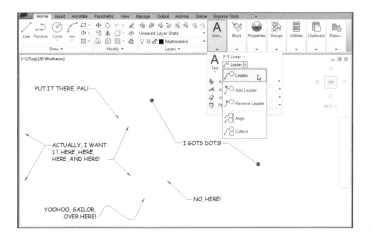

Figure 13-10: No loss for (multi)leaders.

You can use grips to manipulate a multileader's individual components, just as if it were several objects instead of a single object. Hold down the Ctrl key and click a multileader to select different pieces. You can even use grips to adjust the width of multileader text as if it were a plain everyday Mtext object.

Multi options for multileaders

In addition to the MLEADER command itself, which we walk you through in the preceding steps, multileaders come with a slew of formatting, drawing, and editing commands:

✔ **MLEADEREDIT:** Use this command to add or remove leader lines from multileader objects. You'll find each of those functions on the Multileader drop-down list (refer to Figure 13-10).

- **MLEADERSTYLE:** Multileaders, like text, tables, and dimensions, are formatted according to named styles. To display the Multileader Style Manager dialog box (which looks a lot like a simplified version of the Dimension Style Manager) click Multileader Style on the Home tab's Annotation slideout.

- **MLEADERALIGN:** A tedious chore in earlier AutoCAD versions was getting all the leaders to line up; it usually involved drawing a construction line and then using object snaps to move common points on the leaders to the construction line. To line up multileaders, choose Align from the Multileader drop-down list.

- **MLEADERCOLLECT:** Multileaders can contain blocks as well as text (we cover blocks in Chapter 17). Choose Collect from the Multileader drop-down list to gather a group of leaders containing blocks; they'll rearrange themselves as a single multileader containing the multiple blocks.

For more information on any of these commands, look them up by name in the Command Reference section of the online help.

Multileaders and multileader styles can be annotative or non-annotative. Making them annotative and assigning appropriate annotation scales is a huge timesaver for creating them initially and for creating detail views at different scales.

Entering New Dimensions

In This Chapter

▶ Placing dimensions in drawings

▶ Choosing a dimensioning method

▶ Creating and modifying your own dimension styles

▶ Adjusting dimension sizes to suit the drawing plot scale

▶ Placing and modifying annotative dimensions, including details at other scales

▶ Modifying dimensions

*1*n drafting — either CAD or manual drafting — *dimensions* are special text labels with attached lines that together clearly indicate the size of something. Although it's theoretically possible to draw all the pieces of each dimension by using AutoCAD commands, such as LINE and MTEXT, *dimensioning* is so common of a drafting task that AutoCAD provides special commands for doing the job more efficiently. These dimensioning commands group the parts of each dimension into a convenient, easy-to-edit package much like a block. In fact, AutoCAD actually produces each dimension as something it calls an *anonymous block*. We discuss blocks in Chapter 17.

Even better, as you edit an object — by stretching a line, for example — AutoCAD automatically updates the measurement displayed in the dimension text label to indicate the object's new size, as shown in Figure 14-1. And perhaps best of all, AutoCAD's *annotative* dimensions adjust their text height and arrowhead size automatically to suit the annotation scale on the model tab or the viewport scale in a layout. We explain the general principles of annotative objects in Chapters 13 and 15; in this chapter, we take a close look at annotative dimensions.

Original dimension

Dimension updates
when you change the object.

Current annotation
scale

Figure 14-1: Changing objects automatically updates dimensions.

How Do You Measure Up?

Start off with a quick exercise to introduce AutoCAD's dimensioning functionality:

1. **Start a new drawing, using the `acad.dwt` template file.**

 This puts AutoCAD into imperial mode, even if your installation is metric. This saves us lazy writers from having to duplicate everything for metric users.

2. **Use the LINE command to draw a *non-orthogonal* line — that is, a line segment that's not horizontal nor vertical.**

 Make the line about 6 units long, at an angle of about 30 degrees upward to the right.

3. **Set a layer that's appropriate for dimensions as current.**

 Okay, you started from a blank template, so it won't have any specific layers, but we included this step as a gentle reminder. As we discuss in Chapter 6, correct procedure is normally to have dedicated layers for visible edges, hidden edges, text, dimensions, section lines, hatching, and so on.

4. **Start the DIMLINEAR command by clicking the Dimension button on the left side of the Annotate tab's Dimensions panel, or type DLI and then press Enter.**

 If the Dimension button isn't displayed, click the down arrow at the bottom of whichever button is showing and then select Dimension.

 AutoCAD prompts with

   ```
   Specify first extension line origin or <select object>:
   ```

5. **To specify the origin of the first extension line, snap to the lower-left endpoint of the line by using Endpoint object snap.**

 If you don't have Endpoint as one of your current running object snaps, specify a single endpoint object snap by holding down the Shift key, right-clicking, and choosing Endpoint from the menu that appears. (See Chapter 7 for more about object snaps.)

 AutoCAD prompts you:

   ```
   Specify second extension line origin:
   ```

 You <u>must</u> use object snaps when applying dimensions in order to make later editing work properly.

6. **To specify the origin of the second extension line, snap to the other endpoint of the line by using Endpoint object snap again.**

 AutoCAD draws a *horizontal* dimension — the length of the displacement in the left-to-right direction — if you move the crosshairs above or below the line. It draws a *vertical* dimension — the length of the displacement in the up-and-down direction — if you move the crosshairs to the left or right of the line.

 AutoCAD prompts you:

   ```
   Specify dimension line location or
   [Mtext/Text/Angle/Horizontal/Vertical/Rotated]:
   ```

7. **Move the mouse to generate the type of dimension you want — horizontal or vertical — and then click wherever you want to place the dimension line.**

 AutoCAD draws the dimension.

 When you're specifying the dimension line location, you usually *don't* want to object-snap to existing objects. Rather, you want the dimension line and text to sit in a relatively empty part of the drawing rather than have it bump into existing objects. If necessary, temporarily turn off running object snap (for example, click the OSNAP button on the status bar) to avoid snapping the dimension line to an existing object.

If you want to be able to align subsequent dimension lines easily, turn on Snap Mode and set a suitable snap spacing — more easily done than said! — before you pick the point that determines the location of the dimension line. See Chapter 4 for more information about Snap Mode. The DIMSPACE command can also be used to select several existing dimensions and then automatically space them equally.

 8. **Repeat Steps 4 through 7 to create another linear dimension of the opposite orientation (vertical or horizontal).**

 9. **Click the line to select it.**

 10. **Click one of the grips at an end of the line and drag it around.**

 Watch in amazement as the dimensions automatically update, live and in real time, to reflect the current values as you move the mouse.

Your second reaction, after the shock and awe wear off, will probably be to say (hopefully not out loud if other people are within earshot), "Yes, that's cute, but we don't dimension to four places of decimal, and normal text in our drawings uses a different font, and we need to dual-dimension in imperial and metric units, and some of our dimensions need to show manufacturing tolerances. . . ."

Why dimensions in CAD?

You may think that CAD would have rendered text dimensions obsolete. After all, you comply with all our suggestions about using AutoCAD precision techniques when you draw and edit, and you're careful to draw each object at its true size, right? The contractor or machinist can just use AutoCAD to query distances and angles in the DWG file, right? Sorry, but no (to the last question, anyway). Here are a few reasons why the traditional dimensioning that CAD drafting has inherited from manual drafting is likely to be around for a while:

 ✔ **Some people need to or want to use paper drawings when they build something.** Even with iPads and AutoCAD WS, we're still some time away from the day when contractors haul computers around on their tool belts (never mind mousing around a drawing while hanging from scaffolding).

 ✔ **In many industries, paper drawings still rule legally.** Your company may supply both plotted drawings and DWG files to clients, but your contracts probably specify that the plotted drawings govern in the case of any discrepancy. The contracts probably also warn against relying on any distances that the recipient of the drawings measures — using measuring commands in the electronic drawing file or a scale on the plotted drawing. The text dimensions are *supposed* to supply all the dimensional information that's needed to construct the object.

 ✔ **Dimensions sometimes carry additional information besides the basic length or angle.** For example, dimension text can indicate the allowable manufacturing tolerances or show that a particular distance is typical of similar situations elsewhere on the drawing, or can simultaneously show imperial and metric values.

Not a problem. AutoCAD controls the look of dimensions by means of *dimension styles,* just as it controls the look of text with text styles, and tables with table styles. In fact, AutoCAD also uses text styles to control the appearance of the text in dimensions. We cover dimension styles in more detail later in this chapter, but suffice it to say that AutoCAD has about 80 variables that can be used to warp dimensions into just about any perversion that your industry or company can imagine.

Meanwhile, look at the other basic types of dimension that AutoCAD can apply, as shown in Figure 14-2.

Figure 14-2: Examples of dimensioning commands.

A Field Guide to Dimensions

AutoCAD provides several types of dimensions and commands for drawing them; most commands are shown in Figure 14-2. These commands are found on the Dimensions panel of the Annotate tab of the Ribbon. If you can't find the button you want, it's probably hidden in the drop-down list under the larger button on the left side of this panel. This panel remembers the last button used, so at any given time, it may be displaying any one of the following buttons:

✔ **Linear:** DIMLINear. Indicates the linear extent of an object or the linear distance between objects. Most linear dimensions are either horizontal or vertical, but you can draw dimensions that are rotated to other angles, too.

✔ **Aligned:** DIMALIgned. Similar to linear dimensions, but the dimension line tilts to the same angle as a line drawn through the origin points of its extension lines.

You don't always have to pick points when placing dimensions. Watch the Command window; it may ask you to

```
Specify first extension line origin or <select object>:
```

If you press Enter instead of picking the first point, AutoCAD will ask you to select an object. And when you do, it automatically selects each end of the object for you.

✔ **Angle:** DIMANGle. Indicates the angular measurement between two lines, the two endpoints of an arc, or two points on a circle. The dimension line appears as an arc that indicates the sweep of the measured angle.

✔ **Radial:** DIMDIAmeter, DIMRADius. This has nothing to do with AM or FM electromagnetic radiation. A *radius* dimension shows the radius of a circle or an arc, and a *diameter* dimension calls out the diameter of a circle or an arc. You can position the dimension text inside or outside the curve; refer to Figure 14-2. If you position the text outside the curve, AutoCAD (by default) draws a little cross at the center of the circle or arc. AutoCAD automatically adds the diameter and radius symbols to the appropriate dimension type.

If you're wondering when you should use which (because radius and diameter dimensions seem to do the same thing), the convention in most drafting disciplines is to use diameter dimensions for whole circles (for example, a hole) and radius dimensions for part circles or arcs (for example, a fillet).

You can also use DIMLINear to dimension a circle or arc. Trying to pick the endpoints of a circle can keep you busy for several hours, but if you press Enter at the first prompt and then select an arc or circle, it will apply a linear dimension across the diameter.

✔ **Arc Lenth:** DIMARC. Measures the length of an arc as though it were stretched out straight, and then applies a curved dimension line concentric with the arc.

✔ **Jog:** DIMJOGGED. No, this has nothing to do with dimensioning your morning exercise run. Standard drafting practice when dimensioning arcs is to create a dimension line that starts at the center of the arc and proceeds outward to the arc itself. A problem arises, however, when dimensioning arcs with a very large radius. The center may be at an inconvenient location

where the dimension line would interfere with other geometry — or worse yet, may be well beyond the edge of the final drawing. DIMJOGGED neatly solves this problem for you. It works almost exactly like DIMARC except that it asks you to specify two extra points. After you select the arc (or circle, strangely enough), it then asks you to specify a center override point and then for a location for the jog itself. The resulting dimension line consists of three segments, starting at the center override point: The first and last point to the real center, and the middle segment connects the ends of the other two to put a jog in the line.

✔ **Ordinate:** DIMORDinate applies X or Y coordinate dimensions from an origin point. Certain types of mechanical parts can have a great many holes and other features. The drawing would get impossibly cluttered if you were to apply two traditional dimensions to show the X and Y locations of each detail. Common practice in this situation is to use ordinate dimensioning. Each ordinate dimension appears simply as a single extension line and a number showing the X or Y distance from the origin of the drawing or from the origin of the current User Coordinate System (UCS) if there is one. We cover UCSs in Chapter 7. Normal practice is to specify the lower-left corner of the part to be the origin. The X and Y values are usually aligned neatly in a row and column along the edge of the part. There are no dimension lines or arrowheads.

These basic dimension commands are also found in the upper-right corner of the Annotation panel of the Home tab on the Ribbon.

Leaders used to be placed by using a command from the dimensioning set, but they are now much more powerful and versatile, and so are considered to be text annotations. We cover them in Chapter 13.

The lazy drafter jumps over to the quick dimension commands

Three dimensioning commands can help you place multiple dimensions very quickly. They are found on the right side of the Dimensions panel of the Annotate tab of the Ribbon.

✔ **Continue:** DIMCONTinue. Having placed one linear dimension, you can now carry on to place a series of end-to-end dimensions. AutoCAD automatically picks the end of the previous dimension as the start of the next one, so you need to pick the end of only the next one.

✔ **Base:** DIMBASEline. This works much like DIMCONTinue except that AutoCAD selects the start of the previous one as the start of the next one. You thus end up with a series of dimensions, all measuring from a common starting point.

- **Quick Dimensions:** QDIM. Interestingly, this is one of the very few dimensioning commands that doesn't start with DIM*xxx*. When you invoke it, it invites you to select objects. The best bet usually is to use one or more Window selections (pick left to right), each of which completely surrounds several objects. Now, when you press Enter to continue, AutoCAD automatically applies DIMLINear dimensions wherever it can (and you might be surprised at some of those places!). It can place dimensions in several formats, including continue, baseline, staggered, ordinate, and several others. For convenience in repeat operations, it remembers the last mode you used.

If you want to be superefficient, memorize the three-letter keyboard aliases for the dimension commands you use the most. The aliases for the most common commands are shown in Figure 14-2.

The AutoCAD dimensioning commands prompt you with useful information at the command window or dynamic-input prompts. Read the prompts during every step of the command, especially when you're trying a dimensioning command for the first time. When all else fails. . . .

Dimension associativity

By default, AutoCAD groups all the parts of each dimension — the extension lines, dimension lines, arrowheads, and text — into a special *associative dimension* object. *Associative* means two things:

- **The different parts of the dimension function as a single object.** When you click any part of the dimension, AutoCAD selects all its parts.

- **The dimension is connected to the points on the object that you specified when you drew the dimension.** If you change the size of the object (for example, stretch a line), the dimension updates appropriately. The lines and arrows move, and the text changes to reflect the line's new size.

The associative dimensions we're talking about here first appeared in AutoCAD 2002. Before that, AutoCAD had a more primitive kind of dimensioning. Dimensions were single objects, and they did update if you stretched an object *if* you were very careful to include the dimension itself in the crossing selection for the STRETCH command. Here's where things can get a bit confusing: AutoCAD used to call these old-style, single-object dimensions *associative* but now calls them *non-associative.* And what used to be called *non-associative dimensions* before AutoCAD 2002 are now called *exploded dimensions* — but if you Explode a dimension, you get four lines, two arrowheads, and a piece of text. Sometimes you can't tell the players even with a program. For more information about how to determine which kind of dimension AutoCAD draws, see the "Controlling and editing dimension associativity" section, later in this chapter. We mention the old style here only because you will probably encounter it in old drawings.

As much as we like the Drafting & Annotation workspace and the Ribbon, one task where using the classic interface just might be more efficient is in dimensioning. The classic Dimension toolbar provides access to more dimension tools than the Ribbon, and it does so while maintaining consistent one-click access to each command. With the Ribbon, you may find it takes a couple of clicks to get to the command you want, and some dimension commands aren't even there.

Here's how to turn on the Dimension toolbar in a Ribbon-based workspace:

1. **Click the View tab on the Ribbon.**

2. **On the User Interface panel, click Toolbars.**

 AutoCAD displays a menu of loaded customization files. If your system doesn't have Express Tools installed, or if you're using AutoCAD LT, you may see only AutoCAD (or AutoCAD LT) on this menu. If you're working for a large company, you may well see additional custom menus on this list.

3. **Click AutoCAD or AutoCAD LT to display a list of classic toolbars.**

4. **Choose Dimension from the menu.**

 AutoCAD closes the Toolbars menu, and the classic Dimension toolbar appears either floating or docked on an edge of the drawing area.

Where, oh where, do my dimensions go?

In this section, we explain where to *put* your dimensions, not where to *place* them. Huh? Right. We aren't going to tell you to place dimensions outside the part outline, with smaller ones closer to the part and longer ones farther away, and so on. What we're covering next is the location in the file where your dimensions will live. Okay, if that still isn't clear, then read on, and you'll find that it is actually quite simple. You can choose one of three different methods for dimensioning your drawings:

✔ **You can place your dimensions in model space by using non-annotative dimensions.** This is the oldest method, and for many years was the only possible way. We mention it here because you are bound to encounter many of the millions and millions of existing drawings that were created this way.

 • *Advantage:* Dimensions are available in model space as you edit the drawing.

 • *Disadvantage:* As with text (Chapter 13) and hatching (Chapter 15), dimension objects have to be scaled to suit the drawing scale. Placing dimensions on details at other scales can get really ugly. We cover scale factors in Chapter 4 as well as later in this chapter.

✔ **You can place your dimensions in paper space.**

This was introduced as the second-generation method in an attempt to overcome the scaling issue. You can reach from paper space through a layout viewport and snap onto the model space objects. Dimensions remain associative and will usually change when the model space objects change.

• *Advantage:* You don't need to set a dimension scale factor to suit the drawing scale. The dimension scale factor is always 1:1 because paper space layouts are usually plotted full-size, and the viewport scale sets the model space scale factor.

• *Disadvantages:* The dimensions aren't available when editing in model space, so you're flying blind. In addition, the associative connections between the paper space dimensions and the model space objects are very fragile and are easily broken. There is a repair command, but it's a nuisance to have to use it.

✔ **You can place dimensions in model space by using annotative dimensions.**

This is the newest, latest, greatest, and best way of placing dimensions. Annotative dimensions automatically size themselves to suit the drawing scale that you choose. We discuss annotative text in Chapter 13, annotative hatching in Chapter 15, and annotative dimensions later in this chapter.

• *Advantages:* Dimensions are available in model space while you're drawing and editing, you don't need to mess with dimension scale factors, and applying dimensions to drawing details that are at a different scale from the main drawing becomes trivial.

• *Disadvantage:* Annotative dimensions have been slow to catch on because people are stuck in the older ways ("That's how we've always done it!") and because they don't understand a couple of subtleties about them that we reveal in Chapter 13. If you're the first in your office to adopt annotative dimensions, then everyone else will hail you as the Great AutoCAD Guru and will be pestering you to help them learn how to use them.

The Latest Styles in Dimensioning

Near the beginning of this chapter, we show a quick exercise on placing dimensions. At the end of it, you perhaps said to yourself, "Yes, that's cute, but we don't dimension to four places of decimal, and normal text in our drawings uses a different font, and we need to dual-dimension in imperial and metric units, and some of our dimensions need to show manufacturing tolerances. . . ."

Now that we've progressed this far in dimensioning, you're probably still asking yourself the same question. Note that talking to yourself isn't a problem, and arguing with yourself is getting borderline, but losing those arguments is a definite sign of trouble.

In this section, we discuss how to set those factors that control the format and appearance of dimensions, but we start with a brief anatomy lesson. AutoCAD uses the names shown in Figure 14-3 and described in the following list to refer to the parts of each dimension:

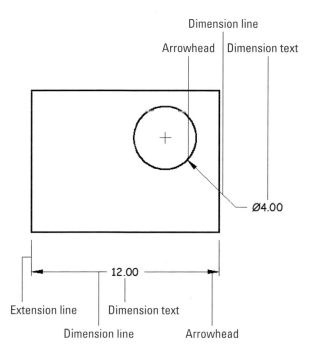

Figure 14-3: The parts of a dimension.

- ✓ **Dimension text:** The numeric value that indicates the true distance or angle between points or lines. Dimension text can also include other information in addition to or instead of the number. For example, you can add a suffix, such as TYP., to indicate that a dimension is typical of several similar configurations; you can add manufacturing tolerances; and you can show dual dimensioning in alternate units.

- ✓ **Dimension lines:** In linear dimensions, the *dimension lines* indicate the true distance between points. Angular dimensions have curved dimension lines with the center of the curve at the vertex point of the objects being dimensioned. For radius and diameter dimensions, the dimension

line simply points at or through the center of the object being dimensioned.(See Figure 14-2 for examples of these dimension types.)

- **Arrowheads:** The dimension's *arrowheads* appear at the end or ends of the dimension lines and emphasize the extent of the dimensioned length. AutoCAD's default arrowhead style is the closed, filled type shown in Figure 14-3, but you can choose other symbols, such as dots or tick marks, to indicate the ends of the dimension lines. (Don't get "ticked off," but AutoCAD calls the line ending an *arrowhead* even when, as in the case of a tick mark, it doesn't look like an arrow.)

- **Extension lines:** These extend outward from the definition points (also known as *defpoints*) that you select (usually by snapping to points on an object) to the dimension lines. By drafting convention, a small gap usually exists between the defpoints and the beginning of the extension lines. Also by convention, the extension lines usually extend just past the dimension lines — refer to Figure 14-3 for examples. AutoCAD makes dimensions look tidier by assigning fixed gap sizes and projection lengths for the extension lines, and if you need to dimension to circles or center lines, you can assign dash-dot linetypes to either or both extension lines.

- **Defpoints:** When you create any kind of dimension, AutoCAD places one or more definition points (universally known as *defpoints*) on a special layer named (what else?) Defpoints, which the program creates when a dimension command is issued for the first time. These points are usually invisible because the objects being dimensioned are on top of them, but you can see where they sit by selecting a dimension to turn on its grips. The grips on the objects being dimensioned are on the dimension's definition points. Because you wouldn't want these points to appear when you plot your drawings, the Defpoints layer has a special property: Nothing created on the Defpoints layer will ever print.

Because of the Defpoints layer's nonprinting property, experienced users have been using it for years as a place to put sketches, guidelines, and important notes (for example, "Don't forget to buy bread on the way home!"). We don't endorse this practice because a convoluted relationship exists between the Defpoints layer and Layer0. Namely, it can be very hard to tell what's on which layer, and that can make the drawing harder to edit. If you want a "scratch" layer for those important notes, create one named Scratch and set it to NoPlot in the Layer Properties Manager palette. (For more about layers and the Layer Properties Manager, see Chapter 6.)

In the early days, AutoCAD controlled the appearance of dimensions by using about 20 dimensioning *system variables*. For example, to switch dimension text from showing decimal values to showing fractions, the setting of DIMLUNIT would be changed from 2 to 5. Similarly, DIMDEC sets the number of places of decimal, or the smallest fraction (would you believe 1/256 of an inch?). We discuss system variables in Chapter 26.

The problem was that every time you wanted to switch back and forth between decimals and fractions, you had to change these two variables. To set a system variable, or SysVar, you enter its name, followed by a suitable value as determined from Help. The only reason we mention this is because you're bound to run into older drawings that were done this way.

The good news is that AutoCAD later added named dimension styles. You can now set up a decimal style, a fractional style, a style with specific manufacturing tolerances, and so on. All it takes is a couple of quick mouse clicks to switch between them.

Some people will try to warn you that AutoCAD dimensioning is a big, complicated, difficult subject. Don't be alarmed, however. The basic principles are actually quite simple. The problem is that every industry has its own dimensioning conventions, habits, and quirks. As usual, AutoCAD tries to support them all — and, in so doing, makes things a bit cumbersome for everyone.

The good news is that you should have to adjust things to suit your specific industry or company only once, and then all dimensions will suit the specified standard. The really good news is that it usually takes only a bit of fine-tuning of the default settings to cover most of your dimensioning needs.

Dimension styles are saved within the current drawing. The really, really good news is that you can save this drawing as a *template* file (we cover templates in Chapter 4) so that all new drawings created from this template will have the dimension styles predefined. The really, really, really good news is that you're working in an office where someone has already set up suitable dimension styles. If this is the case, you can skim over the next section a little more quickly.

You add dimensions to a drawing *after* you've drawn at least some of the geometry; otherwise, you won't have much to dimension! (Well, duh.) Your dimensioning and overall drafting efficiency improve if you add dimensions in batches rather than draw a line, place a dimension, draw another line, place another dimension. . . .

Creating and managing dimension styles

A *dimension style* (or *DimStyle* for short) is a collection of drawing settings called *dimension variables* (or *DimVars* for short), which are a special class of the *system variables* that we describe in Chapter 26.

If you *do* need to create your own dimension styles or you want to tweak existing ones, use the DIMSTYLE command. You can invoke it by clicking the small diagonal arrow in the lower-right corner of the Dimensions panel of the Annotate tab of the Ribbon. This brings up the Dimension Style Manager dialog box, as shown in Figure 14-4.

Figure 14-4: Yet another manager, this one for dimension styles.

Every drawing comes with a default dimension style named Standard (for imperial [feet-and-inches] drawings) or ISO-25 (for metric drawings) and a matching Annotative style. We cover Annotative dimensions later in this chapter. Although you can use and modify the Standard or ISO-25 style, we suggest that you leave them as-is and create your own dimension style(s) for the settings that are appropriate to your work. This approach ensures that you can use the default style as a reference. More important, it avoids a potential naming conflict that can change the way your dimensions look if the current drawing gets inserted into another drawing. (Chapter 17 describes this potential conflict.)

When you install AutoCAD, it checks with Windows to see what country was selected when Windows was installed, and then sets its measurement system accordingly. If you're in the United States or one of the few other (backward) countries that still use imperial units, the default dimension style is Standard; most of the rest of the world defaults to ISO-25. Canada, on the other hand, is nominally metric, but most people still use imperial. The system variable MEASUREINIT controls the default action. If set to 0 (zero), AutoCAD uses imperial units; if set to 1, metric units are used. Among other things, this setting also affects text styles (see Chapter 13), hatching (see Chapter 15), and noncontinuous line types (see Chapters 4 and 6).

Starting a new drawing from an ISO template (for example, `acadiso.dwt`) forces everything to metric, and starting a new drawing from a non-ISO template (for example, `acad.dwt`) forces everything to imperial, regardless of the setting of MEASUREINIT.

The system variable MEASUREMENT can be used to override the default for a specific drawing, but it affects only text, hatching, and noncontinuous line types.

Let's get stylish!

The following steps describe how to create your own dimension style(s):

1. **On the Ribbon's Home tab, click the label of the Annotation panel to open the panel slideout, and then click the Dimension Style button.**

 Alternatively, if that just sounds like too much work, you could type **D** and press Enter. The Dimension Style Manager dialog box appears.

2. **In the Styles list, select the existing dimension style whose settings you want to use as the starting point for the settings of your new style.**

 For example, select the default dimension style named Standard or ISO-25.

3. **Click the New button to create a new dimension style that's a copy of the existing style.**

 The Create New Dimension Style dialog box appears.

4. **Enter a New Style Name and then select or deselect the Annotative check box. Click Continue.**

 Select the Annotative check box to create an annotative dimension style, or deselect it for a non-annotative style. Refer to Chapter 13 and later in this chapter for more about annotative objects.

 The New Dimension Style dialog box appears. (This dialog box is virtually identical to the Modify Dimension Style dialog box.)

5. **Modify dimension settings on any of the seven tabs in the New Dimension Style dialog box.**

 See the descriptions of these settings in the next section of this chapter.

6. **Click OK to close the New Dimension Style dialog box.**

 The Dimension Style Manager dialog box reappears.

7. **Click Close.**

 The Dimension Style Manager dialog box closes, and your new dimension style becomes the current dimension style that AutoCAD uses for future dimensions in this drawing.

8. **Draw some dimensions to test your new dimension style.**

Avoid changing existing dimension styles that you didn't create unless you know for sure what they're used for. When you change a dimension style setting, *all* existing dimensions that use that style change to reflect the revised setting. Thus, one small dimension variable setting change can affect a large number of existing dimensions! To play it safe, instead of modifying an existing dimension style, create a new style by copying an existing one and modifying the new one.

A further variation on the already convoluted dimension styles picture is that you can create dimension *substyles* (also called *style families*), which are variations of a main style that affect only a particular type of dimension, such as radial or angular. If you open the Dimension Style Manager dialog box and see names of dimension types indented beneath the main dimension style names, be aware that you're dealing with substyles.

Adjusting style settings

After you click New or Modify in the Dimension Style Manager dialog box, AutoCAD displays a tabbed New Dimension Style or Modify Dimension Style dialog box (the two dialog boxes are identical except for the title bar) with a mind-boggling — and potentially drawing-boggling, if you're not careful — array of settings.

Fortunately, the dimension preview that appears on all tabs — as well as on the main Dimension Style Manager dialog box — immediately shows the results of most setting changes. With the dimension preview and some trial-and-error changing of settings, you can usually home in on an acceptable group of settings. For more information, use the dialog box help feature: Just hover your mouse pointer over the setting that you want to know more about.

Before you start messing with dimension style settings, it's important to know what you want your dimensions to look like when they're plotted. If you're not sure how it's done in your industry, ask others in your office or profession, or look at a plotted drawing that someone in the know represents as being a good example. A general rule we've found to be helpful in virtually all aspects of life is to stick with the defaults unless you know specifically what you want to change — and why.

The following sections introduce you to the more important tabs in the New/Modify Dimension Style dialog boxes and highlight useful settings. Note that whenever you specify a distance or length setting, you should enter the desired *plotted* size. We discuss plotting size scale factors in Chapters 13 (text) and 15 (hatching), and later in this chapter.

Following lines and arrows

The settings on the Lines tab and the Symbols and Arrows tab control the basic look and feel of all parts of your dimensions, except text.

Symbolically speaking

The settings on the Symbols and Arrows tab control the shape and appearance of arrowheads and other symbols.

A useful setting is Center Marks. Depending on which radio button you select, placing a radius or diameter dimension will also identify the center by placing a small center mark, or center lines that extend just beyond the circle or arc, or none. The default is tick marks, but we prefer lines because normal drafting practice is usually to show center lines.

Tabbing to text

Use the Text tab to control how your dimension text looks — the text style and height to use (see Chapter 13) and where to place the text with respect to the dimension and extension lines. In particular, note the Text Style dropdown, which contains a list of the text styles available in the drawing. The three-dot button at the right end of the list gives direct access to the text style dialog box so you can edit or create a suitable text style if one doesn't already exist in your current drawing. See Chapter 13 for more information on text styles. The default Text Height in imperial units is too large for most situations — set it to 1/8", 3mm, or another height that makes sense.

Even if you're opposed to defacing books, get out a bright red marker and put a circle around this warning, even if you borrowed the book from the library or a friend. Here goes: You *must* define the text style that you specify for a dimension style with a height of 0 (zero) in the Text Style dialog box. (See Chapter 13 for more information about variable-height and fixed-height text styles.) If you specify a fixed-height text style for a dimension style, the text style's height will override the Text Height setting in the New/Modify Dimension Style dialog boxes. Use a zero-height style to avoid the problem — and bear in mind that using nonzero-height text styles in dimensions is one of the most common mistakes made by new AutoCAD users.

Getting fit

The Fit tab includes a bunch of options that control when and where AutoCAD shoves the dimension text if it doesn't quite fit between the extension lines. The default settings leave AutoCAD in "maximum attempt at being helpful" mode — that is, AutoCAD moves the text, dimension lines, and arrows around automatically so that things don't overlap. On rare occasions, AutoCAD's guesses might be less than perfect. It's usually easier to adjust the

text placement by grip editing the placed dimension, as we describe in the section "Editing dimension geometry," later in this chapter, instead of messing with dimension style settings.

Even at its most helpful, AutoCAD sometimes makes a bad first guess about how you want your dimension text and arrows arranged. If you're having problems getting the look you want, don't flip your wig — flip your arrows to the other side of the dimension lines by selecting the dimension and choosing Flip Arrow from the multifunction grip on the arrow.

Most important, the Fit tab includes the Annotative check box. Using annotative dimensions, as we recommend in this chapter, will make your dimensioning go a lot more smoothly!

We highly recommend that you get comfortable with annotative dimensioning in model space. Unfortunately, old-style (that is, non-annotative) dimensioning is still part of the program, and many offices will probably keep doing it that way for a while to come.

The Use Overall Scale Of setting corresponds to the DIMSCALE system variable, and you'll hear long-time AutoCAD drafters refer to it as such. In Chapters 13 (text) and 15 (hatching), we refer to a scale factor by which text height and hatch patterns need to be multiplied so they plot properly. This also applies to dimensions. If you are using old-style non-annotative dimensions, this is where that number goes. It resizes text height, arrowhead sizes, and gaps accordingly. When Scale Dimensions to Layout (for paper space layout dimensioning) is selected, DIMSCALE is automatically set to 0 (zero). When Annotative is selected, DIMSCALE is ignored, and a suitable scale factor is applied to each dimension when it's created.

Using primary units

The Primary Units tab gives you highly detailed control over how AutoCAD formats the characters in the dimension text string. You usually want to set the Unit format and Precision and maybe specify a suffix for unitless numbers if it's not clear from your drawing what units you're using. You may also change the Zero Suppression settings, depending on whether you want dimension text to read 0.5000, .5000, or 0.5. ("Zero Suppression!" also makes a great rallying cry for organizing your fellow AutoCAD drafters.)

AutoCAD 2010 introduced an interesting tweak to dimension text: Dimension *subunits*. If the main unit of measure on your drawing is meters — rather than have a bunch of smaller distances dimensioned as, say, 0.450 — you could create a centimeter subunit so that any dimension of less than 1 meter would be shown in centimeters. We were always taught a very strict drafting standard that says that all dimensions on a drawing must be in the same units. In other words, in a drawing with meters as the dimension unit, 0.45 would

be correct, and 45cm would be incorrect. Check your own office standards before you incorporate this feature, which you can find on the Primary Units tab of the New/Modify Dimension Style dialog box.

Other style settings

If your work requires that you show dimensions in two different systems of measure (such as inches and millimeters), use the Alternate Units tab to turn on and control alternate units. Alternate Units display both dimensions at once.

If your work requires listing construction or manufacturing tolerances (for example, 3.5 +/-0.01), use the Tolerances tab to configure the tolerance format that you want.

 AutoCAD also includes a separate TOLERANCE command that draws special symbols called *geometric tolerances.* If you need these symbols, you probably know it (and you have our sympathies); if you've never heard of them, just ignore them. Look up *Geometric Tolerance* dialog box in the AutoCAD help system for more information.

Size Matters

As discussed in Chapter 13, Chapter 15, and earlier in this chapter, the size of text and dimensions applied in model space has to be adjusted to suit the final plotting scale of the drawing. As we repeat several times in several chapters, by far the best way of doing this is to use annotative dimensions. To see what we mean, try this:

1. **Start a new, blank imperial drawing.**

 Use the `acad.dwt` template.

2. **Draw a horizontal line about 20 units long.**

3. **Apply a linear dimension (DimLin, or DLI) to the line.**

 Pretty hard to read, isn't it?

4. **Switch to the Annotative dimension style.**

 Find the window in the upper-right corner of the Dimension panel of the Annotate tab of the Ribbon that reads `Standard`. Click it and then choose Annotative from the drop-down list.

5. **Change the drawing scale.**

 Select the 1:5 scale from the drop-down list under the Annotation Scale button in the lower-right corner of the drawing window.

6. **Dimension the line again.**

Ah, that's better, and it didn't require any esoteric calculations.

 To avoid confusing results, which is what has turned most users off from using annotative annotations, make sure that the Automatically Add Scales button in the lower-right corner is turned off. We discuss this more in Chapter 13.

Details at other scales

Dimensioning details at different scales was always the hardest type of dimensioning, and still is unless you use annotative dimensions.

The hard way

We used to draw the complete object full-size, including all the fine details, zooming in as necessary. Next, we would copy those elements that made up the fine detail and then use the SCALE command to resize them to suit the detail scale. Finally, we would apply dimensions to the scaled one that had two suitable scale factors: First, we had to set the dimension scale factor to suit the overall drawing scale (say 1:2), and then we had to set the DIMLFAC (DImension Linear FACtor) to suit the detail scale.

The problem is that we have been telling you all along to draw "full size" so that dimensions automatically measure the object to which they are applied, but now our detail is at a different scale. DIMLFAC is a fudge factor applied to dimensions that corrects the measured value, so a 1" line in a 5:1 detail will measure as 1 inch, not 5 inches. Ouch. And we haven't even gone into all the gruesome details about how to calculate all those scale factors, and heaven help you should you need to edit the main view or the detail. Again, we mention the hard way only because a lot of existing drawings are lurking out there.

The easy way

Here's the easy way to create a multiscale drawing, such as the one in Figure 14-5.

1. **Draw the object full-size in model space, including the small notch detail.**

2. **Select the 1:10 scale from the drop-down list under the Annotation Scale button in the lower-right corner of the AutoCAD window.**

3. **Apply the three dimensions that show in the Scale 1:10 view in Figure 14-5, using an annotative dimension style.**

 The figure shows paper space, but you're working in model space.

Figure 14-5: A drawing with a detail at another scale.

4. **Apply an annotative hatch, as we discuss in Chapter 15, and then draw the center line.**

5. **Edit the properties of the hatch pattern and the 1.400 dimension to add 1:2 scale factors, as we describe in Chapter 13.**

6. **Make sure that the Automatically Add Annotative Scales button is turned off, and change the Annotation Scale to 1:2.**

 Three existing dimensions disappear, and the hatch and the 1.400 dimension resize themselves.

7. **Add the 1.500 and 2.400 dimensions.**

8. **Now comes the magic part. Switch to the paper space Layout 1 tab. Click the viewport boundary and then grip edit it approximately to the size and location shown.**

 Your model space drawing is probably not properly located, and the hatch and dimensions won't show.

9. **Click the viewport boundary again, and then click the Viewport Scale button (it probably reads something like 0.694694) and select 1:10 from the scale list.**

 The viewport zooms accordingly, and the hatch and 1:10 dimensions appear. If necessary, double-click in the viewport to enter model space and then pan accordingly.

 Don't zoom, or you lose the scale setting!

10. **Double-click outside the viewport to return to the paper space layout.**

11. **Create a second viewport by using the VPORTS command, or simply COPY and then modify the existing one.**

12. **Repeat Steps 8 and 9 on the new viewport, but use a Viewport Scale of 1:5.**

Use the Lock/Unlock button to lock the viewports to prevent inadvertent messing with them.

There you have it! A multiview, multiscale detail drawing without duplicating any geometry or annotations. To see the real magic of this, go to the model space tab and observe that there is still only one model of the part and no detail at the other scale. Now use the STRETCH command to play with the depth and location of the notch. Go back to the Layout 1 tab to see how everything has automatically updated in both views. Magic!

Editing Dimensions

After you draw dimensions, you can edit the position of the various parts of each dimension and change the contents of the dimension text. AutoCAD groups all the parts of a dimension into a single object.

Editing dimension geometry

The easiest way to change the location of dimension parts is to use grip editing, which we describe in Chapter 10. Just click a dimension, click one of its grips, and maneuver away. You'll discover that certain grips control certain directions of movement. In general, selecting a dimension displays grips at the text, the ends of the dimension lines, and the defpoints. Experiment for a few minutes to see how they work.

In AutoCAD 2012, dimensions joined the group of objects that feature multifunction grips. Click the text grip on a linear dimension and use the grip menu to adjust the text location. Click an arrow grip, and you can create a continuous or baseline dimension from that end of the dimension, or you can flip the arrow. You can do these things by selecting a dimension and changing items in the Properties palette, but the multifunction grips make it a lot more efficient.

If you want to change the look of a component of a specific, individual dimension (for example, substitute a different arrowhead or suppress an extension line), use the Properties palette. (See Chapter 11 for more on the Properties palette.) All the dimension settings in the New/Modify Dimension Style dialog boxes (see "Adjusting style settings," earlier in this chapter) are available from the Properties palette when you select one or more dimensions.

More fine tweaking

In manual drafting, it's considered bad form to cross object lines (that is, real geometry) with dimension lines or extension lines, or to have anything cross a dimension line. Dimension Break (DIMBREAK) prompts you to select a dimension and then an object to break it. The really wild thing here is that this is a smart break. If you do anything to the dimension or to the object being broken to change where they cross, then the break follows accordingly — and if you change either item so that they no longer cross — the break heals itself. Better yet, if you change things yet again so that they cross again, the break reappears!

The Dimension Space (DIMSPACE) command applies a specified separation between existing linear or angular dimensions. Spacing dimensions equally — if you don't use the DIMBASELINE command as they're created — requires tedious manipulation with Snap and MOVE.

A fundamental mantra in AutoCAD is that you should always draw everything full-size. There may be occasions, however, where this isn't always practical. For example, you may be designing a power-transmission shaft for a large machine. The shaft is 4" in diameter and 12' long. It has a variety of splines, keyways, and bearing shoulders on each end, but the 11' section in the middle is simply a straight cylinder. If you draw it full-size and scale the plot to fit a suitable paper size, you'll never see the details at each end.

Common practice is to draw the interesting end details but to break out and remove the boring center section, bringing the ends closer together. Now you can create a reasonable plot. The problem is that any dimension that crosses over the break, such as the overall length, won't show the correct value. The solution is to override the value (we explain how a little later in this chapter) and then to use the DIMJOGLINE command to insert a jog in the dimension line to indicate that the dimension line isn't the true length.

In spite of the name similarities, don't confuse DIMJOGLINE with the DIMJOGGED command covered earlier. DIMJOGLINE is for linear dimensions and DIMJOGGED is for radial dimensions.

If you select one or more dimensions and right-click, the menu displays a number of useful options for overriding dimension settings or assigning a different style.

When you change a setting in the Properties palette, you're *overriding* the default style setting for that dimension. If you need to make the same change to a bunch of dimensions, it's usually better to create a new dimension style and assign that style to them. You can use the Properties palette or the right-click menu to change the dimension style that's assigned to one or more dimensions.

Earlier in this chapter, we describe the pre-DimStyle days when we had to manually change DimVars to get different dimension appearances. This process still works, but it can cause all sorts of problems. If you manually change a DimVar setting, this gets applied to the current dimension style as an override, and all subsequent dimensions that are placed by using this style have the overridden appearance. This can cause much the same problem as overriding object properties instead of using different layers; if you edit a dimension style, then all existing dimensions that use it update, including the ones that you hadn't expected because they seem to be different from the desired ones.

You can use the Properties palette to turn on AutoCAD's background mask feature (described in Chapter 13) for the text of individual dimensions: Select the dimensions, display the Text area in the Properties palette, and find the Fill Color item. Click in the list box, scroll down, and select Background to use the drawing background color (which usually gives the best results). To ensure that dimension text lies on top of other objects, use the DRAWORDER or TEXTTOFRONT command — see Chapter 13 for more information.

The AutoCAD EXPLODE command on the Home tab's Modify panel will blow a dimension to smithereens — or at least into a bunch of line and multiline text objects. Don't do it! Exploding a dimension makes it much harder to edit cleanly and eliminates AutoCAD's ability to update the dimension text measurement automatically.

Editing dimension text

In most cases, you shouldn't have to edit dimension text. Assuming that you draw your geometry accurately and pick the dimension points precisely, AutoCAD displays the right measurement. If you change the size of the associated object, AutoCAD updates the dimension and its measurement. However, you may occasionally want to *override* the dimension text (that is, replace it with a different measurement) or *add* a prefix or a suffix to the true measurement.

AutoCAD creates dimension text as multiline text, so dimension text has the same editing options as ordinary text. There are several ways of launching the dimension text editor, but the easiest is to simply double-click the dimension text.

AutoCAD displays the true dimension length as text in the actual dimension (and keeps the text up-to-date if you change the size or location of the object). You can override the true length by typing a specific length or other text string. You can preserve the true length but add a prefix or suffix by inserting <> (that is, the left and right angle-bracket characters) as placeholders for the dimension value. For example, if you enter **About <>** and the actual distance is 12.000, AutoCAD displays About 12.000 for the dimension

text. If you stretch the object later on so that the actual distance changes to 14.528, AutoCAD changes the dimension text automatically to read About 14.528. Now you can appreciate the importance of drawing and editing geometry precisely!

Avoid the temptation to override the default dimension text by replacing the angled brackets with a numeric value unless you plan on using the DIMBREAK command on the dimension. Doing so eliminates AutoCAD's ability to keep dimension measurements current, but even worse, you get no visual cue that the default distance has been overridden (unless you edit the dimension text). If you're overriding dimension text a lot, it's probably a sign that the creator of the drawing didn't pay enough attention to using precision techniques when drawing and editing. We're not going to point any fingers, but you probably know whom to talk to.

Controlling and editing dimension associativity

When you add dimensions by selecting objects or by using Object Snap modes to pick points on the objects, AutoCAD normally creates associative dimensions, which are connected to the objects and move with them. This is the case in new drawings that were originally created in any release of AutoCAD starting with 2002.

If you have to work on drawings created or last edited in versions older than AutoCAD 2002, you must set the DIMASSOC system variable to 2 before later releases will create associative dimensions. An easy way to make this change for the current drawing is to open the Options dialog box (click the Application button and choose Options from the bottom of the Application Menu), click the User Preferences tab, and turn on the Make New Dimensions Associative setting. Be aware that this setting affects only new dimensions that you draw from now on. To make existing non-associative dimensions associative, use the DIMREASSOCIATE command described in the following list. Look up *DIMASSOC system variable* in the AutoCAD help system for more information.

You aren't likely to need any of these three commands very often, but if you do, look up the command name in the online help system:

 ✓ **DIMREASSOCIATE:** If you have dimensions that aren't currently associative (probably because they were created in older versions of AutoCAD) or are associated with the wrong objects, you can use the DIMREASSOCIATE command to associate them with points on the objects of your choice. DIMREASSOCIATE can be found on the Annotate tab's Dimensions panel slideout, or you can just type **DRE** and press Enter.

- **DIMDISASSOCIATE:** You can use the DIMDISASSOCIATE (DDA) command to sever the connection between a dimension and its associated object.

- **DIMREGEN:** In a few special circumstances, AutoCAD doesn't automatically update geometry-driven associative dimensions. (Maybe Autodesk should call them "usually-fully-awake-but-occasionally-asleep-at-the-wheel associative dimensions.") In those cases, the DIMREGEN (no command alias) command will fix things.

The bad puns and witty jokes in this chapter came from our resident DimWit.

15

Down the Hatch!

In This Chapter

▶ Adding hatching to your drawings
▶ Using predefined and user-defined hatch patterns
▶ Making solid fills
▶ Choosing hatching boundaries
▶ Using annotative hatching
▶ Copying existing hatches
▶ Editing hatches

*I*f you were hoping to hatch a plot (or plot a hatch), see Chapter 16. If you want to hatch an egg, look for *Raising Chickens For Dummies,* by Kimberly Willis and Robert T. Ludlow. If you need to fill in closed areas of your drawings with special patterns of lines (*cross-hatching*, or more commonly just *hatching*) or solid fills, this is your chapter.

An AutoCAD *hatch* is a separate object that fills a space; has an appearance dictated by the hatch pattern assigned to it; and by default is associated with the objects that bound the space, such as lines, polylines, or arcs. If you move or stretch the boundaries, AutoCAD normally updates the hatching to fill the resized area.

Batten Down the Hatches!

Drafters often use hatching to represent the type of material that makes up an object, such as insulation, metal, and concrete. In other cases, hatching helps emphasize or clarify the extent of a particular element in the drawing — for example, showing the location of walls in a

building plan or highlighting a swampy area on a map so you know where to avoid building a road. Figure 15-1 shows an example of hatching in a structural detail. In mechanical design, it's used to show the cut faces of cross sections.

Figure 15-1: A big batch o' hatch.

This section gives you a quick jump-start on the basic process used to create hatching and shows you how easy it is. We'll also cover many of the options included in the Hatch Creation contextual Ribbon tab, shown in Figure 15-2, and how to edit existing hatched areas.

The following steps show you how to hatch an enclosed area by using the *pick points* method of selecting the hatch area:

1. **Start a new drawing, using the acad.dwt template for imperial units or acadISO.dwt for metric.**

 Draw a circle with a radius of 5 units (imperial) or 50 units (metric). Draw a second circle inside the first with a radius of 2 units (imperial) or 20 units (metric).

2. **Start the HATCH command by typing H and pressing Enter, or click the Hatch button on the Draw panel of the Ribbon's Home tab.**

 The Hatch Creation contextual Ribbon tab (see Figure 15-2) appears, but just ignore it for the time being.

3. **Move the cursor around on the screen.**

 As the cursor moves within any enclosed area in your drawing, a quick preview appears to show you how the final hatching would look like if you picked a point inside that particular area. Starting from outside the larger circle, move it into the space between circles; then into the inner circle, and then back into the space between circles — and note the changes.

4. **Change some of the hatch options.**

 The quick preview updates as you select any variants or change any values in the Hatch Ribbon panels. Try different patterns. The three little arrows along the right side of the Pattern panel scroll you through all the different patterns that are available. Our personal favorite is Escher.

5. **Pick a point in the region between the circles.**

 Press Enter or the spacebar, or right-click and then click Enter.

 Congratulations! You've just done in a few seconds — something that would have taken an hour or more in pencil-and-paper days.

 But wait! There's more!

6. **Time for a change.**

 Click the outer circle, and then click and drag one of the four outer grips to change the diameter of the circle. Watch in shock and awe as the hatching updates to match. This is *associative hatching*.

 Now click the inner circle, and then click and drag its center grip to change its location. What happens when you move the smaller one outside the larger one? And what happens when you move it back inside?

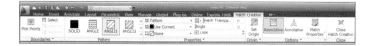

Figure 15-2: The Hatch Creation contextual Ribbon tab.

Don't Count Your Hatches. . .

Now that you've seen how easy it is to create hatched areas, explore the main options within the contextual Hatch tabs of the Ribbon. If you start the HATCH command, you get the Hatch Creation tab you used previously. But if you double-click an existing hatch, you get the Hatch Edit tab — they are virtually identical.

Working from left to right, you find:

- **Boundaries**

 If you followed the earlier example in this chapter, you already used the easiest, most intuitive, and most common way of defining the boundary of a hatch when you simply picked inside the desired region. If you pick multiple regions within one run of the HATCH command, each region is hatched, and the result is one hatch object. This means that later, when you edit the properties of any region, all regions are updated. This is commonly used when hatching the cut faces of a cross section; all faces common to a single item automatically maintain matching hatch properties.

 You can also select an area to be hatched by picking specific objects to define the boundary, but you must select enough objects to define a fully enclosed region. In the previous section, our pick points exercise shows how the hatch pattern behaves when you select the region between the circles — it doesn't hatch the inner circle. This is *island detection*. If you select specific objects for the boundary, island detection is turned off. In the exercise, if you had selected the outer circle, the hatching would run right over the inner circle.

 No matter which selection method you choose, the boundary must be airtight. Boundary objects can overlap, but there can't be any leaks, not even microscopic ones. Okay, technically, it is possible to set a fuzz factor to allow for very tiny leaks, but because this defeats the purpose of drawing with precision, we're not going to tell you about it.

 The A Closed Boundary Could Not Be Determined error message means that you need to repair lines or other objects so they define a fully airtight boundary. Sometimes you can use the FILLET command with a 0 (zero) fillet radius to force two lines to meet exactly. Another possibility is to use grip editing to align one endpoint precisely with another. Chapters 10 and 11 discuss these two editing techniques. The HATCH command displays one or more red circles at gaps in the not-quite-enclosed area you want to hatch. Even if it won't fix the gaps, it does show you where *you* should fix them.

Moving right along, the next panel in the Hatch tab is Pattern.

- **Pattern**

 If you think a bride planning a wedding has a wide range of patterns to choose from, take a peek at AutoCAD's collection of hatch patterns. The scroll arrows at the right-hand edge of this panel give access to the 82 predefined hatch patterns, including 9 solid and gradient fills that ship with AutoCAD.

Hatch patterns are defined by external files named `acad.pat` or `acadlt.pat` (imperial units), or `acadiso.pat` or `acadltiso.pat` (metric units). Each file includes the definitions for all the patterns. You can also create your own hatch patterns — the online help system's Customization Guide explains how — or you can buy libraries of custom hatch patterns. Any patterns not defined in `acad.pat` or `acadiso.pat` are referred to as *custom patterns*, but you must be careful when using them. Because they are external files, they must be available to AutoCAD when you open a drawing containing them. If you send the drawing to someone else, you must also send the pattern definition file, which can have copyright issues if you bought the patterns.

Autodesk created the hatch patterns whose names begin with *AR-* particularly for use in architectural drawings, and unlike the non-AR patterns, they *do* represent real objects such as brick and roof shakes. The AR patterns were designed with a final hatch scale of 1.0 in mind, but in some cases, you'll have to adjust up or down in order to achieve a suitable scale.

⌐ **Properties**

This panel contains buttons for as many as ten different properties that can be attached to hatches, but many of them can be covered in other ways. We identify them by their default values. Your results may differ.

- *Pattern:* See the Pattern panel.

- *Use Current:* This button refers to color, and should nearly always be ByLayer, which is what the current general color override should be.

- *None:* This button refers to background color, which can be useful when using hatching to portray actual objects. For example, a brick pattern could have a red background so the hatched region looks like red bricks, as shown in Figure 15-3.

- *Hatch Transparency:* The options for this button range from 0 (opaque) to 90% transparent.

- *Angle:* Hatch patterns can be rotated as desired. For example, in mechanical design, you may be cutting a cross section of an assembly. Standard practice is to hatch the resultant cut faces, usually with ANSI31, and to adjust the rotation angles so that each part has a different angle to help distinguish one from another. Note that some patterns — the ANSI series, in particular — usually have an initial 45-degree rotation built in.

- *Scale:* Ah, here's the big one (pun intended). We cover it in more detail in the "Size Matters!" section, a little later in this chapter.

✔ **Origin**

Typically, AutoCAD creates hatched areas by having them radiate outward from the origin, effectively turning them on and off as they encounter boundaries. This can cause problems with some of the real-object patterns, however. You wouldn't want a brick wall to start with 68.3% of a brick, so the Origin option lets you snap to an exact point, as shown in Figure 15-3.

Figure 15-3: Poorly laid red bricks (top). Properly laid red bricks (bottom).

✔ **Options**

- *Associative:* By default, hatches are associative to their boundaries. This means that they know about each other, which explains what happened when you change and move the circles in the earlier pick points exercise.

- *Annotative:* Just like text (Chapter 13) and dimensions (Chapter 14), hatches must be scaled properly to match the drawing scale. We cover this in more detail in the "Size Matters!" section, later in this chapter.

- *Match properties:* This function lets you select an existing hatch object and then copy its properties onto another hatch object, just like the Format Painter in many Windows applications.

✔ **Close**

This closes the Hatch tab. Well, duh.

Size Matters!

Hatches are actually annotation objects just like text (Chapter 13) and dimensions (Chapter 14) in that they don't directly contribute to the geometry of what you're drawing. However, they do impart additional information.

Just like text and dimensions, hatches also need to be scaled to suit the final drawing scale. Start with the common ANSI31 pattern. As defined, it produces parallel lines spaced 1/8" apart. So far, so good, but what if you're drawing the cross section of a large part, such as the 10'-long boom for a backhoe? Remember to always draw full size and then scale when you plot. If you were to apply hatching at the nominal 1:1 scale and then plot at 1:10 to get your boom to fit onto a smaller sheet of paper, then your 1/8" hatch spacing becomes 0.0125", which effectively becomes a solid fill. As with text and dimensions, you need to apply a scale factor of 10 to your hatches. The hatch lines in your drawing file then turn out to be 1.25" apart, which scale down to 1/8"- when you plot. We also discuss scale factors in Chapter 4.

We can do this the hard way. . .

The hard way (the old way) is to calculate the scale factor before placing the hatching and then enter it into the appropriate window in the Properties panel of the Hatch tab of the Ribbon, hoping you don't need to change the plotting scale later. You don't even want to think about setting the scale for a detail at a different scale in the same drawing.

. . . or we can do this the easy way

The easy way is to select the drawing scale from the Scale List button in the lower-right corner of the AutoCAD screen, the same as we do for text (Chapter 13) and dimensions (Chapter 14), and then to turn on the Annotative button on the Options panel of the Hatch tab of the Ribbon. Now when you create hatches, they will scale themselves correctly to suit the current plot scale. Chapter 14 shows an example of hatching with multiple annotative scales assigned to it.

The setting of the Annotative button is good only for the current editing session, and must be reset if you add more hatching later. AutoCAD's Help facility states that this setting is saved in the drawing, but it isn't.

In Chapter 14 (dimensions), we strongly recommend that you turn off the *Automatically Add Scales* button when placing annotative text and dimensions because you normally don't want everything to show at every scale especially when creating details at other scales. Hatches, on the other hand, normally *do* show in every view at every scale, scaled accordingly. You might be

tempted to turn this button back on for hatching, but if you do, the first time you change the drawing scale, *all* existing annotative objects get the new scale added to them. The best practice is to edit the hatches and manually add the desired scales, the same as we discuss in Chapter 13 for text and Chapter 14 for dimensions.

Don't confuse Annotative with Associative, even though both are polysyllabic words that start with A and are right next to one another in the Hatch Creation tab's Options panel. *Annotative* hatch objects scale themselves automatically to suit the drawing scale. *Associative* hatch objects (enabled by default) update to the new area when you change the hatch boundary. And if that isn't enough, Chapter 19 covers parametrics, which include annotational annotative associative dimensions. Would we lie to you?

Annotative versus non-annotative

Figure 15-4 shows two versions of the same drawing, dressed up with annotative and non-annotative hatch patterns. As the annotation scales displayed on the drawings' status bars show, the annotative hatches change their scale, while the non-annotative hatches remain unchanged.

Chapter 14 shows another example of this. The hatching in both views is actually the same object, but the viewports have different scales, and so the hatching adjusts accordingly.

Before annotative hatching first appeared in AutoCAD 2008, the only way to get the effect in these two views in both drawings was to create two separate layers — one for each hatch scale — hatch the object twice, and then freeze and thaw layers as appropriate.

Figure 15-4: Hatches annotative (and not).

Hatching should be placed on a dedicated layer or layers so it can be easily turned on or off.

Layers for hatching should always use the *Continuous* line type. Many hatch patterns use noncontinuous lines, and if you put them on a layer with a non-continuous line type, it confuses things to no end.

By default, when you select a number of closed areas and then press Enter, the hatched areas will be created as a single object; choose Create Separate Hatches on the Options slideout panel if you want to be able to modify each hatched area.

Set the Draw Order drop-down list to specify whether the hatch objects are in front of or behind the hatch boundary or other drawing objects (see Figure 15-5). By default, they get sent behind their boundary, which is typically what you want. If a hatch is a different color from its boundary and if it's in front of its boundary, the tips of the hatch objects produce a dotted-line effect along the boundary.

Figure 15-5: Hatch options for every occasion.

Pushing the Boundary (Of) Hatch

In the remainder of this chapter, we show you how to refine the techniques presented in the preceding section. We describe how to copy existing hatching, take advantage of the various options in the Hatch and Gradient dialog

box (which offers a bit more control than the Hatch Creation contextual tab), and choose more complicated hatching boundaries.

Your hatching has no style!

A minor problem is that unlike text and dimensioning, you can't create named styles for hatching. The good news is that three workarounds can help offset this.

Plagiarism 101: Editing hatches. Okay, it's not really plagiarism, but it's close. Suppose you have a drawing with several different styles of hatching applied. You now realize that one of them has the wrong specifications. No problem. Simply select the problem hatch, which brings up the Hatch Editor tab of the Ribbon. It's virtually identical to the Hatch Creation tab. From the Hatch Editor tab, you can change any of the properties. The better news is that it also has an Inherit Properties button. Click it, and then click an existing hatch — the original hatch inherits all the properties of the selected hatch.

You can select more than one existing hatch at a time. Any changes you make on the Hatch Editor tab are applied to all the selected hatches.

Plagiarism 201: Cloning hatches. Suppose you have a drawing with several different styles of hatching applied, and now you want to hatch another area. You start the HATCH command, and the Hatch contextual Ribbon appears. Oops, it shows the specifications of the last hatch that was applied, which is quite different from what you want to do now. No problem; simply click the Match Properties button on the Options panel of the Hatch Creation tab, or the Inherit Properties button in the Hatch and Gradient dialog box. Pick an existing hatch, and hey! Presto! All the settings update to match the selected hatch! You can use the cloned settings as is, or you can modify them as desired.

Plagiarism 301: Palettizing hatches. Here's one that even many experienced users miss. It is remarkably easy to customize AutoCAD so that a single mouse-click can produce any hatch style you want. Here's how:

1. **Apply a Hatch with the desired properties.**

 If your existing drawing has such a hatch, this step can be skipped.

 Make sure that the existing hatch is on the correct layer and that the layer has all the correct properties.

2. **Display the Tool Palette window.**

 Select the Tool Palettes tool from the Palettes panel of the View tab of the Ribbon. We discuss tool palettes in Chapter 2.

3. **Display the Hatches and Fills palette by clicking its tab.**

 If you can't see this tab, click the overlapping edges of the tabs at the bottom of the palette window and select Hatches and Fills from the list that appears.

4. **Create your new Hatch tool.**

 Click once to select the existing hatch object, pause, and then select it again. Drag it onto the tool palette and drop it.

 Don't double-click too quickly, and don't click the blue grip, or you'll just end up editing the existing object.

5. **Use your new Hatch tool.**

 Click your hatch tool and then click inside a closed boundary in your drawing. Bingo! Instant hatching to your desired specifications! Note that it even puts hatching on the same layer as the original sample.

 But wait! There's more! If you start a new drawing, create a boundary, and then use your Tool palette to hatch it, you'll be amazed to find that the new hatching in the new drawing is on the correct layer. If the correct layer doesn't exist in the new drawing, AutoCAD creates it to match the original specifications.

 This is *standardization through customization*.

Hatch from scratch

An alternative to using the Ribbon is the Hatch and Gradient dialog box, as shown in Figure 15-6. You don't see your hatch object updating as you change settings the way you do with the Ribbon, but you do have a bit more control over what you're going to end up with. To display the Hatch and Gradient dialog box, click the dialog box launcher (the teeny arrow at the right end of the Options panel of the Ribbon's Hatch Creation tab).

You can use predefined, user-defined, or custom hatch patterns. Most of the time, you'll choose predefined hatch patterns unless some generous soul gives you a custom pattern. On the other hand, we haven't used a user-defined pattern in over 25 years of using AutoCAD. They consist solely of continuous lines. All you can define is the spacing, the rotation angle, and whether the lines are parallel pairs. And all this can be duplicated with standard patterns.

By default, the right third of the Hatch and Gradient dialog box is hidden; to see the additional hatch options at the right side of the dialog box, shown in Figure 15-6, click the More Options arrow beside the Help button.

Figure 15-6: The Hatch tab of the expanded Hatch and Gradient dialog box.

Pick a pattern, any pattern: Predefined hatch patterns

To use AutoCAD's predefined hatch patterns, select Predefined from the Type drop-down list at the top of the Hatch tab in the Hatch and Gradient dialog box. This selection sets the stage for choosing the hatch pattern.

You specify a predefined hatch pattern in one of two ways:

- **Pattern drop-down list:** If you know the name of the hatch pattern, select it from the Pattern drop-down list. The list is alphabetical, except that SOLID (that is, a solid fill) appears at the very beginning.

- **Pattern button:** If you don't know the pattern name or if you prefer the visual approach, click the Pattern button (the tiny button with the ellipsis [three dots] to the right of the Pattern drop-down list and pattern name) to display the Hatch Pattern Palette with pattern previews and names.

Figure 15-7 shows some of the other predefined hatch patterns, which cover everything from Earth to Escher to Stars.

When is a pattern not a pattern? When it's a solid fill

AutoCAD treats filling an area with a solid color as a type of hatching. Simply choose SOLID from the top of the Pattern drop-down list. You'll also see several gradient-fill options.

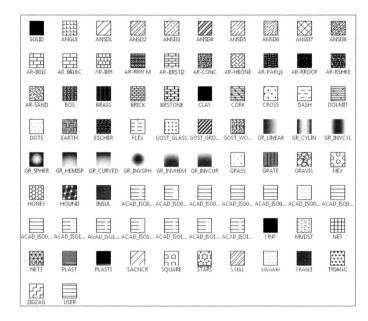

Figure 15-7: A veritable plethora of hatch patterns.

Like any other object, a solid hatch takes on the current object color — or the current layer's color if you leave color set to ByLayer. Therefore, check whether the current object layer and color are set appropriately before you use the Solid hatching option (see Chapter 6 for details).

Here's looking through you, kid

AutoCAD's transparency object property is probably most useful (in 2D, anyway) when applied to solid hatches. You can use transparent solid hatches to demarcate areas on architectural floor plans or aerial photographs of project sites. In addition to the settings we list in the preceding paragraph, make sure that the current object or layer transparency is set correctly, too.

Editing Hatch Objects

Editing an existing hatch pattern is simple after you're familiar with the Ribbon's Hatch Creation tab. Follow these steps:

1. **Select the hatch object.**

 AutoCAD opens the Hatch Editor contextual Ribbon tab and displays the hatch object's current settings.

2. **Make any desired changes and watch the real-time preview as you do. When you're happy, click Close Hatch Editor to keep the changes.**

Alternatively, you can use the Properties palette or the Quick Properties palette (described in Chapter 6) to make most existing hatch pattern changes. By default, AutoCAD displays the Hatch Editor tab when you click a hatch object, and opens the Quick Properties palette when you double-click a hatch object. The Quick Properties palette is especially good for changing several hatches at once.

Simple grip editing is also available. Select a hatch, and then hover the cursor over the round blue center grip. A contextual menu pops up to give you quick access to changing the hatch origin, angle, and scale, all without running the HATCHEDIT command. Don't be misled by the Stretch option on the context menu, though; you can only move a hatch with this option — and when you do, it loses its associativity to its boundary.

Here are a few other hatch tips:

- You can make one hatch look like another without even opening the Hatch Editor tab by using the Match Properties button on the Clipboard panel of the Ribbon's Home tab.

- The MIRRHATCH system variable lets you mirror drawing geometry that includes hatches without mirroring the hatch angle. This can be very useful when creating drawings of symmetrical objects. Model one half, apply the hatching, and then MIRROR (see Chapter 11) to get the other half. The hatch angle remains consistent on both sides of the mirror line.

- You can find the area of any hatch object by simply selecting the hatch object and then opening the Properties palette. The area is listed in the Geometry section, near the bottom of the palette.

Don't go overboard with hatching. The purpose of hatching is to clarify, not overwhelm, the other geometry in the drawing. If your plots look like a patchwork quilt of hatch patterns, it's time to simplify.

Always try to apply hatching last. The HATCH command is smart enough to recognize text and dimensions that fall within the hatched area. It will treat them like sterile eggs and will automatically leave no hatch zones around them. If you forget, or if a need for a note arises later, you'll need to apply background masking to the text. We discuss this in Chapter 13.

The Plot Thickens

*D*espite the infinitesimally small number of offices without a computer (or two) on every desk, many people still want or need to work with easily readable electronic drawings (can you spell PDF?) or actual, dead-tree paper drawings. You may need to give hard-copy prints or PDFs to your less-savvy colleagues who don't have AutoCAD, or to people on construction sites where relatively delicate computers wouldn't survive very long. You may want to make some quick paper prints to pore over during your bus ride home. You may even find that checking drawings the old-fashioned way — with a hard-copy print and a red pencil — turns up errors that managed to remain hidden on the computer screen.

Hard copies may also survive longer as historic records. There are 10-year-old CAD files that can no longer be opened because the company that produced the software that was used to create them no longer exists, and their software won't run on current operating systems. On the other hand, we can still read some Egyptian papyrus scrolls that are several thousand years old.

Whatever the reason, you'll want to print drawings at some point — probably sooner rather than later. Depending on where you are in a project, plotting is the pop quiz, midterm, or final exam of your drawing-making semester. This chapter helps you ace the test.

You Say Printing, We Say Plotting

Plotting originally meant creating hard-copy output on a device that was capable of printing on larger sheets, such as D size or E size (or A1 or A0 for the metrically inclined), that measure several feet (or a meter or more) on a side. (See Chapter 4 for information about drafting-paper sizes.) These plotters often used pens to draw, robot-fashion, on large sheets of vellum or drafting film. The sheets could then be run through *diazo blueline machines* — copying machines that create blueline prints — to create less-expensive copies. *Printing* meant creating hard-copy output on ordinary printers that used ordinary-sized paper, such as A size (letter size, 8½ x 11 inches) or B size (tabloid or ledger size, 11 x 17 inches): A4 or A3 for you metric folk.

Nowadays, AutoCAD and most CAD users make no distinction between plotting and printing. AutoCAD veterans usually say "plotting," so if you want to be cool, you can do so, too.

Whatever you call it, plotting an AutoCAD drawing is potentially more complicated than printing a word-processing document or a spreadsheet. CAD has a larger range of different plotters and printers, drawing types, paper sizes, and output procedures than other computer applications. AutoCAD tries to help you tame the vast jungle of plotting permutations, but you'll probably find that you have to take some time to get the lay of the land and clear a path to your desired hard-copy output. As we indicate in the Introduction section to this book, after you find your sweet spot, plotting actually becomes quite routine.

The Plot Quickens

After reading the preceding paragraph, you probably realize that you're not going to master AutoCAD plotting in five minutes. That doesn't change the fact that your boss, employee, wife, husband, construction foreman, or 11-year-old daughter wants a quick check plot of your drawing.

Plotting success in 16 steps

Here's the quick, cut-to-the-chase procedure for plotting a simple drawing — a mere 16 steps! This isn't as bad as it sounds, however, because you can later see how to save the procedure specifications so they can be reused

with considerably less effort. This procedure assumes that you plot in model space: that is, that clicking the Model button on the status bar shows you the drawing in a way that you want to plot. (We cover plotting paper space layout tabs in the upcoming section, "Plotting the Layout of the Land.") This procedure doesn't deal with controlling plotted lineweights; see the "Plotting Lineweights and Colors" section, later in this chapter, for those details. It should, however, result in a piece of paper that bears some resemblance to what AutoCAD displays on your computer monitor.

Follow these steps to make a simple, not-to-scale, *monochrome* (black-and-white) plot of a drawing:

1. **Open the drawing in AutoCAD.**

2. **Click Model (not the MODEL/PAPER button) on the status bar to ensure that you're plotting the model space contents. If you have the Model and Layout tabs displayed, rather than the status bar buttons, click the Model tab.**

 We explain model space and paper space in Chapters 4 and 5, and how to plot paper space layouts in the section, "Plotting the Layout of the Land," later in this chapter.

3. **Zoom to the drawing's current extents; click the Zoom Extents button on the Navigation bar (if necessary, click the tiny down arrow below the Zoom button and choose Zoom Extents from the menu). Or type Z, press Enter, type E, and then press Enter again.**

 The extents of a drawing consist of a rectangular area just large enough to include all the objects in the drawing.

4. **To display the Plot dialog box, click the Plot button on the Quick Access Toolbar.**

 The Plot dialog box appears, as shown in Figure 16-1.

 AutoCAD automatically appends whatever you're about to plot in the dialog box's title bar. For example, in Figure 16-1, the dialog box title is Plot – Model. If you're plotting a layout and haven't changed the layout name, the title might be Plot – Layout1. If you have changed the layout name, the dialog box title will be Plot – First Floor Plan (or whatever you renamed it). In this book, we call it (simply) "the Plot dialog box."

5. **In the Printer/Plotter area, select a device from the Name drop-down list.**

 For your first quick-and-dirty plot, select *Default Windows System Printer pc3*, assuming that your computer has a generic printer attached to it. If you don't have a system printer connected, choose *Microsoft XPS Document Writer*. This will create a file that can be viewed with Internet Explorer.

More Options button

Figure 16-1: The Plot dialog box.

6. **In the Paper Size area, select a paper size that's loaded in your printer or plotter.**

For most generic Windows desktop printers this will be Letter (8.5" x 11"), ANSI A-size (11" x 8.5"), or ISO A4 (210mm x 297mm)

7. **In the Plot Area area (sponsored by the Department of Redundancy Department), select Extents from the What to Plot drop-down list.**

This will plot all your drawing.

8. **In the Plot Offset (Origin Set to Printable Area) area, select the Center the Plot check box.**

Alternatively, you can specify offsets of 0 (zero) or other amounts in order to position the plot at a specific location on the paper.

9. **In the Plot Scale area, select the Fit to Paper check box.**

 For most real plotting, you'll plot to a specific scale. Select the Fit to Paper check box for now to get our quick-and-dirty plot. We cover plotting to a specific scale in the "Instead of fit, scale it" section, later in this chapter for guidance.

10. **Click the More Options button (at the bottom-right corner of the dialog box, next to the Help button).**

 The Plot dialog box reveals additional settings, as shown in Figure 16-2.

Figure 16-2: The expanded Plot dialog box.

11. **In the Plot Style Table (Pen Assignments) area, choose monochrome. ctb or monochrome.stb from the drop-down list.**

 If AutoCAD asks whether you want to assign this plot style table to all layouts, answer No for the time being.

12. **In the Plot Options area, make sure that the Plot with Plot Styles check box is selected and also that the Save Changes to Layout check box is deselected, as shown in Figure 16-2.**

 Leaving the Save Changes to Layout check box deselected tells AutoCAD to use any plot settings changes that you make *only for this plot.* AutoCAD will revert to the original plot settings the next time you plot the drawing.

After you become confident with plotting, you may want to select this check box so that AutoCAD *does* save your plotting settings changes as the default. Alternatively, click the Apply to Layout button to make the current plot settings the default for future plotting of this tab (that is, the Model tab) in this drawing.

13. In the Drawing Orientation area, choose Portrait or Landscape.

The icon (the letter *A* on a sheet) in the lower-right corner may help you decide on the right orientation. If not, the full preview in the next step will tell you for sure.

14. Click the Preview button and check to make sure that the drawing appears on the paper at the correct orientation and size, shown in Figure 16-3, and then right-click and choose Exit to return to the Plot dialog box.

Figure 16-3: A preview of coming plot-tractions.

15. If you find any problems in the preview, adjust the plot settings (for example, Plot Area, Plot Scale, or Drawing Orientation) and repeat the preview until the plot looks right.

16. Click OK to create the plot.

When AutoCAD finishes generating and sending the plot, it displays a Plot and Publish Job Complete balloon notification from the status bar. If you decide that you don't want to see these notifications, right-click the Plot/Publish Details Report Available icon near the right end of the status bar and deselect Enable Balloon Notification.

There! — 16 steps, as promised. On the other hand, we never promised that this plot would be usable. For example, if you tried to plot a large, complex D-size or E-size architectural drawing on an A-size sheet of paper, it won't be very readable without a microscope. The bottom line, however, is that you produced a plot! Read the rest of this chapter for all the details about the numerous other plotting options available in AutoCAD. If you had trouble with this quick plot, you may want to jump ahead in this chapter to the troubleshooting section, "The Plot Sickens," later in this chapter.

Get with the system

One of the complications you face in your attempts to create a hard copy is that AutoCAD has two distinct ways of communicating with your plotters and printers. Operating systems, and the programs that run on them, use a special piece of software called a *printer driver* to format data for printing and then send it to the printer or plotter. When you configure Windows to recognize a new printer connected to your computer or your network, you're actually installing the printer's driver. AutoCAD, like other Windows programs, works with the printers you've configured in Windows. AutoCAD calls these *system printers* because they're part of the Windows operating system.

But AutoCAD, unlike other Windows programs, can't leave well enough alone. Some output devices, especially some larger plotters, aren't controlled very efficiently by the Windows system printer drivers. For that reason, AutoCAD comes with specialized *nonsystem drivers* (that is, drivers that are not installed as part of the Windows system) for plotters from companies such as Hewlett-Packard, Xerox, KIP, and Océ. These drivers ignore the tidy rules for communicating with Windows printers in order to get things done a bit more quickly and flexibly.

Most of the time, using already-configured Windows system printers is easiest, and they work well with many devices, especially devices such as laser and inkjet printers that print on smaller paper. However, if you have a large-format plotter, you *may* be able to get faster plotting, better plot quality, or more plot features by installing a nonsystem driver. To find out more, choose Installation & Deployment➪Driver and Peripheral Guide➪Use Plotters and Printers on the AutoCAD online help system's home page.

Configure it out

For now, you should simply make sure that AutoCAD recognizes the devices that you want to use for plotting. The following steps show you how:

1. **Launch AutoCAD and open an existing drawing or start a new, blank drawing.**

2. **Choose Options on the Application Menu — or type** OP **and press Enter — to open the Options dialog box; then click the Plot and Publish tab.**

3. **Click the drop-down arrow to view the list just below the Use as Default Output Device option, as shown in Figure 16-4.**

 The list includes two kinds of device configurations, designated by two tiny, difficult-to-distinguish icons to the left of the device names:

 - *Windows:* A little printer icon with a sheet of white paper coming out the top indicates a Windows system printer configuration.

 - *Nonsystem:* A little plotter-with-legs icon with a piece of paper coming out the front indicates a nonsystem (that is, AutoCAD-specific) configuration.

 The nonsystem configuration names always end in .pc3 because they're stored in special AutoCAD Plotter Configuration version 3 files. So, if you can't distinguish the difference between the icons, look for the .pc3 at the end of the name.

System printers List of devices

Non-system printers

Figure 16-4: System and nonsystem printer configurations.

4. **Verify that the list includes the printers and plotters that you want to have available in AutoCAD.**

 If they're not in the list, how you add one depends on your operating system:

 - *Windows XP:* Choose Start⊏⟩Printers and Faxes and then click the Add a Printer link under Printer Tasks on the left side of the window.

 - *Windows Vista:* Choose Start⊏⟩Control Panel⊏⟩Hardware and Sound⊏⟩Printers⊏⟩Add a Printer and then click Add a Local Printer.

 - *Windows 7:* Choose Start⊏⟩Devices and Printers⊏⟩Add a Printer and then click Add a Local Printer.

 If your printer isn't in the default Windows list, cancel the wizard and hunt down a driver disc that came with your printer. Better yet, download the current driver from the printer manufacturer's website.

5. **Choose the output device that you want to make the default for new drawings.**

6. **Click OK to close the dialog box and retain any changes that you made in the previous step.**

You use the AutoCAD Plotter Manager's Add-a-Plotter Wizard to create non-system driver configurations. (Choose Plotter Manager on the Plot panel of the Ribbon's Output tab to display an Explorer window containing a shortcut to the wizard.) This wizard is similar to the Windows Add Printer Wizard; if you can handle adding an ordinary printer in Windows, you can probably handle adding a nonsystem plotter configuration to AutoCAD. When you complete the wizard steps, AutoCAD saves the information in a PC3 (Plotter Configuration version 3) file. If you add an HP Designjet printer or certain Océ wide-format printers, you will be advised by the Add-a-Plotter Wizard to exit and instead install the device as a Windows system printer (for more information, choose Installation & Deployment⊏⟩Driver and Peripheral Guide⊏⟩ Use Plotters and Printers⊏⟩Set Up Plotters and Printers from the online help system's home page). Many people find that the standard drivers work fine, but as we mention later in this chapter, custom drivers may include additional paper sizes as well as other handy settings.

Preview one, two

One of the keys to efficient plotting is liberal use of AutoCAD's preview feature. (To maintain political balance, we recommend conservative use of some other AutoCAD options elsewhere in the book.)

The postage stamp–sized partial preview in the middle of the Plot dialog box is a quick reality check to make sure that your plot fits on the paper and is turned in the right direction. If the plot area at the current scale is too large for the paper, AutoCAD displays thick red warning lines along the side(s) of the sheet where the drawing will be truncated.

Click the Preview button to see a full preview in a separate window. You see exactly how your drawing lays out on the paper as well as how the various lineweights, colors, and other object plot properties will appear. You can zoom and pan around the preview by using the right-click menu.

Any zooming or panning that you do won't affect what area of the drawing gets plotted. Zooming and panning is just a way to get a better look at different areas of the plot preview.

Instead of fit, scale it

In most real plotting situations, you want to plot to a specific scale rather than let AutoCAD choose some oddball scale that just happens to maximize the drawing on the paper. And if you're going to plot the Model tab of a drawing to scale, you need to know its drawing scale factor. Chapter 4 describes setup concepts, and Chapter 13 provides some tips for determining the scale factor of a drawing that someone else created.

If your drawing was created at a standard scale, such as 1:50 or 1/4" = 1'–0", you simply choose the scale from the handy Scale drop-down list in the Plot dialog box. If your scale isn't in the list, type the ratio between plotted distance and AutoCAD drawing distance into the two text boxes below the Scale drop-down list, as shown in Figure 16-5. Usually the easiest way to express the ratio is to type **1** in the upper box and the drawing scale factor in the lower box. (See Chapter 4 for more information.)

Your CAD manager may have edited the Scale drop-down list to add uncommon scales or remove scales that your company never uses. If you're designing espresso machines in Milano, for example, you'll probably never need to plot your drawings at 1/128" = 1'–0".

Creating half-size plots for some purposes is common in some industries. To plot model space half-size, double the drawing scale factor. For example, a 1/8" = 1'–0" drawing has a drawing scale factor of 96, which is equivalent to a plot scale of 1 = 96. To make a half-size model space plot of it, specify a plot scale of 1 = 192 (or choose 1/16" = 1'–0" from the Scale drop-down list).

Figure 16-5: Lots of ways to scale.

Even if you work with drawings created to be plotted at a specific scale, plotting with a Fit to Paper scale may be the most efficient way to make a reduced-size check plot. For example, drafters in your office might create drawings that get plotted on D-size sheets (24 x 36 inches), whereas you have access to a laser printer with a B-size (11 x 17 inches) paper tray. By plotting the D-size drawings scaled to fit on B-size paper, you end up with check plots that are slightly smaller than half size. You won't be able to measure distances on the check plots with a scale, but you *can* give them a visual check for overall correctness.

Plotting the Layout of the Land

In the section "Plotting success in 16 steps," earlier in this chapter, we show you how to plot the model space representation of your drawing by making sure that the Model tab is active when you open the Plot dialog box. In most industries, however, model space plotting went the way of the dodo 20 years ago. Paper space gives you many additional options for controlling the look of your output without having to modify the underlying geometry. So most of the time, you will want to plot a paper space layout instead.

Paper space is the environment that's specifically designed for outputting hard copy of your drawings. If you need a refresher on paper space or layouts, have another look (or a first look!) at Chapter 5.

As we explain in Chapter 5, AutoCAD gives you two alternative ways of switching between full-screen model space and the paper space layouts stored in the drawing. If you choose to display the Model and Layout tabs, you simply click the appropriate tab to select the one you want. If instead you hide the Model and Layout tabs, use the Model and Layout buttons, plus Quick View Layouts, on the status bar. For the complete lowdown on using Quick View Layouts, refer to Chapter 5. In this section, we explain using this feature to print your paper space layouts.

Plotting a paper space layout is pretty much like plotting model space except that you need to find the appropriate layout first and make sure that its tab is selected before you open the Plot dialog box, as follows:

1. **Click Quick View Layouts on the status bar and scroll through the image panel.**

 The Quick View image panel opens in the lower part of the drawing area and displays a preview panel of model space and each layout stored in the drawing.

2. **Move your mouse pointer across the images in the Quick View panel and pause over the image of the layout that you want to plot.**

 As you move your mouse over each image, icons appear: Publish at the upper-right corner, and Plot at the upper left. We describe the PUBLISH command briefly in Chapter 20. In this chapter, we're sticking with PLOT.

3. **Click the Plot button in the upper-left corner of the image panel of the layout that you want to plot.**

 The Plot dialog box appears with the name of the layout to be plotted displayed in the title bar. (In Figure 16-6, we're plotting a layout named D-Size Layout.)

If no one has set up a layout yet, AutoCAD creates a default layout. (If the Show Page Setup Manager for New Layouts setting on the Display tab of the Options dialog box is turned on, you'll see the Page Setup Manager dialog box first — just click the Close button.) The default layout probably won't be useful for real projects, but you can use it to find out about the layout plotting procedure. Refer to Chapter 5 for instructions on creating a real layout.

4. **Specify a Printer/Plotter Name and a Paper Size.**

If you don't have a printer capable of outputting larger than letter- or tabloid-size sheets, you can still experiment by selecting a device that outputs to file, such as DWG To PDF.pc3.

5. **In the What to Plot drop-down list, choose Layout, as shown in Figure 16-6.**

The Layout option is available only when plotting a layout tab; Limits is available only when plotting the Model tab.

6. **Specify the Plot Offset (such as 0 in both the X and Y directions).**

Specifying the Plot Offset as 0 in both X and Y directions places the lower-left corner of the plotted drawing at the lower-left corner of the printable area.

7. **In the Plot Scale area, select 1:1 from the Scale drop-down list, as shown in Figure 16-6.**

One of the big advantages of layouts is that you don't need to know anything about drawing scale in order to plot the drawing; hence, the name *paper space*. Figure 16-6 shows the proper settings for plotting a layout.

To create a half-size plot of a layout, select 1:2 from the Scale drop-down list. In addition, select the Scale Lineweights check box to reduce lineweights proportionally. (We cover plotting lineweights in the next section.)

If you find that the layout is too big for your plotter's largest paper size at a plot scale of 1:1, you can select Extents from the What to Plot drop-down list and then select the Fit to Paper check box in the Plot Scale area. Alternatively, you can close the Plot dialog box and fix the problem if you want to have a paper space layout that permanently reflects a new paper size. Use the Page Setup dialog box to modify the layout settings, or copy the layout and modify the new copy.

8. **Click the More Options button and change any additional plot options that you want to.**

Refer to Steps 11 through 13 in the earlier section, "Plotting success in 16 steps."

Figure 16-6: Settings for plotting a paper space layout.

9. **Click the Preview button, ensure that the drawing displays on the paper at the correct orientation and size, right-click, and choose Exit from the menu that appears to return to the Plot dialog box.**

 If you found any problems in the preview, change your plot settings and preview again until it looks right.

10. **Click OK to create the plot.**

Plotting Lineweights and Colors

In previous sections of this chapter, we help you gain some plotting confidence. Those sections show you how to create scaled, monochrome plots with uniform lineweights in model space or paper space. Those skills may be all you need, but if you care about controlling plotted lineweights and colors or adding special effects such as *screening* (plotting shades of gray), read on.

Plotting with style

Plot styles provide a way to override object properties with alternative plot properties. (See Chapter 6 for information about object properties.) The properties include plotted lineweight, plotted color, and screening. Figure 16-7 shows the full range of options. Plot styles come in two exciting flavors:

- Color-dependent plot styles
- Named plot styles

Color-dependent plot styles are based on the standard way of plotting in earlier versions of AutoCAD (before AutoCAD 2000), whereas named plot styles provide a newer (but not necessarily better) way.

Figure 16-7: Editing a color-dependent plot style table.

It's remotely possible that you won't need to bother with plot styles. If the drawings you want to plot have layer and object properties (especially lineweights) that reflect how you want objects to plot, you can dispense with plot styles. But most people and most drawings use plot styles, so you should at least be familiar with them.

A couple of common reasons for using plot styles are to

- **Map screen colors to plotted lineweights.** If this idea seems completely loony to you, try to suspend judgment until you read the "Plotting through thick and thin" section, a bit later in this chapter.

- **Create screened lines on monochrome plots.** Lines that are screened display in various shades of gray, not black. Drafters sometimes use screened lines to de-emphasize secondary objects that otherwise would overwhelm the main objects in the drawing. Screening is expressed as a percentage, with 100 percent being completely black and 0 percent being invisible. For example, on a subdivision layout, you might want to de-emphasize all the property and house outlines except one.

Using plot styles

If you want objects in your drawing to plot with properties that differ from their display properties, you need plot styles. For example, you can plot with different lineweights or colors from the ones you're using for display purposes. Or, as we mention in the preceding section, you may need to map display colors to plotted lineweights. AutoCAD groups plot styles into plot style tables, each of which is stored in a separate file.

Color-based plot styles live in *color-dependent plot style table* (CTB) files, and they map the 255 AutoCAD display colors to 255 plot styles. AutoCAD automatically attaches the color-dependent plot styles to every object, based on (you guessed it)the object's color. (Are those AutoCAD programmers brilliant, or what?) Color-dependent plot style tables mimic the old color-mapped-to-lineweight plotting approach of AutoCAD R14 and earlier releases; this remains the most common method in most companies.

Named plot styles were introduced in AutoCAD 2000, and are object properties, just like color, linetype, and lineweight. Named plot styles live in (wouldn't you know it?) *named plot style table* (STB) files. After you create a named plot style table, you create one or more plot styles and give them any names you like. Then you can assign the named plot styles to layers or to individual objects. (See Chapter 6 for more information about object and layer properties.)

To use the plot styles in a plot style table (whether they're color-dependent or named), you must attach the plot style table to model space or a paper

space layout. The attached plot style table affects plotting only for that layout or for model space. This approach lets you plot the same drawing in different ways by attaching different plot styles to different tabs.

You can attach a plot style to model space or a paper space layout by selecting its image in the Quick View Layouts panel and opening the Plot dialog box; or, by right-clicking an image, choosing Page Setup Manager, and then clicking the Modify button. Choose the plot style table name from the Plot Style Table (Pen Assignments) area of the expanded Page Setup or Plot dialog box. See the section "Controlling plotted lineweights with screen colors," later in this chapter, for an example.

When you start a new drawing in the usual way — that is, by using a template drawing (see Chapter 4) — the template drawing's plot style behavior determines whether you can choose CTB or STB files. If you want to change from color-dependent plot styles to named plot styles (or vice versa) in a particular drawing, use the CONVERTPSTYLES command.

Creating plot styles

If you're lucky, someone will provide you with the plot files you need. If that's the case, you must put the CTB or STB files in your Plot Styles folder for AutoCAD to recognize them. (To find the location of your Plot Styles folder, open the Options dialog box, choose the Files tab, and look for the Printer Support File Path⇨Plot Style Table Search Path setting.)

If you're not lucky, you'll need to be smart — that is, you'll want to know how to create your own plot style table files. (Personally, we'd rather be lucky than smart; hey, it's worked so far in life!) Here's how to create plot style table files:

1. **Click the Application button to open the Application Menu, choose Print, and then choose Manage Plot Styles.**

 Use the tiny down arrow at the bottom of the list to scroll farther down if necessary. The Plot Styles folder opens in a separate Windows Explorer window.

2. **Double-click the Add-a-Plot Style Table Wizard program shortcut.**

3. **Read the opening screen and then click Next.**

4. **On the Add Plot Style Table – Begin page, choose the Start from Scratch option or one of the other three options if you want to start with settings from another file. Then click Next.**

 The remaining steps in this procedure assume that you chose Start from Scratch. If you chose another option, simply follow the wizard's prompts.

If the creator of a drawing provides you with an AutoCAD R14/AutoCAD LT 98 PC2 (version 2) or AutoCAD R12/AutoCAD LT 95 PCP (version 1) file, choose the Use a PCP or PC2 File option. With this option, the wizard imports color-to-plotted-lineweight settings automatically.

5. **On the Add Plot Style Table – Pick Plot Style Table page, choose whether you want to create a color-dependent plot style table (CTB file) or a named plot style table (STB file). Then click Next.**

 Choose Color-Dependent Plot Style Table to map screen colors to plotted lineweights. Choose Named Plot Style Table to create named plot styles that you can apply to layers or objects.

6. **On the Add Plot Style Table – File Name page, type a name for the new CTB or STB file and then click Next.**

7. **Click the Plot Style Table Editor button on the Add Plot Style Table – Finish page.**

 The Plot Style Table Editor dialog box opens to the Form View tab if you're creating a color-dependent plot style table (refer to Figure 16-7), or to the Table View tab if you create a named plot style table.

If you choose a named plot style in Step 5, the Plot Style Table Editor dialog box opens in Table view, with one plot style named Normal in the first data column, a blank column to its right, and Add Style and Delete Style buttons at the bottom. New named plot styles that you create continue to be added in columns to the right of the previous column. For more information, click the Help button in the Plot Style Table Editor.

8. **If you created a color-dependent plot style table, assign Lineweight, Screening, or other plot properties to each color that's used in the drawing. If you created a named plot style table, click the Add Style button and then assign plot properties to each of the named styles that you create.**

 To determine which colors are used in a drawing, switch to the AutoCAD window and open the Layer Properties Manager palette by clicking the Layer Properties button located on the Layers panel of the Ribbon's Home tab.

To change a setting for all colors or named styles, select them all first by clicking the first color or named style, holding down the Shift key, scrolling to the end of the list, and then clicking the last color or named style. Any subsequent changes you make get applied to all the selected colors or named styles.

9. **Click the Save & Close button to close the Plot Style Table Editor dialog box. Then click Finish to complete the steps for the wizard.**

 The Plot Styles folder now displays your new CTB or STB file.

10. **Close the Plot Styles folder by clicking the X in its title bar.**

Creating your first plot style table can be a harrowing experience because you have so many options. Just remember that your most likely reason for creating one is to map screen colors to plotted lineweights (as we describe in greater detail in the next section). Also remember that you may be able to minimize your effort by getting a CTB or STB file from the person who created the drawing that you want to plot.

In Chapter 6, we recommend that you limit yourself to the first 9 Standard AutoCAD Colors when defining layers, and not a patchwork of the 255 colors that AutoCAD makes available. If you follow our advice, your work to create a color-dependent plot style table will be much reduced because you'll have to assign plot properties for only 9 colors, rather than worrying about 255 of them.

For systematic testing of your CTB files, you can download the file named `plot_screening_and_fill_patterns.dwg` from the AutoCAD 2010 Sample Files group at `www.autodesk.com/autocad-samples` (LT users, feel free to help yourselves to this file too — it's not included with the downloads at `www.autodesk.com/autocadlt-samples`). This drawing shows an array of color swatches for all 255 AutoCAD colors. The layouts (such as Grayscale and Screening 25%) demonstrate how different CTB files attached to the same layout produce radically different results.

Named plot styles hold a lot of promise, but there are at least a couple of places — dimensions and tables, for example — where they don't work as well as traditional color-based plotting. Dimension properties allow you to assign different colors to dimension lines, extension lines, and text. The purpose for this is to allow different parts of a dimension object to print with different lineweights; for example, you can have your dimension text print with a medium lineweight, the same as your annotation text, while keeping extension and dimension lines to a fine lineweight. But because named plot styles are based on objects or layers, you don't have that lineweight control over individual dimension components. The same limitation applies to tables, where you can set your text to be one color and your grid lines to be another.

If you *really* get carried away and decide to take advantage of the 16 million-odd colors in AutoCAD's True Color or Color Book modes, you're not going to be controlling lineweights with color-dependent plot styles. CTB plot styles affect the lineweights only of objects that use the traditional 255 colors of the AutoCAD Color Index set. If you want True Color or Color Book colors, use object lineweights or named plot styles to control plotted lineweight.

Plotting through thick and thin

Long ago, manual drafters developed the practice of drawing lines of different thicknesses — *lineweights* — to distinguish different kinds of objects.

Manual drafters did it with different technical ink pen nib diameters or with different hardnesses of pencil lead and varying degrees of pressure on the pencil. Because a computer mouse usually doesn't come with mouse balls of different diameters (and we're going to resist the urge to jump in with a comment about mouse reproduction, especially because these days, most mice are optical), AutoCAD developers had to figure out how to let users indicate lineweights onscreen and on a plot. They came up with two different ways to indicate lineweight:

✔ **Mapping onscreen colors to plotted lineweights:** We describe this common approach in Chapter 6.

✔ **Displaying lineweights onscreen to match what the user can expect to see on the plot:** This approach appeared in AutoCAD 2000.

Controlling plotted lineweights with object lineweights

Plotting object lineweights is trivial, assuming that the person who created the drawing first took the trouble to assign a lineweight property to layers or objects (see Chapter 6 for details). Just make sure that the Plot Object Lineweights check box in the expanded Plot dialog box is selected. You may also want to deselect the Plot with Plot Styles check box because plot styles can override the object lineweights with different plotted lineweights. You can also make these settings in the Page Setup dialog box for the appropriate Layout or Model tab. To access the Page Setup Manager, right-click the Quick View Layouts button on the status bar and choose Page Setup Manager.

Plotting with plodders

Color-as-color and lineweight-as-lineweight seem like great ideas, but Autodesk knew when it added object lineweights back in 1999 that longtime users of AutoCAD weren't going to abandon the old colors-mapped-to-lineweights approach overnight. Thus you can still control plotted lineweight by display color in AutoCAD.

AutoCAD veterans, by and large, have chosen to stick with the old way for now. They've done so for a variety of reasons, including inertia, plotting procedures and drawings built around the old way, third-party applications that don't fully support the newer methods, and the need to exchange drawings with clients and subcontractors who haven't upgraded. In summary, the ripple effect of those who need to or want to continue using colors-mapped-to-lineweights is lasting a long time. Don't be surprised if you find yourself going with the flow for a while.

The default setting in AutoCAD 2013 is to plot object lineweights, so that's the easiest method if you don't have to consider the historical practices or predilections of other people with whom you exchange drawings. Mapping screen colors to lineweights requires some initial work on your part, but after you've set up the mapping scheme, the additional effort is minimal.

If you want object lineweights to control plotted lineweights, make sure that the Plot Object Lineweights check box is selected in the Plot Options area of the Plot or Page Setup dialog box. If you *don't* want to plot the lineweights assigned to objects, you must deselect both the Plot Object Lineweights and Plot with Plot Styles check boxes in the Plot or Page Setup dialog box. Selecting Plot with Plot Styles selects Plot Object Lineweights as well.

Controlling plotted lineweights with screen colors

To map screen colors to plotted lineweights, you need a color-dependent plot style table (CTB file), as we describe in the earlier section, "Plotting with style." If you're plotting a drawing created by someone else, that someone else may be able to supply you with the appropriate CTB file — or, at least, with a PCP or PC2 file from which you can create the CTB file quickly. At the very least, the creator of the drawing should be able to give you a printed chart showing which plotted lineweight to assign to each AutoCAD screen color. Use the instructions in the "Plotting with style" section to copy or create the required CTB file.

Unfortunately, no industry-wide standards exist for mapping screen colors to plotted lineweights. Different offices do it differently. That's why it's so useful to receive a CTB, PCP, or PC2 file with drawings that someone sends you.

After you have the appropriate CTB file stored in your Plot Styles folder, follow these steps to use it:

1. **Click the Quick View Layouts button on the status bar to open the Quick View Layouts panel. Move the mouse pointer to the image of model space or the layout that you want to plot.**

 As you move the pointer over each image panel, icons for the PLOT and PUBLISH commands appear at the upper corners.

2. **Click the Plot button in the upper-left corner of the selected image.**

 The Plot dialog box opens. Click the More Options button if the dialog box doesn't open in expanded mode, as shown in Figure 16-8.

3. **In the Plot Style Table (Pen Assignments) area on the Plot dialog box, select the CTB file from the drop-down list, as shown in Figure 16-8.**

 This action attaches the plot style table (CTB file) to the layout or model space tab that you clicked in Step 1.

4. **Click the Apply to Layout button.**

 AutoCAD records the plot setting change with the current layout's configuration information. Assuming that you save the drawing, AutoCAD uses the CTB that you selected as the default plot style when you (or other people) plot that layout in the future.

5. **Continue with the plotting procedures described earlier in this chapter.**

Page Setup - D-Size Layout

Page setup

Name: <None>

Printer/plotter

Name: DWG To PDF.pc3 Properties

Plotter: DWG To PDF - PDF ePlot - by Autodesk

Where: File

Description:

Paper size

ARCH expand D (36.00 x 24.00 Inches)

Plot area
What to plot:
Layout

Plot offset (origin set to printable area)
X: 0.000000 inch Center the plot
Y: 0.000000 inch

Plot scale
Fit to paper
Scale: 1:1

1 inches =
1 unit
Scale lineweights

Plot style table (pen assignments)
Pellucid.ctb
None
acad.ctb
DWF Virtual Pens.ctb
Fill Patterns.ctb
Grayscale.ctb
monochrome.ctb
Pellucid.ctb
Screening 100%.ctb
Screening 25%.ctb
Screening 50%.ctb
Screening 75%.ctb
New...
☑ Plot object lineweights
☐ Plot transparency
☑ Plot with plot styles
☑ Plot paperspace last
☐ Hide paperspace objects

Drawing orientation
○ Portrait
● Landscape
☐ Plot upside-down

Preview... OK Cancel Help

Figure 16-8: Selecting a plot style table that maps screen colors to plotted lineweights.

If your drawing uses a named plot style table instead of a color-dependent plot style table, you follow the same procedure, except that you select an STB file instead of a CTB file in Step 3.

You can tell whether the current drawing was set up to use color-dependent plot styles or named plot styles by looking at the Properties panel on the Ribbon's Home tab. If the upper-right drop-down list is grayed out, shows ByColor, and doesn't display a tooltip, the drawing uses color-dependent plot styles. If this list isn't grayed out and displays the Plot Style tooltip, the drawing uses named plot styles.

Plotting in color

Plotting the colors that you see onscreen requires no special tricks. In the absence of a plot style table (that is, if you selected None from the drop-down list in the Plot Style Table [Pen Assignments] area in the Plot or Page Setup dialog box), AutoCAD sends color information as it appears onscreen to the plotter. As long as your output device can plot in color, what you see should be what you get.

If you attach a plot style table to the layout that you're plotting (as described in thepreceding section), you can — if you really want to — map screen colors to different plotted colors. In most cases, you don't want that kind of confusion. Instead, leave the Color property in the plot style table set to Use Object Color.

If your goal is *not* to plot color, make sure that you set the Color property for all plot styles to Black. If you try to plot colors on a monochrome device, you may find that objects appear in various shades of gray, with lighter colors mapped to lighter shades of gray and darker colors to darker shades of gray. This process of mapping colors to shades of gray is *dithering*, and it usually is *not* what you want in a CAD drawing. To override it, use the Plot Style Table Editor, as described in the section "Creating plot styles," earlier in this chapter, to set the Color option for all colors to Black. (The default setting is Use Object Color.) If you don't already have a plot style table that you want to use, select `monochrome.ctb` for color-based plot styles or select `monochrome.stb` for named plot styles — both of which come with AutoCAD — from the drop-down list in the Plot Style Table (Pen Assignments) area of the Plot dialog box.

When in doubt, send it out

Whether you plot to scale or not, with different lineweights or not, or in color or not, consider using a service bureau for some of your plotting. In-house plotting on your office's output devices is great for small check plots on faster laser or inkjet printers. Large-format plotting, on the other hand, can be slow and time consuming. If you need to plot lots of drawings, you may find yourself spending an afternoon loading paper, replenishing ink cartridges, and trimming sheets.

Good plotting service bureaus have big, fast, expensive plotters that you can only dream about owning. Also, *they're* responsible for babysitting those fancy devices, feeding them, and fixing them. As a bonus, service bureaus can make blueline prints from your plots if you need to distribute hard-copy sets to other people.

The only downside is that you need to coordinate with a service bureau to make sure that it gets what it needs from you and can deliver the kinds of plots you need. Some service bureaus plot directly from your DWG files while others ask you to make PLT (plot) files. Some service bureaus specialize in color plotting while others are more comfortable with monochrome plotting and making blueline copies.

When you're choosing a service bureau, look for one that traditionally has served drafters, architects, and engineers. These service bureaus tend to be more knowledgeable about AutoCAD, and they should have more plotting expertise than the desktop-publishing, printing, and copying shops.

Whomever you choose, do some test plots well before the day that important set of drawings is due. Talk to the plotting people and get a copy of their plotting instructions. Have the service bureau create some plots of a couple of your typical drawings and make sure that they look the way you want them to.

If you do lots of plotting with a service bureau, look into whether you can charge it to your clients as an expense (just like bluelines or copying).

To see the full range of AutoCAD colors available on your plotter, or to see how a particular plot style table affects plotting, open and then plot the sample file `plot_screening_and_fill_patterns.dwg`, which you can download from `www.autodesk.com/autocad-samples`. The Screening 100% layout in this drawing contains color swatches for all 255 AutoCAD colors (and this file is available to AutoCAD LT users as well).

It's a (Page) Setup!

Page setups specify the plotter, paper size, and other plot settings that you use to plot a particular layout or the model space of a drawing. AutoCAD maintains separate page setups for model space and for each paper space layout. When you click the Apply to Layout button in the Plot dialog box (or select the Save Changes to Layout check box and then click OK to plot), AutoCAD stores the current plot settings as the page setup for the current layout.

You can also give page setups names and save them. The advantage of doing so is that you can switch quickly between different plot settings and copy plot settings from one drawing layout to another. Named page setups are stored with each drawing, but you can copy them from another drawing into the current one with the Page Setup Manager dialog box (described later in this section).

If you want to get fancier, you can create named page setups in order to plot the same layout (or model space) in different ways, or to copy plot settings from one layout to another or one drawing to another. Click the Add button in the Page Setup area of the Plot dialog box to create a named page setup from the current plot settings. After you create a named page setup, you can restore its plot settings by choosing it from the Page Setup Name drop-down list.

For even greater control, right-click Quick View Layouts on the status bar and choose Page Setup Manager to create, change, and copy page setups. In the Page Setup Manager dialog box, shown in Figure 16-9, you can create new page setups and modify existing ones. Click the Modify button to open the Page Setup dialog box, which is almost identical to the Plot dialog box. The primary difference is that you're changing plot *settings* rather than actually plotting. The Set Current button copies the page setup that you've selected on the Page Setups list to the current layout tab. With the Import button, you can copy a page setup from another drawing or drawing template (DWT) file.

Figure 16-9: The Page Setup Manager dialog box.

Continuing the Plot Dialog

In previous sections of this chapter, we cover most of the important options in the Plot dialog box. This section reveals a few more fine points that will make your plotting life easier. We don't cover every minute, obscure, useful-only-at-cocktail-party-discussions detail. (And if this sounds like your kind of cocktail party, remind us that we're busy that night!) We do point out some occasionally useful options that will increase your vocabulary when you're communicating with the Plot dialog box.

Use the Plot dialog box's tooltips to find out more about any part of the dialog box:

1. **Hover your mouse pointer over the part of the dialog box that you want to know more about.**

2. **Press F1 or click the Help button at the bottom of the dialog box if the pop-up help isn't enough.**

3. **For a more conceptual take on plotting, click the Learn about Plotting link to view the Quick Start to Plotting section of the online help.**

The following list explains most of the remaining controls, check boxes, and lists in the Plot dialog box:

✔ **Printer/Plotter:** As we describe in the earlier section "Configure it out," you use the Name drop-down list to select the Windows system printer or nonsystem driver configuration that you want to use for plotting.

Clicking the Properties button opens the Plotter Configuration Editor dialog box, with which you can change *media* (type of paper) and other properties that are unique to the currently selected plotter or printer. In particular, you can define custom paper sizes.

As if AutoCAD's Plot dialog box settings weren't overwhelming enough, depending on your plot device, you may also have to deal with the Plotter Configuration Editor dialog box. Some plotter drivers hide important settings in this dialog box. To access them, you typically click the Custom Properties button near the bottom of the Plotter Configuration Editor dialog box. For example, if you're using the enhanced Windows system driver for HP plotters, available at www.designjet.hp.com, you can click the Custom Properties button and then the More Sizes button to specify which paper sizes are available to you on the Paper Size drop-down list of the main Plot dialog box.

To make matters even *more* confusing, if you make any changes in the Plotter Configuration Editor dialog box, AutoCAD prompts you to save the changes to a separate PC3 file. You should choose Save Changes to the Following File (that is, create a new AutoCAD-specific configuration that includes the revised settings) and type a configuration name that you'll recognize later. When you want to plot with custom settings, remember to choose the AutoCAD-specific PC3 configuration near the end of the Printer/Plotter Name drop-down list, and not the original Windows system printer configuration near the beginning of the list.

✔ **Plot to File:** If you need to plot to a file, rather than directly to your plotter or network printer queue, select the Plot to File option. When you click OK to plot, AutoCAD asks you for a plot filename and location. You may need to use this option to create files to send to a plotting service bureau.

AutoCAD includes DWFx to its ePlot options. DWFx is a flavored version of DWF that conforms to Microsoft's XPS page description language. For most people, the handiest thing about this format is that if you plot to DWFx, the resulting file can be displayed in Internet Explorer.

Plotting to the DWG to PDF.pc3 file creates versions of your drawing files that can be opened and viewed in the free and widely available Adobe Reader software.

✔ **Plot Stamp On:** Use this option to turn on and off and configure the contents of a text string that AutoCAD adds automatically to the corner of each plot. The plot stamp can include useful information, such as the drawing's filename and plot date and time.

✔ **Plot Area:** Specify the area of the drawing to plot. Your choices include Display, Extents, and Window, regardless of whether you're plotting a paper space layout or model space. If you defined named views in the drawing, AutoCAD adds a View option. The additional choice is Layout for a paper space layout or Limits for model space.

- *Display:* The drawing as it's currently displayed in the drawing window (including any empty space around the drawing objects).

- *Extents:* The rectangular area containing all the objects in the drawing.

- *Limits (full-screen model space only):* The model space area that you may or may not have specified when you set up the drawing. If you didn't specifically set your drawing's limits (as we demon-strate in Chapter 3), plotting limits will give unpredictable results. Use one of the other options instead.

- *Layout (Layouts only):* The paper space area you defined when you set up the layout.

- *Window:* A rectangular area that you specify.

- *View:* A named view that you select from a drop-down list. (Chapter 12 describes named views and how to create them.)

Usually, you'll choose to plot Layout in paper space. For model space, the choice depends on how the drawing was set up and what you want to plot. If you're trying to plot a drawing in which the limits weren't set, try Extents instead. Use Window or View if you want to plot just a portion of model space.

✔ **Plot Offset:** A plot offset of X=0 and Y=0 positions the plot at the lower-left corner of the plottable area. If you want to move the plot from this default position on the paper, enter nonzero numbers or select the Center the Plot check box. (The Center the Plot check box isn't available if you select Layout from the What to Plot drop-down list.)

✔ **Shaded Viewport Options:** If your drawing includes viewports show-ing shaded or rendered 3D models, use this area to control the plotted appearance.

✔ **Plot Options:** The Plot Object Lineweights and the Plot with Plot Styles check boxes control whether AutoCAD uses the features described in the "Plotting with style" and "Plotting through thick and thin" sections, earlier in this chapter.

The Hide Paperspace Objects check box controls whether AutoCAD hides objects that are behind other objects when a 3D model is displayed in a viewport.

🖊 **Plot Upside-Down:** Select this check box if you want to rotate the plot 180 degrees on the paper. (It's a handy option for plotting in the Southern Hemisphere or for avoiding having to cock your head at an uncomfortable angle as you watch plots come out of the plotter.)

AutoCAD normally generates plots in the foreground — that is, the plotting process takes over the program for the entire time that the program is creating the plot. AutoCAD includes a background plotting feature that returns control of the program to you more quickly. If you have a reasonably fast computer with adequate memory, turn on this feature in the Options dialog box: Type **OPTIONS** (or **OP**) and press Enter, click the Plot and Publish tab; from in the Background Processing Options area, select Plotting.

If you want to automate plotting for a batch of drawings, check out the sheet sets feature in AutoCAD and AutoCAD LT. One of the tasks that sheet sets are designed to accomplish is the publishing of a set of drawing sheets at one fell swoop. If this sounds like your ticket to plotting bliss, go to the online help system and type **Work with Sheets in a Sheet Set** in the Search Help Resources box.

The Plot Sickens

No matter how many times you read this chapter or how carefully you study the AutoCAD documentation, you'll occasionally run into plotting problems. You're especially likely to encounter problems when trying to plot other people's drawings because you don't always know what plotting conventions they had in mind. (*Plotting conventions* aren't where spies meet; they're a standardized approach to plotting issues.)

By far, one of the most common plotting problems occurs because people have used object property overrides instead of sticking to ByLayer. For example, you want to plot an architectural drawing to show the client the general room layout. You don't want to confuse them with all the dimensions, so you freeze the Dimension layer. Oops, only half of the dimensions go away, but so do several walls, a couple of windows, and the bathtub.

Table 16-1 describes some of the more common plotting problems and solutions.

Table 16-1	Plotting Problems and Solutions
Problem	*Possible Solution*
Nothing comes out of the plotter (system printer driver).	Check that the printer is plugged in, that it is turned on, that it has paper, that the paper is not jammed, that it is not low on toner or ink, that it is connected to the computer, and if the drawing is a large one that takes a long time to rasterize.
	Check whether you can print to the device from other Windows applications. If not, it's not an AutoCAD problem.
	Try the Windows Print Troubleshooter
	Windows XP: Start⇨Help and Support⇨ Printing and Faxing⇨Fixing a Printing Problem⇨ Printing Troubleshooter.
	Windows Vista and Windows 7: Start⇨ Help and Support, type **printing troubleshooting** in the Search box and press Enter; then click Troubleshoot Printer Problems or Open the Printer troubleshooter.
Nothing comes out of the plotter (nonsystem printer driver).	Choose Plotter Manager on the Plot panel of the Ribbon's Output tab, double-click the plotter configuration, and check the settings.
Objects don't plot the way they appear onscreen.	Check for a plot style table with weird settings or try plotting without a plot style table.
Objects appear ghosted or with washed-out colors.	In the plot style table, set Color to Black for all colors.
Scaled to Fit doesn't work right in paper space.	Change the What to Plot drop-down list from Layout to Extents.
The HP-enhanced Windows system driver that you down-loaded from HP's website doesn't have the right paper sizes (for example, no archi-tectural paper sizes).	In the Plot dialog box's Printer/Plotter area, click the Properties button to display the Plotter Configuration Editor dialog box, click the Custom Properties button (near the bottom), and then click the More Sizes button to specify the stan-dard and custom paper sizes.
Something else is wrong.	Check the plot log: Click the Plot/Publish Details Report Available icon near the right end of the status bar and look for error messages.

Part IV
Advancing with AutoCAD

After you get the lines and text right, you may be justified in thinking that your work in AutoCAD is done. But AutoCAD enables you to do so much more! Blocks and external references help you manage data within drawings, between drawings, and across a network. Parametric drawing lets you maintain the intent of your designs. If you plan to share drawings (whether among your own projects, with people in your office, or with folks in other companies), you need to think about consistency in presentation and drawing organization.

The Internet is the biggest ongoing swap meet in human history, and AutoCAD offers some unique trading possibilities — and potential pitfalls — via e-mail and the Web. And if you think the Internet is big, wait until you learn about *The Cloud* and how AutoCAD can use it.

With the information in this part, you'll be teaching AutoCAD how to give and receive in no time.

17

The ABCs of Blocks

*I*n Chapter 11, you can see how to copy objects within a drawing, or even *to* another drawing. That's one way to use AutoCAD to improve drafting efficiency. You can copy a DWG file and then modify it to create a similar drawing — an even better productivity booster, as long as you're in the habit of making similar drawings. But all those are baby steps compared with the techniques that we cover in this chapter and Chapter 18: treating drawings, parts of drawings, drawings saved in web format (*DWF,* or *Design Web Format*), Autodesk Inventor 3D models, PDFs, MicroStation DGN files, and raster images as reusable and updateable modules. If you want to make drafting production more efficient with AutoCAD, you want to know how to use blocks, xrefs, IPTs, IAMs, PDFs, DWFs, DGNs, and raster files.

In this chapter, we present the ABCs of blocks — basic creation and insertion, adding attributes, and getting rid of block definitions you no longer need or want. In Chapter 18, we show you how to make even more of already-created drawing data, including dynamic blocks, associative array objects, and several flavors of external reference files (including PDFs and MicroStation DGN files) and raster images.

Rocking with Blocks

A *block* is a collection of objects grouped to form a single object. You can insert this collection more than once in the same drawing, and when you do, all instances of the block remain identical. By redefining the block definition, you can automatically change all instances of the block insertion (officially called a "block reference") at once. Although a block lives within a specific drawing, you can transfer copies of it into other drawings. And you can add fill-in-the-blank text fields — *attributes* — to blocks.

You can create single-line or multiline attributes; in addition to having more than one line, multiline attributes have many of the formatting options of multiline text. And blocks both with and without attributes can be defined as annotative objects to boot. (See Chapter 13 for a rundown on annotative objects.)

To use a block in a drawing, you need two things: a block *definition* and one or more block *insertions.* AutoCAD doesn't always make the distinction between these two things very clear, but you need to understand the difference to avoid terminal confusion about blocks. (Maybe this syndrome should be called "blockheadedness"?)

A block definition lives in an invisible area of your drawing file: the *block table.* (It's one of those sets of named symbols that we describe in Chapter 6.) The block table is like a book of graphical recipes for making different kinds of blocks. Each block definition is like a recipe for making one kind of block. When you insert a block, as described in the upcoming section, "Inserting Blocks," AutoCAD creates a special object called a "block reference." The block reference points to the recipe and tells AutoCAD, "Hey, draw me according to the instructions in this recipe!"

Although a block may look like a collection of objects stored together and given a name, it's really a graphical recipe (the block definition) plus one or more pointers to that recipe (one or more block references). Each time you insert a particular block, you create another pointer to the same recipe.

The advantages of blocks include

- ✔ **Grouping objects when they belong together logically:** You can draw a screw, using lines and arcs, and then make a block definition out of all these objects. When you insert the screw block, AutoCAD treats it as a single object for purposes of copying, moving, and so on.
- ✔ **Saving time and reducing errors:** Inserting a block is, of course, much quicker than redrawing the same geometry again. And the less geometry you draw from scratch, the less opportunity there is to make a mistake.

✔ **Efficiency of storage when you reuse the same block repeatedly:** If you insert the same screw block 15 times in a drawing, AutoCAD stores the detailed block definition only once. The 15 block references that point to the block definition take up much less disk space than 15 copies of all the lines, polylines, and arcs. No matter how big the block definition is, each insertion adds only about 100 bytes to the drawing file size.

✔ **The ability to edit all instances of a symbol in a drawing simply by modifying a single block definition:** If you decide that your design requires a different kind of screw, you simply redefine the screw's block definition. With this new recipe, AutoCAD then replaces all 15 screws automatically. That's a heck of a lot faster than erasing and recopying 15 screws!

✔ **Varying the appearance of block references by using dynamic blocks:** If your design requires a different kind of screw, you simply change the view of the screw to the other kind (assuming, of course, you've defined your screw as a dynamic block). Every instance of the screw in the drawing could show a different kind of screw. And *that's* a heck of a lot more efficient than creating 15 different block definitions! For the lowdown on creating, inserting, and manipulating dynamic blocks, see Chapter 18.

Blocks *aren't* all that great for drawing elements that might be used in multiple drawings, however, especially if several people are working on and sharing parts of drawings with one another. That's because blocks, after they get into multiple drawings, stay in each drawing; a later modification to a block definition in one drawing does *not* automatically modify all the other drawings that use that block. If you use a block with your company's logo in a number of drawings and then you decide to change the logo, you must make the change within each drawing that uses the block. Using external reference (xref) files can overcome this problem. We cover XREFs in Chapter 18.

If all you need to do is group some objects so that you can more easily select them for copying, moving, and so on, use AutoCAD's Group feature. We describe groupies a little more fully in Chapter 10. Type **GROUP** (or the command alias **G**) and press Enter, or simply click the Group button on the Home tab's Groups panel. Then just select some objects, and you're done. When you're editing drawings that contain groups, press Ctrl+Shift+A to toggle "group-ness" on or off. If you've toggled group-ness on, picking any object in a group selects all objects in the group. If you've toggled it off, picking an object selects only that object, even if it happens to be a member of a group. For more information, refer to Chapter 10 or visit the online help index.

Blocks — along with external references, DWF and PDF underlays, raster images, and DGN files — enable you to reuse your work and the work of others, giving you the potential to save tremendous amounts of time — or to cause tremendous problems if you change a file on which other people's

drawings depend. Use these features when you can to save time, but do so in an organized and careful way so as to avoid problems.

How you use blocks and xrefs depends a lot on the profession and office in which you work. Some disciplines and companies use these drawing organization features heavily and in a highly organized way, but others don't. Ask your colleagues what the local customs are and follow them.

Creating Block Definitions

To create a block definition from objects in the current drawing, use the Block Definition dialog box. (The other way to create a block definition is by inserting another drawing file into your current drawing as a block, which we explain in the next section.) The following steps show you how to create a block definition by using the Block Definition dialog box:

1. **On the Ribbon's Home tab, click the Create button on the Block panel.**

 The Block Definition dialog box appears (see Figure 17-1).

Figure 17-1: The Block Definition dialog box.

Pay attention to layers when you create the objects that make up a block. As a rule, block geometry created on most layers retains the color, linetype, lineweight, transparency, and plot style properties of those layers. The exception to the rule is object geometry created on Layer 0. If you create a block by using geometry drawn on Layer 0, the block takes on the features of any layer into which you insert it.

2. **Type the block definition's name in the Name text box.**

 If you type the name of an existing block definition, AutoCAD will warn you when you click OK at the end of the process. This isn't always a bad thing because AutoCAD will ask whether you want to replace that block definition with the new objects you select. This process is *block redefinition.* If you have a drawing with a large number of block insertions — for example, numerous bathtubs in a 1,000-room hotel — you can use a simplified block representation during the design process and then redefine it to a more complex definition just before final plot time.

 To see a list of the names of all the current blocks in your drawing, open the Name drop-down list.

3. **Specify the base point (also known as the *insertion point*) of the block, using any of the following methods:**

 - Enter the coordinates of the insertion point in the X, Y, and Z text boxes.

 - Click the Pick Point button and then specify a point on the screen. (In this case, use an object snap or other precision technique, as described in Chapter 7, to grab a specific point on one of the block's objects.)

 The *base point* is the point on the block by which you insert it later, as we describe in the next section.

 Use an obvious and consistent point on the group of objects for the base point, such as the lower-left corner, so that you know what to expect when you insert the block.

4. **Click the Select Objects button and then select the objects that you want as part of the block.**

 AutoCAD uses the selected objects to create a block definition and displays an icon showing those objects next to the block name. Figure 17-2 shows the base point and group of selected objects during the process of creating a new block definition.

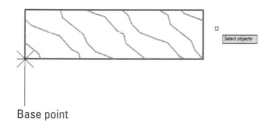

Base point

Figure 17-2: Building a block.

5. **In the Objects area, select one of the radio buttons to tell AutoCAD what to do with the objects used to define the block: Retain them in place, convert them into a block instance, or delete them.**

 The default choice, Convert to Block, is usually the best. See Step 9 for a description of what happens with each choice.

6. **Specify the insert units to which the block will be scaled in the Block Unit drop-down list.**

 When you or someone else drags the block from one drawing into another via the DesignCenter palette (see Chapter 6) or Tool Palettes (described later in this chapter), the units you specify here and the units of the drawing you're dragging into will control the default insertion scale factor. The list contains 17 different units from Angstroms to Parsecs, but unfortunately doesn't include fathoms or furlongs.

 Three additional features in AutoCAD's Block Definition dialog box give you even more control over what happens to your blocks as they're inserted:

 - *If the Annotative check box is selected:* The block insertion will be scaled to suit the current drawing scale, and additional scales can be applied so the insertion will be scaled differently to suit other drawing scales. This would typically be applied only to symbols (such as north arrows) and not to insertions of blocks depicting actual objects (such as toilets or motors). (We explain the nuts and bolts of annotative objects in Chapter 13.)

 - *If the Scale Uniformly check box is selected:* Blocks will be inserted with the same X, Y, or Z scale factors. (Scale Uniformly is selected automatically if Annotative is selected.)

 - *If the Allow Exploding check box is selected:* Blocks can be exploded during or after their insertion in a drawing.

7. **Enter a description for the block in the Description text area.**

 You don't have to enter a description to create a block, but it's not a bad idea. Think like a database manager and enter a useful description that will identify the block to yourself and others.

8. **Make sure that the Open in Block Editor check box is deselected.**

 You don't need to use the Edit Block Definition dialog box unless you're going to add dynamic features to the block. (See Chapter 18 to find out more about dynamic blocks.)

9. **Click OK to complete the block definition process.**

 AutoCAD stores the block definition in the current drawing's block table. The radio buttons you choose from in Step 5 do the following:

- If you select the *Convert to Block* radio button (the default) in Step 5, AutoCAD creates a block reference pointing to the new block definition. The objects look the same onscreen, but they are now an instance of the block rather than the original, separate objects. Most of the time, this is your best choice.

- If you select the *Retain* radio button, the objects remain in place but aren't converted into a block reference. They remain individual objects with no connection to the new block definition.

- If you select the *Delete* radio button, the objects disappear, but the block definition still gets created.

When you define a block, you can include a special kind of variable text object called an *attribute definition*. When you insert a block that contains one or more attribute definitions, AutoCAD prompts you to fill in values for the text fields. Attributes are useful for things like variable title block information (sheet number, sheet title, and so on), electric motor nameplate information, and symbols that contain different codes or callouts. We describe how to create and use attribute definitions later in this chapter.

Keep your common symbol drawings in one or more specific folders that you set aside just for that purpose. You may want to use one of the following techniques to develop a library of symbols that you use frequently:

- Create a separate DWG file for each block.

- Store a bunch of symbols as block definitions in one drawing and use DesignCenter to import block definitions from this drawing when you need them.

- If you have a block definition in one drawing that you would like to use in other drawings, use the WBLOCK (WriteBlock) command to extract and write a copy of it out to disk as a new DWG file and then insert it into other drawings as required.

Inserting Blocks

AutoCAD provides a number of ways to insert a block or a whole drawing file, but the most commonly used and most flexible is the Insert dialog box. Here's the procedure for inserting a block:

1. **Set an appropriate layer current, as described in Chapter 6.**

 Insert each block on a layer that has something to do with the block's geometry or purpose:

- *If all the objects in the block definition reside on one layer,* it's usually best to insert the block on that layer.

- *If the block geometry spans several layers,* choose one of them to insert the block on.

If any of the block definition's geometry was created on Layer 0, that geometry will inherit the color, linetype, and other object properties of the layer on which you insert the block. It's like the chameleon changing color to match its surroundings or a politician changing his position to match the day's opinion polls.

2. **On the Ribbon's Home tab, click the Insert button on the Block panel.**

 The Insert dialog box appears, as shown in Figure 17-3.

Figure 17-3: The Insert dialog box.

3. **Enter the block definition name (or external filename) by using one of the following methods:**

 - *Use the Name drop-down list* to select from a list of block definitions in the current drawing.

 - *Click the Browse button* to select an external DWG file and have AutoCAD create a block definition from it.

 You can browse to any existing drawing and insert it into the current drawing. This creates a new block definition within the host drawing. The new definition doesn't retain any connection at all to the inserted drawing.

 You can use an external drawing to replace a block definition in your current drawing. If you click Browse and choose a file whose name matches the name of a block definition that's already in your drawing,

AutoCAD asks you to confirm the update and, if you agree, updates the block definition in your drawing with the current contents of the external file. This process is *block redefinition,* and AutoCAD automatically updates all block references that point to the block definition.

4. **Enter the insertion point, scale, and rotation angle of the block.**

 You can either select the Specify On-Screen check box in each area to specify the parameters onscreen at the command prompt; or type the values you want in the text boxes in the Insertion Point, Scale, and Rotation areas.

 Select the Uniform Scale check box to constrain the X, Y, and Z scaling parameters to the same value (which is what you want in almost all cases).

5. **If you want AutoCAD to create a copy of the individual objects in the block instead of a block reference that points to the block definition, select the Explode check box and click OK.**

6. **If you selected the Specify On-Screen check box for the insertion point, scale, or rotation angle, answer the prompts on the command line to specify these parameters.**

After you insert a block, all the objects displayed in the block reference behave as a single object. When you select any object in the block reference, AutoCAD highlights all the objects in it.

Another way to insert a block is to drag a DWG file from Windows Explorer and drop it anywhere in the current drawing window. AutoCAD then prompts you to choose an insertion point and optionally change the default scale factor and rotation angle. Similarly, you can drag a block definition from the Blocks section of the DesignCenter palette and drop it into the current drawing window. (Chapter 6 describes DesignCenter.)

You can now import Inventor part (.IPT) and assembly (.IAM) models directly into AutoCAD 2013. Inventor is AutoCAD's 3D parametric and associative sibling, intended primarily for mechanical design. Imported Inventor files come across as dumb 3D solids that lose their parametrics and associativity, but they can be modified and edited like any other AutoCAD 3D solid. We cover AutoCAD's 2D parametrics in Chapter 19, and introduce you to 3D modeling in Chapters 21 through 23.

AutoCAD provides one additional way of inserting blocks: the Tool Palettes window, which we describe in Chapter 2. As is true of using a tool palette for hatching (Chapter 15), you first must create and configure appropriate tools. The easiest method is right-clicking a drawing in DesignCenter and choosing Create Tool Palette. A new tabbed page is added to the Tool Palettes window,

containing all the block definitions from the drawing that you right-clicked. Simply click and drag a tool to insert its corresponding block into a drawing.

Dragging blocks from a tool palette doesn't give you the chance to specify a different insertion scale, nor can you use all AutoCAD's precision tools to specify the insertion point precisely — you may need to move the block into place after inserting it. We recommend that you first master the other block insertion methods described in this chapter — especially using the Insert dialog box and DesignCenter palette. Then if you find yourself inserting the same blocks frequently, consider creating a tool palette containing them. Check out "Add Content with DesignCenter" in the AutoCAD online help system for more information.

Although the preceding paragraph refers to the *Tool Palettes window,* palettes in AutoCAD are not like regular windows or dialog boxes. They are *modeless,* which means that they can stay open while you carry on with other tasks outside them. The official programmer-ese term for palettes is *enhanced secondary window,* or ESW for short. (We think we're sticking with *palettes.*)

Be careful when you insert one drawing into another. If the host (or parent) drawing and the inserted (or child) drawing have different definitions for layers that share the same name, the objects in the inserted drawing take on the layer characteristics of the host drawing. For example, if you insert a drawing with lines on a layer called Walls that's blue and dashed into a drawing with a layer called Walls that's red and continuous, the inserted lines on the Wall layer will turn red and continuous after they're inserted. The same rules apply to linetypes, text styles, dimension styles, table styles, multileader styles, and block definitions that are nested inside the drawing you're inserting. As you probably remember from when you were little . . . parents rule!

If you need to modify a block definition after you've inserted one or more instances of it, use the Block Editor (BEDIT command); choose Block Editor on the Home tab's Block panel. Look up *BEDIT* in the AutoCAD online help system.

Locate Using Geographic Data is an option in AutoCAD's Insert dialog box. *Geographic data* refers to locating drawing geometry with reference to specific locations on planet Earth (so far) defined in one of a number of recognized global coordinate systems. This feature promises to be very big in the civil engineering community, or possibly for very large architectural projects, where a ground-based coordinate system is in place. If it sounds like something you need, look in the online help (and visit your local dealer or training center for further direction).

Attributes: Fill-in-the-Blank Blocks

You may think of attributes as the good (or bad) qualities of your significant other, but in AutoCAD, *attributes* are fill-in-the-blank text fields that you can add to your blocks. When you create a block definition and then insert it several times in a drawing, all the ordinary geometry (lines, circles, regular text strings, and so on) in all the instances are exactly identical. Attributes provide a little more flexibility in the form of text strings that can be different in each block reference.

For example, suppose that you frequently designate parts in your drawings by labeling them with a distinct number or letter in a circle for each part. If you want to create a block for this symbol, you can't simply draw the number or letter as regular text by using the MTEXT or TEXT command. If you create a block definition with a regular text object (for example, the letter *A*), the text string will be the same in every instance of the block (always the letter *A*). That's not much help in distinguishing the parts!

Instead, you create an *attribute definition,* which acts as a placeholder for a text string that can vary each time you insert the block. You include the attribute definition when you create the block definition. (Refer to the "Creating Block Definitions" section, earlier in this chapter.) Then each time you insert the block, AutoCAD prompts you to fill in an *attribute value* for each attribute definition.

When they were first introduced, and for a long time afterward, block attribute values were limited to a single line of variable text with a maximum of 255 characters. AutoCAD 2008 and later supports multiline attributes; as well as offering more than one line, multiline attributes have many of the formatting options of multiline text. For more information on creating and inserting blocks with multiline attributes, look up *Define Block Attributes* in the online help system.

The AutoCAD documentation and dialog boxes often use the term *attribute* to refer indiscriminately to an *attribute definition* or an *attribute value.* We attribute a lot of the confusion about attributes to this sloppiness. Just remember that an attribute *definition* is the text field or placeholder in the block definition, and an attribute *value* is the specific text string that you type when you insert the block.

Creating attribute definitions

You use the Attribute Definition dialog box to create attribute definitions (clever, eh?). The procedure is similar to creating a text string except that you must supply a little more information. Create attribute definitions with the following steps:

1. **Change to the layer on which you want to create the attribute definition.**

2. **Choose Define Attributes on the Home tab's Block panel slideout to run the ATTDEF command.**

 The Attribute Definition dialog box appears, as shown in Figure 17-4.

 You rarely need to use any of the first four Mode settings (Invisible, Constant, Verify, or Preset). Just leave them deselected. If you're curious about what the modes do, hover your mouse pointer over an item; if that doesn't give you enough information, use the dialog box Help button to find out more.

 Attribute Definition

Mode	Attribute
☐ Invisible	Tag: PT_NUM
☐ Constant	Prompt: Enter Part Number:
☑ Verify	Default: -
☐ Preset	
☑ Lock position	**Text Settings**
☐ Multiple lines	Justification: Left
Insertion Point	Text style: S-Text
☑ Specify on-screen	☐ Annotative ⓘ
X 0"	Text height: 1/8"
Y 0"	Rotation: 0
Z 0"	Boundary width: 0"

 ☐ Align below previous attribute definition

 [OK] [Cancel] [Help]

 Figure 17-4: The Attribute Definition dialog box.

3. **Select or deselect the Lock Position check box.**

 If Lock Position is selected, the attributes can't be relocated within the block reference — the whole thing is treated as a single object. Deselecting Lock Position allows attributes to be moved by dragging their grips, without moving the block reference as a whole.

4. **Select or deselect the Multiple Lines check box.**

 Selecting Multiple Lines in the Mode area disables the Default text box and displays a button to open the Multiline Editor. By default, you don't get the whole panoply of formatting options that you get in the MTEXT command's In-Place Text Editor, but you can overscore or underscore text;

and from a right-click menu, you can import text, assign a background mask, or choose from a number of other options. Setting the value of the system variable ATTIPE to 1 enables *all* formatting options in the In-Place Text Editor, See the online help system for more information.

5. **In the Attribute area, type values for the *tag* (the unique identifier for the attribute), the user prompt, and the default value.**

 The name you type into the Tag text box can't contain any spaces. The Prompt and Default text boxes may contain spaces, though.

 Attribute values can include *fields* that automatically update, such as date, filename, or system variable settings. Click the Insert Field button to the right of the Default text box to insert a field. See Chapter 13 for more information on fields.

6. **(Optional) If you select the Multiple Lines check box in Step 4, click the Multiline Editor button (it shows three periods) to enter the multi-line default attribute value and add any formatting; then click OK.**

 The value you enter here is the default text stored in the attribute definition, and you can change it when you insert the block.

7. **In the Text Settings area, specify the Justification, Text Style, Annotative property, Text Height, Rotation, and Boundary Width (the last for multiline attributes only).**

 The text properties for attribute definitions are the same as those for text objects — see Chapter 13.

8. **Select Specify On-Screen to choose an insertion point for the attribute definition.**

 An attribute definition's insertion point is like a text string's base point. Remember to use snap, object snap, or another precision tool if you want the eventual attribute values to be located at a precise point.

9. **Click OK to create the attribute definition.**

10. **Repeat Steps 1 through 9 for any additional attribute definitions.**

 If you need to create a series of attribute definitions in neat rows, create the first one by using Steps 1 through 9 and then select the Align Below Previous Attribute Definition check box for the subsequent definitions. To make a series of nonadjacent attributes, create the first one by using Steps 1 through 9 and then copy the first attribute definition and edit the copy with the Properties palette. You can prevent your attributes from being dragged around the block by selecting the Lock Position check box in the Attribute Definition dialog box.

Defining blocks that contain attribute definitions

After you create one or more attribute definitions — and any other geometry that you want to include in the block — you're ready to create a block definition that contains them. Follow the steps in the section "Creating Block Definitions," earlier in this chapter.

At Step 4 in the section "Creating Block Definitions," you can select any attribute definitions before or after you select the other geometry. However, you should select each attribute definition one by one (clicking each attribute definition rather than selecting multiple attributes with a selection window) in the order that you want the attribute value prompts to appear in the Edit Attributes dialog box (see Figure 17-5 in the next section). If you don't select the attributes one by one, your block and attributes will still work, but the order of the attribute prompts in the Edit Attributes dialog box may not be what you want.

You can use the Block Attribute Manager to reorder the attribute definitions in a block definition. Choose Attribute, Block Attribute Manager on the Home tab's Block panel slideout. You also can use this dialog box to edit other attribute definition settings, such as the prompt, text style, or layer.

Inserting blocks that contain attribute definitions

After you create a block definition that contains attribute definitions, you insert it just like any other block. Follow the steps in the section "Inserting Blocks," earlier in this chapter. At the end of the steps, AutoCAD displays the Edit Attributes dialog box, as shown in Figure 17-5. The dialog box contains one row for each of the attribute definitions and has any default values filled in. You simply edit the values and then click OK.

The ATTDIA (ATTribute DIAlog box) system variable controls whether AutoCAD prompts for attribute values in a dialog box (ATTDIA=1) or at the command line (ATTDIA=0). If you insert a block and see command-line prompts for each attribute value, type a value and press Enter for each attribute value you want to set. When you return to the command prompt, type **ATTDIA**, press Enter, type **1**, and press Enter again. When you insert blocks with attributes into this drawing in the future, AutoCAD displays the Edit Attributes dialog box instead of prompting you at the command line.

Figure 17-5: The Edit Attributes dialog box.

Edit attribute values

After you insert a block that contains attributes, you can edit the individual attribute values in that block reference with the EATTEDIT command. Click the Single drop-down button on the Home tab's Block panel and click any object in the block reference. AutoCAD displays the Enhanced Attribute Editor dialog box with the current attribute values, as shown in Figure 17-6. The most common attribute editing operation is to edit the *text value* — that is, the text string that appears in the block reference. You also can change properties of the attributes, such as layer and text style.

Figure 17-6: The Enhanced Attribute Editor dialog box.

Many people use attributes in the way we've described so far — as fill-in-the-blank text fields in blocks. But attributes also can serve as data extraction tools. For example, you can export attribute values, such as part numbers and quantities, to a table object in AutoCAD or to a text, spreadsheet, or database file for analysis or reporting.

Extracting data

Selecting Extract Data from the Linking & Extraction panel on the Ribbon's Insert tab starts the Data Extraction Wizard. You can find out much more about this specialized function in the online help. Check out User's Guide⇨Share Data between Files⇨Extract Data from Drawings and Spreadsheets. And, AutoCAD LT users, although you don't have this wizard, you can still extract attribute information to space- or comma-delimited text files by using the Attribute Extraction dialog box. For more information, visit the online help.

Exploding Blocks

In regular block definitions (not dynamic blocks), the objects in each block reference act like a well-honed marching squadron: If you move or otherwise edit one object in the block reference, all objects move or change in the same way. Usually this cohesion is an advantage, but occasionally you need to break up the squadron in order to modify one object without affecting the others.

To *explode* a block reference into individual objects, click Explode on the Home tab's Modify panel or type **X** and press Enter, and then select the block reference. When you explode a block reference, AutoCAD replaces it with all the objects — lines, polylines, arcs, and so on — specified in the block definition. You then can edit the objects individually or perhaps use them to make more block definitions.

If you explode a block that contains attributes, the attribute values change back to become attribute definitions. This usually isn't the sort of change that you want. If you really need to explode the block reference, you'll probably want to erase the attribute definitions and draw regular text strings in their place. If you've installed the AutoCAD Express Tools (not available in AutoCAD LT), you can perform this task automatically with the BURST command. Just type **BURST** and press Enter.

Both AutoCAD and AutoCAD LT have an NCOPY command that you can use to copy objects contained within blocks without having to explode the block. AutoCAD users familiar with the Express Tools may already be familiar with NCOPY; the command is now in the core of the program and therefore available to LT users. In both versions, you can find the Copy Nested Objects tool on the Home tab's Modify panel slideout (or you can simply type **NCOPY**).

Purging Unused Block Definitions

Each block definition increases the size of your DWG file, as do other named objects, such as layers, text styles, and dimension styles. In the case of a large, complex block definition, the size increase can be significant. If you delete (or explode) all the block references that point to a particular block definition, that block definition no longer serves any purpose.

You should run the PURGE command periodically in each drawing and purge unused block definitions. Click the Application button to open the Application Menu, choose Drawing Utilities on the left side, and then choose Purge to display the Purge dialog box. Click the Purge All button to purge all unused named objects in the current drawing.

PURGE isn't only for blocks: You can also remove empty layers, blank text strings, zero-length lines, empty groups, and unused style definitions. In Figure 17-7, the Purge dialog box shows the unused dimension, multileader, and text styles that can be removed from this drawing with a click of the Purge All button.

Figure 17-7: Purging your drawing of unneeded named objects.

Note the Purge Nested Items check box. Some items may not become unused until something else is purged. For example, a block definition can contain one or more other block definitions as components of it, and they in turn can contain others. If the parent contains the only use of a child or grandchild, purging the parent releases the child and so on down. When Purge Nested Items is selected, AutoCAD tunnels down through the nestings, looking for new orphans. These may include block definitions, and/or things like layer, text style, and dimension style specifications.

Everything from Arrays to Xrefs

*W*e introduce simple arrays in Chapter 11. They've served us well for many years, but they're basically just a quick way of producing multiple copies of drawing objects in regular patterns.

In this chapter, we discuss AutoCAD's associative array feature. Associative arrays are also *dynamic:* that is, you can edit them by changing the number of items, changing the definition of the objects being arrayed, or substituting a different object set for one or more object sets in an array.

An *external reference drawing* — xref — is like an industrial-strength block. An xref is a pointer to a separate drawing file outside the drawing you're working on. When you attach a reference drawing, it appears onscreen and on plots as part of your drawing, but it continues to live as a separate document on your hard drive or network. If you edit the externally referenced drawing, the appearance of the drawing changes in all drawings that reference it. Like a block insertion, an xref attachment increases the drawing file only slightly, regardless of the size of the xref file.

A *raster image* file stores a graphical image as a series of dots. BMP and JPG images seen on the Internet or from a digital camera are typical examples. Raster files are good for storing photographs, logos, and other images. AutoCAD *vector* files are good for storing geometrical objects, such as lines and arcs, along with text and other annotations for describing the geometry. Sometimes combining raster images with AutoCAD vector files by attaching them to your drawing files is handy, and the External References palette makes the process straightforward.

Before AutoCAD 2007, *external references* meant AutoCAD drawing files (and only AutoCAD drawing files) that you attached to your current drawing. Images were (and still are) raster graphics files that you attached in a similar way but with a different command. In AutoCAD 2007 and later, you use the External References palette to attach and manage not only externally referenced AutoCAD drawings (xrefs) and 2D MicroStation DGN drawing files, but also image files and DWF or PDF underlays. (*DWF* stands for Design Web Format; a DWF is a lightweight version of a DWG file intended for design review or posting on a website.) We discuss attaching DWFs or PDFs as external references at the end of this chapter, and describe the web functions of DWFs in Chapter 20.

Both AutoCAD and AutoCAD LT enable you to attach DGN files to current drawings via the External References palette. *DGN* files are drawing files created by one of AutoCAD's competitors: MicroStation from Bentley Systems. (You can also import and export DGN drawing data in both AutoCAD and AutoCAD LT.) If you're new to AutoCAD, you're not likely to encounter DGN files unless you're working for a large company that exchanges a lot of drawings with partners and consultants. For more information on DGN files in AutoCAD 2013, enter **DGN Files** in the Search box at the top of the online help home page.

As we mention in Chapter 17, blocks, external references, DWF underlays, PDF underlays, raster images, and DGN files enable you to reuse your work and the work of others, giving you the potential to save tremendous amounts of time — or to cause tremendous problems if you change a file on which other people's drawings depend. Use these features when you can to save time, but do so in an organized and careful way to avoid problems.

In Chapter 17, we introduce *blocks* as collections of object geometry that are treated as single entities in AutoCAD. In that chapter, we also describe giving blocks a little more oomph by adding *attributes* — changeable text tags that can differ with each insertion. Other than that kind of slight variation, though, the blocks that we describe in Chapter 17 tend to be pretty static.

Blocks, however, don't have to be static creations. Instead of having a half dozen regular blocks for a half dozen different door sizes, you can create a single *dynamic block* that includes all those sizes. Unlike a regular block, in which every instance of a particular block is geometrically identical, each instance of a dynamic block can display geometric variations. For example, you can insert one furniture block three times and have one instance display as a sofa, one as a loveseat, and one as an armchair. We introduce *block authoring* — the process for creating and editing dynamic blocks — in this chapter.

Arraying Associatively

Things used to be so simple back around . . . oh, AutoCAD 2011. ARRAY was unequivocally a modifying command, just like COPY or ROTATE. You filled in values in a dialog box, and after a bit of tweaking, you ended up with multiple copies of the source objects, neatly arranged in geometric patterns: either in evenly spaced rows and columns, or evenly distributed radially about a center point. Then Autodesk programmers decided that old-fashioned arrays weren't enough, so Autodesk took the old ARRAY command into the lab, wired electrodes to its brain, and threw the switch — and up rose the new super ARRAY!

Try this quick example, and then we'll come back a little later to dig into more detail.

The following exercise works only in AutoCAD 2013 and later.

1. **Start a new drawing, and create a couple of simple objects (for example, a line passing through a circle) in the lower left of the screen.**

2. **Type the command ARRAYREC in the command window and then press Enter.**

3. **Select the line and the circle that you just drew and then press Enter.**

4. **AutoCAD displays a three-row-by-four-column preview with six blue grips.**

5. **Experiment by clicking and dragging the grips to see what they do.**

6. **Press Enter to create your first associative array.**

7. **To see what associative means, click any of the objects in the array.**

 Magic! The blue grips come back, and you can change the number of rows and columns and their spacing.

Comparing the old and new ARRAY commands

The results of using the ARRAY command in AutoCAD 2012 and later are so different from those in previous releases that we really wish that Autodesk would give it a new name. We're going to do our best to clarify the muddy waters, so here's the terminology we use in this book:

- **Associative array:** This is an object type created as a single object from separate source objects, using the current (AutoCAD 2012 and later) ARRAY command.

- **ARRAY:** Use this command for creating associative rectangular, polar, path, and 3D arrays of existing objects. The ARRAYRECT, ARRAYPATH, and ARRAYPOLAR are subsets of the ARRAY command.

- **Simple or non-associative array:** Individual copies of source objects are created in regular rectangular or polar patterns or by using the –ARRAY command. You can create the exact equivalent of a simple array by repeatedly using the COPY command.

- **–ARRAY:** This command-prompt version of the original ARRAY command has been present in AutoCAD for more than 20 years. This version only creates what we refer to as non-associative or simple arrays. We cover this in Chapters 3 and 11.

- **ARRAYCLASSIC:** If you type this command, the Classic Array dialog box appears. It produces simple arrays.

Some of the differences between simple arrays and associative arrays are

- **A simple array is just multiple copies**. When you array objects with –ARRAY, the source objects are simply copied in rectangular or radial patterns. They remain as separate lines or circles or whatever the original entity type.

An array with a large number of objects in the array and a large number of objects within each copy can rapidly reach government-spending file sizes. Best practice is to create a block of the objects first. We discuss blocks in Chapter 17. A further advantage of this practice is that if you change the block definition, all insertions of it in the array also update.

- **An associative array is a single object**. When you create an associative array, the source objects are deleted from the drawing and replaced by a new associative array object. An array object is effectively a block. We discuss blocks in Chapter 17.

- **The two array types interact differently with layers**. When you create a simple array, the copies of the selected drawing objects are placed on the same layers as the source. On the other hand, an associative array follows the same rules as any block insertion: The new object is placed

on whatever layer happens to be current. Source objects located on layer 0 (zero) take on the properties of the current layer, while source objects on other layers retain the properties of their layers.

🗸 **There are two types of simple arrays, but three associative types.** Associative Simple arrays can be either rectangular (that is, in evenly spaced rows and columns) or polar (evenly arranged around a center point). Associative arrays have a Path option, as well as Rectangular and Polar patterns.

🗸 **Associative arrays can be edited.** An associative array is a single object, and so it can be edited as such. Associative arrays (think of them as *intelligent* arrays) have far more editing options than non-associative arrays do. Okay, anything much above *pretty well none* counts as *more*. With an associative array, you can change the quantity values (rows, columns, spacing, and so on), you can move and suppress individual items within the array, and you can replace individual items with different ones. You can redefine the source objects, and every repetition updates. The really good news is that you can always put the array back like it was if you mess up too badly.

Associative array objects are recognized as such in AutoCAD 2012 and later, and can be edited only by using the ARRAYEDIT command. In earlier versions, associative arrays are treated as anonymous blocks, and their content can be edited only by exploding them. This turns them into simple arrays, and if you receive the file back into AutoCAD 2013, the array isn't associative anymore. We discuss exploding in Chapter 17.

AutoCAD 2013 files cannot be opened by earlier versions. If you need to send a drawing to someone running an earlier version, you need to use the SAVEAS command and select the appropriate version from the Files of Type drop-down list at the bottom of the File Save dialog box.

Hip, hip, array!

When associative arrays were introduced in AutoCAD 2012, many reviewers were startled to see that the dialog box used for simple arrays had gone away and seemed to be replaced by command window input, just like the good — oops, we mean bad — old days. The disadvantage to command window input is that you must follow a step-by-step sequence, and if you make a mistake or change your mind, you have to cancel and start over again. The good news is that the ARRAY command displays a live preview so you can see exactly how your array will turn out. The bad news is that AutoCAD 2012's interface was a little clunky, much like the old command window version.

And even more good news is that the ARRAY command interface has been significantly reworked for AutoCAD 2013. We won't point out each and every difference, so you can consider everything from here to just before the section "Going External," later in this chapter, to be new in 2013. The final outcome is the same — it's just the interface that changed.

Start with a rectangular array, using the ARRAYRECT command. When you have finished this exercise, you will have multiple copies of a set of drawing objects, neatly arranged in a grid pattern of several rows and columns.

1. **Open a drawing containing some objects you want to array, or draw some simple geometry for your source objects.**

2. **On the Home tab's Modify panel, choose Rectangular Array from the Array drop-down list.**

 Choosing the specific array type from the drop-down list saves you from answering one prompt you'd get if you typed ARRAY.

 When drop-down lists are available, the Ribbon remembers the last selection chosen. The Array button may show any one of three different icons. If you like the one that's showing, you can simply select it instead of initiating the drop-down list.

3. **At the Select Objects prompt, select one or more objects that you want to array.**

 When you finish selecting, AutoCAD displays a three-row-by-four-column preview with six blue grips (shown in Figure 18-1) and prompts:

   ```
   Select grip to edit array or [ASsociative/Base point/
           COUnt/Spacing/COLumns/Rows/Levels/eXit]<eXit
   ```

 If Dynamic input is turned on, the cursor prompt displays:

   ```
   Select grip to edit or <eXit>:
   ```

 The Ribbon changes to display the Array Creation contextual tab, as shown in Figure 18-1.

4. **Enter the number of rows and columns of your source objects that you want to be arrayed, and also their spacing.**

 As we mention earlier, when AutoCAD 2012 introduced associative arrays, many people commented on what appeared to be a regressive step away from a dialog box and back to command window input. The good news is that AutoCAD 2013 gives you most of the advantages of both methods but few of the disadvantages — and adds yet another variant: the Ribbon.

Row spacing Row and column quantity

Row quantity

Column spacing Column quantity

Base: move your array

Figure 18-1: You're ready to dynamically define your associative array.

Start with the editing method that we believe most users will adopt — grip editing. As you play with the following options, observe how the dynamic preview constantly updates. Each grip controls a different aspect of your array, as follows:

- *Row 1, column 1:* Base. You can move your array to a different location as you create it. After you select this grip, you can drag and drop it to a new location (object snaps work), or you can enter X and Y values at the dynamic cursor prompt.

- *Row 1, column 2:* Column spacing. Drag this grip (or enter a value at the dynamic prompt) to change the spacing of all columns.

 You can enter a negative value, or you can drag to the left of row 1, column 1 to make your array grow in the opposite direction.

- *Row 1, column 4:* Column quantity. Drag this grip (or enter a value at the dynamic prompt) to change the quantity of columns.

- *Column 1, row 2:* Row spacing. Drag this grip (or enter a value at the dynamic prompt) to change the spacing of all rows.

 You can enter a negative value, or you can drag below row 1, column 1 to make your array grow in the opposite direction.

- *Column 1, row 3:* Row quantity. Drag this grip (or enter a value at the dynamic prompt) to change the quantity of rows.

- *Row 3, column 4:* Row and column quantity. Drag this grip (or enter values at the dynamic prompt) to change the quantity of rows and columns at the same time.

5. **Check out the other methods of specifying your array.**

 The AutoCAD 2013 changes to the ARRAY interface give you three basic methods for defining your array. If you followed the scenario in this step list, you already played with grip editing. The interesting option is that the command window continues to show almost all the prompts. Typically, command-line input forces you to follow a specific sequence, but ARRAY in AutoCAD 2013 allows you to enter any command window option at any time.

 Earlier, we mention that the Ribbon displays the Array Creation contextual tab while you're defining your array. At any time, you can enter specific values for anything we have discussed so far, but it also has an extra functionality: the Columns and Rows tabs each have a Total window, referring to a total distance. If you enter values in either window, the column and/or row spacing will be adjusted so that the number of rows and/or columns fit exactly within the specified distance.

6. **Finish building your array.**

 If you don't have a grip selected, the default mode is eXit. Simply press Enter or the spacebar, or click the Close Array button in the Ribbon, and you're done!

But wait! There's more! The Rows tab of the Array Creation contextual tab of the Ribbon includes options for vertical (Z axis) values. If you're working in 3D, you can easily create a set of bleacher seats, for example, where the higher-numbered rows are at a higher elevation so everyone gets a good view.

But it's not even Christmas!

AutoCAD also has the ARRAYPOLAR command for creating polar (circular) arrays, such as the bolt holes in a pipe flange, horses on a carousel, or chambers in a revolver. As we indicate earlier, it may be hidden in the drop-down list under the Array button on the Modify tab of the Home panel of the Ribbon.

The basic principles of a polar array are the same as a rectangular one.

- Each polar array is a single, associative object.
- Objects within an array can be edited separately. We cover this a little later in this chapter.
- As you create them, you see a dynamic preview of what the final array will look like.
- You can specify your input to the command through grip edits, the command window, the dynamic cursor, and/or the Polar version of the Array Creation tab of the Ribbon.

But polar arrays also have a few differences.

- ✔ When you finish selecting the objects to be arrayed, you are asked for a center point for the array. Note that normal object snaps can be most helpful here.

- ✔ After you select the center point, a six-item dynamic preview with editing grips appears, along with the polar variant of the Array Creation tab of the Ribbon.

- ✔ Input specifications include

 - *The radius of the array*

 - *The number of items in the array*

 - *The angle to fill*

 A gear sector, for example, might need only ten teeth in a 60-degree segment.

 - *The number of rows*

 Although this seems to be strange terminology for a circular pattern, you can specify the number of concentric repeats of the circular pattern and the radial distance between them, like the growth rings of a tree.

 - *Whether items are rotated (for example, gear teeth) or not (Ferris wheel seats) as the array is produced*

 - *The number of levels and the Z direction spacing between them*

Down the garden path

Associative arrays have a third type that isn't available when you use ARRAYCLASSIC or –ARRAY to produce a simple array.

Unlike rectangular and polar arrays, which require only source objects and some input parameters, path arrays require an additional piece of drawing geometry — a path. A path can be as simple as a line or a circle, or it can be a spline or a 2D or 3D polyline. Other than that, they behave very much like rectangular and polar arrays.

In the following steps, we show you how to use the ARRAYPATH command to bring some chairs to an elliptical dining room table and use the table itself as the path.

1. **Open a drawing containing some objects you want to array along a path, or draw some simple geometry for your source object, and a line or an open or a closed spline or polyline for your path.**

2. **On the Home tab's Modify panel, choose Path Array from the Array drop-down list.**

 Path Array may be hidden in the drop-down list under the Array button on the Modify tab of the Home panel of the Ribbon.

3. **At the Select Objects prompt, select one or more objects that you want to array along a path.**

 AutoCAD prompts:

   ```
   Select objects:
   ```

 You can select any and all AutoCAD object types, including block insertions and text.

 Object arraying is done based on the position of the objects relative to the starting end of the path object. If you want the arrayed objects to land on the path, they must be on the path before you select them.

 When you finish selecting objects, AutoCAD prompts:

   ```
   Select path curve:
   ```

4. **Select the object you want to serve as the path.**

 Valid object types include straight lines, open or closed polylines and splines, arcs, circles, and ellipses, as well as helixes and 3D polylines.

 You don't have to press Enter after you select the path. AutoCAD immediately responds with a lengthy, multioption prompt, displays a dynamic preview, and displays the path version of the Array Creation contextual Ribbon tab.

5. **Enter the specifications for your array.**

 As with rectangular and polar arrays, you can specify the number of items, the distance between them, and/or the length of a portion of the path to fill. A bit of experimentation will show that these options are often interrelated; changing one forces another one to change. You can also specify whether the arrayed objects stay horizontal, or whether they rotate to stay parallel to the path.

 Again, just like the other array types, you can jump back and forth between grip editing, Ribbon entries, the command window options, and dynamic cursor input.

6. **Finish building your array.**

 If you don't have a grip selected, the default mode is eXit. Simply press Enter or the spacebar, or click the Close Array button in the Ribbon, and you're done!

Put the path object on a separate layer. After you complete the array, freeze that layer, and the path object becomes invisible. We cover layers in Chapter 6.

Figure 18-2 shows the finished path array.

Figure 18-2: Down the garden path, using a path array.

Associatively editing

If you click any arrayed element (not the path of a path array), AutoCAD displays the Array contextual tab on the Ribbon. From here, you can revise pretty much every aspect of the array definition. In addition, the Options panel appears near the end of the Array tab.

You need a special tool for tinkering with the entrails of associative arrays, and AutoCAD provides it with the ARRAYEDIT command. The three items on the Options panel link to the three options of this command. Start with a typical scenario: You just finished the drawing of the garden path when the client comes in and announces that the steppingstones need to be bigger.

No problem. Select any one of the steppingstones (but not the spline path curve itself) in the array. Now click the Edit Source button in the Options panel of the Array tab, and then select any one of the arrayed items. Edit it to your heart's content, including adding and moving objects, changing layers, and deleting objects. When you're finished, select Save Changes from the Edit Array panel at the end of the Home tab of the Ribbon, and all the arrayed items update.

So far, so good, but now the client wants a square steppingstone to replace one of the circular ones halfway down the path (see Figure 18-3). No problem. Step through the following steps (pun intended):

1. **Draw the new steppingstone.**

 The easiest way to do this is to use the RECTANG command from chapter 8.

2. **Select the array you want to edit.**

 Select any object in the path array. Don't select the path itself or you will be editing the path, not the array.

3. **Select the replacement stone.**

 Select the Replace Item tool in the Options tab of the Array context ribbon and then select the replacement rectangular stone. Press Enter to continue.

4. **Select the base point of the replacement rectangular stone.**

 Select a point about in the center of the rectangle. This is the point that will end up sitting exactly on the path.

5. **Select the stone to be replaced.**

 Select one or more existing circular stones in the array that you want to replace with the new rectangular one, and then press Enter to continue.

6. **Finish it off.**

 Press Enter, or select eXit from the context menu.

Figure 18-3: Going down a different path: The results of editing an associative array.

Oops! You replaced the wrong steppingstone. No problem. Select the array, and then select Reset Array from the Options panel of the Array tab. Voilà! Your changes are undone. Now you can replace it with the correct one.

Earlier, we emphasize the importance of selecting an arrayed item in a path array, and not the path. The reason for this is simple: The path can be edited

separately. Simply select it and then edit it like the object that it is. When you're finished, the path array updates to match the revised path.

And no matter how much tinkering you do, you can always revert to the original state by clicking Reset Array on the Options panel of the Array tab.

Going External

In AutoCAD, an *xref* (external reference) is a reference to another *external* drawing file — one outside the current drawing — that acts as though it's part of your drawing. Technically, a reference is simply a pointer from one file to another. The xref is the actual pointer, but many people call the combination of the pointer and the external file the "xref."

In both AutoCAD and AutoCAD LT, external drawing files are just one of several file types you can attach to your current drawing via the Select Reference File dialog box. You use this dialog box to attach externally referenced AutoCAD drawings (xrefs), raster image files, DWF and DWFx files, PDF files, and MicroStation DGN drawing files, among others.

Use the Attach button of the Insert tab Reference panel to open the Select Reference File dialog box. When you attach an external drawing to your current drawing, you become the host of the external file. No need to break out the cocktails and canapés, though, because it's actually your current drawing that's doing the hosting — and in AutoCAD, it's called (what else?) the *host drawing.* You can think of the attached xrefs as guests, but most of the time they're pretty well-behaved ones — and like the best of guests, they go away as soon as you want them to.

Xrefs have a big advantage over blocks: If a drawing is inserted as a block into another drawing, its geometry doesn't change if the original drawing is changed in any way — it always looks the way it looks when it's inserted. If that drawing is attached as an xref, however, AutoCAD will automatically update every host drawing to which it's attached when the host drawing is reopened. You can also manually reload the changed xref if you don't want to close and reopen the host drawing.

When you open a drawing that contains xrefs, AutoCAD displays a little symbol (looks like papers with a binder clip) on the right end of the status bar. This symbol alerts you that some of the things you see in the drawing are actually parts of other, xref-ed drawings. If an xref changes while you have the host drawing open (because you or someone else opens and saves the referenced drawing), the status bar xref symbol displays an External Reference Files Have Changed balloon notification. Simply click the

Reload link in the balloon notification to show the updated xrefs. (If you want to change how AutoCAD checks for changes, look up XREFNOTIFY in the online help.)

Another advantage that xrefs have over blocks is that their contents aren't stored in your drawing even once. The disk storage space taken up by the original drawing (the xref) isn't duplicated, no matter how many host drawings reference it. This characteristic makes xrefs much more efficient than blocks for larger drawings that are reused several times.

Sure, you can always buy a larger hard drive, so the storage issue isn't crucial. The key benefit of xrefs is that they enable you to organize your drawings so the changes you make to a single drawing file automatically ripple through all the host drawings into which it's xref-ed. This benefit is even greater on larger projects involving multiple drafters, each of whose work may be incorporated in part or in whole in the work of others.

You can use xrefs to your advantage in almost any type of drawing. For example, several drafters might be working on the components for a large machine, while one master drawing brings them all together in the final assembly. Similarly, a set of separate architectural drawings could show electrical, plumbing, HVAV, and so on with everyone referencing the same floor plan. The host file would contain nothing but a title block and xrefs to the other files.

However, the automatic update feature of xrefs is a big advantage only if you're organized about how you use xrefs. Suppose that an architect creates a plan drawing showing a building's walls and other major features that are common to the architectural, structural, plumbing, and electrical plan drawings. The architect then tells the structural, plumbing, and electrical drafters to xref this background plan into their drawings so that everyone is working from a consistent and reusable set of common plan elements. If the architect decides to revise the wall locations and updates the xref-ed drawing, everyone will see the current wall configuration and be able to change their drawings. But if the architect absent-mindedly adds architecture-specific objects (toilets and furniture, for example) to the xref-ed drawing, or shifts all the objects with respect to 0,0, everyone else will have problems. If different people in your office share xrefs, create a protocol for who is allowed to modify which file when, and what communication needs to take place after a shared xref is modified.

Becoming attached to your xrefs

Attaching an external reference drawing is similar to inserting a block, and almost as easy. Just use the following steps:

1. **Set an appropriate layer current, as described in Chapter 6.**

 Insert xrefs on a separate layer from all other objects.

 Note that if you freeze the layer on which an xref is inserted, the entire xref disappears. (This behavior can be a handy trick, a nasty surprise, or a fun trick.)

2. **If the External References palette isn't already open, click its icon (it looks like a sheaf of papers with a bulldog clip and a silhouetted user) on the Palettes panel of the View tab to open it.**

 Use the toolbar at the top of the palette to attach an external DWG file, a DWF underlay, a PDF underlay, a MicroStation DGN drawing file, a raster image file, or a point cloud. We cover attaching images and DWFs or PDFs later in this chapter. If you need to attach DGN files, visit the online help.

3. **Click Attach DWG. Click the down arrow if the tooltip offers to attach something else — see Figure 18-4.**

 The Select Reference File dialog box appears.

4. **Browse to find the file you want to attach, select it, and then click Open.**

 The Attach External Reference dialog box appears.

5. **Specify the parameters for the xref in the dialog box.**

 Parameters include the insertion point, scaling factors, location based on geographic data, and rotation angle. (We describe geographic location briefly in Chapter 17.) You can set these parameters in the dialog box or specify them onscreen, just like you can do when inserting a block, as described in Chapter 17.

 The Path Type drop-down list provides more flexibility in how the xref path is stored. See the "Forging an xref path" section, later in this chapter, for more information.

 We recommend that you choose Relative Path instead of Full Path.

6. **Click OK.**

 The externally referenced file appears in your drawing.

In drawings that contain many xrefs, locating the one you want can be difficult. When you select an object that's part of an xref in the drawing area, the xref name is highlighted in the External References palette. Likewise, selecting an xref in the External References palette highlights the attached file geometry in the drawing editor.

List View

Attach DWG

Tree View

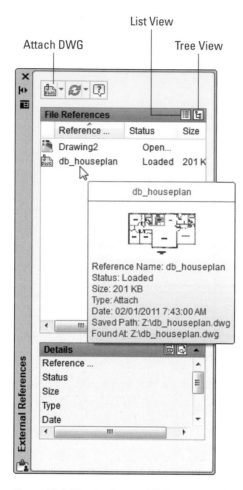

Figure 18-4: Use the External References palette to attach an xref.

You can select either the Attachment or Overlay radio button to tell AutoCAD how to handle the xref. The choice matters only if you create a drawing that uses xrefs, and then your drawing is, in turn, used as an xref. Attachment is the default choice, and it dictates that the xref-ed file will always be included with your drawing when someone else uses your drawing as an xref. Overlay, the other choice, means that you see the xref-ed drawing, but someone who xrefs *your* drawing won't see the overlaid file. By choosing Overlay, you can xref a map, for example, to your drawing of a house, but the map won't show up when someone else xrefs your house drawing. (That person can xref the map, if needed.) We recommend that you use the default Attachment reference type unless you have a specific reason not to.

One use of Overlay mode is to avoid circular references. If drawing A references drawing B, which references drawing C and then C references A, you have an infinite loop. If C references A as an overlay, though, C doesn't see B, and so the loop is broken.

Layer-palooza

When you attach or overlay an xref, AutoCAD adds new layers to your current drawing that correspond to the layers in the xref-ed DWG file. The new layers are assigned names that combine the drawing name and layer name. For example, if you xref the drawing MYSCREW.DWG (which has the layer names GEOMETRY, TEXT, and so on), the xref-ed layers will be named MYSCREW|GEOMETRY, MYSCREW|TEXT, and so on. By creating separate layers corresponding to each layer in the xref-ed file, AutoCAD eliminates the potential problem with blocks that we warn you about in Chapter 17, when layers have the same name but different color or linetype in the two drawings.

Creating and editing an external reference file

To create a file that you can use as an external reference, just create a drawing and save it. That's it. You can then create or open another drawing and create an external reference to the previous one. The xref-ed drawing appears in the host drawing as a single object, very much like a block insert. In other words, if you click any object in the xref, AutoCAD selects the entire xref. You can measure or object snap to the xref-ed geometry, but you can't modify or delete individual objects in the xref. Instead, you open the xref drawing to edit its geometry.

The XOPEN command provides a quick way to open an xref-ed drawing for editing. You just start the command and pick any object in the xref. Alternatively, you can select the xref from the External References palette and then right-click and choose Open to open one or more xrefs for editing. See the "Managing xrefs" section, later in this chapter, for more information.

An alternative to opening the xref-ed file when you need to edit it is to use the REFEDIT command. Use REFEDIT (short for *Reference Edit*) to edit the external file from within the host drawing, rather than having to open the reference in its own window. Look up REFEDIT in the AutoCAD online help system's Command Reference.

With several xrefs attached to your drawing, or with a very complex xref, it can be difficult to tell which objects belong to the drawing you're editing, and which are part of the xref. You can fade your xrefs as follows:

1. **Open a drawing containing an external reference drawing.**

 Alternatively, you can attach a drawing to your current drawing by following the steps in the "Becoming attached to your xrefs" section, earlier in this chapter.

2. **On the Insert tab, click the Reference panel label to open the Reference slideout.**

 The Reference slideout also contains the Edit Reference button, which runs the REFEDIT command.

3. **Click the Xref Fading button to toggle reference fading off and on.**

4. **Drag the Xref Fading slider to increase or decrease the level of fading in the reference file.**

 The default value is 70; increasing the value toward 90 (the maximum) increases the degree of fading, and lowering it reduces the fade level.

Forging an xref path

When you attach an xref, one option is to have the host drawing store the xref's *full path* — that is, the drive letter and sequence of folders and subfolders all the way down to the folder in which the DWG file resides — along with the filename. This behavior corresponds to the Full Path setting in the Path Type drop-down list. Figure 18-5 shows the three xref path options. Full Path works fine as long as you never move files on your hard drive or network and never send your DWG files to anyone else — which is to say, it almost never works fine!

Figure 18-5: Follow the path less traveled when you attach an xref.

At the other end of the path spectrum, the No Path option causes AutoCAD not to store any path with the xref attachment — only the filename is stored. This is the easiest and best option if the host drawings and the xrefs reside in the same folder. However, if the host and the xref are in different folders, you have to browse to find the reference file every time you open the host drawing.

If you prefer to organize the DWG files for a particular project in more than one folder, you'll appreciate AutoCAD's Relative Path option, as shown in Figure 18-5. This option permits xref-ing across more complex folder structures but avoids many of the problems that the Full Path option can cause. For example, you may have a host drawing

```
H:\Project-X\Plans\First floor.dwg
```

that xrefs

```
H:\Project-X\Common\Column grid.dwg
```

If you choose Relative Path, AutoCAD will store the xref path as

```
..\ Common\Column grid.dwg
```

instead of

```
H:\Project-X\Common\Column grid.dwg
```

This way, if you decide to move the \Project-X folder and its subfolders to a different drive (or send them to someone else who doesn't have an H: drive), AutoCAD can still find the xrefs.

When attaching an external reference we strongly recommend you check the Path Type window and make sure it says Relative Path. If not, select Relative Path from the drop-down list from this window.

When you use Relative Path, you'll see xref paths that include the special codes — . and . . (single and double period). The single period means *this host drawing's folder,* and the double period means *the folder above this host drawing's folder.*

You can report on and change xref paths for a set of drawings with the Reference Manager (not in AutoCAD LT). See Chapter 20 for more information.

If all these path options and periods leave you feeling punchy, you can keep your life simple by always keeping host and xref drawings in the same folder and using the No Path option when you attach xrefs. On the other hand, it can get a little messy when a file such as a standard title block and border is

xref-ed into many different drawings for several different projects, and you
want to keep each project's files in separate folders. The best solution is usu-
ally a bit of each; the title block and border can have a specific path in each
host, but the other project files don't.

Managing xrefs

The External References palette includes many more options for managing
xrefs after you attach them. Many of these options are hiding in right-click
menus. Important options include

- **List of external references:** You can change between the List view and
 Tree view of your drawing's external references by clicking the appropri-
 ate button at the top of the palette (refer to Figure 18-4). You can resize
 the columns by dragging the column dividers or re-sort the list by click-
 ing the column header names, just like in Windows Explorer.

- **Unload:** Right-click an xref and choose Unload to make the selected
 xref disappear from the onscreen display of your drawing and from any
 plots you do of it, but yet retain the pointer and attachment information.
 Right-click again and choose Reload to redisplay an unloaded xref.

- **Reload:** Right-click an xref and choose Reload to force AutoCAD to
 reread the selected xref-ed DWG file from the disk and update your
 drawing with its latest contents. This feature is handy when you share
 xrefs on a network and someone has just made changes to a drawing
 that you've xref-ed.

- **Detach:** Right-click an xref in the External References palette and choose
 Detach to completely remove the selected reference to the external file
 from your drawing.

- **Bind:** Right-click an xref and choose Bind to bring the selected xref into
 your drawing and turn it into a block. You might, for example, use this
 function to roll up a complex set of xrefs into a single archive drawing.

 In many offices, binding xrefs without an acceptable reason for doing
 so is a crime as heinous as exploding blocks indiscriminately. In both
 cases, you're eliminating an important data management link. Find out
 what the policies are in your company. When in doubt, keep yourself out
 of a bind. And even when you do have a good reason to bind, you gener-
 ally should do it on a copy of the host drawing.

- **Open:** Right-click an xref and choose Open to open one or more xref
 drawings in separate drawing windows. After you edit and save an xref
 drawing, return to the host drawing and use the Reload option in the
 External References palette to show the changes.

None of these options (other than opening and editing the xref) affects the xref-ed drawing itself; it continues to exist as a separate DWG file. If you need to delete or move the DWG file that the xref refers to, do it in Windows Explorer.

The fact that the xref-ed drawing is a separate file is a potential source of problems when you send your drawing to someone else; that someone else needs *all* the files that your drawing depends on, or it will be useless. Make sure to include xref-ed files in the package with your drawing. See Chapter 20 for a procedure.

Both AutoCAD and AutoCAD LT include an additional xref feature called *exref clipping.* You can clip any kind of externally referenced file or block insertion so only part of it appears in the host drawing. Use the CLIP command to trim away unwanted parts of xref drawings, DWF and DWFx files, raster images, MicroStation DGN files or PDFs. You can even clip block insertions. For more information, look up CLIP in the online help's Command Reference section.

Blocks, Xrefs, and Drawing Organization

Blocks and xrefs are useful for organizing sets of drawings to use and update repeated elements. When to use blocks and when to use xrefs isn't always clear, though. Applications for xrefs include

- ✔ The parts of a title block that are the same on all sheets in a project
- ✔ Reference elements that must appear in multiple drawings (for example, wall outlines, site topography, and column grids)
- ✔ Assemblies that are repeated in one or more drawings, especially if the assemblies are likely to change together (for example, repeated framing assemblies, bathroom layouts, and modular furniture layouts)
- ✔ Pasting up several drawings (for example, details or a couple of plans) onto one plot sheet
- ✔ Temporarily attaching a background drawing for reference or tracing

On the other hand, blocks remain useful in simpler circumstances. Situations in which you might stick with a block are

- ✔ **Components that aren't likely to change**
- ✔ **Simple components**
- ✔ **A simple assembly that's used repeatedly but in only one drawing**

✔ **When you want to include *attributes* (variable text fields) that you can fill in each time you insert a block**

Blocks let you include attribute definitions; xrefs don't. Refer to Chapter 17 for the lowdown on attributes.

Everyone in a company or workgroup should aim for consistency as to when and how they use blocks and xrefs. Check whether guidelines exist for using blocks and xrefs in your office. If so, follow them; if not, it would be a good idea to develop some guidelines.

Mastering the Raster

AutoCAD includes four more xref-like features: the ability to attach raster images, DWF files, PDF files, and DGN files to drawings. We cover DWF and PDF files in the next section and refer you to the online help if you should find some DGN files on your hands. The image feature is useful for adding a raster logo to a drawing title block or placing a photographed map or scene behind a drawing. A *raster,* or *bitmapped,* image is one that's stored as a field of tiny dots.

AutoCAD drawings are vector files. A *vector* drawing is a graphic file defined by storing geometrical definitions of a bunch of objects. Typical objects include a line (defined by its two endpoints) and a circle (defined by its center point and radius). Vector-based images are typically smaller (in terms of the disk space they occupy) and more flexible than raster images, but also are less capable of displaying visually rich images, such as photographs.

Raster images often come from digital cameras or from other programs, such as Photoshop. Raster images can also come into the computer from some kind of scanner that imports a blueline print, photograph, or other image.

Whether you're doing your own scanning or having a service bureau do it for you, you need to know that AutoCAD handles most popular image file formats, including: the Windows BMP format; the popular Web graphics formats GIF and JPEG; common print formats such as PCX, PNG, and TIFF; the less popular DIB, FLC, FLI, GP4, MIL, RLE, RST, TGA formats, and several even more obscure ones.

Three scenarios in which you could incorporate raster images in your drawing include

✔ **Small stuff:** You can add logos, special symbols, and other small images that you have in raster files.

✔ **Photographs and maps:** You can add photographs (such as a future building site) and maps (for example, showing the project location).

✓ **Vectorization:** To convert a raster image into a vector drawing by tracing lines in the raster image, you can attach the raster image in your drawing, trace the needed lines by using AutoCAD commands, and then detach the raster image. (This procedure is okay for a simple raster image; add-on software is available, from Autodesk and others, to support automatic or semiautomatic vectorization of more complex images.)

Your raster image may be distorted a bit; for example, the aspect ratio (ratio of width to height) may not be correct, but AutoCAD won't let you change it. No problem; simply attach the raster image, make a block that contains it, and then insert the block with different X and Y scale factors. We love cheating.

Using raster images is much like using external references. The raster image isn't stored with your drawing file, though. Instead, a reference to the raster image file is established from within your drawing, like an xref. You can clip the image and control its size, brightness, contrast, fade, and transparency. These controls fine-tune the appearance of the raster image onscreen and on a plot.

When you attach raster images, you have to make sure that you send the raster files along when you send your drawing to someone else. Raster images are simply referenced from the drawing and aren't part of it. If you don't send the raster image file along with the drawing, the drawing displays a rectangle containing the name of the missing file in its place. The best way to make sure that you get all the required files when sending a drawing file to someone else is to use the ETRANSMIT command, which we cover in Chapter 20.

Some raster image files that you find on the Internet may not be appropriate AutoCAD attachments.

Attaching a raster image

Follow these steps to bring a raster image into AutoCAD:

1. **If the External References palette isn't already open, click its icon on the Palettes panel of the View tab.**

 Use the drop-down list on the first toolbar button to attach a drawing, an image, or a DWF, PDF, or DGN file.

2. **Click Attach Image and locate the image file you want to attach.**

 The Attach Image dialog box appears, as shown in Figure 18-6.

3. **Browse to find the file you want to attach, select it, and then click Open.**

 The Attach Image dialog box appears.

 Click the Show Details button in the Attach Image dialog box to see more information about the resolution and image size of the image you're attaching.

Figure 18-6: The Attach Image dialog box.

4. **Specify the parameters for the attached image in the dialog box.**

 Parameters include the insertion point, scale factor, and rotation angle. You can set these parameters in the dialog box or specify them onscreen, similar to what you can do with blocks and external references, as described earlier in this chapter.

 The Attach Image dialog box includes the same Full Path, Relative Path, and No Path options as those for attaching xrefs. (See the "Forging an xref path" section, earlier in this chapter.)

5. **Click OK.**

 The image appears in your drawing.

6. **If you need to ensure that the raster image floats behind other objects in the drawing, select the raster image, right-click, choose Draw Order, and then choose Send to Back.**

 The DRAWORDER command provides additional options for which objects appear on top of which other objects. If you need this kind of flexibility, look up DRAWORDER command in the AutoCAD online help system.

Maintaining your image

You manage the images in your drawing via the External References palette. You can view a list of image files that appear in the current drawing, detach (remove) image references, and unload and reload images when needed. You can't bind an image to your drawing, though; it always remains an external file.

You can clip images so that only part of the image is displayed in your drawing. Choose Clip from the Insert tab's Reference panel and follow the prompts

to clip the image. You can have multiple overlapping or distinct pieces of any number of images in your drawing, and only the parts you need are loaded into memory when you have your drawing open.

Raster image files often are larger than DWG files of corresponding complexity; raster file size can affect performance within AutoCAD because the raster file loads into memory when you're working on your drawing. If you find raster attachments slowing down AutoCAD's response, then follow these tips:

- ✔ Attach raster images late in the production process.

- ✔ Create a lower-resolution version of the raster file, just large enough to create the desired effect in your drawing.

- ✔ Right-click an image in the External References palette and choose Unload from the menu that appears to temporarily hide an image without losing the attachment information.

In addition, raster files can also dramatically increase the time that AutoCAD takes to generate plots (and the plot file sizes). Before you settle on using large raster files in your AutoCAD drawing, do some testing on zooming, editing, and plotting.

You Say PDF, We Say DWF

The Adobe PDF format has been around for a very long time, and for a while, it seemed like Autodesk was trying to supplant it with its own universal file format — DWF (Design Web Format). That didn't happen, but if you can't beat them. . . . AutoCAD includes a very acceptable PDF printer driver, and both PDF and DWF are suitable candidates for external reference files.

You could think of a DWF as "DWG Lite" because it looks just like a drawing file and contains some of the actual drawing file data. We talk more about the web side of DWFs in Chapter 20; in this section, we explain how you can use DWFs as well as PDFs as reference files in your own drawings. (Some people call DWF files "dwiffs," but we're going to hold off on that one until we start hearing DWG files called "dwiggs". And why is *phonetic* spelled that way?)

You create both DWFs and PDFs from within AutoCAD in one of two ways. Either choose Plot and select a DWF or PDF option in the Printer/Plotter name list, or choose Print⇨Batch Plot from the Application Menu and then select DWF, DWFx, or PDF from the Publish To area of the Publish dialog box.

Both file types are compact and secure. Because you can't edit either PDFs or DWFs in AutoCAD, both formats are ideal for two purposes:

✔ You can post DWFs or PDFs on the web.

✔ You can send your drawings to consultants and clients in a form that they can't mess up.

You can attach PDFs or DWFs to your drawing files in pretty much the same way you attach drawings as external references. DWFs and PDFs attached to drawing files are referred to as DWF underlays or PDF underlays.

As with DWF and DGN attachments, you can object-snap to entities in the PDF underlay by enabling the Snap to Underlays function in the Reference panel slideout on the Insert tab. Setting PDF parameters is virtually identical to setting DWF parameters, and you can attach a PDF to your drawing by using exactly the same steps as the ones that follow.

The previous sections show how to attach a DWG and a raster image. Follow these steps to attach a DWF (or a PDF!) file as an underlay:

1. **If the External References palette isn't already open, click its icon on the Palettes panel of the View tab to open it.**

 Use the toolbar at the top of the palette to attach an external file as an xref, a raster image file, or a DGN or DWF underlay. We cover attaching xrefs and images earlier in this chapter. See the online help for information on attaching DGN files.

2. **Click Attach DWF or Attach PDF and then locate the file you want to attach.**

 The Select Reference File dialog box appears.

3. **Browse to find the file you want to attach, select it, and then click Open.**

 The Attach DWF Underlay or Attach PDF Underlay dialog box appears.

4. **Specify the parameters for the DWF or the PDF in the dialog box.**

 Parameters include specifying a sheet, the insertion point, scaling factors, rotation angle, and path type (see Figure 18-7). You can set these parameters in the dialog box or specify them onscreen, just like you can do when inserting a block, attaching an xref, or attaching an image, as described earlier in this chapter.

5. **Click OK.**

 The externally referenced DWF or PDF file appears in your drawing.

Neither PDF nor DWF files are as precise as DWGs, and that's why they're a lot smaller. When using object snaps to locate points in DWFs, you may see the word `approximate` on the Object Snap tooltip. If this is a problem, you can increase the precision of your DWF file when you create it.

Figure 18-7: The Attach PDF Underlay dialog box.

AutoCAD allows you to import about 20 different file formats into an AutoCAD drawing. Most of these are 3D modeling formats. They are imported into model space (not attached or xref-ed), and are used as the basis for additional 3D modeling and editing and/or for generating 2D working drawings from them. We discuss 3D to 2D in Chapter 23.

Theme and Variations: Dynamic Blocks

You can add variety to your blocks by making them dynamic. The two most useful applications for dynamic blocks are multiple presentations of similar objects and manipulation of components within individual block inserts.

AutoCAD dynamic blocks feature offers you a great deal of flexibility to block creation and insertion, but using them is also a very complicated system with its own set of commands and system variables. We recommend that you become *very* familiar with regular block creation and insertion techniques for creating and inserting blocks (which we describe in Chapter 17) before you tackle dynamic blocks.

Spend some time planning your dynamic blocks. Sketch out the geometry for each variation in appearance (visibility state) and decide where the common base point should be. Unless you're a lot smarter than we are, you'll probably find that creating dynamic blocks is complex enough without trying to design your blocks as you go.

Now you see it

If your drawing shows six different kinds of windows, one approach is to create six different standard blocks to represent them all. Alternatively, you can create a single dynamic block and define visibility states to cover all six different types. The following steps show you how to make your blocks do double (or sextuple?) duty by using the Edit Block Definition dialog box:

1. **Open a drawing that contains some block definitions you'd like to combine, or draw some simple geometry to make some similar types of objects.**

 You can find the files we use in this sequence of steps at this book's companion website. Go to www.dummies.com/go/autocad2013fd and download afd18.zip. The drawing named afd18b.dwg contains the three-piece furniture suite (see Figure 18-8) we use to create a dynamic block.

 You can create dynamic blocks from scratch, or you can work with existing standard (nondynamic) block definitions. Figure 18-8 shows a drawing with three nondynamic blocks.

2. **On the Block panel of the Home tab, choose Block Editor to open the Edit Block Definition dialog box.**

3. **In the Block to Create or Edit box, specify a new block name or select Current Drawing and then click OK to display the Block Editor window.**

 The Block Editor is a special authoring environment with its own Ribbon tab plus a passel of command-line commands. You also have access to the rest of the Ribbon tabs, so you can draw and edit just like you would in the regular drawing window. The background color is different from the drawing editor's background color to help you remember where you are.

 The Block Editor tab's Geometric, Dimensional, and Manage panels (see Figure 18-9) are elements of the AutoCAD parametric drawing feature. (AutoCAD LT doesn't fully support parametric drawing, so the LT Block Editor lacks the Geometric and Dimensional panels and gets a miniversion of the Manage panel.) In this book, we don't have room to cover parametric constraints in dynamic blocks, but we do cover parametric drafting in Chapter 19. The concepts are pretty similar to adding parametric features to dynamic blocks.

 If you enter a new block name, AutoCAD displays an empty block-authoring environment where you draw geometry or insert existing blocks. If you instead select Current Drawing, AutoCAD places all drawing objects inside the block authoring environment.

Figure 18-8: Three blocks to make three seats.

4. **Create some geometry for the first visibility state. Alternatively, click the Home tab, choose Insert on the Block panel, and select an existing block definition to serve as the first visibility state.**

 When creating geometry from scratch, pay attention to where the common base point should be. Although you use different blocks to assemble a multiple-view block, they should all have the same base point. (0,0 is a good one for blocks.) You don't want your chairs jumping around between different insertion points!

5. **If you inserted an existing block in Step 4, deselect all three Specify On-Screen check boxes, make sure that the Explode check box is *not* selected, and then click OK.**

6. **Repeat Steps 4 and 5, drawing or inserting all the necessary geometry.**

 At this point, your drawing screen may look pretty strange (see Figure 18-9). Don't worry; you're going to fix it in the next steps.

7. **Click the Parameters tab of the Block Authoring Palettes and then click Visibility, as shown in Figure 18-9.**

 If the palettes aren't open, click Authoring Palettes on the Manage panel on the highlighted Block Editor contextual tab of the Ribbon.

 AutoCAD prompts you to specify the parameter location.

Visibility Status controls

Block Editor panels

Block Authoring palettes Visibility Parameter marker

Figure 18-9: Three seats in the Block Editor.

8. **Click to place the parameter marker somewhere other than the base point location you chose in Step 4.**

 AutoCAD places a parameter marker at the selected point and returns to the command line. As shown in Figure 18-9, the label Visibility1 appears next to the Visibility Parameter marker, and a yellow Alert symbol indicates that no action has been assigned to the parameter yet. The controls on the Ribbon's Visibility panel become active.

 The parameter location that you specify will be the spot on the block where the dynamic block option grip will be displayed. It's not crucial where you locate this point, but try to pick a sensible location on the object. If you specify the same point for the parameter location as the base point for the block, you may have a hard time selecting the dynamic option grip.

9. **Click Visibility States on the Visibility panel. Click Rename and change VisibilityState0 to something more descriptive. Then click OK.**

 As is the case with other named objects in AutoCAD, best practice is to assign useful, descriptive names rather than accept the default generic labels.

10. **On the Visibility panel, click the Make Invisible button. At the Select Objects prompt, select the geometry or block inserts that should be invisible in the current visibility state — that is, those that are *not* associated with the current visibility state — and then press Enter.**

AutoCAD prompts:

```
Hide for current state or all visibility states
        [Current/All] <Current>: C
```

11. **Click Visibility States again and then click New to create a new visibility state. In the New Visibility State dialog box, enter a descriptive name. Select the Show All Existing Objects in New State radio button and then click OK.**

 All your geometry should reappear.

12. **Repeat Steps 9 and 10 to create additional visibility states associated with the remaining geometry or blocks.**

 The geometry or block insert associated with the last created visibility state should be visible onscreen.

13. **Click OK to close the Visibility States dialog box, and then click Close Block Editor on the Ribbon. Save the changes to your new block or to Current Drawing.**

 AutoCAD displays an alert box asking whether you want to save changes to your block. Click Cancel to return to the block editor or Discard the Changes to close the Block Editor without saving your changes. Click Save the Changes to update the block and exit. AutoCAD closes the block authoring environment and returns to the standard drawing editor window.

The Block Editor tab includes a Test Block tool you can use to see what your finished product will look like without the hassle of closing the editor and inserting or manipulating the block inside the drawing editor. Test Block displays the geometry and lets you try different parameters; then you can easily return to the Block Editor to tweak your masterpiece. You'll find the Test Block button on the Open/Save panel of the Block Editor contextual tab.

Lights! Parameters!! Actions!!!

You can modify the appearance of individual instances of the same block by defining parameters and actions to move, rotate, flip, or align parts of them. You can adjust the block's appearance while you insert it or at any time afterward. The following steps show you how to use the Block Editor to add some action to a block definition:

1. **Open a drawing that contains some block definitions whose appearance you'd like to spice up a little, or draw some simple geometry that might make a suitably dynamic block.**

 Action parameters are most effective in block definitions that contain groups of related objects — for example, an office desk and chair or a furniture arrangement.

2. **On the Block panel of the Ribbon's Home tab, choose Block Editor to open the Edit Block Definition dialog box.**

3. **In the Block to Create or Edit box, type a new block name or select Current Drawing, and then click OK.**

4. **Create some geometry or insert some blocks.**

When you insert blocks, make sure that the Explode check box at the lower-left corner of the Insert dialog box is *not* selected, and then click OK.

Draw the geometry or insert the blocks in a group so that you can insert the finished arrangement into your drawings. For example, upcoming Figure 18-10 shows the creation of a dynamic block for a coffee shop or cafeteria.

5. **Repeat Step 4 until you've drawn all the needed geometry or inserted all the necessary blocks.**

6. **Click the Parameters tab of the Block Authoring Palettes and then click Rotation Parameter.**

AutoCAD prompts you to specify the parameter location.

7. **Click to place the parameter marker somewhere on the object geometry other than the base-point location.**

If you specify the same point for the parameter location as the base point for the block, you may have a hard time selecting the dynamic option grip.

8. **AutoCAD places a parameter marker at the selected point and returns to the command line, prompting you to specify the radius of the rotation parameter and the default rotation angle.**

The parameter marker's label appears next to the rotation parameter marker.

9. **Click the Actions tab of the Block Authoring Palettes and then click Rotate. Select the Rotate Parameter, select the objects that should be modified when the grip is used, and specify a point for the action's label.**

AutoCAD returns to the command prompt. At this point, it's fine to go with default values and onscreen pick points.

10. **Repeat Steps 6 through 9, trying different parameters and actions.**

For example, choose a Point Parameter and a Move Action.

Figure 18-10 shows a set of block components, several of which have action parameters assigned. After the block is inserted, you can manipulate the components to which you've added parameters to vary the appearance of the blocks. We explain how a little later in this chapter.

Point Parameter marker Rotation Parameter marker

Figure 18-10: A passel of parameters ready for action.

11. **Click Close Block Editor on the Ribbon and save or discard your changes.**

 AutoCAD closes the block-authoring environment and returns to the standard drawing editor window.

Manipulating dynamic blocks

After a dynamic block is inserted in a drawing, you can select it and modify its display through a special set of custom grips. (That's what AutoCAD calls them, so I'm following suit.)

When you select a nondynamic block, you see a single grip at the insertion point. When you select a dynamic block, you see at least two — and maybe more — custom grips, as well as the insertion point grip. The custom grips usually look different from the regular object grips, but not always, so be careful while clicking grips.

The following steps show you how to make your dynamic blocks do the things you just spent all this time teaching them to do:

1. **Insert a few blocks that contain some dynamic parameters, such as visibility or action parameters.**

 If your block inserts don't have any action parameters, go to Step 4.

2. **Select a block that includes some action parameters.**

 The block insert displays a number of grips (see Figure 18-11). If the insert displays only a single square grip, it isn't a dynamic block.

Figure 18-11: Variations on dynamic blocks (original on the right, and a handy grip tip on a chair at left center).

3. **Click one of the custom grips — for example, clicking a round grip opens the rotation parameter of the object. Rotate the component as required.**

4. **Select a block that includes a visibility parameter and then click the visibility grip. Choose the desired visibility state from the menu that appears.**

 For additional information on manipulating actions and visibility states, look up Dynamic Blocks in the online help system.

Dynamic blocks, as we suggest more than once, are a powerful — and complicated — feature. Prior to AutoCAD 2010, the Block Authoring Palettes contained 10 selectable parameters, 8 actions, and 20 parameter sets. AutoCAD 2010 added 12 geometric constraints and 6 dimensional constraints. We could write a book on the topic. Until we do, AutoCAD's online help system is your best resource for more information on all the possibilities of dynamic blocks. The quickest and most direct way to AutoCAD's own help on the subject is to type **Dynamic Blocks** into the Search box on the program title bar.

19

Call the Parametrics!

In This Chapter

▶ Introducing parametric drawing

▶ Understanding constraints

▶ Applying geometric and dimensional constraints

▶ Using inferred constraints

▶ Editing parametric drawings

A few releases back, AutoCAD included a set of parametric drawing tools, and, offhand, we can't think of a more significant new feature in recent years. (Don't worry; we're going to offer a definition of *parametric* in just a few more paragraphs.) In fact, if you work primarily in 2D — and especially if you're in the manufacturing business — parametrics in AutoCAD (and, to a very limited degree, in AutoCAD LT) might just be the most significant new feature *ever* since the beginning of engineering drawings in Roman times.

If you know what we're talking about, you're probably pretty interested in finding out more about what you can do with parametrics in AutoCAD. If, on the other hand, you think parametrics are the folks who show up when you dial 911, the following paragraphs should straighten you out.

Imagine this. Your boss has been in a meeting all morning with an important client. At two minutes before noon, they emerge. Your boss hands you a marked-up print and rather imperiously commands, "We need these 12 dimensions changed and the drawing updated by the time we get back from lunch." The drawing involves multiple views, several cross sections, and a couple of details at different scales.

By the time they get their coats on, you meet them at the door and hand them a print of the revised drawing. The client invites you to join them for lunch.

This chapter shows you how to make this scene come true.

Maintaining Design Intent

Parametric (rule-based) drawing is by far the best way of enforcing design intent in 2D drafting. *Design intent* in AutoCAD (or any other engineering software) means that when drawings are edited — "this part" made wider, "that hole" made larger — all the attached or related objects behave in a predictable way that honors the designer's intentions when she created the drawing in the first place.

Before AutoCAD 2010, there was simply no way of maintaining the design concepts that went into an AutoCAD drawing. You could use AutoCAD drawing and editing commands to draw accurate, precise plans, sections, and details, but as far as AutoCAD was concerned, they were just a bunch of lines and circles.

Take, for example, that base-plate drawing example in Chapter 3. Maybe the engineer has had a second look and determined that those 1 1/2" (38mm for the metric crowd) bolts aren't quite up to the job — they need to be changed to 1 3/4" (44mm). To revise the drawing by using AutoCAD in the traditional way, you draw a new, larger circle for the bolt and erase the old one. Now the nut is too small, and so is the hole in the plate. (Maybe you can't see it, but you know and we know it's there.) There's a whole lot of editing required to fix this drawing.

In AutoCAD, you can add some intelligence to those lines and circles by applying parametric constraints to them. Instead of trying to explain what this means, the easiest way is to show you.

Unfortunately, the following exercise won't work in AutoCAD LT.

1. **Start a new drawing.**

2. **Draw a circle and a line anywhere in the drawing.**

 Exact sizes and alignments aren't critical. You'll see why in a moment, and we'll explain even more a little later.

 Apply a tangent constraint between the circle and the line.

 Parametric functions are found on the Parametric tab (what a surprise!) of the Ribbon. Click the Tangent button, and then select the circle and the line (sequence doesn't matter) and observe how they move until

they are tangent to each other, and also how a little gray icon — a constraint bar — appears to indicate the type of constraint. Note that "tangent" doesn't necessarily mean that they have to touch.

3. Grip edit the line and the circle.

We cover grip editing in Chapter 10. You can move the circle or line, you can change the diameter of the circle, you can move either end of the line — but no matter what you do, the other object obediently remains tangent. But wait! There's more!

4. Apply a diameter dimension to the circle.

Don't use the normal DIMDIAmeter command from Chapter 14, but use the Diameter button in the upper-right corner of the Dimensional panel of the Parametric tab of the Ribbon. When you select the circle as prompted, AutoCAD places a gray, funny-looking dimension that reads something like `dia1=5.3716`. It has the same background color as the MTEXT edit box (see Chapter 13); in fact, that's exactly what it's inviting you to do. Enter a suitable value (say, 7.5), and the circle resizes itself to suit the dimension value you entered, and the line adjusts itself to remain tangent!

5. Apply an Aligned dimension to the line.

Again, be sure to use the Aligned button from the Dimension panel on the Parametric tab, and select each end of the line in turn (or press Enter and then select the line). This time, when it places the dimension, enter **=dia1*2** (including the = sign, no spaces). The line automatically resizes itself to be twice as long as the diameter of the circle.

6. Change things.

You can still grip edit the position of the line and circle, but you can't grip edit the diameter or the line length, nor can you STRETCH the line length any more. Now double-click the diameter dimension and change its value. Surprise! The circle changes size, and the line changes its length so it's still twice as long as the new diameter of the circle! Now that is one smart drawing. Imagine the effect that this can have on your productivity in creating and editing drawings.

7. Close your mouth.

You're drooling all over the keyboard.

Defining terms

The word *parameter* is derived from two Greek roots. *Para* means to work with, to assist, to work alongside (think of *paramedic* ambulance attendants; you were right when you thought "ambulance" when we mentioned "parametrics" earlier), and *metros* means measure (and hence meter, and metric). For

the purposes of making drawings in AutoCAD, think of a *parameter* as a rule that works alongside AutoCAD objects — and therefore think of *parametric drawing* as rule-based drawing.

AutoCAD's parametric rules — officially called *constraints* — fall into two categories:

- ✔ **Geometric constraints:** Based on object types and relationships between objects; different object types have different potential constraints. In the earlier example in the preceding step list, we show you how to apply a Tangent constraint between the line and the circle — and as you moved or changed one, the other followed along.

- ✔ **Dimensional constraints:** Based on dimensioned distances on or between objects or points on objects. In the earlier example, you see how to apply a dimensional constraint to the circle. Changing the dimension value changes the circle size. Better yet, you can establish a relationship between the circle and the line so that changing the circle diameter also changes the length of the line.

Both AutoCAD and AutoCAD LT support constraints, but as is usually the case, the feature is limited in LT. If you use the full version, you can create and modify geometric and dimensional constraints, as we describe in the steps in this chapter. If you're using LT, you can't *create* either type of restraint, but you can work with existing constraints in drawings that were created in AutoCAD itself. Figure 19-1 shows the difference between the AutoCAD and AutoCAD LT Parametric tabs.

If you're using AutoCAD LT, or if you just want to check out some ready-made parametric possibilities, you can download the sample drawing datasets from either www.autodesk.com/autocad-samples or www.autodesk.com/autocadlt-samples. The parametric samples are architectural_example-imperial.dwg, civil_example-imperial.dwg, and mechanical_example-imperial.dwg.

Figure 19-1: Parametric tabs in AutoCAD (above) and AutoCAD LT (below).

Forget about drawing with precision!

"Are you serious? All through this book you continually nag about the need for drawing with precision!"

We're sure that you're familiar with (or at least have come across) computer acronyms and abbreviations, such as RAM, ROM, DVD, USB — and, of course, CAD. Okay, here's a new one we coined for a magazine article a few years back: NAD. It has been our observation that the vast majority of design projects start life as a sketch on a coffee shop napkin: hence, NAD or *Napkin-Aided Design*.

A big strength of CAD is that drawings can (and should) be very precise and so you can make use of information within them, such as areas. A big weakness of CAD is that you are forced to be very precise, even early in the design process when things are likely to change. Yes, commands like MOVE and STRETCH make editing relatively simple, but "relatively" is a relative term. "Easy to use" is easy to say.

With parametrics, you can start out with a NAD sketch that shows the general idea of our design. Remember our parametric motto: "Close enough is good enough" (by the way, this also applies to horseshoes, hand grenades, and dancing). Then apply geometric and dimensional constraints and formulas to control the behavior of the drawing, and fine-tune the values until you get your final design.

Constrain yourself

You can apply dimensional or geometric constraints to new geometry as you create it, or you can assign constraints to existing geometry in old drawings. You can even convert existing associative dimensions to dynamic dimensional constraints. The following sections describe the available constraints in each of the two categories. We start with geometric constraints because we've found that it's usually best to pin objects down (pun intended) before applying dimensional constraints so that the drawing objects will behave in a predictable manner when dimension values are changed.

Understanding Geometric Constraints

Adding geometric constraints to object geometry is quite simple because it's much like using normal object snaps. In fact, in several cases, AutoCAD's geometric constraints have equivalent object snaps. There are tangent, parallel, concentric (center), and perpendicular object snaps and tangent, parallel, concentric, and perpendicular geometric constraints. The difference between

these relations as object snaps and as geometric constraints is that constraints are *persistent*.

For example, in the example earlier in this chapter, you can see how the line always stays tangent to the circle, no matter what. The objects remember how to get along with their siblings. Now if we could just figure out a way to make that work with our kids.

Twelve geometric constraints are at your disposal that you can apply to your drawing objects, and the easiest way to apply them is by clicking buttons on the Geometric panel of the Ribbon's Parametric tab. Table 19-1 presents a list of the geometric constraints and explains what they do.

Table 19-1		Geometric Constraints
Button Icon	**Constraint Name**	**Description**
	Coincident	Forces two or more points, such as endpoints or midpoints, to coincide; can also constrain a point to lie anywhere on an object
	Collinear	Forces two or more lines to lie along an infinitely long projection of the first line selected
	Concentric	Forces the centers of two or more arcs, circles, ellipses, or arc segments of polylines to share the same center point
	Fix	Locks the location of an object or a point on an object to a specific location in the drawing
	Parallel	Forces two lines to be parallel; the second line selected becomes parallel to the first line
	Perpendicular	Forces two lines to be perpendicular to one another
	Horizontal	Forces a line or two points to be horizontal relative to the current coordinate system

Button Icon	Constraint Name	Description
	Vertical	Forces a line or two points to be vertical relative to the current coordinate system
	Tangent	Forces an object to be tangent to a selected arc or circle
	Smooth	Joins a selected spline object with another spline, line, arc, or polyline while maintaining curvature (also known as G2) continuity
	Symmetric	Forces two objects, or two points on objects to be symmetrical about an imaginary line, and is like a persistent Mirror command
	Equal	Forces two lines or linear polyline segments to be the same length; forces two arcs or circles to have the same radius

Text objects can also be geometrically constrained. You can apply horizontal or vertical constraints to text, and you can make text parallel, perpendicular, or collinear with lines. Anyone who's had to label utility lines on civil engineering drawings in earlier releases so that the text aligns with the linework (who . . . *moi??*) will be very happy with this feature!

Applying a little more constraint

If you're using the full version of AutoCAD (not AutoCAD LT), you can constrain drawing objects geometrically by clicking buttons on the Geometric panel of the Parametric tab. In the following steps, we show you how to get started with geometric constraints.

This procedure may seem a little tedious, but we want you to become familiar with the basic properties of each type of constraint. Later, we show you a couple of shortcuts that greatly speed things up.

You can find the files we use in this sequence of steps at this book's companion website. Go to www.dummies.com/go/autocad2013fd and download afd19.zip. The drawing named afd19c.dwg contains the unconstrained geometry, and drawing afd19d.dwg contains the end product.

1. **Start a new drawing. Make the Ribbon's Parametric tab current and turn off Snap, Ortho, Polar, Osnap, and Otrack at the status bar.**

 For real drafting, you probably want to use these precision aids, but for this example, you get a better sense of parametrics with a *really* imprecise drawing.

2. **Draw some linework by using the PLINE command and then add a couple of circles.**

 Draw something similar to Figure 19-2 if you want to follow closely.

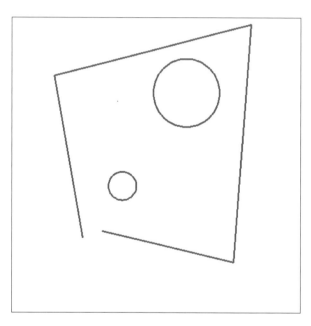

Figure 19-2: Random shapes that badly need constraining.

Every drawing is going to be tackled differently, so think ahead and figure out the most efficient way to apply the constraints you need so that your design intent is maintained. In this example, you want to end up with two concentric circles in the middle of a square.

As we mention earlier, you'll find it a lot easier to apply constraints if at least one point on the geometry is fixed in space. In many cases, one of the first constraints you should think about applying is Fix, the one that constrains a point to one location in the drawing area. This has nothing to do with tomcats.

In this example, you're going to lock one of the endpoints of the polyline into position.

3. Click Fix in the Geometric panel and then click a point you want to fix in space.

A blue padlock icon is displayed beside the pickbox, and the red pick point marker appears when you're over a point you can constrain (see Figure 19-3). In this example, we click one of the endpoints on the polyline. A padlock icon appears in the constraint bar, indicating that the endpoint of the polyline segment is fixed in place.

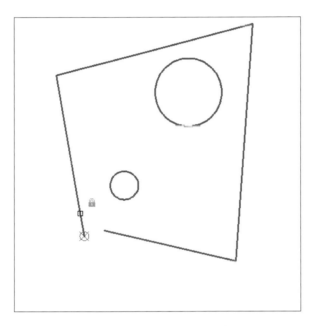

Figure 19-3: Locking down an object in drawing space.

With at least one point on the geometry fixed in place, you can start constraining the geometry by closing the gap in the linework.

4. Click Coincident in the Parametric tab's Geometric panel.

You use a coincident constraint to make two points coincide. A blue coincident icon appears near the pickbox, and as you move your crosshairs over an object, a marker appears over relevant points — in the case of lines or polyline segments, at the endpoints and midpoint.

Use appropriate drawing commands based on your design intent. We use a polyline in this example because the ends of the segments are already coincident-constrained by being part of a single polyline object. If you had drawn this shape with lines, you'd have to apply individual coincident constraints to each corner.

5. **Click an endpoint on the first polyline segment that you want to connect and then click an endpoint on the second segment.**

 The endpoint of the second polyline segment jumps to the endpoint of the first line, and a small blue square — the marker for coincident constraints — appears at the intersection. (If you don't see the little blue square, click Show All in the Geometric panel.)

6. **Apply some orthographic parameters so that the linework starts to look a little more like a rectangle. Click Horizontal in the Parametric tab's Geometric panel and then click a line or polyline segment that you want to be aligned with the drawing's X axis.**

 In this example, we picked the bottom segment of the polyline. The segment realigns itself horizontally from the endpoint nearest to where you picked the line (unless a Fix constraint is added first), and a horizontal constraint marker — a *constraint bar* — appears near the object. A single item is still called the constraint bar because if you add additional constraints to the object, they get added to the existing one, like a toolbar.

7. **Click Vertical to align a line or polyline segment with the drawing's Y axis.**

 In this example, we pick the left vertical-ish polyline segment. The segment realigns itself at 90 degrees to the horizontal segment, and a constraint bar showing a vertical constraint appears. With one horizontally and one vertically constrained line segment, you're halfway to a geometrically precise rectangle!

8. **Because rectangles have parallel and perpendicular sides, next you apply those constraints to your linework. Click Parallel in the Parametric tab's Geometric panel, click the vertically constrained line segment, and then click the line segment opposite.**

 Because there's already a vertical constraint applied to one segment, it doesn't matter which line you pick first. If neither line had an existing constraint, the second line you picked would become parallel to the first line.

 Always keep your design intent in mind as you think about which constraints to apply and when to apply them. As a general rule, start with the most important and drill down to the least important. And, as we remind you earlier in the chapter, applying a fix constraint early in the game can prevent your geometry rearranging itself in ways you don't expect.

 To make the final side of the almost-rectangle orthogonal with the other three, you could use another parallel constraint and click the bottom line. However, you don't want to wear out our Parallel button, so use Perpendicular on the final segment.

9. Click Perpendicular on the Geometric panel, click either vertical side, and then click the non-orthogonal side.

Again, because three of the four sides are already constrained to horizontal and vertical, it doesn't matter which segment you pick first.

"Perpendicular" means "at right angles to." It isn't restricted to "a vertical line going upward from one end of a horizontal line." A line at an angle to the X axis can still be perpendicular to another.

Some constraints work on one object (horizontal, vertical), while others work on two objects (parallel, tangent, perpendicular). If you roll the cursor over a two-object constraint, its soul mate lights up.

To delete a constraint, move the mouse pointer over the constraint marker to display the constraints bar (see Figure 19-4), right-click, and choose Delete from the menu that appears.

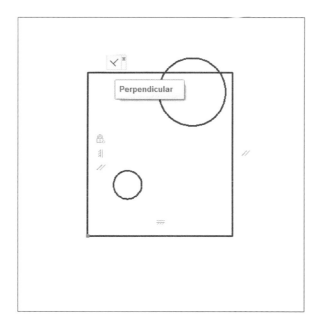

Figure 19-4: Constraining to orthogonal.

From four non-orthogonal, not-even-closed line segments, applying a handful of constraints yields a perfect rectangle. However, you *really* want a square! Here's where the Equal constraint comes in.

10. Click Equal on the Geometric panel, click the bottom side, and then click either of the vertical sides.

A perfect square! Now you want to constrain those circles.

The design intent in this example is to have the circles to be concentric and to locate their centers in the exact center of the rectangle. First the easy part: Making the circles concentric.

11. Click Concentric in the Geometric panel, click one circle, and then click the other.

The two circles are concentrically constrained (try saying that ten times in a hurry!), and a new constraint bar appears in their vicinity. Try moving one circle by clicking it and then watch the other tag along.

As we suggest, concentric was the easy constraint. We'd love to be able to use the Mid Between 2 Points object snap and just click two diagonally opposite corners to locate the circles dead center in the rectangle. However, because you can constrain only objects or points on objects, you have to add some construction geometry in order to maintain the design intent.

12. Draw a line between diagonally opposite corners by using Endpoint object snaps, and then apply coincident constraints between the endpoints of this line and the corners of the rectangle (see Figure 19-5).

Figure 19-5: Adding some construction geometry.

TIP

Draw construction geometry on a separate layer and set that layer to NoPlot in the Layer Properties Manager. If you don't want to even see it — let alone, not plot it — you can turn off your construction geometry layer or even freeze it — and the geometric constraints will still work.

13. **Click Coincident in the Geometric panel. Click either circle so that the parametric marker appears in the center, move the pickbox over the construction line, and click when the parametric marker is over the midpoint of the line.**

 You're done! You can test your design intent by using the STRETCH command on the corner of the rectangle that doesn't display a little square, blue coincident icon. As you drag the corner, you should see the two circles moving, too, always maintaining their position in the middle of the rectangle (see Figure 19-6).

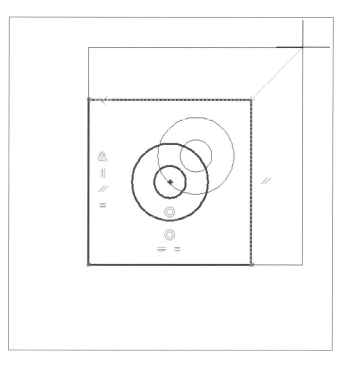

Figure 19-6: Full-on geometric constraints.

Parametrics was a new feature in AutoCAD 2010, and it got a considerable enhancement in AutoCAD 2011 with the addition of *inferred constraints*. A status bar button (to the left of the Snap button) toggles Infer Constraints mode off and on. When Infer Constraints mode is enabled, you don't have to specifically apply many of the geometric constraints.

To get the best results, you should go at least part way back to drawing with precision. For example, a coincident constraint is applied pretty much any time you use an object snap, while horizontal and vertical constraints are placed if polar or ortho modes are on.

Inferred constraints also work when editing existing geometry.

Inferred Constraints mode is a powerful component of parametric drafting in AutoCAD, but we recommend that first you make yourself familiar with manually applying constraints in the ways we show in this chapter.

AutoConstrain yourself!

The geometric constraints listed in Table 19-1 are meant to be applied one at a time. That flexibility is great, but it can be pretty darned time consuming to go around a complex object, trying to figure out what the best constraint option would be and then applying it.

The Auto Constrain button on the Parametric tab's Geometric panel can apply a whack of constraints to a selection of objects with a single click — but before you execute that single click, it's worth taking a look at the Auto Constrain settings. Click the dialog box launcher (the little arrow at the right end of the Geometric panel label) to open the Constraint Settings dialog box and make the AutoConstrain tab active (see Figure 19-7). Choose which constraints you want to apply automatically, and in what order you want them in the list, so that the ones that should take precedence have a higher priority. Your best bet initially is to stick with the defaults until you become more familiar with things.

Auto Constrain works only with geometric constraints, not with dimensional constraints.

AutoCAD won't let you overconstrain an object. For example, if you have a horizontal constraint on one line and a parallel constraint between it and a second line, AutoCAD will object if you try to add a horizontal constraint to the second line.

The three buttons at the right side of AutoCAD's Geometric panel — and the *only* buttons on AutoCAD LT's Geometric panel — are for controlling the visibility of geometric constraint markers. Show All shows them all, and Hide All (surprise!) hides them all. Use the Show/Hide button to display the constraints on selected objects. This last button is a little clunky. It would be nice to be able to hover the mouse pointer over an object and have the constraints show, but you actually have to click an object and then press Enter to see any results.

Figure 19-7: Auto-constrainable geometric relations in the Constraint Settings dialog box.

Understanding Dimensional Constraints

The normal practice in AutoCAD is to create some geometry — of course, using all the precision techniques we discuss in Chapter 7 — and then apply dimensions as we describe in Chapter 14. Assuming that you're using fully associative dimensions, you can then edit the geometry and watch the dimensions update automatically. The length of the line or the radius of the circle are in control, and those dimensions are called *driven dimensions* because they change when the object geometry changes.

Dimensional constraints, unlike regular AutoCAD dimensions, are *driving dimensions,* which means that when you change the value of a dynamic dimension on a line, the line changes to match. In other words, the dimension is driving the length of the line, not the other way around.

There are only eight dimensional-constraint options, but they cover all the bases. Table 19-2 lists them and describes their purposes.

Table 19-2		Dimensional Constraints
Button Icon	**Constraint Name**	**Description**
	Linear	Applies a horizontal or vertical dimensional constraint (similar to DIMLINEAR)
	Horizontal	Applies a dimensional constraint aligned with the X axis of the coordinate system (similar to DIMLINEAR's Horizontal option)
	Vertical	Applies a dimensional constraint aligned with the Y axis of the coordinate system (similar to DIMLINEAR's Vertical option)
	Aligned	Applies a dimensional constraint aligned with the object or with the points being dimensioned (similar to DIMALIGNED)
	Radial	Applies a set value or formula to the radius of an arc or a circle (similar to DIMRADIUS)
	Diameter	Applies a set value or formula to the diameter of an arc or a circle (similar to DIMDIAMETER)
	Angular	Applies a set value or formula to the angle between two lines or three points (similar to DIMANGULAR)
	Convert	Converts an existing associative dimension object to a dimensional constraint

Practice a little constraint

The objects that you add to your drawing from the Dimensional panel are not the same as the dimension objects you add from the Annotate tab. Dimensional constraints are *driving dimensions,* meaning that when you change the value of one of these dimensions, the geometry changes.

A lot is happening behind the scenes as you apply parametric constraints. You can get a great sense of how these constraints work at keeping your drawing objects in order by trying the STRETCH command on objects after you apply a constraint to them.

You can find the files we use in this sequence of steps at this book's companion website. Go to www.dummies.com/go/autocad2013fd and download afd19.zip. The drawing named afd19a.dwg contains the unconstrained geometry, and drawing afd19b.dwg contains the end product.

The following steps present a very simple example of dimensional constraints:

1. **Start a new drawing and make the Ribbon's Parametric tab current.**

 Turn on some appropriate precision drawing aids on the status bar, such as Snap, Ortho, and Osnap.

2. **Draw some reasonably precise geometry by using some of those precision techniques we describe in earlier chapters.**

 In the following example, we use the RECTANG and CIRCLE commands to draw the geometry you see in Figure 19-8. The rectangle is 10 units square, and the 2.5-unit–radius circle is deliberately drawn away from the middle of the square.

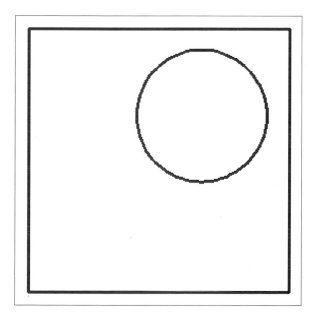

Figure 19-8: Simple geometry badly in need of constraining.

3. **On the Dimensional panel of the Parametric tab, click the top part of the Linear split button.**

 A linear dimension icon appears beside the pickbox, and AutoCAD prompts you to specify the first constraint point or to pick an object.

 Just like the DIMLINEAR command, the Linear dimensional constraint tool is *inferential:* that is, which way you drag the crosshairs controls whether you get a horizontal or vertical dimension. Also, just like DIMLINEAR, you can press Enter at the command prompt and select an object to dimension.

4. **Press Enter at the command prompt to confirm that you want to select an object and then select the bottom horizontal line segment.**

 If you see red markers at the midpoint and ends of the bottom line, you didn't press Enter, and you're in point-selection rather than object-selection mode.

 AutoCAD generates a preview of a dimensional constraint and prompts you for a location.

5. **Click to locate the dimension position.**

 AutoCAD draws a dimensional constraint with a highlighted text field displaying the dimension name (*d1* in this example) and the value returned by AutoCAD. You could type a new value in the edit box, but for now, just press Enter to confirm the value and the dimension location (see Figure 19-9).

 If your dimensional constraints disappear as soon as you place them, click the Show All button on the Parametric tab's Dimensional panel (refer to Figure 19-1).

 Dimensional constraints are not regular dimension objects — they're not going to plot, so it doesn't really matter where you put them or what they look like. (We show you how to turn dimensional constraints into properly styled, plottable dimensions in the next section.)

6. **Repeat Steps 3 through 5 and add a dimensional constraint to the right vertical edge of the rectangle.**

 AutoCAD draws a second dimensional constraint, this one named *d2*.

As you mouse over the Linear button, you can see that unlike its Aligned neighbor, it's split into two parts. You can force a linear dimensional constraint to be either horizontal or vertical (rather than dependent on the direction in which you drag your crosshairs) by clicking the bottom part of the Linear button and making your choice from the drop-down menu.

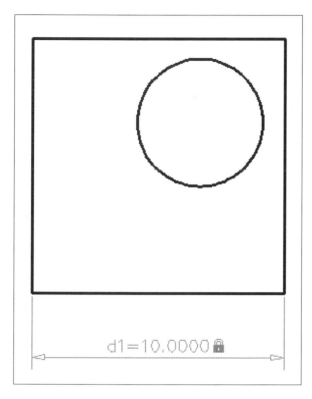

Figure 19-9: Placing a dimensional constraint.

Making your drawing even smarter

If this were a traditional mechanical drawing that followed the rules of drafting, those two dimensions would be enough: Whoever is reading your drawing understands that if sides are parallel and perpendicular, a dimension on one side applies to the opposite side as well. But in this chapter, we're talking about *intelligent* drawings that respect design intent, not dumb collections of lines and circles, even if they *do* follow the rules of drafting!

If you try stretching the rectangle in various ways (from the upper-left corner, for example), you can see that only the bottom and right sides are constrained to 10 units in length. You could add two more linear dimensional constraints to the unconstrained sides, but then you'd have to remember to edit both dimensions. Rather than constraining both sides to be 10 units long, the way to maintain design intent is to make both sides equal in length.

You can make the two sides equal by using either dimensional or geometric constraints. It's usually a good idea to apply most or all of the geometric constraints to your drawing before adding dimensional constraints. This way, the objects will behave in a more predictable manner when you change dimension values.

We cover geometric constraints in the "Understanding Geometric Constraints" section, earlier in the chapter, so if you read that section, you should understand why we're going to apply three geometric constraints.

1. **On the Geometric panel of the Parametric tab, click Fix (the padlock icon) and then click the lower-left corner of the rectangle.**

2. **On the Geometric panel, click Horizontal and then click the bottom side of the rectangle. Then click Vertical and click the left side.**

 Icons appear near the drawing geometry, showing that those three geometric constraints are active.

3. **On the Dimensional panel of the Parametric tab, click Linear and add a dimensional constraint to the top horizontal line.**

4. **Click to locate the dimension, type** d1, **and then press Enter when AutoCAD prompts for the dimension text.**

 Instead of having numeric values like the first two linear constraints, this new dimensional constraint displays fx: d3=d1.

The main part of this expression sets the d3 dimension to equal the value of the d1 dimension. The fx: is there just to remind you that other variables in other dimensions are being referenced.

5. **Repeat Steps 3 and 4, this time adding a constraint to the vertical line at the left and then entering** d2 **as the dimension text.**

 All four dynamic dimensional constraints display their names, plus a value or expression for each.

Dimensional constraints have names as well as values. They can also include expressions or formulas. You can set the default appearance of dynamic dimensional constraints by clicking the dialog-box launcher (the little arrow at the right end of the Dimensional panel label) to open the Constraint Settings dialog box with the Dimensional tab active (see Figure 19-10). The options are

 ✔ **Name:** The first linear dimension is named *d1*, the second *d2*, and so forth. You use the dimension names in expressions.

 ✔ **Value:** The numeric value that you enter into the dimensional constraint or that AutoCAD enters if you don't override it.

✔ **Name and Expression:** The dimension name shown as equal to an expression. The expression can be a value, as in this example, or it can be a formula.

Figure 19-10: Format the appearance of dimensional constraints in the Constraint Settings dialog box.

Using the Parameters Manager

Both AutoCAD and AutoCAD LT include the *Parameters Manager* palette, accessible from the Manage panels of their Ribbon's Parametric tab. You can use the Parameters Manager to give all those dimensional constraints more sensible names than d1 and d2, but even more usefully, you can enter expressions instead of plain numeric values, as we explain in the following steps.

1. **Click Parameters Manager in the Manage panel.**

 The Parameters Manager palette appears, showing a list of dimensional constraints currently applied in the drawing (see Figure 19-11).

 In Figure 19-11, the Expression column shows the numeric values we specified for d1 and d2 and the expressions we entered for d3 and d4. The read-only Value column shows the calculated value. You can't change a value in the Value column (it's grayed out to remind you); you can only edit the cells in the Expression column.

Figure 19-11: The Parameters Manager palette.

2. **In the d1 row, click in the Expression field to highlight the current value (10 in this example); then click again and type a new value. For example, type 13 and press Enter.**

 The rectangle resizes itself in the drawing editor, and because the d3 constraint on the top side was made equal to the d1 constraint on the bottom side, both sides change equally.

 Next, use an equation as an expression.

3. **In the d2 row, click in the Expression field to highlight the current value and then type an expression. For example, type d1*0.75 and then press Enter.**

 The read-only Value column and the drawing geometry show that the new d1 distance of 13 has been multiplied by 0.75 and is now 9.75 (see Figure 19-12).

4. **Close the Parameters Manager.**

 Finally, constrain the circle so that its center is always at dead center of the rectangle, no matter how the rectangle's size changes.

Figure 19-12: Editing constraints in the Parameters Manager.

5. **Apply a horizontal dimensional constraint from the upper-left corner of the rectangle to the center of the circle. Locate the dimension, type d3/2, and then press Enter.**

 Because the rectangle is now dimensionally constrained on all four sides, it doesn't really matter which corner you start from. And note that you don't have to type the whole expression d5=d3/2. AutoCAD knows what you mean!

6. **Repeat Step 5, this time adding a vertical constraint from one of the corners to the center of the circle. Locate the dimension and then type d4/2.**

 Figure 19-13 shows the object geometry with all constraints added in this section. Who knew that drafting could be such fun?

Figure 19-13: All locked down — dimensionally, at least.

If your drawing starts getting overwhelmed with parameters, you can add parameter filters in the Parameters Manager palette. Right-click any parameter and choose Show Filter Tree, or click the double-right arrow at the top left

of the palette to open the Filters pane. Click the funnel icon in the toolbar to create a new filter group, and then simply drag and drop parameters into the group. Figure 19-14 shows the two constraints added in Steps 5 and 6 (of the preceding step list) dragged into a new group filter.

Figure 19-14: Filter your parameters to keep them organized.

Dimensions or constraints — have it both ways!

After all that hard work adding dimensional constraints to your drawings, it would be a downright shame to have to go back and apply regular dimensions, wouldn't it? Well, you don't have to. You can make dimensional constraints look and behave like regular dimensions. You can go the other way, too, and make your regular dimensions act like dimensional constraints.

Dimensional constraints are available in two flavors:

✓ **Dynamic constraints:** The default form. Dynamic constraints appear gray with a padlock icon next to them in the drawing area. You can make them appear and disappear by clicking Show All in the Dimensional panel. They don't plot, and they resize as you zoom in and out of the drawing, so they're always legible.

✔ **Annotational constraints:** This form is controlled as an object property, so you have to set it in the Properties palette. Annotational constraints do plot, don't resize as you zoom in and out, and don't disappear as you toggle the Show All button on and off. Annotational constraints conform to dimension style settings.

The dimension name format of annotational constraints can be set to Name, Value, or Name and Expression, just like dynamic constraints (refer to Figure 19-10 for another look at the Constraint Settings dialog box). If you're going to plot your drawing with annotational constraints, remember to reset the format so it doesn't show the dimension name or the expression.

Here's how to turn dynamic dimensional constraints into annotational constraints.

1. **Open a drawing that contains some geometry with dimensional constraints.**

 You can also start a new drawing, draw some simple geometry, and add a dimensional constraint to two.

2. **Select a dynamic constraint, right-click, and choose Properties.**

 The Properties palette opens with the object properties of the selected dimensional constraint listed in table form.

3. **Click in the Constraint Form field, and in the drop-down list, change Dynamic to Annotational (see Figure 19-15).**

 The dynamic constraint becomes annotational, and takes on the appearance of the current dimension style. If you change the dimension style in the Properties palette, the annotational constraint updates to the new dimension style format.

 You can go the other way, too, from regular dimension objects to dimensional constraints.

4. **Add a linear, radius, diameter, aligned, or angular dimension (that is, a regular dimension, not a dimensional parameter) to your drawing geometry.**

 Nearly every type of dimension object has a parametric analog; the exceptions are arc length, jogged radius, jogged linear, and ordinate dimensions.

Figure 19-15: Turning dynamic constraints into annotational ones.

5. **Click Convert in the Dimensional panel, select one of the dimension types in Step 4, and press Enter.**

The Dimensional Constraint text box displays as soon as you click an associative dimension, and the dimension becomes a dynamic constraint as soon as you press Enter.

The only clue that a dimension is an annotational constraint rather than a regular old associative dimension is the padlock icon that appears next to the dimension value. You can turn off the display of the padlock in the Constraint Settings dialog box, but we recommend that you leave it on. It doesn't plot anyway, and you might decide to delete the dimension without realizing that's it's controlling your object geometry.

Annotational dimensions can also be annotative so that they size themselves automatically to the drawing scale. We cover annotative dimensions in Chapter 14. Annotational and annotative dimensions are also associative, so you can have annotative annotational associative dimensions. Try saying that after a few drinks.

In this chapter, we present the two varieties of parametric constraints separately, but you'll get the most mileage from this feature when you incorporate both geometric *and* dimensional constraints with all those other precision techniques that we tell you about in Chapter 7. In fact, if you start a drawing by using Snap, Ortho, Osnap, and other precision techniques before you start adding dimensional and parametric constraints, you'll be well on the way to creating a library of intelligent drawings that maintain your design intent.

Geometric and dimensional constraints can be equivalent. For example, a 90-degree angle dimensional constraint is equal to a perpendicular geometric constraint, and AutoCAD won't let you apply both.

All the examples in this chapter involve a single drawing view. Geometric constraints actually apply "to infinity," and so you can synchronize objects in one orthographic view with those in another. For example, coincident and collinear constraints can link objects in the front view with their equivalents in the top and right-side views, and liberal use of the Equal constraint means that you should never have to measure or dimension anything twice, you should only ever need minimal construction geometry, any changes in one view reflect through to the others, and your views always remain orthogonally aligned.

20

Drawing on the Internet

In This Chapter

▶ Understanding AutoCAD Internet features

▶ Exchanging drawing files via e-mail and FTP

▶ Using Reference Manager to view and fix file dependencies

▶ Using Design Web Format

▶ Protecting drawings with passwords and digital signatures

▶ Sharing and collaborating with AutoCAD WS and Autodesk Cloud

*U*nless you've been living under a rock for the past 20 years, you know that the Internet is causing major changes in the way people work. Because of the 'Net, most of us communicate differently, exchange files more rapidly, and phone out for pizza less frequently. (Well, ordering pizza over the Internet is very easy, but they still have to work out a few of the details to be able to deliver it that way.)

In this chapter, we show you how and when to use AutoCAD Internet features. We also cover how the Internet features can connect with traditional CAD tasks, such as file sharing. The emphasis of this chapter is on useful, no-nonsense ways to take advantage of the Internet in your CAD work.

The Internet and AutoCAD: An Overview

The web is changing so quickly that it's almost impossible to write the definitive chapter that spells out exactly how everything works and what's best for you. Our intention in this chapter is to steer you toward the features that we feel are of most interest.

You send me

E-mail and FTP (File Transfer Protocol) have largely replaced blueline prints and overnight delivery as the standard means of exchanging drawings. Snail mail is dead! Sending and receiving drawing files doesn't differ much from sending and receiving other kinds of files, except for the following:

- ✔ **DWG files tend to be bigger than word-processing documents and spreadsheets.** Consequently, you may need to invest in a faster Internet connection.

- ✔ **You can easily forget to include all the dependent files.** An AutoCAD file may not be an island unto itself, but may also require other files to go with it. We tell you in the next section how to make sure that you send all the necessary files.

- ✔ **It's often not completely obvious how to plot what you receive.** Read Chapter 16 as well as the "Bad reception?" section, later in this chapter, to solve plotting puzzles.

Whenever you send DWG files, ask the recipient to try opening the drawings you sent as soon as they get them so you both have more time to respond if there's any problem.

Send it with eTransmit

Many people naively assume that an AutoCAD drawing is always contained in a single DWG file, but that's often not the case. Each drawing file created in AutoCAD can contain references to more than a dozen other kinds of files, the most important of which are described in Table 20-1. Thus, before you start exchanging drawings via e-mail or FTP, you need a procedure for assembling the drawings with all their dependent files.

Table 20-1	Kinds of Files That DWG Files Commonly Reference		
Description	*File Types*	*Consequences If Missing*	*Explained In*
Custom font files	SHX, TTF	AutoCAD substitutes another font.	Chapter 13
Other drawings (xrefs)	DWG, DGN, DWF, DWFx, PDF	Stuff in the main drawing disappears.	Chapter 18
Raster graphics files	JPG, PCX, TIF, and so on	Stuff in the drawing disappears.	Chapter 18
Plot style tables	CTB, STB	Lineweights and other plotted effects won't look right when you plot the drawing.	Chapter 16

Table 20-1 doesn't exhaust the types of files that your DWG files might refer to. Custom plotter settings (such as custom paper sizes) may reside in PC3 or PMP files. If you use sheet sets, a DST file contains information about the sheet structure. (We don't cover sheet sets in this book. If you're interested, check the online help.) An FMP file controls some aspects of font mapping. Look up *sheet sets* and the *FONTALT* and *FONTMAP system variables* in the AutoCAD online help system for detailed information.

Rapid eTransmit

Fortunately, AutoCAD's ETRANSMIT command pulls together all the files that your main DWG file depends on. Follow these steps to assemble a drawing with all its dependent files by using ETRANSMIT:

1. **Open the drawing that you want to run ETRANSMIT on.**

 If the drawing is already open, save it. ETRANSMIT prompts you to save before you proceed; it's not essential to do this, but it's usually a good idea.

2. **Click the Application button and choose Publish and then eTransmit from the Application menu.**

 The Create Transmittal dialog box appears, as shown in Figure 20-1.

![Create Transmittal dialog box]

Figure 20-1: Rapid eTransmit.

3. **On the Files Tree or Files Table tab, remove the check mark next to any file that you want ETRANSMIT *not* to copy with the main drawing.**

Unless you have assigned custom font mapping, you can omit the Acad.fmp file.

If you're an AutoCAD LT user, the equivalent file is named Acadlt.fmp.

4. **Select a transmittal setup from the list.**

Transmittal setups contain settings that control how ETRANSMIT processes the drawings and creates the transmittal package. Click the Transmittal Setups button to create new or modify existing setups. The default Standard transmittal setup works fine for most purposes. In any case, you should view the settings (click the Modify button) just to see what options you can change if you need to later.

If you want AutoCAD to include SHX and TTF font files, including any custom fonts that you're using, you must turn on the Include Fonts setting in the transmittal setup. As we discuss in Chapter 13, however, many custom fonts work like licensed software: Sending them to others is just like sharing your AutoCAD program DVD with others. No, we don't mean that it's easy and fun; we mean that it's illegal and unethical. That's why we strongly advise against using custom text fonts.

5. **Click the View Report button.**

You see a report listing the files that ETRANSMIT will copy, along with warnings about any files that it can't locate.

6. **Review the report and make sure that ETRANSMIT was able to find all the files.**

7. **Click OK.**

ETRANSMIT displays a file dialog box so that you can specify the name and location of the transmittal package.

8. **Click Save.**

ETRANSMIT creates the transmittal package (which is a Zip file by default). Zipping creates a single, tidy package of all your DWG, DGN, DWF, PDF, raster image, plot style table, and font files all ready to be e-mailed.

FTP for you and me

File Transfer Protocol (FTP) is a system for copying files over the Internet. A computer that's connected to the Internet can act as an FTP *server,* which means that part of its hard drive is accessible over the Internet. The person who configures the FTP server can place restrictions so that only people who

enter a particular logon name and password can see and download files. FTP overcomes the file size limitations that often occur with e-mail.

Because of all these FTP benefits, it's common for people at larger companies to place drawing files on their company's FTP site and tell you to go get them. This approach relieves them of having to e-mail you the files, and relieves you of waiting for that 10MB e-mail download when you least expected it.

The person making the files available to you via FTP will usually send you a Uniform Resource Locator (URL) that looks like a web page address, except that it starts with `ftp://` instead of `http://`. Simply enter the FTP URL into the address field of your web browser and follow any instructions regarding login name, password, filename, and/or password that may appear. As an alternative to FTP, see "Cloudy with a Shower of DWGs," later in this chapter.

Bad reception?

As soon as you receive an e-mail message or FTP download that contains drawings (zipped, we hope!), copy the file to a new folder on your hard drive or a network disk and unzip the files.

Check at least a few of the drawings in the package to make sure that all the xrefs and other reference files, fonts, and raster image files were included. You can perform this check by opening each main drawing in that folder. After you open each file, press F2 to view the AutoCAD text window and look for missing font and xref error messages of the following sort:

```
Substituting [simplex.shx] for [helv.shx].
Resolve Xref "GRID": C:\Here\There\Nowhere\grid.dwg
Can't find C:\Here\There\Nowhere\grid.dwg
```

Write down each missing file and then tell the sender to get on the ball (in a nice way, of course) and send you the missing pieces. While you're at it, tell that person to buy this book and read this chapter! Or buy it for them yourself!

If you receive drawings with custom TrueType font files (files whose extensions are TTF), you must install those files in Windows (not AutoCAD) before Windows and AutoCAD will recognize them. Refer to your Windows version's online help for instructions on installing fonts.

Help from the Reference Manager

In Chapter 18, we warn you about the complications of xref paths and the potential perils of AutoCAD not being able to locate xrefs if you move project folders around or transfer drawings to or from someone else. A similar

danger exists for raster image files and DWF/DWFx, DGN, and PDF underlays (Chapter 18) and for font files (Chapter 13). The ETRANSMIT command, described in the section "Rapid eTransmit," earlier in this chapter, does a good job of gathering dependent reference files, raster files, and font files, but it can't gather what AutoCAD can't locate.

The AutoCAD Reference Manager utility (not included with AutoCAD LT) is a real lifesaver if you find yourself suffering from file-path perils — whether they occur in your own company or when sending files to or receiving them from others.

Reference Manager is a separate program, not a command inside AutoCAD. Follow these steps to launch the utility from your Windows desktop:

1. **Choose Start➪All Programs➪Autodesk➪AutoCAD 2013➪Reference Manager.**

 The Reference Manager program opens, as shown in Figure 20-2.

Figure 20-2: The Reference Manager.

2. **Click the Add Drawings button to add one or more DWG files to the Drawings pane on the left.**

 Navigate to the folder that contains the drawings you want to send, select them, and then click Open.

3. **In the Reference Manager – Add Xrefs dialog box, choose Add All Xrefs Automatically Regardless of Nesting Level.**

 The Reference Manager processes the drawings and displays all referenced objects in its right pane.

4. **Click Export Report to create a text report listing all the dependent files and their paths, or click Edit Selected Paths to modify paths of selected reference files.**

5. **If you do choose to modify any selected paths, click Apply Changes.**

 When you're finished exporting reports and repathing reference files (or finding reference files you may never suspected you had if you hadn't run the Reference Manager), close the Reference Manager window. Click the Help button in Reference Manager to find out more about the utility's capabilities.

If you always keep parent and child DWG files in the same folder — the simplest approach to dealing with xref paths — you probably won't need to use the Reference Manager.

Design Web Format — Not Just for the Web

Earlier in this chapter, we explain how you can exchange drawings via e-mail and FTP. That's all the Internet connectivity that many AutoCAD users need, but if you're curious about connecting drawings to the web or sharing drawings with people who don't have AutoCAD, this section is for you.

The AutoCAD web features are built on three pieces of technology:

- ✓ A special "lightweight" drawing format called DWF that Autodesk originally developed especially for putting drawings on the web.

- ✓ An updated, XML-compliant version of the DWF format called DWFx that can be viewed by using the Microsoft XPS Viewer that's built in to Windows Vista and Windows 7 or available as a plug-in for Windows XP.

- ✓ A free program from Autodesk called Autodesk Design Review 2013 that enables anyone to view, mark up, and print DWF files without having AutoCAD.

All about DWF and DWFx

The AutoCAD DWG format works well for storing drawing information on local and network disks, but the high precision and large number of object properties that AutoCAD uses make for comparatively large files.

To overcome this size problem and encourage people to publish drawings on the web, Autodesk developed an alternative lightweight vector format for representing AutoCAD drawings: DWF (Design Web Format). A DWF file is a

more compact representation of a DWG file. DWF uses less space — and less transfer time over the web and e-mail — because it's less precise and doesn't have all the information that's in the DWG file.

Use the EXPORTDWF command to create a DWF file. This command is found under the Export button in the drop-down list under the Application Menu (the big red A in the upper-left corner of the screen).

DWFx is a version of regular DWF that's compliant with Microsoft's XML Paper Specification (or XPS for short — had your fill of alphabet soup yet?). Everything about DWF in this chapter also applies to DWFx. The DWFFORMAT command determines whether the PUBLISH, 3DDWF, and EXPORT commands output to DWF or DWFx. If this sounds like something that might be important in your work, look up *DWFFORMAT* in the online help system. Windows Vista and Windows 7 include an XPS Viewer, and the long and the short of this feature is that drawings plotted to DWFx can be viewed automatically in these Windows versions without AutoCAD or any special viewing software.

DWFx files are essentially electronic paper, or more specifically like a sheet of paper with transparent overlays stacked on top of it. Recipients can zoom, pan, turn layers on and off, apply markups, and can print, but they can't edit anything.

You can create DWF or DWFx files from your drawings and send those files to people who don't have AutoCAD. Your recipients can view and plot the DWF files after they download the free Autodesk Design Review 2013 program, which is available at the Autodesk website, `http://usa.autodesk.com/design-review/`.

Many people outside CAD-using companies don't have access to large-format plotters. They're limited to 8 1/2 x 11" — or, at best, 11 x 17" — reduced-size check plots. Consequently, many people won't be able to plot your DWF files to scale and may not even be able to plot them large enough to read everything.

Autodesk Design Review 2013

After you create DWF files, you or the recipient of your DWF files can use Autodesk Design Review to view and print them. (Autodesk Design Review 2013, the current release, is a free viewer from Autodesk.) If you send DWFs to people without AutoCAD, they can download Design Review 2013 from Autodesk's Web page, `http://usa.autodesk.com/design-review/`.

When you install AutoCAD 2013, the setup program, by default, installs Autodesk Design Review 2013 as well. From your Windows desktop, choose Start➪All Programs➪Autodesk➪Autodesk Design Review 2013 — or simply double-click a DWF file in Windows Explorer to launch the viewer.

The Drawing Protection Racket

Whether you're sending DWG or DWF files, you may be concerned about their misuse (that is, by the wrong people or for the wrong purposes), abuse (for example, modification without your consent), or reuse (on other projects or by other people without due compensation to you). AutoCAD has two features for securing your drawings when you send them to others:

✔ **Password protection:** Enables you to lock a DWG or DWF file so that only those who type the password that you've specified can open, insert, or xref it.

AutoCAD LT users can't apply a password, but they can open password-protected files — if they know the password, of course!

Add password protection to drawings only when you really need it:

- If you forget the password, you'll no longer be able to open the drawing. Neither AutoCAD nor Autodesk has any magical way to extract the password or unlock the drawing.

- After you password-protect a drawing, others can't insert the drawing as a block or attach it as an xref.

If you're using a password, you probably should do it on a *copy* of the drawing that you send; keep an *unprotected* version for yourself.

✔ **Digital signature:** Original paper drawings can't be modified without leaving evidence, and copies are obviously copies. Electronic files can be copied and/or modified without leaving any evidence, so a dispute can arise as to which version is the original. Solution: AutoCAD supports digital signatures. Digital signatures don't prevent unauthorized people from opening the file, nor do they prevent anyone from modifying it. All they do is to verify that a file has or hasn't been modified since it was signed if there is ever a dispute. You must first get an account with a digital-certificate provider before you can apply them. For more information, see *digital signatures, about* in the AutoCAD online help system.

Although electronic security features such as the ones described in this section can be useful as part of a strategy to protect your work from misuse, they're not a substitute for communicating clearly — preferably in the form of written contracts — what constitutes appropriate use of drawings that you send to or receive from others.

Autodesk Weather Forecast: Increasing Cloud

Even if you just came out from under your rock in the past *two* years, you may not have heard of "the cloud," or may not really understand what it means. Okay, here's the truth; *the cloud* really just means the Internet, which

in turn really just means a huge network of interconnected computers. Some organizations have put together a large number of computers — a "cloud" of them, if you will — and connected them through and to the Internet. Collectively, they have tremendous computing and storage capabilities.

So far, there are two fundamental uses for the cloud:

 ✔ **Computing:** Application software can live and run on the cloud, so your computer simply becomes a keyboard and monitor with very long cords back to the cloud of computers. This can involve relatively simple applications, such as AutoCAD WS (covered a little later in this chapter), but the collective power of the cloud of computers makes it possible to do things that are impossible, or at least highly impractical, on stand-alone units.

 Probably the best example of this is the entertainment industry. Before you start producing your own blockbuster computer-generated movie, do the math. AutoCAD can produce high-quality photorealistic images, but it can take anywhere from several minutes to a few hours to produce a single frame. Now you need 24 or 30 frames per second (fps; movies versus TV) for several hours. You soon hit geologic time frames. 3D movies like *Avatar* and *How to Tame Your Dragon* were produced on rendering farms containing 20,000 to 30,000 (that's right; twenty to thirty *thousand*) computers. I have heard it claimed that if your personal computer costs one dollar per hour to run, several thousand cloud computers still cost you only about one dollar per hour.

 ✔ **File storage:** Cloud servers can collectively contain literally tens of thousands of hard drives, each with many terabytes (TB) of storage capacity. A secondary benefit of cloud storage is collaboration. If you set things up properly, you can share your files instantly, live, with anyone anywhere in the world.

The term "infinite computing" has been applied to the cloud, which is obviously a little silly. (After all, if you cut an infinite line in half, how long is each piece?) On the other hand, the computing power and storage available today would have been beyond comprehension just a few years ago.

Working Solidly in the Cloud

Take a look at cloud computing, starting with one of the simplest applications.

Free AutoCAD!

No, this isn't the rallying cry of demonstrators trying to liberate AutoCAD. You actually can run a baby version of AutoCAD for less than for free. Yes, over the years, a number of lower-cost AutoCAD clone programs have

appeared on the market with prices as low as free, but how can you run AutoCAD for less than that?

Answer? AutoCAD WS. It's such a low-cost program that you don't need a program or even a computer. The software itself and your drawing files live on an Autodesk web server (hence AutoCAD *WS*). All you need is an Internet-enabled device like a smartphone or tablet, plus a free app for it. Okay, so maybe it isn't realistic to do full-time drawing creation on an iPhone, but one can be suitable for quickly reviewing drawings or checking on a specific dimension.

On the other hand, if you do want to run AutoCAD WS on your personal computer, you can simply access it through almost any web browser. You don't need a plug-in for your browser, so you can even run it from Internet café stations.

AutoCAD WS has been available for a couple of years as an Autodesk Labs experimental project called Project Butterfly, but it was recently released as a mainstream product. What's new about it is how it connects to AutoCAD 2013, which we cover a little later.

Try it yourself. Simply go to www.autocadws.com, create a free account even if you don't have an AutoCAD license, and log in. You'll find three sample drawings to play with. As you play with it, you'll soon realize that AutoCAD WS isn't quite full-blown AutoCAD. Realistically, it isn't even AutoCAD LT. On the other hand, the price is right, and we think that you'll be amazed at what it can do. *Disclaimer:* Autodesk is always working on it, so we might state that certain things don't work, but you'll likely find they do by the time you try them.

When you open a drawing, you're faced with a simplified version of the now-familiar Ribbon interface, as shown in Figure 20-3.

Figure 20-3: AutoCAD WS runs on the web, not your computer.

Autodesk is continually upgrading AutoCAD WS. The following lists of what you can and cannot do in AutoCAD WS are always changing.

What you can do

Here's a quick list of what you can do with AutoCAD WS:

- ✔ **Draw most 2D objects (including revision clouds).**
- ✔ **Use object snaps and Ortho.**
- ✔ **Use most of the editing commands, including Undo and Redo.**
- ✔ **Create and manage layers.**
- ✔ **Pan and zoom.**
- ✔ **Switch between model pace and paper space layouts.**
- ✔ **Insert and edit blocks.**
- ✔ **Use many of the keyboard mnemonics: L for Line, C for Circle, M for Move, and so on.**
- ✔ **Upload existing files from your computer.**
- ✔ **Download AutoCAD WS files, which are standard AutoCAD DWG files.**
- ✔ **Print files.**
- ✔ **Create folders and move files between them.**

 XREFs are supported, including attached raster image files. See Chapter 18 for a discussion on XREF attachments. Plot styles, discussed in Chapter 16, are supported, but the style definition files have to be uploaded separately.

So far there doesn't seem to be any limitation on the file space available to individual users. Better yet, you can upload and download any file type (docs, spreadsheets, and so on), but you can only open file types supported by AutoCAD, which includes DWG, DXF, and several raster formats such as BMP and JPG. My brain hurts.

What AutoCAD WS can do that AutoCAD can't

What you'll probably find to be really surprising is that AutoCAD WS can do a few things that full AutoCAD can't.

Does this scenario sound familiar? You're trying to sell a component to someone, or are trying to buy a component from someone, or your company has another operation somewhere else, or you are a consultant, and you need to discuss the drawing with them. In the (so)-called good old days, you'd have snail mailed or couriered prints back and forth, with a turnaround time of several days for each iteration. These days you probably e-mail the files and

then phone the other party. You know the typical conversation: "No, the other hole on the other side!" So far, so good, but what if the recipient doesn't own AutoCAD, or may not even be CAD-literate? AutoCAD WS to the rescue!

Just upload the file to AutoCAD WS, click the Share button, and enter one or more e-mail addresses. An e-mail invitation goes out to each person, inviting them to review the drawing. When the recipients click the link in their e-mail, they get signed into your account on AutoCAD WS, even if they don't have an account. AutoCAD WS then opens the one drawing that you invited them to share. Two or more people can log in to the same drawing at the same time, and everyone can see everyone else's cursor. Anyone can make changes, and a text chat box is available. But wait! There's more! AutoCAD WS keeps a history of all changes. Just click to jump back and forth anywhere along the timeline. Try doing *that* in standard AutoCAD.

You can specify a variety of file rights when you issue the invitation. Perhaps you want some people to *look but don't touch* or *look but don't download*, or maybe you just want them to see a smaller cropped region of the drawing. You can also un-share a file.

What AutoCAD WS can't do

As hinted earlier, there is a surprisingly short list of things that AutoCAD WS can't do (yet).

- You can't create new files. However, as a work-around, simply upload a blank file, or erase everything from an existing one, and away you go.

- 3D objects (Chapters 21 and 22) don't display on your web browser, but the 2D viewports created from them (Chapter 23) do display. 3D objects do display on your mobile device if you download the free app.

- Hatching can be created, but can't be edited. It loses its associativity (Chapter 15) if the boundary is edited.

- Layer management (Chapter 6) is limited to changing the color of layers and to moving objects to different layers.

- Parametrics (Chapter 19) can't be applied or edited, and don't update. On the other hand, they do survive a round trip, and upon returning, will update any changes made to the related objects.

- Annotative objects (Chapters 13, 14, and 15) display only the configuration of the first scale factor applied to them, but they survive a round trip.

You may have noticed an almost complete absence of *New in 2013* indicators in the book. The vast majority of what's new in AutoCAD 2013 lands in this chapter and Chapter 23. About the only thing not totally new is AutoCAD WS, which we just covered, but even then its relationship to AutoCAD has changed. For all practical purposes, the rest of this chapter is *New in 2013*.

Going once, going twice, going 123D

123D Catch — — can be very useful if you need to document existing real objects. You can download this free Autodesk product from www.123dapp.com/catch. Then simply "shoot circles" around any existing real-world object with any generic digital camera. Literally, shoot 20 to 30 pictures that overlap about 40 percent each and then upload them to an Autodesk cloud site by using the upload link in the software.

Now here's where the power of cloud computing kicks in. Within minutes, the Autodesk cloud service hands back a 3D CAD model of your object, as shown in Figure 20-4. Now all we need is a 3D printer (which does exist, by the way), and we have the Matter Replicator.

Figure 20-4: Four different views of a 3D CAD model generated from 30 2D photos.

We have seen samples that range in size from a watch gear to people, cars, buildings, (and even Mount St. Helens!) produced from 30 screen captures of Google Earth, to a mountain that someone flew around in a light plane. The UNESCO World Heritage Center has collected postcards, travel brochures, and private tourist's photos and has managed to create a 3D model of the giant statue of Buddha in Afghanistan that was destroyed by the Taliban.

Your head planted firmly in the cloud

As we indicate earlier in this chapter, the other main use for the cloud at this time is file storage. Many commercial sites will store your files for you for a range of fees, including free sites such as Google Docs.

Although the cloud is being touted as the next big thing, some critics have been quick to point out that it's mainly being touted as such by the software companies. One major advantage to them to running software from a cloud server is that it completely eliminates the piracy issue. Yes, some applications like AutoCAD WS are currently free, but some companies have been hinting that they would like to eliminate all stand-alone versions of their major software products. They might then sell annual access fees, and/or taxi-meter for occasional users.

Ralph Grabowski's upFronteZine (www.upfrontezine.com) is a weekly e-mail magazine devoted to the CAD industry. In late 2011, Ralph editorialized that, "The cloud is dead," and unleashed a veritable torrent of e-mail responses both for and against. At the end of the day, everything basically boiled down to two major points, which we summarize in the next two sections.

The pros

Here are some advantages of using the cloud for file storage:

- **Security:** Do you keep your money under your mattress, or do you put it in a bank? The *pro* side claims that your personal computer is the least-secure place in the world to keep your data files. Viruses sneak in, hard drives fail, computers get stolen, buildings burn down, and you may not (or more likely, probably don't) have a proper backup procedure.

 A competent cloud server service is probably using RAID (Redundant Array of Independent Disks) technology. The users see it as a single disk drive, but in reality, your files are automatically copied to several physical drives. If one drive fails, the RAID operating system automatically disconnects that drive and continues working with the other drives. A technician swaps out the dead drive on the fly, plugs in the new one, and the RAID system automatically refreshes it from the good drives. The users don't even know anything has happened.

- **Convenience:** Because the cloud server is part of the Internet, you can access your files anytime from anywhere in the world. Some services, such as Autodesk Cloud, can allow simultaneous access. Several people scattered all over the globe can access, discuss, and edit files at the same time. AutoCAD WS (discussed earlier in this chapter) is an example of this.

The cons

Here are some disadvantages of using the cloud for file storage:

- ✔ **Security:** How do you know whether your cloud service is actually following proper RAID and backup procedures? Are your files stored in their native format or are they encrypted? How secure is their site against hackers and intruders? Who really owns your files? Can they jack their rates way up and then hold your files for ransom until you agree to pay the new rates? What if they go bankrupt? Banks fail. . . .

 Anything you post to anywhere on the Internet is there *forever*. You may think you have deleted a file, but all you have really done is to flag the space it occupied as available. The raw data will survive until its disk space is needed and a new file overwrites it. (By the way, this is also true for your local hard drive. Many an embarrassing file has been recovered from a discarded drive.) In addition, RAID servers by definition hold multiple copies of the same file, and/or a competent cloud service will be doing regular backups.

- ✔ **Convenience:** We want to go back and slightly amend one sentence fragment from the "Pros" section so it now reads, ". . . you can *usually* access your files *almost* anytime from *almost* anywhere . . ." Here's the scenario: Your four-hour flight to visit an important client has just taken off. The seat belt signs turn off indicating that it's okay to use electronic equipment. You have about an hour of work to do on one last critical drawing. You fire up your laptop, launch AutoCAD, and open. . . . Oh, rats! (or words to that effect). No Internet connection. No cloud service. No files. You're doomed.

Cloudy with a shower of DWGs

If you haven't read the pros and cons of using cloud services, we strongly recommend that you go back a tad before you actually use any of what's coming up next.

Autodesk has entered the cloudy skies with its new Autodesk Cloud service, which gives anyone up to 1 gigabyte of free storage space. Now back up for a moment. There are two ways of acquiring AutoCAD (okay, two legal ways of acquiring AutoCAD):

- ✔ **Buy a license.**
- ✔ **Pay an annual subscription fee.** Being on subscription gives a number of extra benefits, including 3GB of cloud storage space.

AutoCAD 2013 cloud connectivity

AutoCAD 2013 adds a whole new Ribbon tab, shown in Figure 20-5, specifically for connecting directly to the Autodesk Cloud for online file sharing, customized file syncing, and more.

Figure 20-5: Tie a ribbon around a cloud.

We won't bore you with all the details of every option under every panel, because after we discuss the general principles, the options are pretty obvious.

We strongly suggest that you read through this section to see the options and some of the implications before you actually dive in to try anything.

In the following sections, we show the actual command name right after the Ribbon button name. Working from left to right, we start with the Online Documents panel:

✔ **Autodesk 360:** ONLINEDOCS is the basic command for signing in to Autodesk 360. After you're signed in, you can save and upload files to the cloud, share and collaborate with others, and download from the cloud. The first time, you're asked to set up your preferences. These can always be changed later, using the other Ribbon buttons that we cover a little later.

You sign in to Autodesk 360 by using your Autodesk Single Sign-on Account. You create your account when you install and activate AutoCAD. For a variety of reasons, though, you may not have an account or may not know your account information; for example, you may not be the person who installed AutoCAD on the computer that you're using. No problem; you can always create an account on the fly as you log in.

For that matter, you can also go directly to

```
https://documents.cloud.autodesk.com/Landing/Index
```

and create an account, even if you don't own AutoCAD. All you need is a valid e-mail address that isn't already linked to an Autodesk account.

After you're logged in, ONLINEDOCS opens your Autodesk Cloud Documents list and folders in a browser, as shown in Figure 20-6.

Figure 20-6: Have you ever seen the inside of a cloud?

From here, most of the actions are self-explanatory or are easy to figure out with a bit of experimenting, and/or are duplicated by AutoCAD commands. Rather than duplicate the descriptions here, we discuss them a little later in this chapter.

Right-click a file to bring up a contextual menu of the various things that you can do to or with the file.

You're not restricted to uploading AutoCAD drawing files to your Autodesk Cloud account. The Select Documents button of the Upload Documents dialog box lets you browse to any drive or folder accessible on your computer, including network drives, and it lets you select any type of file.

Your Autodesk Cloud documents are also available from many Select File dialog boxes throughout AutoCAD. For example, when you open, save, or attach a file, you can access the cloud directly from the Places list on the left side of the dialog box.

Now here's one of the many magic things about uploading drawing files to Autodesk Cloud. As we discuss in Chapters 13 (text), 14 (dimensions), 15 (hatch), 16 (plot), and 18 (XREFs), an AutoCAD drawing may not be an island unto itself but <u>may</u> require access to several supporting files. This is often a problem when you try to send a drawing to someone, because if you miss one of the required supporting files, the recipient can have problems opening your drawing. Now comes the magic: When you upload drawings directly from AutoCAD to the cloud, external references and other dependent files are automatically included with the upload. Problem solved.

Don't select the Keep Me Signed In check box in the Account Sign In dialog box if you are using a computer to which other people have access. If you do, and then simply close your browser when you're finished, ONLINEDOCS won't ask for a sign-in name or password the next time it's invoked. It will just sign in directly to your account, no matter who is using the computer. To deselect this box after you've signed in, don't just close your browser but instead move the cursor over your sign-in name in the upper-right corner of the browser window and then choose Sign Out from the scroll list that appears.

✓ **Online Options:** ONLINEOPTIONS actually starts the normal OPTIONS command and then selects its Online tab.

From the left side of this tab, you can control automatic or semiautomatic cloud storage. You can have AutoCAD automatically save an encrypted copy to the cloud every time you save a file, or only copy files that you select. Autodesk recommends the save-every-time option, but you might want to read "The pros" and "The cons" sections, earlier in this chapter, before you decide.

The right side of this tab enables Sync My Settings, which we cover a little later in this chapter.

✓ **Open on Mobile**: OPENONMOBILE. Use this when you have a drawing open on your computer but now you want to open it on your mobile device.

Assuming your mobile device already has the AutoCAD WS app loaded on it and that you're already signed in with the same Autodesk ID as your main computer, the Open on Mobile tool sends a push notification to the mobile device. This opens the current drawing without you having to open AutoCAD WS and without you having to browse to the file.

We're not sure why you would want to open a drawing on your mobile device when it's already open on your computer. Do you sometimes get the feeling that program features exist because they can be done, and not necessarily because they need doing?

✓ **Upload Multiple:** ONLINEUPLOAD lets you browse for and upload multiple drawings in one hit. What a surprise!

Next, we come to the Customization Sync panel.

✓ **Pimp My Ride** (oops, we mean **Sync My Settings**): ONLINESYNC could be your Dream Come True button if you have customized AutoCAD and its settings and if you often use two or more different computers. If you enable this, your personal settings and customizations are saved to the cloud on the fly while you work.

Now go to a different computer and turn this same button on. Presto! All your settings and customizations are downloaded from the cloud, and

AutoCAD on the second machine looks and runs exactly the same as your personalized computer. The two machines stay synchronized. When you log out, you're prompted to either keep the new settings on the second machine (perfect if you switch back and forth between your main computer and a laptop) or restore the original settings (Kindergarten 102: Be polite. After all, after you finish playing with someone else's toys you should always put them back where you found them.)

✒ **Choose Settings:** ONLINESYNCSETTINGS is a command name that you probably don't want to type in from the keyboard very often. This tool lets you specify which settings to synchronize and which to ignore. The list includes options (almost everything in the OPTIONS dialog box), customization files, printer support files, custom hatch patterns, custom fonts, shapes, and linetypes, tool palettes, and drawing templates. You may not want to synchronize everything. For example, different computers may have different printers.

Moving right along, we encounter Share & Collaborate. No, this isn't a law firm.

✒ **Share Document:** ONLINESHARE is used when you want to share the current drawing with other users. It signs you in to the cloud and copies the current drawing to the cloud if it isn't already there. You can specify the e-mail addresses of specific individuals or you can declare it to be *public*, and you can control the access level of shared documents.

✒ **Collaborate Now:** ONLINECOLNOW launches AutoCAD WS in your web browser and starts a collaboration session with another WS user. We describe AutoCAD WS earlier in this chapter.

Now all we need is a margin symbol for this book to apply to the SHARE command to indicate "New in 2012 but dead in 2013 and replaced by CLOUDCOLNOW." The SHARE command has to be one of the shortest-lived commands in AutoCAD history.

So you may well ask why Autodesk provides such obviously valuable services as AutoCAD WS and Autodesk Cloud for free. How can they make a profit from that? Well, the obvious MBA answer is that they'll make it up in volume. The less-obvious answer is that Autodesk hopes that this service will encourage more people to run out and buy AutoCAD and/or other Autodesk products.

Tomorrow's Forecast

At Autodesk University 2011, several Autodesk executives were quite adamant that they would not forcefully push anyone onto the cloud. "The cloud where appropriate, but not just for its own sake."

Part V
On a 3D Spree

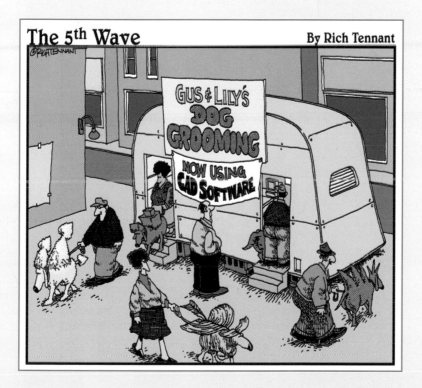

The 5th Wave — By Rich Tennant

GUS & LILY'S DOG GROOMING
NOW USING CAD SOFTWARE

*Y*our world isn't flat, and your drawings don't need to be either! It's been nothing but Xs and Ys up until now, but there's a whole new axis out there, and you're about to shinny up (or down) it in this part. In the chapters in this part of the book, you discover how your AutoCAD designs can escape the bounds of the X,Y plane and gain some height as well as length and breadth. You give your designs some volume by specifying Z-coordinates along with X- and Y-values. You can do some rapid visualization by changing to one of AutoCAD 2013's predefined visual styles.

The real world may be 3D, but it still uses a lot of 2D drawings. We show you how to rapidly generate 2D working drawings from your 3D models. All in all, AutoCAD has taken drafting a long way from the drawing board!

21

It's a 3D World After All

The addition of a third coordinate — the Z coordinate — releases your design work in AutoCAD from the planar world of two dimensions into a much more lifelike three-dimensional space. AutoCAD's 3D capabilities have grown by leaps and bounds since AutoCAD 2007 appeared with a souped-up 3D engine. Not only have its model creation and editing tools advanced, but AutoCAD is now also a dab hand at visualization and rendering. You can view your 3D models from any angle or slice through them to see what they look like inside. And finally, because the world of technical drawing is still a two-dimensional one, you can use AutoCAD's viewing options to create 2D views from 3D models.

If you're an AutoCAD LT user, you're going to have to sit out most of this and the next two chapters. One of the major areas where AutoCAD LT differs from regular AutoCAD is in its extremely limited 3D functionality. Even viewing 3D models is much more difficult in AutoCAD LT than it need be. LT users can acquire nearly all the 3D *viewing* capabilities of the full version of AutoCAD, but you need a separate — and free — program to do so. Just go to www.autodesk.com/trueview and download DWG Trueview.

This chapter takes a look at some of the tools available in AutoCAD 3D Modeling workspace and introduces you to many of the general concepts of creating 3D objects. You also discover how to look at your model from different viewpoints, and how to change the way it appears onscreen.

3D modeling and visualization is a lot more demanding on computer hardware than 2D drafting. 3D models tend to be bigger than 2D drawings, so you may need more disk space. And you'll certainly be happier with more than the bare minimum of RAM required for 2D in AutoCAD. In Chapter 2, we list AutoCAD system requirements and point out the increased resources needed for 3D work. In particular, note the desirability of using an engineering graphics card as opposed to a gaming card for heavy-duty 3D work.

Understanding 3D Digital Models

Here are the three basic types of 3D computer models:

- **Wireframe models:** Consist of edges and vertices only. Although they do occupy 3D space, they're totally unrealistic and difficult to read correctly. AutoCAD can create wireframe models, but nobody does any more. You only need to view a complex 3D model in wireframe mode to understand why.

- **Surface models:** Consist of infinitely thin skins that stretch from edge to edge of a model. AutoCAD can create two different types of surfaces: mesh surfaces, composed of thousands and thousands of three- or four-sided faces, and NURBS surfaces (Non-Uniform Rational Bezier Splines, if you must know). Mesh surfaces tend to be a little imprecise; they're most often used for 3D animation or terrain modeling. Think of the mirror disco ball in a nightclub. From a distance, it looks like a sphere, but as you get closer, you can see that it is made up of many small flat patches. NURBS surfaces are far more precise (as you'd expect with a name like that!) and are frequently used in product design. Due to space limitations, we don't cover either type of surface modeling in this book

- **Solid models:** Have edges, surfaces, and mass. They are true 3D models, and so you can do interference checking between them to make sure that an assembly will fit together properly. You can also find the surface area, volume, center of gravity, and moments of inertia of 3D models. Unfortunately, AutoCAD always assumes the material has a density of 1. If your real-life part is going to be made from something other than water, you will need to multiply the mass values by a suitable conversion factor, depending on the actual material being used.

AutoCAD has several commands related to applying materials to solids, but they affect only the appearance — not the density.

Although surface and solid models are created and modified differently, the 3D objects that make up the models are made up of the same subobjects. The subobjects that a 3D object is made up of are

- **Vertex:** The 3D equivalent of an AutoCAD point object. Vertices are defined by a single X, Y, Z coordinate that can exist anywhere in 3D space and are located where the edges of a 3D object meet.

- **Edge:** The boundary of a face, as defined by two X, Y, Z coordinates, one at each vertex.

- **Face:** The surface area bounded by three or more edges.

Figure 21-1 shows a simple 3D object — a six-sided cubic shape created with the AutoCAD BOX command — and its subobjects.

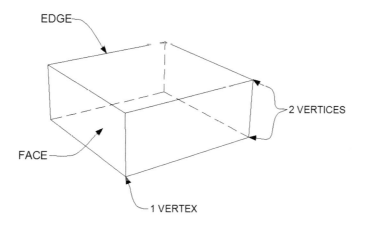

Figure 21-1: Subobjects of a 3D object.

Tools of the Trade

AutoCAD includes a plethora of tools for creating, editing, viewing, and visualizing 3D models. You can find the most commonly used tools for 3D modeling on the 3D Modeling workspace's Ribbon.

AutoCAD comes with two 3D workspaces: 3D Modeling and 3D Basics. We suppose the idea is that if you're new to 3D, you get your feet wet with the 3D Basics workspace and then graduate to the 3D Modeling workspace after you gain some experience. Personally, we think the 3D Basics workspace is a waste of time; our preference is to have the whole enchilada available from the get-go. For this book, we work exclusively with the 3D Modeling workspace.

AutoCAD's 3D environment is a lot like its 2D version, but there are some important differences. You should be aware of the following program settings and elements:

- ✔ **Hardware Acceleration:** Graphics functions, such as changing visual styles and running 3D Orbit, can be processed on the main CPU — or, if hardware acceleration is enabled, on the graphics card itself. Turning on hardware acceleration, if your graphics card supports it, (which we cover in the next section) nearly always improves 3D performance.

- ✔ **Workspaces:** AutoCAD 2013 comes with two 3D workspaces. We highly recommend that you use the 3D Modeling workspace. (We introduce workspaces in Chapter 2.) For more about the tools in the 3D Modeling workspace, see "Entering the third dimension," later in this chapter.

- ✔ **Drawing Window:** The drawing window's background, crosshairs, and dynamic tooltip colors change when you switch between 2D and 3D views, and in 3D views, when you switch between parallel and perspective projection. Click Options on the Application Menu, click the Display tab, and then click the Colors button to access color settings for the different interface elements. Note that we've tweaked the background colors on our systems so they're clearer on the printed page. Unless you've made changes already, you'll be looking at a very dark gray background, rather than the light gray one in this chapter's figures.

- ✔ **UCS Icon:** When working in 3D, the UCS icon shows the orientation of the current X, Y plane and the direction of the Z axis. For information on using the UCS icon, see "Changing Planes," later in this chapter.

 Prior to AutoCAD 2012, the UCS icon merely showed you the orientation of the X, Y, and Z axes. If you used the UCS command to set a new UCS, the icon reoriented itself accordingly. Starting in AutoCAD 2012, the selectable UCS icon is in the driver's seat — you can directly manipulate the icon to change the UCS. We introduce you to the new UCS icon in the "Changing Planes" section, later in the chapter.

Warp speed ahead

When you start AutoCAD for the first time after installing it, the program assesses your computer's graphics card, and — if it's up to the task — enables hardware acceleration. With hardware acceleration, you can change the view of your model — even models with lighting and applied materials — in real time, without any deterioration in quality. Hardware acceleration also boosts the overall visual quality of drawing objects as well as regeneration performance.

Autodesk tests a wide range of cards and drivers with each new release. To find out whether your graphics card is supported for AutoCAD, check out the graphics hardware list online at

www.autodesk.com/autocad-graphicscard

Entering the third dimension

If you're new to the 3D game and you've been working in 2D up until now, you need to do a couple of things before you can start a new 3D model in AutoCAD. You have to change the workspace and then you have to open a new file by using a 3D template. The following steps explain how:

1. **Open the Workspaces drop-down list on the Quick Access Toolbar, or click the Workspace Switching button on the status bar and then choose 3D Modeling.**

 Toolbars, palettes, and Ribbon panels flash on and off, and soon AutoCAD settles down to display the Ribbon, as configured for the 3D Modeling workspace with a few additional panels.

2. **Click the Application button and choose New; then click Drawing.**

 The Select Template dialog box appears.

3. **Choose `acad3d.dwt` if you're working in imperial units or `acadiso3d.dwt` if you're working in metric. Click Open.**

 A 3D modeling space appears (see Figure 21-2) where, instead of looking straight down at the drawing area, you look at it at an angle from above.

Figure 21-2: Ascending the Z axis.

4. **To switch from 3D to the 2D world, simply reverse the steps just given.**

Untying the Ribbon and opening some palettes

Most of AutoCAD 3D modeling tools can be accessed from the Ribbon and 3D–related palettes. The following list introduces you to the Ribbon tabs and palettes available in the 3D Modeling workspace. (Note that not all items in this list are visible in Figure 21-2 and that this list omits some items that are not unique to 3D.)

- ✔ **Home tab:** Contains a subset of the most frequently used 3D tools for creating and editing solids, surfaces, and meshes; as well as user coordinate system command options, view tools, 2D drawing and editing commands, and layer and group tools.

- ✔ **Solid tab:** Contains tools for creating and modifying 3D solids. We show you some of the finer points of solid modeling in Chapter 22.

- ✔ **Surface tab:** Contains tools used to create, edit, and analyze NURBS surfaces.

- ✔ **Mesh tab:** Contains tools used to create and modify meshes, convert them to solids, and generate live sections.

- ✔ **Render tab:** Contains tools to add lighting and materials to a 3D model, and generate rendered output. Chapter 23 presents the basics of rendering in AutoCAD.

- ✔ **View tab:** Contains tools to navigate, visualize, and change the current view and UCS of a 3D model. We cover navigation tools, coordinate systems, and visual styles in this chapter.

- ✔ **Output tab:** Contains tools to output a 3D model to a DWF or PDF file or even generate a 3D print. We cover plotting 2D drawings in Chapter 16, and outputting 3D designs to paper isn't significantly different (see the online help for specifics). We don't cover exporting to 3D DWF or 3D printing in this book.

- ✔ **Plug-ins tab:** Contains the Inventor Fusion panel with the single Edit in Fusion button. Inventor Fusion is a free-standing 3D modeling application installed (optionally) with AutoCAD 2013. The Inventor Fusion plug-in lets you select 3D objects from your AutoCAD drawing, edit them in Fusion, and then return to AutoCAD when you're done. The prime feature of Fusion is that you can create and edit flowing, free-form solids — such as the body of a hair dryer — that would be extremely difficult, or even impossible, in AutoCAD.

The following palettes are found on the View tab of the Ribbon:

- ✔ **Materials Browser palette:** Use to apply materials to the objects in the current model, and to manage materials in saved material libraries.

- ✔ **Materials Editor palette:** Use to apply, create, and modify materials in the current model. Chapter 23 introduces you to materials.

Applying materials in AutoCAD affects only the appearance and not the density.

- **Advanced Render Settings palette:** Use to manage rendering presets.
- **Visual Styles Manager palette:** Use to create, modify, and manage visual styles in the current model.

The following palettes are found on the Render tab of the Ribbon:

- **Lights in Model palette:** Use to manage lights in the current model.
- **Sun Properties palette:** Use to specify the lighting settings for the Sunlight system in the current model.

Modeling from Above

So far in this book, you've been working with X and Y coordinates only. X and Y coordinates by themselves define a two-dimensional plane known (logically enough) as the *X, Y plane*.

In this and the following two chapters, you supply a third value, a Z coordinate, in order to locate geometry above or below the X,Y plane. You use the same methods to specify Cartesian (X, Y, Z) coordinates as the ones we set out in Chapter 7. You just add a comma and another number. The following techniques can be used to specify points in 3D:

- **Coordinate and direct distance entry**
- **Point filters**
- **Object snaps**
- **3D object snaps**
- **Object snap tracking**

Using 3D coordinate input

We introduce you to 2D coordinate entry in Chapter 7. To recap, the input formats are

- **Absolute Cartesian coordinates:** Expressed as *X, Y* — the distances along the X and Y axes from the origin (0,0).
- **Relative Cartesian coordinates:** Expressed as *@X, Y* — the distances parallel to the X and Y axes from last point.
- **Relative polar coordinates:** Expressed as *@d<a* — the distance and angle in the X, Y plane from the last point.

Although you can use these 2D coordinate input methods in 3D, you usually have to give AutoCAD just a little more information when you want to work in three dimensions. You can use absolute or relative Cartesian coordinates by simply adding a Z coordinate to the end. In addition, there are two 3D–only coordinate formats, both based on 2D polar coordinates. You can enter 3D coordinates with the following methods:

- **Absolute Cartesian coordinates:** Expressed as *X, Y, Z*. Working with absolute coordinates in 3D should look familiar because the input is like working in 2D except that you add a Z coordinate at the end.

- **Relative Cartesian coordinates:** Expressed as *@X, Y, Z*. Relative coordinates in 3D work just like they do in 2D except that you add the Z coordinate.

- **Cylindrical coordinates:** Expressed as *@d<a,z*. Cylindrical coordinates are similar to relative polar coordinates (*d* is the distance and *a* the angle from the last point *in* the X, Y plane) with the addition of a Cartesian Z coordinate to locate the point above or below the X, Y plane.

- **Spherical coordinates:** Expressed as *@d<a1<a2*. Spherical coordinates are also based on relative polar coordinates, but instead of a Z coordinate to specify a location above or below the X, Y plane, you specify an angle from the X, Y plane.

Using point filters

Coordinate entry (as described in the preceding section) is fine if you already know the coordinate values or distances in 3D space where you want to locate your points. Often, however, you may need to derive 3D points from existing geometry without knowing those exact values. Using point filters, you can locate new points based on existing points. You can use point filters to construct 2D and 3D coordinates.

When AutoCAD prompts you to specify a point, you can either enter point filter values at the command line, or bring up the right-click menu and choose a filter option from the Point Filters submenu. After selecting a point filter option, specify a point to filter out part of the coordinate value and then enter the requested value. For example, use the .XY filter to enter your own Z coordinate value after specifying a point on the current working plane.

Object snaps and object snap tracking

Object snaps allow you to accurately specify points on existing objects in a 3D model. You can use object snaps such as endpoints, midpoints, and center on 3D objects, but AutoCAD also provides a set of object snaps specific to 3D modeling.

 3D object snaps allow you to specify points on 3D objects that regular object snaps won't recognize — for example, the center of a face, or a vertex. You enable 3D object snaps by clicking the 3D Object Snap button on the status bar. Right-click the 3D Object Snap button and choose the running 3D object snap modes you want to use.

 Object snap tracking allows you to calculate points that are not on an object by using object snap points on existing objects. When working in 3D, you can not only track points on the current X, Y plane but also along the Z axis. While tracking points along the Z axis, AutoCAD provides feedback in the form of a tooltip that lets you know you're moving along the Z axis in the positive or negative direction.

 The ELEVATION system variable allows you to specify a height above or below the current working plane. When you enter a 2D coordinate, AutoCAD uses the value assigned to ELEVATION system variable (by default, it's 0) to create a 3D coordinate. You can set the OSNAPZ system variable to 1, to substitute the Z coordinate value of a point specified by using an object snap with the value of ELEVATION.

Changing Planes

Come fly with us while we explain changing planes in AutoCAD. (Just step through this metal detector over here while we X-ray your bags.)

Okay, it's not *that* kind of plane. This section covers using the user coordinate system (UCS) to control the current working (or X, Y) plane. The UCS icon displayed either at the lower-left corner of the drawing window or at the origin (0, 0, 0) shows you the orientation of the current work plane and the positive direction of the Z axis.

Displaying the UCS icon

By default, the UCS icon is displayed in both 2D and 3D views. You can lose your bearings pretty easily when working in 3D, and we strongly recommend that you keep the UCS icon in your sights at all times. If you don't see a UCS icon, you can turn it on from the Coordinates panel of the View tab on the Ribbon. Click the button with the burned-out light bulb and choose either Show UCS Icon or Show UCS Icon at Origin.

 In addition to controlling the display of the UCS icon, you can also tweak its size, color, and location by using the UCS Icon dialog box. To display the UCS Icon dialog box, choose UCS Icon, Properties on the Coordinates panel of the Home tab.

In previous releases, the UCS icon was merely a graphic indicator of the current coordinate system. If you set a new user coordinate system in model space, the UCS icon adjusted itself to show you the orientation of the new X, Y plane and Z axis. In other words, the UCS icon was *driven* by the current coordinate system. Beginning with AutoCAD 2012, the UCS icon moves across to the driver's seat! You can now select the UCS icon and see new multifunction grips that allow you to set a new UCS by dragging the grips on the origin and the legs of the icon. There's also a new right-click menu. You can enable or disable UCS icon selectability on the Settings tab of the UCS dialog box — type **UCSMAN** to open it. In the next section, we show you how to create a new user coordinate system by selecting and manipulating the UCS icon.

Adjusting the UCS

Every drawing you create uses the World Coordinate System (WCS), but when working in 3D, you need to create additional work planes. User coordinate systems (UCSs) are necessary when you need to draw objects on work planes other than the WCS. In the real world, think of latitude and longitude as the WCS; street naming, house numbering, and hotel room numbers are all local systems and are equivalent to UCSs. Traditional UCSs are static; create one, and it stays current until you change it. By default, such coordinate systems are unnamed, but you can assign a name and save it for future use. A couple of releases back, AutoCAD introduced dynamic UCSs. Because dynamic is the opposite of static, what you get is a temporary coordinate system that changes as you move your mouse pointer over different planar faces of a 3D object. Use the status bar Allow/Disallow Dynamic UCS button on the status bar, or press the F6 key to toggle dynamic UCS on and off.

Name that UCS

The UCS command offers ten options to help you define a new UCS. Access the UCS command options from the Coordinates panels on either the View or Home tab of the Ribbon.

The most commonly used options of the UCS command are listed below. After you select one of these options from the Ribbon, follow the command prompts at the command line or the Dynamic Input prompt.

- **World:** Align the UCS to match the WCS.
- **Face:** Align the UCS to the face of a 3D solid.
- **View:** Align the UCS so that the X plane is perpendicular to your current viewing direction.
- **3 Point:** Specify a new origin for the UCS, and then the positive direction of the X and Y axes. Alternatively, use the multifunction grips on AutoCAD's UCS icon to create a new UCS by moving and realigning the icon.

For more information on all the UCS command's options, refer to AutoCAD's online help system.

The more UCSs in your drawing, the more you need help managing them. AutoCAD offers a handy dandy UCS dialog box for doing just that. Open it by clicking the dialog box launcher (the little arrow at the right end of the panel label) on the Coordinates panel of the View or Home tab, or simply type **UCSMAN** and press Enter. The three tabs in the UCS dialog box are

- **Named UCSs:** Lists World and other user coordinate systems. Set a UCS current with the Set Current button, or right-click a UCS to rename or delete a named UCS. (You can't rename or delete the World UCS.)

- **Orthographic UCSs:** Lists the six default orthographic coordinate systems (front and back, left and right, top and bottom) relative to the WCS. These UCSs are automatically created by AutoCAD and can't be deleted or renamed.

- **Settings:** Controls properties of both the UCS icon and the UCS itself.

After you define a UCS that you think you might want to use again, you can save it in the UCS dialog box. We explain how in the following steps, which you begin by creating a solid box.

1. **Start a new 3D drawing by selecting** `acad3d.dwt` **(or** `acadiso3d.dwt` **for the metric crowd) for your template, and ensure that the 3D Modeling workspace is current.**

 Refer to the steps in the "Entering the third dimension" section, earlier in the chapter, if you need a refresher.

2. **On the Modeling panel of the Home tab, click Box.**

 AutoCAD prompts:

   ```
   Specify first corner or [Center]:
   ```

3. **Type** 0,0,0 **and then press Enter.**

 AutoCAD anchors the first corner of the box at the origin of the WCS and prompts:

   ```
   Specify other corner or [Cube/Length]:
   ```

4. **Drag your crosshairs away from the first corner and click a point to set the length and width of the box.**

 Exact distances don't matter in this example. AutoCAD prompts:

   ```
   Specify height or [2Point]:
   ```

5. Drag the crosshairs upward from the second corner and click to set the height of the box.

AutoCAD creates the 3D box and exits the command.

Preliminaries are over. Now it's time to start making some UCSs.

6. Move the crosshairs over the UCS icon.

The UCS icon shows the orientation of the World Coordinate System. As you move the crosshairs over the icon, it turns a greenish-gold color, indicating that it can be selected.

7. Click to select the UCS icon.

A square multifunction grip appears at the origin, and round multifunction grips appear at the ends of the icon's legs.

8. Move the crosshairs over each multifunction grip and look at the grip menus.

Hovering over one of the round grips at the end of a leg lets you choose between realigning the selected axis, or rotating the UCS around one of the unselected axes. Hovering the mouse pointer over the origin grip lets you move the UCS origin to a new location and either keep the current alignment of the X and Y axes or realign them. The third grip option, World, restores the WCS.

Now you use the UCS icon's multifunction grips to set a new UCS.

9. Click the UCS icon to select it, and then move the crosshairs over the square multifunction grip at the origin.

The crosshairs jump to the origin and the grip menu appears.

10. From the grip menu, choose Move and Align.

AutoCAD prompts:

```
** MOVE AND ALIGN **
        Specify origin point or align to face,
        surface, or mesh:
```

Move the crosshairs to a different corner of the box, and when the UCS icon origin is over the corner, click to set the new origin.

If you want, you can drag the round grips on the axes to realign the new UCS. After you have it the way you want, it's worth saving it. The next steps show how.

11. On the Coordinates panel of the Home tab, choose UCS, Named UCS.

AutoCAD displays the UCS dialog box.

12. With the Named UCSs tab current, select Unnamed in the UCSs list.

The new, unnamed UCS is the current UCS in the drawing and is listed at the top of the list.

13. **Right-click Unnamed and choose Rename from the shortcut menu.**

 An in-place editor is displayed that allows you to rename the UCS.

14. **Type a name for the new UCS press Enter.**

 The Unnamed UCS is renamed (see Figure 21-3).

Figure 21-3: Naming a custom UCS.

15. **Click OK.**

 The UCS dialog box closes, and the new UCS is saved in the drawing.

16. **On the Coordinates panel of the Home tab, choose UCS, World.**

 The current UCS is now aligned with the WCS.

17. **On the Coordinates panel of the Home tab, click in the Named UCS drop-down list and choose the name of the UCS you just saved.**

 The new UCS is restored.

AutoCAD likes giving you lots of choices. You can also restore a named UCS from the UCS drop-down list at the bottom of the ViewCube. (We fill you in on the ViewCube in the "Taking a spin around the cube" section, later in this chapter.) Or you can right-click the UCS icon, choose Named UCS, and then choose the UCS from the menu.

Using Dynamic UCS

A named UCS allows you to work on different work planes, but it can take a bit of effort to set up and that can distract you when you're focused on 3D modeling. With Dynamic UCS, you can focus on modeling, not on creating a UCS. To enable or disable the dynamic UCS feature, click the Dynamic UCS button on the status bar.

Figure 21-4 shows an example of drawing a circle on the side of a 3D solid. With Dynamic UCS enabled, AutoCAD highlights the face of the 3D solid that

the UCS will be aligned with. Click over the face to align the UCS with the face, and then finish the command. The circle is aligned with the face of the 3D solid, and the previous UCS is then restored.

Figure 21-4: Dynamically create a UCS on 3D solids.

Navigating the 3D Waters

If you're brand new to 3D in AutoCAD, you may be wondering how to look at whatever it is you're modeling from whatever angle you desire.

One way to change viewpoints that works in both AutoCAD and AutoCAD LT is to use the preset views from the Ribbon by selecting the View tab, and then clicking the down arrow at the bottom of the 3D preset views drop-down menu on the Views panel (shown in Figure 21-5) to switch to one of the standard orthographic 3D views or an isometric view.

- ✓ The six standard orthographic (straight-on) views are Top, Bottom, Left, Right, Front, Back.
- ✓ The four standard isometric views are SW (left-front), SE (right-front), NE (right-back), and NW (left-back). (An *isometric view* is one in which you see the object from above — or below, but AutoCAD's standard views don't do below.)

Figure 21-5: 3D Preset Views drop-down menu.

An isometric view is an unrealistic 3D view because all lines that are parallel in reality are also parallel in the view. In a perspective view, lines that are parallel in reality appear to meet at a vanishing point, as parallel lines *appear* to do in reality (think of railroad tracks heading across the prairie). The isometric views we mention previously are parallel projection views, and you can view 3D models by using those views in either the full version of AutoCAD or AutoCAD LT. Perspective views are more commonly used in architectural applications, and parallel views are more commonly used in mechanical design.

This warning is for AutoCAD LT users (users of the full version of AutoCAD don't need to worry). As we point out earlier, AutoCAD LT can open drawings created in the full version. Those AutoCAD drawings can be saved with perspective projection current, and if you open such a drawing in AutoCAD LT, you can see it in perspective. You can switch from perspective to parallel projection by changing the PERSPECTIVE system variable's value from 1 to 0. Be very careful if you do this because you can't change it back again! You could use UNDO to reverse the change, but if you save and close the drawing, you're sunk.

The six orthographic and four isometric views work well for showing 3D models of common objects such as mechanical components and buildings. You can also change to *plan view,* which is a top-down view of either the world coordinate system or a user coordinate system.

AutoCAD LT has limited 3D viewing capabilities. The same preset views are in both AutoCAD and AutoCAD LT, and you can also use the Viewpoint Presets dialog box (DDVPOINT command) in which you set a viewing position by specifying angles in and from the XY plane. Finally, there's the really ugly command line only VPOINT command. (Man, that one's soooo ugly, it's not even on the Ribbon!)

Orbit à go-go

 Preset views are fine for many 3D modeling tasks, but if you really want to have fun, 3DOrbit (not in AutoCAD LT) is your ticket to it. (Orbiting a 3D model in AutoCAD is similar in concept to orbiting around the Earth in a satellite — only a lot cheaper.) The two orbiter modes are Constrained and Free. Constrained mode is pretty much like the Free mode with training wheels.

 Free Orbit displays an *arcball* on the screen — a circle representing a sphere around your object. You click various places inside, outside, and on the arcball and then drag to change the 3D view. The idea is that you're spinning an imaginary sphere containing your model. As you drag the cursor, AutoCAD updates the screen dynamically.

You can start Constrained orbiting, the 3DOrbit command, by holding the SHIFT key down and then holding the middle mouse button while dragging the mouse.

You might also want to experiment with different projection modes:

- ✓ *Parallel projection* is the default AutoCAD projection. Lines that are parallel in the 3D object remain parallel in the projected view on the screen.

- ✓ *Perspective projection* makes objects look more realistic (for example, train tracks appear to converge in the distance), but lines that are parallel in the model don't appear parallel in perspective projection.

If you manage to 3DOrbit out of control and can no longer see your model, right-click to display the 3DOrbit shortcut menu and choose Zoom Extents. The Zoom, Pan, and Preset Views options offer other ways of getting your model back in your sights.

 When you start orbiting with no objects selected, AutoCAD tries to update the display of everything in your model, and this can take some time. To speed things up or to simply regain your bearings, try selecting some objects before you start orbiting. Then AutoCAD updates the display of the selected objects only. When you exit orbit mode, the entire model redisplays based on the new viewpoint.

Taking a spin around the cube

With so much talk about hybrid devices these days, Autodesk decided to create its own in the form of the ViewCube (not in AutoCAD LT). The ViewCube (see Figure 21-6) is an interactive tool that provides visual feedback about the current viewpoint, allows you to set a preset view current or orbit the model, restore a named UCS, and define and restore the Home view of a model.

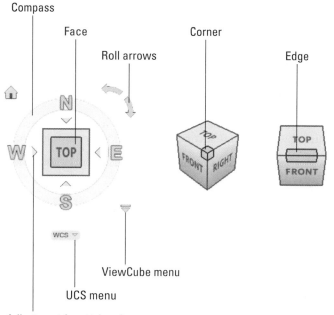

Figure 21-6: ViewCube, the multifunctional viewing device.

To change the view of the model by using the ViewCube, you can do one of the following:

- Click a corner, an edge, or a face to align the current view with the same viewpoint represented on the ViewCube.
- Click and drag the main area of the ViewCube to orbit the view of the model.
- Click one of the roll arrows to rotate the current view 90 degrees.
- Click one of the adjacent face triangles to switch to the adjacent orthographic view that is indicated by the triangle.
- Click one of the letters (N, E, S, W), or click and drag the compass to rotate the view around the center of the drawing.

Home view is a special view that you can define so you have a known reference view in the model. That way, if you lose your bearings, you always have a way to get back home. You can restore the Home view from the ViewCube or the SteeringWheels right-click menus.

Grabbing the SteeringWheels

SteeringWheels act as a kind of navigation hub that allows you to access several different 2D and 3D navigation tools from a single user interface. (AutoCAD LT includes only the 2D Navigation wheel.) AutoCAD (the full version) comes with the 2D Navigation wheel and three other wheels that are designed to be used with 3D modeling. The three additional wheels are

- ✔ **View Object:** Contains tools to center a model in the current view, zoom in and out, or orbit around a model.

- ✔ **Tour Building:** Contains tools to move the viewpoint forward and backward, look around the model from a fixed location, and change the elevation of the current viewpoint.

- ✔ **Full Navigation:** Contains a combination of the tools found on the 2D Navigation, View Object, and Tour Building wheels with the addition of tools to walk around or fly through a model.

All wheels include a Rewind tool, which allows you to restore a previous view. The Rewind tool is similar to the Previous option of the ZOOM command.

When a wheel is active, move the cursor over the wedge that contains the tool you want to use. For many of the tools, you either click over the tool, or click and drag to use the tool. Some tools support alternate versions of themselves when you press and hold the Shift key. To get an idea of what each tool does, hover the cursor over the tool to display a tooltip message. To learn more about each of the wheels and the tools on them, see AutoCAD's online help. To display the help specific to the wheels, right-click when a wheel is displayed and choose Help from the shortcut menu.

Visualizing 3D Objects

It really doesn't seem like that long ago when the only way of viewing 3D models was wireframe mode, but the last several releases have dramatically improved AutoCAD's visualization capabilities. There are almost a dozen different display modes — *visual styles* — that you can set with the click of a drop-down menu. Figure 21-7 shows the default visual styles — and you can add your own if you want — in the Visual Styles Manager palette.

Visual styles are collections of settings that build on the SHADEMODE settings found in earlier incarnations of AutoCAD. AutoCAD 2008 introduced five default visual styles, and that number doubled with AutoCAD 2011 to a total of ten:

- ✔ **2D Wireframe:** AutoCAD's classic 2D viewing mode: full wireframe, dot-based grid, the 2D UCS icon, and no perspective.

- ✔ **Conceptual:** An illustrative kind of shaded view. Colors are unrealistic and edges are heavy, but you get a good sense of the model's form. Figure 21-3 shows an example of the Conceptual visual style.

- ✔ **Hidden:** Looks slightly like a wireframe view (no surfaces are visible) but edges behind faces are hidden.

- ✔ **Realistic:** Fully shaded, but not rendered visual style; edges are not displayed, and a default ambient lighting highlights the faces with different intensities of the object color. Materials and textures are visible if they've been applied. Have a look at Figure 12-8 for an example.

- ✔ **Shaded:** Similar to Realistic, but with more subdued lighting. Textures do not appear in this visual style.

- ✔ **Shaded with Edges:** Same as the Shaded visual style, except that isolines are set to be displayed.

- ✔ **Shades of Gray:** Like Shaded, only all object colors are changed to different intensities of gray.

- ✔ **Sketchy:** Visual style that does not apply any shading to the faces of 3D objects but give the edges of 3D objects a hand-sketched look. Somehow we're not sure of the logic in spending several thousand dollars on hardware and software so you can produce something that looks hand sketched.

- ✔ **Wireframe:** Pretty much the same as 2D wireframe, except for background color, optional perspective, and the 3D rather than the 2D UCS icon. Figure 21-4 shows a simple model in Wireframe visual style.

- ✔ **X-ray:** Similar to Shaded with Edges, except that Materials and Textures are applied like the Realistic visual style and faces are set to 50% opacity.

AutoCAD 2013's ten preconfigured visual styles are only the beginning. You can modify any of the styles or create new ones in the Visual Styles Manager palette (see Figure 21-8).

Figure 21-7: Some new styles to try on.

Figure 21-8: A manager for your visual styles.

 To display the Visual Styles Manager, click the dialog box launcher (the little arrow at the right end of the panel label) on the Visual Styles panel of the View tab, or simply type **VSM** and press Enter.

22

From Drawings to Models

*F*or millennia, people have documented the design and construction of three-dimensional objects by drawing two-dimensional views of them. Most people have continued to use these "classical" methods with CAD drafting because the methods are well understood and work reasonably well. After all, if 2D drawing was good enough for guys like Leonardo da Vinci and Andrea Palladio, it should be good enough for us, right?

Nonetheless, the past decade (or so) has seen a trend toward creating 3D CAD models and letting the software generate the 2D views more-or-less automatically. This approach seems more logical, especially if the project documentation requires numerous, complex views of the same object. 3D modeling also is an absolute necessity when you want to create rendered views for presentation purposes.

And although AutoCAD 3D construction and visualization tools have improved dramatically over the years (trust us — you should have seen what they were like as recently as AutoCAD 2006!), it's still a complex process that requires sophistication on the part of the AutoCAD user. Although 3D modeling requires only one more dimension than 2D drafting, developing 3D CAD models can seem to be more complicated. Users must master new techniques and contend with the 2D limitations of most display screens and input devices. On the other hand, after you have the 3D model, generation of traditional 2D drawing views is almost trivial.

In Chapter 21, we show you how to move around models that others have made, and explain the principles of 3D coordinate systems that you need to understand to work in AutoCAD's 3D environment. This chapter introduces you to the concepts, tools, and techniques of AutoCAD 3D modeling itself; here, you can get your feet wet creating your own 3D objects.

Full 3D support is one of the main differences between full AutoCAD and AutoCAD LT. If you're using AutoCAD LT, you can look at and plot 3D models created in AutoCAD, but you can't do much 3D object creation or editing yourself. Also, viewing 3D models is less flexible in AutoCAD LT because it lacks nearly all the 3D navigation and rendering tools included in the full version of AutoCAD.

Is 3D for Me?

Traditional 2D drawings provide clues to help the viewer's mind construct a 3D model from the 2D image on paper. Multiple views from different viewpoints in 3D space give experienced designers, drafters, and builders the information they need to make 3D sense of 2D drawings. Design and drafting have succeeded pretty well by using 2D representations as the guide to creating 3D objects. But at some point, nothing can replace a true 3D model, such as in helping someone understand how a building will look when constructed or how two parts fit together.

What does using 3D in AutoCAD mean? Fundamentally, it means creating *models* instead of *drawings*. Rather than generate cross sections of an object or individual views of it from certain perspectives, you create a three-dimensional model of the object. This 3D depiction of each object includes all the necessary information for AutoCAD to create a drawing view from any point of view. With a properly constructed 3D model, AutoCAD can output commands to machines to create actual 3D objects, whether plastic prototypes carved from a tank of jelly by 3D printers, or an actual bolt, valve, or piston created by computer-controlled machine tools.

As we explain in Chapter 21, AutoCAD can create three types of 3D models: wireframe, surface, and solid. In most practical applications of 3D, you select one of these types for all or most of the objects in the drawing, based on ease of construction and intended use of the model. However, AutoCAD doesn't prevent you from mixing all three types of 3D objects in the same drawing.

After you determine the type of 3D representation to use, you decide on the appropriate level of detail and construct the model, using the commands and techniques introduced in this chapter. If you need, you can go on from there to create any required 2D and/or rendered views for plotting or viewing onscreen.

Getting Your 3D Bearings

The first challenge in 3D modeling is being able to see your three-dimensional model on a two-dimensional computer screen. The normal model space view on the Model tab in the drawing area shows a single, projected 2D view of your model — the top-down, "plan" view by default.

AutoCAD provides two model space capabilities that enable you to escape this visual flatland:

- ✔ With view*ports*, you can carve the model space drawing area into smaller rectangular areas, each of which shows a different view of the model.

- ✔ With view*points*, you can change the point in 3D space from which you look at the model. By setting a different viewpoint in each viewport, you can look at several sides of your model at the same time. It's like looking at one of Picasso's cubist paintings, only what you see is more orderly.

No matter how much or how little 3D modeling you're thinking about doing, it's well worth your while to set up a template. (We fill you in on drawing templates in Chapter 4.) If you've ever started a new drawing, you're probably aware that AutoCAD already comes with a template for 3D modeling named `acad3d.dwt` (or `acadiso3D.dwt` for the metrically inclined). This is fine as far as it goes, but it only shows you a single view of your model. The next section explains how to improve on this template.

Creating a better 3D template

Model space viewports enable you to see several views of your model at one time, each from a different viewpoint. For this reason, model space viewports are especially useful when you're creating and editing objects in 3D. As you draw and edit, the different views help ensure that you're picking points that are located correctly in 3D space.

Chapter 5 discusses viewports in paper space, which are useful for creating layouts for use in plots and presentations in both 2D and 3D. Model space viewports, cousins of paper viewports, are less flexible but simpler, and are a great help in constructing 3D models.

Model space viewports divide the screen into separate rectangles with no gaps between them. Unlike paper space viewports, you can't move, stretch, or overlap them. You can't plot multiple model space viewports (that's what paper space is for). And, unlike the situation in layouts, a layer that's visible in one model space viewport always is visible in all of them.

You may hear or read references to *tiled viewports*, which is just another name for model space viewports. *Tiled* refers to the way in which model space viewports always fill the drawing area, with no gaps and no overlapping allowed. Conversely, paper space viewports are sometimes called *floating* viewports because you can move them around, leave gaps between them, and overlap them.

One of the best new features introduced in AutoCAD 2012 goes by the somewhat obscure title of in-canvas viewport controls. Those little text labels that you may have noticed at the top-left corner of the graphics area (see Figure 22-1, for example) are clickable controls that let you set the visual style and the view. What's especially nifty is that double-clicking the plus or minus sign toggles the drawing area between multiple tiled viewports already configured for 3D viewing, and a single, maximized viewport. Out of the box, double-clicking the minus (–) sign switches to four equal-sized viewports showing different views of the geometry. Figure 22-1 illustrates what we're talking about: In this example, you see four viewports, four different viewpoints, and four different visual styles. That's a bit extreme for everyday work, but it gives you an idea of the possibilities.

Figure 22-1: 3D viewing from every which way.

We highly recommend working with multiple viewports when you're modeling in 3D — that way you get to see exactly what you're doing in all three dimensions, in real time. Our preference is to work mostly in the isometric viewport, so we make that one larger than the other three. The in-canvas

viewport toggle will switch back and forth between the last multiple viewport you set up, and a maximized viewport. In the following steps, we explain how to set up the tiled-viewport configuration you see in Figure 22-3.

1. **If you're not already in the 3D Modeling workspace, click the Workspace drop-down list on the Quick Access Toolbar and choose 3D Modeling.**

 You can also click the Workspace Switching button on the status bar and again, select 3D Modeling. If the Materials Browser palette opens, close it.

2. **Click New on the Quick Access Toolbar to open the Select Template dialog box.**

 If a new blank drawing appears and you don't see the Select Template dialog box, someone has assigned a default template to this button in the Options dialog box. In that case, click the Application button (the Big Red A) and choose New, and then choose Drawing from the submenu.

3. **Choose `acad.dwt` (choose `acadiso.dwt` if metric is your preference), and click Open.**

 Yes, we know there are ready-made 3D templates (`acad3d.dwt` and `acadiso3d.dwt`), but trust us — it's easier to start this setup from a 2D template.

4. **From the Viewports panel on the Ribbon's View tab, choose Named.**

 The Viewports dialog box appears.

5. **Click the New Viewports tab to make it current; then choose Four: Left (our preference) or Four: Right from the Standard Viewports list box.**

 The Preview panel shows a large, squarish viewport occupying most of the work area, with three small squarish viewports stacked on the left (or right). The default 2D setup shows the visual style of all four viewports as "2D Wireframe." (We explain visual styles in Chapter 21.)

6. **From the Setup drop-down list, choose 3D.**

 The visual styles remain as 2D Wireframe, but the view direction (listed as "Current" in 2D Setup) is now SE Isometric in the large viewport, while the three small viewports show Top, Front, and Right orthographic views.

 When modeling in 3D, it's nearly always helpful to look at your objects in different ways at the same time. When looking at orthographic views, same as with a drafted drawing, you probably want to see all your linework. But you can get a better sense of the three dimensionality of your model by looking at it in a shaded view. With multiple viewports, you can do both at the same time.

7. In the Preview area, click inside the large SE Isometric viewport and then choose Conceptual from the Visual Style drop-down list.

You're almost finished in here. Rather than go through this setup every time you want to do some modeling, give your new viewport configuration a name.

8. In the New Name box at the top of the Viewports dialog box, enter a name — V3D, for example — for the configuration.

Figure 22-2 shows the new, named viewport configuration. After you close the Viewports dialog box, you can restore this configuration at any time by clicking the Named Viewports tab, choosing V3D, and clicking OK.

New Viewports	Named Viewports

New name: V3D

Standard viewports:

"Active Model Configuration"
Single
Two: Vertical
Two: Horizontal
Three: Right
Three: Left
Three: Above
Three: Below
Three: Vertical
Three: Horizontal
Four: Equal
Four: Right
Four: Left

Preview

View: "Top"
2D Wireframe

View: "Front"
2D Wireframe

View: "Right"
2D Wireframe

View: SE Isometric
Visual style: Conceptual

Apply to: Display Setup: 3D Change view to: SE Isometric Visual Style: Conceptual

OK Cancel Help

Figure 22-2: Setting up a 3D work environment in the Viewports dialog box.

9. Click OK to save the viewport configuration and close the Viewports dialog box.

In Figure 22-3, we turned off the grid in the three small ortho viewports, but whether you leave it on or turn it off is a matter of personal preference.

The ViewCube's Home button can trip you up by changing to a view you don't expect. (We introduce the ViewCube in Chapter 21.) If you want to keep the current SE Isometric viewpoint, be sure to reset the Home view. To do this, simply right-click anywhere in the ViewCube and choose Set Current View as Home from the menu that appears. And because you've gone to the trouble of setting up a shaded 3D viewport, why not make it a little more realistic and turn on perspective mode at the same time?

Figure 22-3: 2D and 3D all at the same time.

10. **In the large 3D viewport, right-click the ViewCube to display its shortcut menu and then choose Perspective With Ortho Faces (see Figure 22-4).**

 Selecting Perspective shows your orthographic views in perspective mode, and usually you don't want that. Selecting Perspective with Ortho Faces resets the projection mode from perspective to parallel when you switch to an orthographic view.

Figure 22-4: Changing settings in the ViewCube's right-click menu.

11. **Repeat Step 10, this time selecting Set Current View as Home.**

 Now you can readily return to this viewport configuration, keeping the same viewpoint in all viewports, perspective projection in the 3D viewport, and parallel projection in the orthographic viewports.

To return to a single viewport later, simply click the plus (+) sign on the in-canvas viewport control.

The last thing to do is save the configuration you've just set up as a template (`.dwt`) file.

12. **Click Save on the Quick Access Toolbar. From the Files Of Type drop-down menu, choose AutoCAD Drawing Template (*.dwt) and enter a filename. Click Save.**

AutoCAD saves your new 3D template file in the same place as your other templates so it's always there for you to select when you want to do some serious 3D modeling.

Seeing the world from new viewpoints

When you choose 3D in the Viewports dialog box's Setup drop-down list, you direct AutoCAD to change the viewpoint in each viewport. The default viewpoints when you choose a four viewport arrangement are top, front, right, and SE ("southeast") isometric. These viewpoints work well for viewing and constructing simple models, but eventually, you'll probably want to specify your own custom viewpoint in a particular viewport.

In both AutoCAD and AutoCAD LT, the best — but not the easiest — way to change viewpoints is to use the drop-down list on the Views panel of the View tab (shown in Figure 22-5) to switch to one of the standard orthographic 3D views or an isometric view:

- ✒ The six standard orthographic (straight-on) views are Top, Bottom, Left, Right, Front, Back.

- ✒ The four standard isometric views are SW (left-front), SE (right-front), NE (right-back), and NW (left-back). An isometric view is one in which you see the object from above, but not too high above — as though you were hovering in a low-flying helicopter.

The easiest — but not the best — way to change viewpoints is to click one of the named faces on the ViewCube (not available in AutoCAD LT). We don't recommend this because the ViewCube is a *viewing* aid, and nothing but. You usually change to an orthographic view because you want to do some drawing or modeling there, and for that, your UCS (user coordinate system) ought to orient itself with the view. (See Chapter 21 for the skinny on UCSs.) Clicking Front on the ViewCube shows you a nice front view of your model, but it leaves the UCS unchanged, and that can make drawing anything difficult. Clicking Front on the View tab's Views panel *does* change the UCS to Front so it matches the view and lets you draw without difficulty.

Figure 22-5: The preset views drop-down menu.

These ten views are called "standard" because they're often used in manual drafting and rendering work. They work well for showing 3D models of common objects such as mechanical components and buildings. You can also change to plan view, which is a top-down view of either the world coordinate system or a user coordinate system. (We describe coordinate systems in Chapter 21.)

The full version of AutoCAD has the ViewCube, the 3DORBIT command, and the Shift+middle button methods of changing 3D viewpoints (all are described in Chapter 21). AutoCAD LT's options are much more limited. LT users can set nonstandard viewpoints by typing **DDVPOINT** and pressing Enter. In the Viewpoint Presets dialog box that appears, specify the following settings:

- ✔ **A viewing angle *in* the X, Y plane:** Imagine moving a camera on a dolly around an object, while keeping the camera at the same elevation.

- ✔ **An angle *from* the X, Y plane:** Imagine using a boom to swoop the camera up to a different height so that you're looking at the object from increasingly steep angles.

AutoCAD users can set viewpoints the same way, but it's grossly inefficient compared with the other viewing options.

By default, AutoCAD shows 3D models in 2D wireframe mode, even if you've created surface or solid objects. If you want to better visualize which objects are in front of which other objects, especially in an isometric or other non-orthogonal view, you have a couple of options:

 ✔ Select a shaded visual style such as Realistic, Conceptual, X-Ray, or
 Shades of Gray, from the Visual Styles drop-down on the Visual Styles
 panel of the View tab. (See Chapter 21 for the low-down on visual styles.)

 ✔ Render the model, as described in Chapter 23.

AutoCAD LT doesn't include visual styles because they're not much use in 2D
drafting. A drawing saved in a visual style in the full version of AutoCAD *does*
display that style when it's opened in AutoCAD LT. However, there's no way of
changing it to 2D wireframe (or anything else) so you can actually work on it.

From Drawing to Modeling in 3D

This section introduces three techniques for creating 3D objects: drawing
3D lines and polylines, creating 3D objects from 2D geometry, and creating
solids. (In AutoCAD LT you can use the first two techniques only.) AutoCAD
is also very capable at surface modeling, offering both freeform mesh and
NURBS surfaces. If you're interested in either of these, check out the online
help system; navigate to User's Guide; then choose Work with 3D Models,
and then Create 3D models. Topics include creating surfaces and meshes
from scratch, and creating solids and surfaces from 2D objects.

When you draw 3D objects, just like when you draw 2D objects, put them on
appropriate layers and use precision techniques to specify each point and
distance. (See Chapter 5 for more information.)

Drawing basic 3D objects

The most basic forms of 3D geometry are wireframe-like objects created by
picking points or entering X, Y, Z coordinates. Such objects have no surfaces,
so they look the same in 2D Wireframe mode or a photorealistic rendering.
They are most useful as paths for sweeps and lofts, or as edges for surface
creation. Such objects include

 ✔ **Lines:** Lines are really 2D objects; although you can specify different Z
 coordinates for start- and endpoints so they're not coplanar with the
 world coordinate system, each individual segment is based on its own 2D
 plane. You can, however, use lines for constructing objects in 3D space.

 ✔ **3D Polylines:** Created with the 3DPOLY command. Similar to the 2D
 polylines that we describe in Chapter 8, except the vertices of 3D poly-
 lines can have different Z coordinates: 2D polylines must be planar. 3D
 polylines are useful as paths for sweeps or for fly-throughs. (We don't
 cover walk-throughs or fly-throughs in this book.)

✔ **Splines:** Splines are free-form curves, created with the SPLINE command and we describe them in a 2D context in Chapter 9. Splines are 3D objects, and vertices can have different Z values. Splines are a better option than 3D polylines for sweeps because they can have smoother curves.

✔ **Helices:** Helices can be either 2D (think of a mosquito coil, or the element on an electric range) or 3D (think of Mr. Slinky). Helices are especially useful as paths for threaded objects.

You can find the LINE, 3DPOLY, and SPLINE commands on the Draw panel of the Ribbon's Home tab; the HELIX command is on that panel's slideout.

The 3DPOLY command is similar to the PLINE (plain old 2D polylines) command. Both commands draw a series of connected line segments, but they have different capabilities:

✔ The 3DPOLY command accepts 3D points for the line segments' vertices. The PLINE command requires that all vertices be on the same plane.

✔ 3DPOLY is limited to straight line segments. PLINE can draw arc segments and create segments with uniform or tapered width.

✔ Segments created with 3DPOLY can't display dash-dot linetypes; 3D polyline segments always display as continuous lines.

The command sequence for drawing 3D segments with the LINE or 3DPOLY command is the same as for drawing 2D segments with the LINE or PLINE command; see Chapter 8 if you need a refresher on drawing lines. The only difference is that you specify 3D coordinates instead of 2D ones. Figure 22-6 shows an example.

Creating 2D representations in this way is straightforward, although tedious, for all but the simplest objects. More important, a wireframe model becomes increasingly difficult to decipher as the complexity of the model increases. You see a mass of lines representing the edges, and you have difficulty telling which parts of which edges are in front of others. To reduce this visual confusion, you need to graduate to surface or solid modeling commands. We introduce you to solid modeling in subsequent sections of this chapter.

Figure 22-6: Entering 3D coordinates to draw a 3D polyline.

Gaining a solid foundation

Solid modeling is in many ways the culmination of 3D CAD. Solids more accurately represent most real-world objects than do wireframes or surfaces. And even when representational accuracy isn't the main issue, it's easier to construct many kinds of models with solids.

Many special-purpose solid modeling programs use a combination of solid and surface modeling techniques for maximum flexibility in constructing and editing 3D models. These kinds of programs — and solid modeling in general — are especially popular in mechanical design.

Constructing the basic building blocks — or solid primitives — for a solid model in AutoCAD isn't difficult. Just follow these steps:

1. **Define a suitable UCS (user coordinate system).**

 The UCS controls the construction plane and basic 3D orientation of the solid. Read about changing planes in Chapter 21.

2. **Click the leftmost button on the Modeling panel of the Home tab, and then choose a solid primitive from the lower half of the split button.**

 As shown in Figure 22-7, your choices are Box, Cylinder, Cone, Sphere, Pyramid, Wedge, and Torus.

Figure 22-7: Everything you need for a solid foundation.

When you see a 3D object in a drawing, you can't tell by looking whether it's a 2D extruded object, surface mesh, or solid. If you want to find out, open the Properties palette and select the object. The drop-down list at the top of the palette shows the type of object that you selected.

Drawing solid primitives

Solids are the easiest kinds of object to work with if you're new to 3D. The two types of 3D solid object are

 ✓ **Primitive solids:** The most basic of 3D building blocks, such as boxes, cones, and spheres. Primitive solids are based on simple geometric shapes, such as lines and circles.

 ✓ **Complex (or compound) solids:** Made by combining primitive solids and optionally editing them with Boolean operations. The following sections focus on creating and modifying 3D solids.

Boolean editing operations (named for the Victorian English mathematician George Boole) use arithmetic-like functions to combine solid objects or remove parts of them. The three primary Boolean commands in AutoCAD are UNION, SUBTRACT, and INTERSECT. See "Boolean operations" later in this chapter for more information.

Adding the Third Dimension to 2D Objects

AutoCAD's 2D roots run deep. Drafting continues to be the primary focus of the program, but recent AutoCAD releases have shifted focus, and the program has become more and more adept at 3D modeling. This section invites you to take what you probably have an abundance of right now (2D objects) and create new 3D objects from them.

Creating 3D objects from 2D drawings

You can create 3D objects from 2D objects by using a number of different techniques. You can add thickness or extrude an open 2D object to create a surface, or take multiple 2D cross sections and create a lofted object that adapts to the shape and size of each cross section selected. Everything mentioned here applies to AutoCAD only (not AutoCAD LT), with the exception of the thickness property.

Add thickness to a 2D object

Most 2D objects, such as lines and circles, have a thickness property. Changing a 2D object's thickness property does not create a true 3D object, but it does create a pseudo-surface that looks like a 3D surface. These pseudo-surfaces can hide objects beyond them, but they do have limitations. If you add thickness to a circle, an open cylinder is created without caps on the top and bottom. If you change the thickness of a rectangle (which is really a polyline), you end up with four walls but no top or bottom.

Extrude open and closed objects

Thickness is one way of adding height to an object, but extruding an object is usually a better approach. You can extrude open or closed 2D objects to create a 3D object. Extruding a closed 2D object, such as a closed polyline,

spline, ellipse, circle, or region, creates a 3D solid. Extruding an open 2D object, such as an open polyline, spline, line, or arc, creates a surface. Figure 22-8 shows results of extruding open and closed objects.

If you want to end up with a 3D solid, you must extrude a single, closed object, such as a circle or a closed polyline. If you want to produce a 3D solid from a boundary composed of multiple objects, read about PRESSPULL later in this chapter.

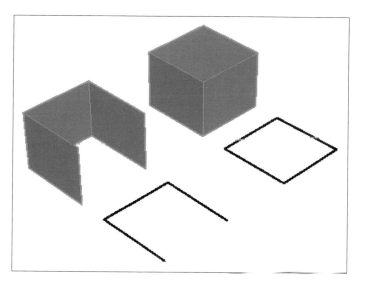

Figure 22-8: 2D to 3D by extrusion is easy as 1, 2, 3.

To extrude an open or a closed 2D object, click Extrude on the Solid panel of the Solid tab, or click the Extrude split button on the Home tab's Modeling panel. If you see a button labeled Loft, Revolve, or Sweep, click the lower part of the split button and choose Extrude from the drop-down menu. Use the MOde option to control whether you create a surface or 3D solid from a closed object, select the objects you want to extrude, and specify an extrusion height or distance to create the 3D solid.

The DELOBJ system variable controls whether the 2D objects you use to create 3D solids are retained or erased. Most of the time, you probably want to keep the source geometry, but the default DELOBJ setting erases it. If you want to keep the original 2D geometry, type **DELOBJ** and set its value to 0. (See Chapter 26 for more about system variables.) DELOBJ also controls whether or not the source objects for associative arrays (introduced in Chapter 18) are retained or deleted.

Press and pull closed boundaries

The PRESSPULL command allows you to create 3D geometry by extruding a closed boundary. PRESSPULL differs from EXTRUDE in that the EXTRUDE command *requires* a single, closed 2D object while PRESSPULL can use closed boundaries formed by other 3D solids, or by several objects that form a closed region. PRESSPULL searches for a suitable boundary in exactly the same manner as the HATCH command, which we cover in Chapter 15.

To press or pull within a closed boundary to create a 3D object, click Presspull on the Solid tab's Solid panel, click inside an enclosed boundary, and then drag or specify the distance on the extrusion you want to create.

Loft open and closed objects

Lofting allows you to select a series of 2D cross sections to create a surface or 3D solid. The selected cross sections are used to define the outer surface that's generated. You must select a minimum of two cross sections. If you select open objects, the resulting loft is a surface; if you select closed objects, the resulting loft can be either a surface or 3D solid, depending on the current value of the MOde option for the LOFT command.

You can loft objects along a path by using guide curves, or just between the selected cross sections (see Figure 22-9). To loft open or closed 2D objects, open the Sweep/Loft drop-down on the Solid tab's Solid panel. Use the MOde option to control whether you create a surface or 3D solid from a closed object cross section, and specify how the loft object should be calculated.

The term "loft" derives from the days of wooden sailing ships. The shipyards had an upstairs area, much like the hayloft in a barn, where they determined the shape of each plank that was required to form the curves of the hull. Because it was performed in the loft, the process became known as "lofting."

Figure 22-9: Using cross sections to create a lofted object.

Sweep open and closed objects along a path

Sweeping is similar to extruding a 2D object except that you specify a path, rather than a height or distance. The object used as the path can be either an open or closed 2D object, and can be only a single object (see Figure 22-10). If you sweep an open object, the resulting swept object is a surface; if you sweep a closed object, the resulting swept object is a surface or 3D solid based on the current value of the MOde option of the SWEEP command.

To sweep an open or closed 2D object, open the Sweep/Loft drop-down on the Solid panel of the Solid tab. Use the MOde option to control whether you create a surface or 3D solid from a closed object, select the objects to sweep, and specify a path for the sweep.

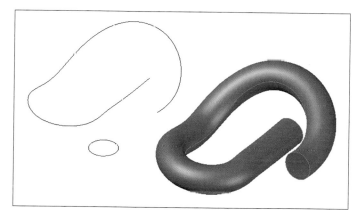

Figure 22-10: Sweeping a closed object along a path.

Revolve open or closed objects around an axis

Revolving allows you to create a surface or 3D solid by turning selected objects around an axis (see Figure 22-11). If open objects are selected, the resulting revolved object is a surface; if you select closed objects, the resulting revolved object is a 3D solid.

To revolve an open or a closed 2D object, click Revolve on the Solid panel of the Solid tab, or click the Revolve split button on the Home tab's Modeling panel. (If you see a button labeled Loft, Extrude, or Sweep, click the lower part of the split button and choose Revolve from the drop-down list. Use the MOde option to control whether you create a surface or 3D solid from a closed object, select the objects to revolve, and specify the axis to use.

Figure 22-11: Revolving a closed object around an axis.

Modifying 3D Objects

Many of the modification techniques and commands that you use in 2D drafting can be applied to 3D modeling. In addition, a specialized set of 3D editing commands is available. All these commands are located on the Modify panel of the Home tab when the 3D Modeling workspace is current.

Selecting subobjects

3D objects themselves are complex objects that can be made up of several hundred — even thousands — of objects. Although these objects never stray from their parent, you can access them individually or in groups through subobject selection. *Subobject selection* means selecting a vertex, edge, or face of a 3D object. After you select a subobject, you can use grip editing and the 3D gizmos to manipulate it. We discuss the 3D gizmos in the following section.

To make it easier to select subobjects, you can enable subobject filtering from the Ribbon. Vertex, edge, and face filters are located on the Subobject Selection Filter split button on the Selection panel of the Home and Solid tabs.

The CULLINGOBJ and CULLINGOBJSELECTION system variables help limit object selection to the faces that are visible in the current view by ignoring faces around the back of the objects being viewed. By default, both of these variables are turned off, so you can select objects in front and behind. If you have a complex model, turn culling on. To turn culling on, click Culling on the Selection panel of the Home tab. To turn it off, click the Culling button again. The button is shaded blue when the feature is enabled.

If you just need to select a face on a 3D object, press and hold the Ctrl key and select the face you want to select. This can be faster than turning subobject filters on and off.

Working with gizmos

Although you can use the MOVE, ROTATE, and SCALE commands to modify 3D objects, they can sometimes give unexpected results in 3D. Enter the 3DMOVE, 3DROTATE, and 3DSCALE commands, which all use a gizmo or grip tool when a non-orthographic view is current (see Figure 22-12).

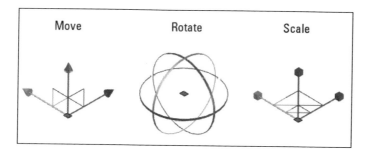

Figure 22-12: Using gizmos to modify objects in 3D.

The gizmos restrict or constrain movement along the X,Y plane and the Z axis. To use a gizmo, click one of the axes on the tool to restrict movement to that axis. You can access the three gizmos by using the following methods:

- ✔ **3DMOVE:** Click 3D Move on the Home tab's Modify panel, or type **3DMOVE** at the command line.

- ✔ **3DROTATE:** Click 3D Rotate on the Modify panel (Home tab), or type **3DROTATE** at the command line.

- ✔ **3DSCALE:** Click 3D Scale on the Modify panel, or type **3DSCALE** at the command line.

You can also access the Move, Rotate, and Scale gizmos in 3D by selecting objects when no command is active. You can set the default gizmo that is displayed when you use grips in 3D by opening the Gizmo drop-down in the Home tab's Selection panel and selecting the gizmo you want to be active. Right-clicking over a gizmo allows you to switch between different gizmos and constraints.

More 3D variants of 2D commands

Moving, rotating, and scaling objects are certainly the big-three operations of 3D editing, but a number of other 3D variations on 2D editing commands are hiding in the wings, awaiting their turn in the spotlight. For more about spotlights, see Chapter 23.

Getting your 3D ducks in a row

Getting objects to align with each other in 3D can be a challenge at times, especially if you need to not only move an object in 3D, but also rotate and scale it based on the specified alignment. AutoCAD has two commands that can be used to align objects:

- **ALIGN:** Used to align 2D and 3D objects based on one, two, or three pairs of points. Based on the number of pairs of points specified and how they're selected, the ALIGN command might move and rotate the selected objects into place. It can also be used to scale objects as well. On the Home tab, choose Align from the Modify panel slideout.

- **3DALIGN:** An improved version of the ALIGN command that includes additional options, as well as the ability to move and rotate a copy of the selected objects and use Dynamic UCS with the command. Click 3D Align on the Modify panel of the Home tab.

Holding up a mirror

The MIRROR command is limited to working on the X, Y plane. If you want to mirror objects in 3D, you need to use the MIRROR3D command. Click 3D Mirror on the Modify panel of the Home tab. The MIRROR3D command is similar to the MIRROR command, but you can control the plane on which the mirroring is performed.

Associative arrays, which we discuss in Chapter 18, work in 3D as well as 2D. AutoCAD has long had a 3DARRAY command; it's still there, and is similar to the old style ARRAY command (refer to Chapter 11 for that one) in that it doesn't create an associative array object. For information on creating rectangular, polar, and path array objects, refer to the online help.

Editing solids

3D solids can be edited in a variety of different ways that other objects can't be. You can use grip editing to change the shape of 3D solids, or Boolean operations on a 3D solid to create complex models. You can fillet and chamfer the edges of a 3D solid by using the FILLETEDGE and CHAMFEREDGE commands.

Using grips to edit solids

Grip editing is one of the most direct ways to modify an object. To edit a 3D solid by using grips, select the 3D solid when no command is running, and then select the grip you want to use to edit the solid. Pay close attention to the grip you select; some grips give you control over changing the overall size of a solid; others might change only part of a solid, such as the face or top radius of a cone. Figure 22-13 shows a pyramid with its top radius (I'll bet you didn't know that pyramids had radii!) being edited with grips.

Ortho: 0.8085 < 90°

Figure 22-13: Grip editing a pyramid.

Boolean operations

As we mention in the "Drawing solid primitives" section, earlier in this chapter, you can join 3D solids by using the UNION command to create a new 3D solid. You can also subtract volume from a 3D solid by using another intersecting 3D solid to determine what should be removed with the SUBTRACT command. The INTERSECT command can be used to calculate a new 3D solid based on the intersecting of two or more 3D solids. See Figure 22-14 for examples. You can find these three commands on the Boolean panel of the Solid tab.

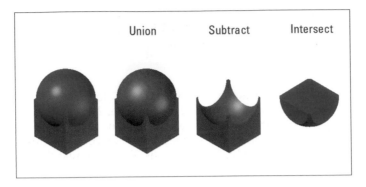

Figure 22-14: Solid primitives on the left, and the result from UNION, SUBTRACT, and INTERSECT commands.

Filleting and chamfering

Because fillets and chamfers are common real-world features, it's logical that tools for creating them are available. You can fillet or bevel the edges of a 3D solid by clicking the Fillet Edge (or Chamfer Edge) split button on the Solid tab's Solid Editing panel.

Both commands allow you to select multiple edges to fillet or bevel. When you select an edge, AutoCAD gives you feedback on how the selected edge will be affected. Figure 22-15 shows an L-shaped 3D solid that's been filleted and chamfered.

Figure 22-15: Before and after filleting and chamfering a 3D solid.

You can remove a fillet or chamfer by starting the ERASE command and, at the Select Objects prompt, holding down the Ctrl key and selecting the fillet or chamfer to be removed. For fillets, you may need to also remove nearby filleted corners that might have been created during the application of the fillet.

The FILLETEDGE and CHAMFEREDGE commands were new in AutoCAD 2011. You can still use the FILLET and CHAMFER commands on 3D solids, but the new commands are much more efficient.

Slice

The SLICE command allows you to cut a 3D solid along a plane. You can slice a 3D solid by using a planar curve such as a circle, 2D polyline, or a surface, among many others. When you slice a 3D solid, you can choose which part of the 3D solid is kept — or you can keep both. Figure 22-16 shows a solid model that's been sliced in half. To start the SLICE command, choose Slice from the Solid Editing panel of the Solid tab. After the command is started, specify a 3D solid to slice, an axis or object to define the cutting plane, and then finally which new 3D solids to keep.

Figure 22-16: Carving up a solid model with the SLICE command.

On a Render Bender

*T*he word *design* has the same Latin origin as *designate*, meaning to point out to or to show to others. If you have an idea and produce it yourself, you aren't a designer: You're an artist or a craftsman (not that there's anything wrong with that). You aren't a designer until you tell someone else about your idea so they can do all the dirty, heavy work of producing it.

2D orthographic drawings go back to Roman times, but only in the past few years have we seen a significant change in how things are designed and how the designers communicate that vision to others. No, we don't mean 2D CAD on a computer because that's just a more efficient way of producing Roman-style drawings. The world we live in is 3D, but paper is 2D. Orthographic engineering drawings were developed for the sole purpose of getting the designer's 3D idea transferred to a 2D format. The recipient of the drawing then transfers the idea back into 3D, first as an image in the mind and then as the physical object.

The big change coming is that low-cost computers are getting powerful enough, and software is getting sophisticated enough, that designers can now work in 3D on a personal computer. At the same time, 3D printers exist

that can take your computer 3D model and produce a real-world object. They were originally developed with mechanical designs in mind, but architectural designers are also using them to print scale models of their buildings. More recently, the scale factor for printing buildings has become 1:1. That's right: Full-scale concrete houses are being 3D printed straight from the computer model! At the end of the day, however, the real world still needs (or at least wants) 2D drawings.

Going the other way, or at least going even farther in the 2D world, relatively low-cost computers and powerful software make it possible for designers to produce photo-realistic images of their 3D models. Clients and customers can see the product before it's real.

We start this chapter by showing you how to generate 2D drawings from 3D models, and then go on to discussing rendering.

Get the 2D Out of Here!

Would you believe that it took less than five minutes to produce Figure 23-1?

Figure 23-1: A drawing in less than five minutes!

Okay, we cheated a little bit. It took about an hour to produce the 3D model first, but the 2D views were produced almost instantly. The rest of the five minutes was spent adding the dimensions. The clock is running. . . .

1. **Switch AutoCAD to the 3D Modeling workspace.**

 Select it from the drop-down list at the end of the Quick Access Toolbar in the upper-right corner of the screen.

2. **Set up a 3D model.**

 Create a new model by using the techniques we discuss in Chapters 21 and 22, or open an existing file that contains a 3D model.

 You can find the files we use in this sequence of steps at this book's companion website. Go to www.dummies.com/go/autocad2013fd and download afd23.zip. The drawing named afd23a.dwg contains the model we use in the following steps.

3. **Switch to paper space.**

 Click the Layout 1 tab near the lower left of the screen.

4. **Delete the existing viewport by clicking the viewport object (the frame of the viewport) and then pressing Delete.**

 By default, new drawings created from a standard template file contain a single viewport. If you're going to be creating new drawings like this quite a bit, we suggest that you set up a template file with the viewport already deleted. We cover templates in Chapter 4.

5. **Start the VIEWBASE command.**

 Click the Base button from the Create View panel of the Layout tab of the Ribbon and then choose From Model Space from the drop-down list.

 The VIEWBASE command creates several new layers. By default, they are the opposite of the screen color, black or white, but they always print black. You can change these layers to any color you want.

6. **Position the base view.**

 AutoCAD automatically selects what it thinks is an appropriate scale, assuming that you'll be placing the standard three orthographic views and one pictorial view. However, this can be changed. Select a suitable place in the lower-left quadrant of the layout sheet.

7. **Define the base view.**

 The Drawing View Creation contextual tab appears on the Ribbon as shown in Figure 23-2, a drop-down list of view options appears at your cursor, and an option list appears in the command window.

Figure 23-2: The Drawing View Creation context tab of the Ribbon.

Using any one of the three selection methods — Ribbon, cursor, or command window — set up the base view as follows:

- *Orientation:* The view shows what appears to be the bottom view of the part because AutoCAD defines top, bottom, and so on relative to the world X, Y coordinates. Select Orientation and the Top to get the view you want.

- *Hidden lines:* The preview image in paper space always displays in shaded mode no matter what the visual style of the model shows in model space. You want Hidden Lines to be Visible and Hidden. The view won't change yet, but don't worry, it will.

- *Scale:* This has defaulted to 1:4, which is suitable for our purposes.

- *Visibility,* or *Edge Visibility:* This specifies how to display edges that are formed where tangent surfaces meet. Normal practice is often to not display them, but this can sometimes cause features to disappear or partially disappear. If you do change this setting, we recommend that you do so from the Edge Visibility button of the Appearance panel of the Ribbon because if you hover your cursor over this button and pause for a few seconds, it produces a much more extensive tooltip list that explains each option in more detail.

- *Move:* Specify a new location for the view before it is finally created. This isn't such a big deal, though, because views can always be easily moved later.

 Exit (or press Enter)

 Any of these view specifications can be edited later on a view-by-view basis.

Hey, what happened? The command didn't end!

8. **Place the other drawing views.**

 When you finish placing and defining the base view, AutoCAD automatically shifts into running the VIEWPROJ command. All you need is three quick clicks to place the top, isometric, and right-side views, and then press Enter to have AutoCAD generate the views.

9. **Edit the isometric view.**

 Isometric views don't normally show hidden lines. Double-click anywhere within the isometric view to bring up the Drawing View Editor tab of the Ribbon, as shown in Figure 23-3.

 Click Hidden Lines on the Appearance tab and then choose Shaded with Visible Lines from the drop-down list.

 If a Ribbon button has a drop-down list, the Ribbon displays the last button that was used. There may be any one of four different buttons in this particular location.

Figure 23-3: The Drawing View Editor context tab of the Ribbon.

10. **Stop the clock.**

Not bad. Figure 23-4 shows three ortho views and a shaded isomeric view that were created in 37.6 seconds.

Figure 23-4: Average creation time was 9.4 seconds per view.

11. **Add annotations.**

Add dimensions and text notes in the paper space layout. Dimensions are associative to their matching geometry if you use object snaps to the geometry when you place them. We cover text in Chapter 13, dimensions in Chapter 14, and object snaps in Chapter 7. While you're at it, perhaps use VIEWDETAIL to create a detail view at a different scale.

12. **Go home, gloat, and come back in three days.**

When you submit your drawing, shown in Figure 23-1, to your boss, she will be impressed that you managed to create such a complex drawing, including the shaded isometric view, in only three days.

Text and dimensions should go on their own layers. We discuss layers in Chapter 6.

An isometric *view* and an isometric *projection* are different. An isometric view is normally drawn so that lines that are parallel to the three principal axes appear in their true length, while an isometric projection foreshortens them due to the tilting and rotating of the viewing angle of the object. AutoCAD creates isometric projections.

If you really want an isometric view, the solution is simply to ignore our usual rule about drawing and inserting full size. When creating an isometric projection, use a scale factor of approximately 1.2247441227836356744839797834917, and you will get an isometric view. You can also edit the insertion later to make it match this scale factor.

A different point of view

You can apply two different types of editing to 2D views that were generated from 3D models.

First, you can edit the view specifications themselves. Start with the easy one. Select the base view, and then select the blue grip box that appears in the center of the view. Now drag and drop the view to a new location. Interesting! If you move the base view, all the ortho views projected from it follow along, with some constraints. The ortho views don't move in perfect unison as a single group, but they do maintain their orthographic relationship to the base view. Similarly, you can move projected ortho views in only the one direction that still maintains their ortho relationship to the base view. Better yet, all (or at least hopefully all) the attached dimensions also follow along.

You can also double-click a view and then change pretty much all the specifications that were used to create it. We did this in Step 9 (in the earlier step list) when we changed the isometric view to a shaded representation.

Now we come to the magic of creating 2D views from a 3D model. Go back into model space and edit the model. For example, add a second hole (hint: subtract a cylinder), extend the length of the peg, and then return to the paper space layout. Presto! Figure 23-5 shows how all your views and their dimensions have updated!

AutoCAD creates the views as a series of *anonymous* blocks. They behave much like regular blocks, but they don't have a normal name, and so you can't access them directly to edit or explode them. We discuss blocks in Chapter 17.

Figure 23-5: If anything changes then everything changes.

But wait! There's more!

So far, we've just touched on the 3D-to-2D capabilities of AutoCAD, but hopefully, it has whetted your appetite for more. To fully cover the 3D capabilities of AutoCAD would easily require a full book on its own (*AutoCAD 3D For Dummies*, perhaps?), but meanwhile here are a few high spots:

- ✔ **Don't want four views?** If you don't want four standard views, you can create only the base view and then change its scale factor to better suit the sheet size.

- ✔ **Need additional base views?** If necessary, you can have more than one base view in a single layout. For example, one large drawing might show an assembly and its component parts.

- ✔ **Didn't create enough views?** Use the VIEWPROJ command to add more projected views later. They don't have to project from the original base view, but can project from an existing projected view.

- ✔ **Don't need a view any more?** You can delete a view, even a base view, without affecting the other views except that doing so breaks the horizontal and vertical links between views that were projected from it.

- ✔ **No 3D model in your drawing?** Earlier in this chapter, we used the VIEWBASE command to generate views from a 3D model that lived in model space of the current drawing. AutoCAD 2013 introduces new functionality that is so significant that it deserves more explanation, which we happily provide in the next section of this chapter.

AutoCAD's top model

You generated 2D drawing views from a 3D model in the previous exercise. In that example there was already a 3D model in model space. If the VIEWBASE command cannot find a 3D model in your current drawing file, then it opens a standard file dialog box so you can browse for an Inventor part or assembly file.

Inventor is the Autodesk 3D parametric modeling software, primarily intended for the mechanical design field. It is fully parametric, in that dimensional constraints drive the profiles that define the solid features that comprise the parts that go into the assembly model that drives the 2D drawing views that Jack built. If you change a dimension on a 2D drawing of a part, *everything* updates all the way down the line.

The Inventor file isn't inserted into the AutoCAD file. Instead, it is attached like an xref. (We cover xrefs and DWG files in Chapter 18.) VIEWBASE creates a 2D drawing view based on it, and additional views can be projected from the base view.

Now here's the magic part. The AutoCAD drawing views are still linked back to the Inventor file so that any changes made to the Inventor file reflect down to the AutoCAD file, bringing it up-to-date.

Better yet, you can send the AutoCAD DWG file to a client or vendor without having to send the source Inventor file. The AutoCAD file contains only anonymous blocks for the 2D views, and has nothing in model space.

On the other hand, whenever the AutoCAD DWG file does have access to the Inventor file the AutoCAD drawing views will update and stay in step with any changes made to the Inventor model.

If VIEWBASE does find an AutoCAD solid in your part you can tell it to ignore it and to let you attach to an Inventor file instead. You can have more than one base view in an AutoCAD drawing, so you can mix and match 2D drawing views. One or more base views can come from an internal AutoCAD 3D model, while others can be linked to external Inventor files.

↳ If model space contains more than one solid, VIEWBASE allows you to switch back to model space, where you can select and unselect solids to appear in the base view. For example, you might have a model of a gearbox assembly consisting of many components. Separate views can be created, perhaps on several different layouts. One might show an outside view of the entire gearbox (which doesn't need to include the internals such as the gears and bearings); another shows only the input shaft, gear, bearings, and seals; and another shows the output shaft and its related components.

↳ The VIEWDETAIL command generates detail views at scales different from the parent view.

✔ The VIEWSECTION command has five options for creating section views: Full, Half, Offset, Aligned, and From Object. It creates section views based on existing views in the layout. The cutting plane line that it generates can be manipulated like any regular polyline, and the section view then updates accordingly.

But wait! There's less!

AutoCAD has gone through several generations of tools to produce 2D views from 3D objects. Each generation generally got better. We list them here because they all still work, and you may encounter older drawings that were made by using them.

✔ **FLATSHOT:** This produces a quick-and-dirty 2D view in model space. Basically, it just sets the Z axis coordinate to 0 (zero) of objects. It creates suitable new layers and then creates a block definition and inserts it.

- *Pro:* If you edit the model, you can run it again and redefine the block.

- *Cons:* It can't create section views, and it takes some complex fiddling to get multiple views to face and align correctly.

✔ **SolView** (Solid View), **SolDraw** (Solid Draw) **SolProf** (Solid Profile), and **MVSetup** (Multi-View Setup): This series of commands is used to create suitable layout viewports and then to generate appropriate 2D views into them. The views are created as anonymous blocks.

- *Pros:* They can produce simple cross-section views, and they are produced directly in layout viewports.

- *Cons:* The commands must be used in a specific order, and the views aren't associative back to the model. If you edit the model, you have to delete the views and start over.

✔ **SectionPlane**, **LiveSection**, **SectionPlaneJog**, and **SectionPlaneToBlock:** This family of commands is used to create a series of blocks containing 2D views, much like FlatShot but with much more versatility and control.

- *Pros:* They can produce more-sophisticated cross sections, such as jogged section planes. If you change the model, the block definitions can be re-created to show the updated version.

- *Cons:* It takes some complex fiddling to get multiple views to face and align correctly.

All in all, the current family of commands that we use in this chapter is by far the best way of producing 2D drawings from 3D models.

Do You See What I See?

In the computer graphics world, *rendering* is the process of illuminating a set of 3D objects with one or more imaginary lights and then creating a more-or-less realistic picture of the results. (No, computer programmers didn't have lard on their minds when they borrowed the word *rendering*. Hand-drawn pictures of building facades were called renderings long before computers got into the act.)

A single example of this technique is called a *still rendering*. Multiple frames strung together produce computer animation. The objects that you see in movies such as *Avatar* or *How to Tame Your Dragon* are first created as 3D models and then rendered frame by frame. This process can take immense amounts of time even on ultrafast graphics workstations, and a major movie is usually done on rendering farms of 20,000–30,000 computers (that's right; 20 to 30 thousand!).

AutoCAD is best at creating still renderings. If you want to create photorealistic rendered animations, you need to use other software programs, such as Autodesk 3ds Max. Even if you use other animation programs, AutoCAD can still be useful for developing the initial 3D models.

Rendering has steadily improved in speed and usability as PCs have become faster and programmers improved their rendering algorithms. Rendering simple scenes is now practical on a mainstream PC, and a fast PC can create some impressive images in a reasonable amount of time. Rendered images are useful for previewing how your models will work in real life and also can be powerful tools for sales and marketing communications for your company. A (rendered) picture can be worth quite a bit more than a thousand words, especially in today's economy.

People who do a lot of rendering and want higher-quality, photorealistic results usually use programs other than AutoCAD to render their models. Autodesk 3ds Max, Cinema 4D (Maxon), and AccuRender (Robert McNeel & Associates) are three popular photorealistic rendering programs. Most rendering programs can import 3D models from AutoCAD DWG files, but some people use specialized 3D modeling programs to do their modeling as well.

Visualizing the Digital World

Rendering allows you to see how a final product might look before it's manufactured or built in the real world (see Figure 23-6); it definitely helps to sell a concept to a client. Although you can show a client a hidden line or shaded view of a 3D model, showing a photorealistic render just helps make it feel that much more real when looking at it.

Figure 23-6: Rendering compared with Conceptual visual style.

Before rendering a 3D model, you need to do the following:

- ✔ **Add lighting to highlight features and define shadows.**
- ✔ **Apply materials to 3D objects by face, object, or layer.**
- ✔ **Set up a background for your 3D model to be rendered against.**

All the above-mentioned items help to bring realism to a 3D model. This chapter focuses on each of these tasks before covering the steps to create a rendering.

Adding Lighting

One of the key ingredients in the soup that makes a rendering look good is *lighting*. Lighting helps give a model depth through the use of highlights and shadows. Just as in the real world, objects that are closest to the light source appear the brightest and those the farthest away appear the darkest.

The two types of lighting in AutoCAD are default and user-defined. Default lighting, as its name suggests, is on and available in every drawing, and it's what gives some basic form to your 3D model when you click the Render button before you add lighting of your own. All types of user-defined lights can cast shadows. Most tools that you use to create and edit lights are located on the Lights and Sun & Location panels of the Render tab.

Default lighting

Over the past few years, AutoCAD's default lighting has improved in quality. Prior to AutoCAD 2007, default lighting consisted of a single, distant light source, always directed toward the target of your current view from behind your back. AutoCAD 2007 added a second default light to help increase the lighting level, and to balance the lighting in a viewport.

Default lighting can't cast shadows, so we don't recommend using it for final renderings. It *does* work pretty well for quick conceptual renderings, however. You can control the brightness, contrast, and midtones levels for default lighting with the slider controls on the slideout of the Lights panel on the Render tab of Ribbon (see Figure 23-7).

Figure 23-7: AutoCAD to lights, extra brightness is a go.

Use the DEFAULTLIGHTING system variable to enable and disable the use of default lighting in the current viewport. Set DEFAULTLIGHTING to 0 when you want user-defined lighting to render your 3D model. If you're using default lighting, the DEFAULTLIGHTINGTYPE system variable controls whether one or two default distant lights are used. When set to 0, one default light is used; when set to 1, two default lights are used.

User-defined lights

Default lights are fine for quick renderings, but they don't bring your render-ings to life in the way that user-defined lights can. User-defined lights are lights that you create — with one exception — and modify in your 3D model. The only user-definable light type that you can enable and modify, but can't create, is the sunlight system.

The first time that a user-defined light is placed in a drawing, the Lighting – Viewport Lighting Mode alert box is displayed, advising you that you need to turn off default lighting in order to see light from user-defined sources. Click Turn Off the Default Lighting to disable default lighting. (To turn default lighting back on, open the Lights panel slideout on the Render tab and click

Default Lighting.) You should always disable default lighting when using user-defined lights; otherwise you can end up overlighting your model, making it look unnatural.

The two types of user-defined lights that you can create are generic and photometric:

- **Generic lights:** Provide advanced control over how they emit light and are much more complex than photometric lights.

- **Photometric lights:** More convenient to use as they are defined to represent how lights work in the physical world.

The LIGHTINGUNITS system variable controls whether user-defined lights in your drawing are represented as generic or photometric lights. When LIGHTINGUNITS is set to 0, generic lights are used. When LIGHTINGUNITS is set to 1 or 2, photometric lights are used; 1 indicates American lighting units, and 2 indicates International lighting units. Lights don't have to be removed and added to switch between generic and photometric lights; you just need to switch the system variable.

To add a user-defined light to your drawing, click the lower half of the Create Light split button on the Lights panel of the Render tab. You can choose from four distinct types of lights on the flyout (for the differences between the light types, see Figure 23-8):

- **Point light:** Emits light uniformly in all directions, but the emitted light falls off the farther it gets from the source. A point light is similar to a candle or a lantern.

- **Spotlight:** Emits light in a specific direction. As light travels farther from the source, it spreads out in the shape of a cone. You can define the *hotspot* — the brightest part of the emitted light — and the fall-off of the light.

- **Distant light:** Emits light along a specified vector and doesn't decay or fall off like other user-defined lights do. A distant light is similar to the sun.

- **Weblight:** A cross between a point light and a spotlight. Weblights are available only when using photometric lights, and the way they emit light is determined by an IES file. IES files are provided by lighting companies for use in products like AutoCAD to mimic the lights that they manufacture.

Point light

Spotlight

Distant light

Weblight

Figure 23-8: Lighting primitives with the four types of user-defined lights.

AutoCAD and we both strongly advise against using distant lights when using photometric lighting. If you decide to ignore this warning, make sure to turn down the intensity factor of the distant light to avoid washing out your rendering.

Point lights, spotlights, and weblights can be selected and edited directly in a drawing because a glyph is displayed to show where the light is located. Distant lights do not have an associated glyph. (A *glyph* is a nonprinting object displayed in a drawing that enables you to select an object that is not part of the actual model.)

Shadows . . . or no shadows?

AutoCAD allows you to define lights that can't generate shadows. This might seem illogical because shadows are cast when light is obscured by an object. This is important because you may want to fill an area with light but not have it affect the way shadows are cast.

To control the shadows a light can generate, select a light, right-click, and then choose Properties to open the Properties palette. The Shadows option in the General category enables or disables shadow creation from the selected light. The Rendered Shadow Details category gives you a large degree of creative control over shadow appearance. For more information on putting your objects in the shade, open the online help and search on *Render 3D Objects for Realism*.

 You can also control how objects themselves affect shadows. Select a 3D object, right-click, and choose Properties. In the 3D Visualization category of the Properties palette, click the Shadow Display drop-down; you can configure your objects to cast shadows, receive shadows, cast *and* receive shadows, or ignore shadows altogether.

The Lights in Model palette

In a complex drawing or one in which you might have added a distant light, you'll want to use the Lights in Model palette (see Figure 23-9). The Lights in Model palette allows you to select, delete, and access the Properties palette for selected lights. To display the Lights in Model palette, click the Lights panel launcher (the little arrow at the right end of the Lights panel label).

Figure 23-9: Ah, yes, you're on the lights list.

Sunlight

You can simulate sunlight via the Sun Properties palette (see Figure 23-10). Adding sunlight to a drawing allows you to perform sunlight studies, as well as add some realism to both indoor and outdoor renderings.

The Sun Properties palette allows you to locate the sun's position based on the nearest large city, or by entering latitude and longitude values. You can also use Google Earth KML or KMZ files to specify your location. In addition to location, you can designate the northern direction in your drawing to get the correct daily movement of the sunlight in your drawing. To adjust the sunlight in a drawing, open the Sun Properties palette by clicking the Sun & Location panel launcher (the little arrow on the panel label).

Figure 23-10: The Sun Properties palette gives you the power to control day and night.

Creating and Applying Materials

Materials can bring your model to life. Materials can be as simple as paint — matte or glossy or anywhere between. You can apply representations of realistic, real-world materials like stone, marble, glass, polished metal, fabric . . . the list is almost endless. They can be opaque, transparent, reflective, or non-reflective. AutoCAD 2013 comes with a material library of literally thousands of different material types, and assigning them to objects can be as simple as dragging from a palette and dropping on an object. Or it can be as complex as you care to make it.

Prior to AutoCAD 2011, you created and stored materials in individual drawings, which made them difficult to manage. AutoCAD 2011 introduced the Materials Browser, which makes managing materials much easier. Material definitions now live in a central repository and are attached to each drawing as an external reference. In addition, all Autodesk products that use material

definitions use the same central library, so a model rendered in AutoCAD will look the same as one done in Inventor, Maya, or in 3ds Max.

Partnered with the Materials Browser is the Materials Editor, accessible from a tool button in the Materials Browser.

The material libraries introduced in AutoCAD 2011 took up vast amounts of hard drive space. That was seen as wasteful for people who never did renderings, so as of AutoCAD 2012, most of the material libraries are online. The first time you click the Render button in AutoCAD 2013, AutoCAD asks whether you want to go online to install the Medium Material Library. If rendering looks interesting to you, go ahead and install the library.

 Use the MATBROWSER command to display the Materials Browser palette (see Figure 23-11), from which you can create, edit, and manage in the current drawing or material libraries. You add materials to your drawing by using a preconfigured material or creating a custom material.

Follow these steps to create and manage a new material:

1. **On the Render tab, choose Materials Browser from the Materials panel.**

2. **On the Materials Browser palette that opens, click Create a Material (in the upper left) and then choose the material template you want to start with. For example, choose Metallic Paint.**

 The Materials Editor palette is displayed (see Figure 23-11).

 3. **On the Materials Editor palette, click in the Name field located below the preview of the material and enter a name.**

4. **Enter new values in the appropriate attributes for the material.**

 The attributes that you can edit vary, based upon the type of material template that you choose to start with. When you finish editing the material, you can close or hide the Materials Editor palette. The material is automatically added to the current drawing.

5. **(Optional) Save the material in a library to use it in more than one drawing. On the Materials Browser palette, at the bottom, click Manage, and then select Create New Library.**

 The Create Library dialog box is displayed.

6. **Enter a name and location for the new library. Click Save.**

7. **On the Materials Browser palette, drag the custom material you created onto the name of the new library.**

 Now you can access the material from any drawing. You can create categories if you want to manage multiple materials within a library. In the Materials Browser, right-click the library name, choose Create Category,

and then enter a name for the new category. After the category is created, simply select the material from the right side of the Materials Browser and drag it to the new category.

Materials Browser palette Materials Editor palette

Figure 23-11: Adding color and texture to a 3D model with the Materials Browser palette (at the left) and the Materials Editor palette (to the right).

TIP

You can open the Materials Editor directly from the Ribbon by clicking the Materials panel launcher (the little arrow at the right end of the Materials panel label).

Which materials you use in a model depends on what you're trying to represent. For example, you might choose to make a material semitransparent to communicate an idea rather than a true material selection. After you create a material, you can apply it to the objects in your 3D model. You can apply materials to objects in the following ways:

✔ **By Layer:** Globally assign materials to all objects on a particular drawing layer by assigning a material to the layer. To assign materials by layer, open the Materials slideout on the Render tab and choose Attach by Layer.

✔ **By Object:** Assign materials to an object by selecting the object and then right-clicking the material you want to assign in the Materials Browser palette. From the menu that appears, choose Assign to Selection. You

can also drag and drop a material from the Materials Browser palette onto an object in a drawing or change an object's Material property by using the Properties palette.

🖊 **By Face:** Assign materials to individual faces of a 3D solid. Select a face using Subobject filtering by holding down the Ctrl key and selecting the face you want to apply a material to. Right-click the material you want to assign in the Materials Browser palette and then choose Assign to Selection from the menu that appears.

Defining a Background

While your model might now be looking a little more realistic with some user-defined lighting and custom materials assigned to it, its setting might look a little, well, empty. You can assign backgrounds to fill that empty space beyond the 3D model in your scene. A background is a property of named views, and you can set them up in the View Manager dialog box. (We cover the VIEW command and View Manager dialog box in Chapter 12.) You can define a background as a solid color, a gradient (two or three colors), a raster image, or a sky with a sun (available only when using photometric lighting).

Follow these steps to create a new named view and assign a background to it:

1. **On the Views panel of the View tab, click Named Views.**

 The View Manager dialog box appears.

2. **Click New to display the New View/Shot Properties dialog box.**

 For a refresher on creating named views, see Chapter 12.

3. **In the Background area, click the Default drop-down, choose an option to override the default background, and then click OK.**

 Choose Solid or Gradient if you want a studio-type scene, or choose Image if you have a suitable raster image to highlight your model. Any of these options displays the Background dialog box where you make your settings (see Figure 23-12). Choose Sun & Sky if you want to place your model in the great outdoors (and it's always fair weather in AutoCAD!). Choosing the last option displays the Adjust Sun & Sky Background dialog box, as shown in Figure 23-13.

4. **After the background is defined, select the view from the Views tree and click Set Current.**

5. **When the View Manager closes, the new background should be displayed.**

 For more information on the View Manager, see Chapter 12.

Figure 23-12: Painting the canvas of the drawing window.

Figure 23-13: Here comes the sun.

> If you don't want to create a named view first, enter the BACKGROUND command at the command line to display the Background dialog box.

Rendering a 3D Model

After you add lights, apply materials, and define a background for your 3D model, you're ready to press the magic button! Clicking Render tells AutoCAD to round up all the materials and apply them to the objects and faces to which they're assigned. After materials are assigned, the background is applied to the current viewport, and then finally AutoCAD calculates light and shadows based on all those property settings you made earlier in the chapter.

By default, rendering is performed in the Render Window (see Figure 23-14). To start rendering your virtual fat into digital lard (and how's that for a grisly image?), click Render on the Render tab's Render panel (another offering from the Department of Redundancy Department)

To help make rendering as easy as possible, AutoCAD comes with five render presets. A *render preset* is a configuration of rendering settings that you can use to get predictable results when rendering a model. The presets range in quality of output, from Draft through Low, Medium, and High to Presentation quality.

Figure 23-14: Rendering a rendering in the Render Window.

To set a render preset current, choose the Render Presets drop-down on the Render tab's Render panel. Choose Manage Render Presets at the bottom of the Render Presets drop-down to open the Render Presets Manager dialog box. The Render Presets Manager allows you to create and edit custom render presets. You can start with an existing render preset when you create a new one.

If the render presets don't seem to offer the look you're striving for, you can experiment with the Advanced Render Settings palette (see Figure 23-15). When you get the settings you like, you can save them to a render preset.

Medium		
General		
Render Context		
Procedure	View	
Destination	Window	
Output file name		
Output size	640 x 480	
Exposure Type	Automatic	
Physical Scale	1500.0000	
Materials		
Apply materials	On	
Texture filtering	On	
Force 2-sided	On	
Sampling		
Shadows		
Mode	Simple	
Shadow map	Off	
Sampling Multiplier	1/2	
Ray Tracing		
Max depth	5	
Max reflections	5	
Max refractions	5	
Indirect Illumination		
Diagnostic		
Processing		

Advanced Render Settings

Figure 23-15: The Advanced Render Settings palette gives you control over all the settings of the rendering process.

In addition to rendering a still image with the RENDER or RENDERCROP commands, you can create an animated walk-through of your model by using the ANIPATH. To find out more about creating animations, see the AutoCAD online help system.

Part VI
The Part of Tens

ens sounds a lot like *tense,* and *tense* is how AutoCAD may make you feel sometimes. *Tens* also may remind you of the metric system, and if you're not used to it, that may also make you feel tense. But never fear — help is on the way! A top ten list is a good way to quickly point out the best — or the worst — of almost anything, AutoCAD included. This Part of Tens features lists that help you understand some of the nuts and bolts that make AutoCAD work, figure out whether you should be using AutoCAD or AutoCAD LT, and hunt for the most valuable AutoCAD resources.

Ten Great AutoCAD Resources

Much as we'd like to make a claim to the contrary, you probably *do* need just a teensy bit more than this book and a copy of the software and the software's help system to reach the very highest peaks of AutoCAD mastery! This chapter lists ten likely aids if you want to find out more about your favorite software program.

Autodesk Feedback Community

Interested in helping shape future releases of AutoCAD? If so, visit Autodesk's Feedback Community Portal (`https://beta.autodesk.com`) and sign up by clicking the New Users Click Here link. In return for small — or sometimes considerable — time commitments, you can contribute your ideas to the AutoCAD Futures group or apply to beta-test the next release of AutoCAD.

Autodesk Discussion Groups

Although some independent, newsreader-based discussion groups are still out there, the majority of the AutoCAD action nowadays happens on Autodesk's own moderated discussion groups. These are user-to-user groups, but even so, you frequently see Autodesk employees jumping in to answer questions in their areas of expertise — sometimes on their own time!

To see what's there, point your browser to `www.autodesk.com/discussion`. You'll find product-based discussion groups for AutoCAD and AutoCAD LT.

Autodesk's Own Bloggers

Several Autodesk employees run their own blogs through the company's servers, and they're chockablock with tips, techniques, and some occasionally highly entertaining digressions. For a list of all Autodesk blogs, go to www.autodesk.com/blogs. The AutoCAD-based blogs we highly recommend are Shaan Hurley's Between the Lines, Heidi Hewitt's AutoCAD Insider, Kate Morrical's LT Unlimited, and Lynn Allen's Blog (that's what it's called, honest!).

Autodesk University

Autodesk University (AU) is an annual event sponsored by Autodesk that usually runs for three or four days around the end of November. For the past few years, the event has settled in Las Vegas, Nevada. If your boss balks at sending you, just quote a few figures: At AU 2011, about 700 instructors presented almost 1,000 classes to more than 8,000 attendees on virtually every conceivable topic related to virtually every Autodesk product. Add in almost 300 exhibitors showing their wares in about 180 booths, plus the AU support staff and techies, and you end up sitting down for lunch with about 10,000 of your best friends. The meals and the evening social sessions are a great time for networking with your peers, and you can often end up learning as much as you do in the classes. Check out http://au.autodesk.com to find out how to schmooze like a pro and come home a guru!

The Autodesk Channel on YouTube

If you use Google to search the web for solutions to particular AutoCAD issues, you've probably already discovered the YouTube Autodesk Channel. You'll find dozens and dozens of video clips here that cover not only AutoCAD and AutoCAD LT, but also other Autodesk products like Inventor and Revit. You can subscribe and receive e-mail notifications of new videos every couple of weeks. Check it out at www.youtube.com/autodesk.

The World Wide (CAD) Web

We're reluctant to list any specific sites because they tend to come and go, but *Cadalyst* magazine (www.cadalyst.com) has been in existence for over 25 years. In particular, click the CAD Software Tutorials link to go to a series

of tutorials called *Circles and Lines,* by Lynn Allen, and *The Learning Curve,* by Bill Fane.

Your favorite search engine can also be a good friend. Apart from Autodesk's own web presence, thousands upon thousands of other sites are scattered around the world. Search by entering *AutoCAD tutorials* for online exercises, or try *AutoCAD blogs* for some independent views and opinions as well as tips and tricks for using AutoCAD.

Your Local ATC

Autodesk Authorized Training Centers (ATCs) are located around the world in both private institutions and public colleges and institutes. At an ATC, you attend scheduled, instructor-led classes where you learn AutoCAD from the ground up. Courses are designed for rank beginners or experienced users who want to learn the latest customization techniques. To find the location of your nearest ATC, browse to www.autodesk.com/atc.

Your Local User Group

AutoCAD has had an incredibly loyal following in the quarter century since its initial release. Of the many reasons why, a main one is the especially enthusiastic individuals who arranges to meet one evening per month and talk about what they discovered they could do with AutoCAD. Those folks are still out there — although some are a bit grayer and more wrinkled than they used to be — and they still love to get together and talk about AutoCAD. And most are especially welcoming to newcomers! Our own local group, the Vancouver AutoCAD Users Society (www.vaus.org), happens to be the first (and therefore oldest) user group in existence, and its newsletter grew and grew until it became *Cadalyst* magazine! To find a nearby group, enter *AutoCAD user group* and your city in your browser's search box.

AUGI

Autodesk User Groups International (AUGI) is the umbrella organization for the global user group community. You don't even have to belong to a group to participate — individuals can join too, and membership is free. AUGI is probably best known for the annual wish list it presents to Autodesk; the list is compiled from requests from members for changes or new features in AutoCAD. It's often the case that top wish-list items find their way into new

releases of AutoCAD, so here's another place where you can help to shape future releases. Browse to www.augi.com to find out more.

AUGI also supports a series of online and live training sessions, and your free membership will get you a discounted rate to attend Autodesk University.

Books

Although we'd like to fill you in on *all* the wonders of AutoCAD, we can do only so much in a 500-page book. As we explain in the Introduction, we simply don't have the space to cover things like data linking and customization, not that either of those is of much use to AutoCAD LT users anyway. There are dozens of books on AutoCAD — just go to www.amazon.com and search on *AutoCAD* if you don't believe us! For a more comprehensive look at AutoCAD (which a thousand pages allows!), have a gander at Ellen Finkelstein's *AutoCAD 2012 and AutoCAD LT 2012 Bible* (John Wiley & Sons, Inc.). Ralph Grabowski, our technical editor for this book, also has a number of specialized e-books at www.upfrontezine.com/ebooks.

Ten (Or So) Differences between AutoCAD and AutoCAD LT

 This book is aimed at users of both the full version of AutoCAD and AutoCAD LT. Throughout the text, you find icons in the margin that highlight places in our descriptions or steps that are significantly different between the two versions.

*R*ather than make you go through the entire text (not that it wouldn't be a highly rewarding task!) looking for tidbits of information, in this chapter we gather the ten most significant differences between the two versions.

Price

Most important to many people — especially if you work in 2D drafting exclusively and don't see a need to spend a lot of time learning AutoCAD's customization languages or 3D capabilities — is the much lower cost of AutoCAD LT. You can buy either version online (visit www.autodesk.com and click Purchase, and then click Shop Online).

Ortho: 0.8085 < 90°

3D Abilities

This may be the most significant difference for some users. If you want to model in 3D, you have no choice but to use the full version. In AutoCAD LT, you can open and view 3D models created in the full version of AutoCAD, but you can't create new ones or edit them, other than to move, copy, or delete them. The only 3D construction you can do in AutoCAD LT is to apply a thickness (height) property to line work. (In AutoCAD, *thickness* means *perpendicular* to the drawing plane; don't confuse it with *width*, which applies to objects *on* the drawing plane.)

And even if you can open 3D models from the full version in AutoCAD LT, it's not easy to view them. Only a limited number of preset viewing positions are available, unlike the full version where you can rotate or orbit around your model to your heart's content.

Finally, because AutoCAD LT is really a 2D drafting program, it has minimal visualization or presentation capabilities, while the full program can display 3D models in several built-in visual styles ranging from a simple wireframe mode through to full photorealistic rendering complete with shadows, reflections, and a humongous materials library.

Customization Options

This one is also a biggie for many people. Talk to seasoned AutoCAD users at work or your local user group, and you'll find that their key to happiness is being able to customize AutoCAD so it does what they want with minimum amounts of time or effort. The full version of AutoCAD supports a number of *Application Programming Interfaces,* or *APIs.* These include AutoCAD's very own programming language — AutoLISP — and its marginally friendlier sibling Visual LISP, ActiveX Automation, and compiled language programming using ObjectARX or Microsoft's .NET framework.

Although you can do simple customization in AutoCAD LT — for example, creating or modifying toolbars, writing scripts, or using custom hatch patterns or linetypes — none of the higher-level programming described in the preceding paragraph is possible in LT.

Network Licensing

Once again, the paradigm is big engineering company versus home-office doodler, and the assumption is that AutoCAD LT users have no need for a network license. With regular AutoCAD, you can get a network license that makes things pretty easy to administer. For example, you can have a 10-seat license that lets AutoCAD run on any 10 out of the 20 machines in your office, providing no more than 10 run at one time. If you're an LT user and you have 20 machines in your office, you'll need 20 licenses, one per machine, even if there are never more than 10 copies of AutoCAD running at one time.

Express Tools

The Express Tools are a set of officially unsupported but nevertheless reliable bonus commands. They include useful utilities and previews of functionality that may end up built right in to future versions of AutoCAD. There are additional drawing and editing commands, a far more elaborate hatch routine

than the regular HATCH command, and commands for working with blocks and xrefs, text, dimensions, and layouts.

Because most of the Express Tools are written by using the APIs mentioned in the "Customization Options" section, they won't work in AutoCAD LT. On the positive side, sometimes a few of the Express Tools are moved into the core of the AutoCAD executable; because they're not using one of those APIs we mention earlier, they can be made available to AutoCAD LT. For example, AutoCAD LT 2012 added the OVERKILL command for weeding out duplicate objects that had previously been an Express Tool.

Parametrics

We cover parametrics in Chapter 19 of this book, and we point out that AutoCAD LT is extremely limited in this area. Yes, there's a Parametric tab, and a Parameters Manager, but in LT, the Manager doesn't have a lot of clout. You can't create parameters with LT, but you *can* delete them, and therefore do a lot of damage to a helpless DWG file. If you like the idea of your drawing geometry changing when you change the value of a dimension, then you really ought to think about the full version of AutoCAD rather than LT.

Standards Checking

Standards — as in *drafting standards* — are important to maintain in design offices. With standards checking, you configure a DWS file (a DWG file set up with your standard layers, text, and dimension styles, layouts, and so forth), and then compare your current drawing, or drawings done by outside consultants, with that DWS file to ensure that they conform to your office standards. AutoCAD LT doesn't support standards checking.

Data Extraction

As we explain in Chapter 17, attributes are variable text strings that you create as part of a block definition. The data in the attributes can be edited or extracted easily in regular AutoCAD and nearly as easily in AutoCAD LT, but AutoCAD LT lacks the full version's Data Extraction Wizard, which extracts information from objects and from attributed or nonattributed blocks. If the ability to use *all* the data in your AutoCAD drawings is important, choose the full version.

MLINE versus DLINE

Here's a case where AutoCAD LT beats its big sibling! AutoCAD (full version) includes an extremely unwieldy command called MLINE for drawing multiple

parallel lines. You can draw such lines in the same way you pick points for the LINE command, but multilines are unintuitive to configure and pretty darned difficult to edit.

AutoCAD LT doesn't have MLINE, but it does have a different command called DLINE. DLINE (Double LINE) may not draw more than two parallel lines, and it can't add colored fills, but it's logical to use and much easier to edit. And sorry, AutoCAD users (we've been waiting to write that for the whole book!), but you don't have DLINE.

Profiles

Throughout the book we reference the Options dialog box. This is the place where you make both drawing-specific and systemwide settings so you can configure the program to work the way you want. In the full version of AutoCAD, you can save these settings as named profiles and switch between them on the Profiles tab of the Options dialog box. For example, you can have one profile with a white drawing background and another with a dark background. Or you can have different profiles that point to different client support files. If more than one person shares a computer, each person can have his or her own profile.

You'll find profiles only in the full version, though — there is no Profiles tab in AutoCAD LT's Options dialog box, because AutoCAD LT doesn't support profiles. Any changes you make to LT's options become the current defaults, but they can't be saved and restored later.

Reference Manager

Reference Manager is a free-standing program that isn't part of AutoCAD or AutoCAD LT. If you have the full version installed, you'll find Reference Manager on the Windows Start menu. Reference Manager helps you make sure that any dependent files (for example, font files, images, or xrefs) are included when you ship a set of files anywhere. There's no technical reason why AutoCAD LT shouldn't include the Reference Manager; but it doesn't. On the other hand, if you have both AutoCAD and AutoCAD LT in your office, then you can use the Reference Manager on drawings created by LT, and why not, because AutoCAD and AutoCAD LT use the same file format.

And The Good News Is . . .

Unless you mess with things, particularly as indicated in the 3D and parametrics sections, drawings will survive a round trip out to LT and back to standard AutoCAD.

Ten System Variables to Make Your Life Easier

*S*ystem variables are settings that AutoCAD checks before it decides how to do something. For example, if you set the system variable SAVETIME to 10, AutoCAD saves your drawing file automatically every ten minutes; if you set SAVETIME to 60, the time between automatic saves is one hour. Hundreds of system variables control AutoCAD's operations.

Most system variables are controlled by the Options command, but you can also change the value of a system variable just by typing its name at the AutoCAD command prompt and pressing Enter. AutoCAD displays the current value of the system variable setting and prompts for a new value. Press Enter to confirm the existing setting, or type a value and press Enter to change the setting.

The three kinds of system variables in the AutoCAD world are

- ✔ **Those saved in the Windows Registry:** If you change this kind of system variable, it affects all drawings when you open them on your system, but not necessarily on other computers.

- ✔ **Those saved in the drawing:** If you change this kind of system variable, the change affects only the current drawing, but on any computer. The drawing icon in the Options command dialog box indicates those that are saved in the drawing. If you change these and then save the drawing as a template, all subsequent drawings started from this template will inherit these values. We cover templates in Chapter 4.

- ✔ **Those not saved anywhere:** If you change this kind of system variable, the change lasts only for the current drawing session.

The System Variables section of the online help's Command Reference tells you which kind of system variable each one is. There are several hundred system variables, but understanding those listed in this chapter will help make you a happy CADster.

APERTURE

APERTURE controls how close the crosshairs must get to an object before an object snap marker appears. (We discuss object snaps in Chapter 7.) You can set APERTURE at the command line anywhere from 0 to 50 pixels, or you can set it in the Options dialog box by adjusting a slider to a maximum of 20 pixels. The default value is 10.

DIMASSOC

DIMASSOC controls how AutoCAD's dimension objects are created (see Chapter 14 for the lowdown on dimensioning). When DIMASSOC is 0, AutoCAD creates exploded dimensions of separate lines, 2D solids, and text. You really don't want to work on DIMASSOC=0 drawings. When DIMASSOC=1, dimensions are referred to as *non-associative* — that means that they're single objects, but they usually don't update if you change an object's size. When DIMASSOC=2 (the default), AutoCAD creates fully associative dimensions. You can set this value at the command line or select the Make New Dimensions Associative check box after choosing Options⇨User Preferences. If you work with older drawings, you'll likely find that the DIMASSOC value is 1, which is the best that releases prior to AutoCAD 2002 could manage. The DIMASSOC setting is stored in the drawing.

MENUBAR

When MENUBAR is 1, AutoCAD displays its traditional classic menu bar below the application title bar. If MENUBAR is set to 0 (the default), the menu bar doesn't appear. MENUBAR is set automatically when you switch between the AutoCAD Classic and Drafting & Annotation workspaces.

If you've been away from AutoCAD for a few years and feel in need of training wheels while you get used to the Ribbon, displaying the classic menu bar is a good approach. (We describe the differences between the traditional AutoCAD Classic and the newer Ribbon-based workspaces in Chapter 2.)

MIRRTEXT

You've got to love it when a system variable's name gives you a clear indication of what it does (ROLLOVERTIPS, anyone?). You'll frequently want to build up a drawing by mirroring already-drawn components of it. That's what the MIRROR command does. Luckily, AutoCAD is smart enough to realize that most of the time you don't want to produce a mirror image of any text that may be included among the set of objects you are mirroring. Having to use a mirror to read the text on your drawing is counterproductive.

On the other hand, suppose you want to draw the mold for a cast part and the finished part has some text molded in it, such as a company name or a part number. The text features in the mold need to be mirror images so the final cast text will read correctly. No problem. Simply set the MIRRTEXT system variable to 1 and now the MIRROR command will mirror the text. When MIRRTEXT is 0 (the default), text is not mirrored and the text still reads the right way around. MIRRTEXT is stored in the drawing.

OSNAPZ

Sometimes drawing in 3D can be a little puzzling, especially if you're looking at 3D objects in orthographic views. Say you have a wireframe cube that you're looking at in Plan view, and you want to draw a line between two diagonal corners on the top of the cube. Using object snaps to pick the corners, as often as not you'll find that you have a line that's not on the plane of the top of the box, but starts at a top corner and ends at a bottom corner. One way around this problem is to set the OSNAPZ variable appropriately. By default, OSNAPZ is set to 0, which means AutoCAD will find the X, Y, and Z coordinate of the snapped-to point. But often you don't want that to happen. Set OSNAPZ to 1, and AutoCAD replaces the Z value of the picked point with the *current* elevation — or the Z value of the first point picked.

Because OSNAPZ affects drawing in three dimensions, it's not available in AutoCAD LT.

PICKBOX

The *pickbox* is the little square box that the crosshairs turn into when AutoCAD prompts you to select something. You control pickbox size by setting a value in pixels for the PICKBOX variable. The initial setting of PICKBOX is 3, which is fine for a lower screen resolution like 1024 x 768. But when you start running at higher resolutions — or when your hair is grayer, your face

more wrinkled, and your vision not *quite* as acute as it once was — a higher setting might be more useful.

REMEMBERFOLDERS

Sometimes, you don't want AutoCAD to start in the same Documents folder where every other program stores its files. Maybe you work on a number of projects and would like a separate desktop icon for each to start in a particular folder. REMEMBERFOLDERS is your ticket to Nirvana. By default, it's set to 1, which means it defaults to storing files in My Documents (just plain Documents in Windows Vista and Windows 7). Set it to 0, and it will open from and save to the folder you specify in your desktop icon when you start, and the last folder you visit as you work. REMEMBERFOLDERS is stored in the Windows Registry.

ROLLOVERTIPS

You were waiting for this one, weren't you? ROLLOVERTIPS controls the tooltiplike message boxes you see when you hover the mouse pointer over objects in the drawing editor. If ROLLOVERTIPS is 1, mousing over your drawing displays a temporary panel showing the object type with its layer, color, and linetype. If, like us, you find this a little intrusive, set its value to 0.

You can get double duty from this command. Not only can you key it into AutoCAD, but if you have a dog named Tips, you can also use it to teach him a neat pet trick! ROLLOVERTIPS is stored in the Windows Registry. (And believe it or not — and we bet you won't — there's another system variable called NOMUTT! Could that be AutoCAD-ese for BAD DOG TIPS!?)

TOOLTIPS

Tooltips themselves are the little text boxes that appear (by default, anyway) when you hover your mouse pointer over a toolbar or Ribbon button, or just about anywhere in a dialog box. Tooltips are really useful when you're getting to know your way around a program, but when you have a sense of where things are, they can get in the way. By default, TOOLTIPS is set to 1, which means that they appear when you hover the mouse pointer over something. Set TOOLTIPS to 0 if you don't want to see them again. The TOOLTIPS setting is stored in the Windows Registry.

VISRETAIN

If you work with xrefs (refer to Chapter 18), you know the potential for competing layer properties. Sometimes, you want your xref to look different from your current drawing so you can tell which is which. You can change layer colors of xrefs in the Layer Property Manager, but whether you have to do that every time you open a drawing with an attached xref depends on the setting of the VISRETAIN system variable. When VISRETAIN is set to 0, the layer properties in the xref take precedence, which means that you *would* have to make those changes every time you opened the host drawing. When VISRETAIN is set to 1 (the default value), changes you make to layer properties in the host drawing remain intact every time you open that host drawing; however, those changes have no effect on the external file itself. The VISRETAIN value is stored in the current drawing.

And the Bonus Round

Here are two system variables that may not help your productivity, but are a bit of fun.

MTJIGSTRING allows you to substitute up to ten characters of your choice to replace the usual *abc* prompt when you start the MTEXT command. For example, *I'm great!* just fits.

The final one is invoked slightly differently. Enter **(setvar "screenmenu" 1)** to turn on the officially dead screen menu from years ago. It is fast, having no icons or tooltips, and is fully context-sensitive. No more right-click to get command options because it was created before three-button mice existed. No matter how you start a command, its options appear automatically. The bad news is that it hasn't been updated in years because it's officially dead.

Index

Apple & Mac

iPad 2 For Dummies,
3rd Edition
978-1-118-17679-5

iPhone 4S For Dummies,
5th Edition
978-1-118-03671-6

iPod touch For Dummies,
3rd Edition
978-1-118-12960-9

Mac OS X Lion
For Dummies
978-1-118-02205-4

Blogging & Social Media

CityVille For Dummies
978-1-118-08337-6

Facebook For Dummies,
4th Edition
978-1-118-09562-1

Mom Blogging
For Dummies
978-1-118-03843-7

Twitter For Dummies,
2nd Edition
978-0-470-76879-2

WordPress For Dummies,
4th Edition
978-1-118-07342-1

Business

Cash Flow For Dummies
978-1-118-01850-7

Investing For Dummies,
6th Edition
978-0-470-90545-6

Job Searching with Social
Media For Dummies
978-0-470-93072-4

QuickBooks 2012
For Dummies
978-1-118-09120-3

Resumes For Dummies,
6th Edition
978-0-470-87361-8

Starting an Etsy Business
For Dummies
978-0-470-93067-0

Cooking & Entertaining

Cooking Basics
For Dummies, 4th Edition
978-0-470-91388-8

Wine For Dummies,
4th Edition
978-0-470-04579-4

Diet & Nutrition

Kettlebells For Dummies
978-0-470-59929-7

Nutrition For Dummies,
5th Edition
978-0-470-93231-5

Restaurant Calorie Counter
For Dummies,
2nd Edition
978-0-470-64405-8

Digital Photography

Digital SLR Cameras &
Photography For Dummies,
4th Edition
978-1-118-14489-3

Digital SLR Settings
& Shortcuts
For Dummies
978-0-470-91763-3

Photoshop Elements 10
For Dummies
978-1-118-10742-3

Gardening

Gardening Basics
For Dummies
978-0-470-03749-2

Vegetable Gardening
For Dummies,
2nd Edition
978-0-470-49870-5

Green/Sustainable

Raising Chickens
For Dummies
978-0-470-46544-8

Green Cleaning
For Dummies
978-0-470-39106-8

Health

Diabetes For Dummies,
3rd Edition
978-0-470-27086-8

Food Allergies
For Dummies
978-0-470-09584-3

Living Gluten-Free
For Dummies,
2nd Edition
978-0-470-58589-4

Hobbies

Beekeeping
For Dummies,
2nd Edition
978-0-470-43065-1

Chess For Dummies,
3rd Edition
978-1-118-01695-4

Drawing For Dummies,
2nd Edition
978-0-470-61842-4

eBay For Dummies,
7th Edition
978-1-118-09806-6

Knitting For Dummies,
2nd Edition
978-0-470-28747-7

Language &
Foreign Language

English Grammar
For Dummies,
2nd Edition
978-0-470-54664-2

French For Dummies,
2nd Edition
978-1-118-00464-7

German For Dummies,
2nd Edition
978-0-470-90101-4

Spanish Essentials
For Dummies
978-0-470-63751-7

Spanish For Dummies,
2nd Edition
978-0-470-87855-2

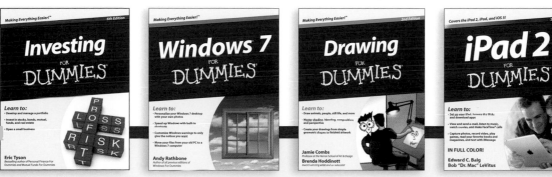

Math & Science

Algebra I For Dummies,
2nd Edition
978-0-470-55964-2

Biology For Dummies,
2nd Edition
978-0-470-59875-7

Chemistry For Dummies,
2nd Edition
978-1-1180-0730-3

Geometry For Dummies,
2nd Edition
978-0-470-08946-0

Pre-Algebra Essentials
For Dummies
978-0-470-61838-7

Microsoft Office

Excel 2010 For Dummies
978-0-470-48953-6

Office 2010 All-in-One
For Dummies
978-0-470-49748-7

Office 2011 for Mac
For Dummies
978-0-470-87869-9

Word 2010
For Dummies
978-0-470-48772-3

Music

Guitar For Dummies,
2nd Edition
978-0-7645-9904-0

Clarinet For Dummies
978-0-470-58477-4

iPod & iTunes
For Dummies,
9th Edition
978-1-118-13060-5

Pets

Cats For Dummies,
2nd Edition
978-0-7645-5275-5

Dogs All-in One
For Dummies
978-0470-52978-2

Saltwater Aquariums
For Dummies
978-0-470-06805-2

Religion & Inspiration

The Bible For Dummies
978-0-7645-5296-0

Catholicism For Dummies,
2nd Edition
978-1-118-07778-8

Spirituality For Dummies,
2nd Edition
978-0-470-19142-2

Self-Help & Relationships

Happiness For Dummies
978-0-470-28171-0

Overcoming Anxiety
For Dummies,
2nd Edition
978-0-470-57441-6

Seniors

Crosswords For Seniors
For Dummies
978-0-470-49157-7

iPad 2 For Seniors
For Dummies, 3rd Edition
978-1-118-17678-8

Laptops & Tablets
For Seniors For Dummies,
2nd Edition
978-1-118-09596-6

Smartphones & Tablets

BlackBerry For Dummies,
5th Edition
978-1-118-10035-6

Droid X2 For Dummies
978-1-118-14864-8

HTC ThunderBolt
For Dummies
978-1-118-07601-9

MOTOROLA XOOM
For Dummies
978-1-118-08835-7

Sports

Basketball For Dummies,
3rd Edition
978-1-118-07374-2

Football For Dummies,
2nd Edition
978-1-118-01261-1

Golf For Dummies,
4th Edition
978-0-470-88279-5

Test Prep

ACT For Dummies,
5th Edition
978-1-118-01259-8

ASVAB For Dummies,
3rd Edition
978-0-470-63760-9

The GRE Test For
Dummies, 7th Edition
978-0-470-00919-2

Police Officer Exam
For Dummies
978-0-470-88724-0

Series 7 Exam
For Dummies
978-0-470-09932-2

Web Development

HTML, CSS, & XHTML
For Dummies, 7th Edition
978-0-470-91659-9

Drupal For Dummies,
2nd Edition
978-1-118-08348-2

Windows 7

Windows 7
For Dummies
978-0-470-49743-2

Windows 7
For Dummies,
Book + DVD Bundle
978-0-470-52398-8

Windows 7 All-in-One
For Dummies
978-0-470-48763-1

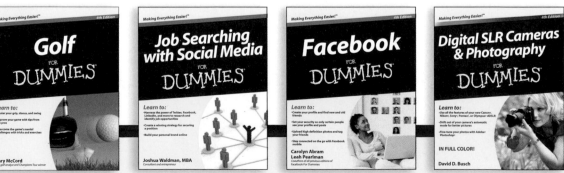